EAST ANGLIAN ARCHAEOLOGY

Iron Age and Roman Settlement: Rescue Excavations at Lynch Farm 2, Orton Longueville, Peterborough

by Stephen G. Upex

with contributions from
P.W. Fifield, Roy Friendship-Taylor, Kay Hartley,
V.C.E. Hughes, Ruth Morgan, Bethan Upex,
Phillipa Walton and Felicity C. Wild

drawings by
Stephen G. Upex

photographs by
Geoffrey Dannell, Roland Sauvaget,
Stephen G. Upex and John Peter Wild

East Anglian Archaeology
Report No.163, 2018

Nene Valley Archaeological Trust

EAST ANGLIAN ARCHAEOLOGY
REPORT NO. 163

Published by
Nene Valley Archaeological Trust
Department of Art History and Archaeology
The Architecture Building
Victoria University of Manchester
Manchester M13 9PL

in conjunction with
ALGAO East
https://www.algao.org.uk/england

Editor: Rebecca Casa Hatton
EAA Managing Editor: Jenny Glazebrook

Set in Times New Roman by Jenny Glazebrook using Corel Ventura™
Printed by Henry Ling Ltd, The Dorset Press

This volume was published with the aid of funding from Historic England

East Anglian Archaeology was established in 1975 by the Scole Committee for Archaeology in East Anglia. The scope of the series expanded to include all six eastern counties and responsibility for publication rests with the editorial board in partnership with the Association of Local Government Archaeological Officers, East of England (ALGAO East).

For details of *East Anglian Archaeology*, see last page

Cover illustration
Excavations in progress at Lynch Farm Site 2 Area A, Ditches 3 and 4. *Photo: J.P. Wild*

Contents

List of Plates

The scales used in photographs vary. Plates 8, 27 and 51–59 are metric; Plates 15, 18, 19, 31, 32 and 44 are both metric and imperial; the remaining plates have imperial scales.

List of Figures

List of Tables

Contributors

Geoffrey Dannell, FSA
Nene Valley Archaeological Trust

P.W. Fifield
Former Masters student, University of Sheffield

Roy Friendship-Taylor, FSA
Upper Nene Archaeological Society

Kay Hartley
Independent, freelance pottery specialist

V.C.E. Hughes
Former Masters student, University of Sheffield

Dr Ruth Morgan
University of Sheffield

Dr Bethan Upex
University of Durham

Dr Stephen G. Upex, MCIfA, FSA
Nene Valley Archaeological Research Committee

the late Rolond Sauvaget
Volunteer with the NVAT

Dr Phillipa Walton
University of Oxford

Felicity C. Wild, FSA
Nene Valley Archaeological Trust

Dr John Peter Wild, FSA
Chairman, Nene Valley Archaeological Trust

Acknowledgements

The Lynch Farm site was excavated by G.B. Dannell and J.P. Wild and I am grateful to them both for making the site archive available and for answering innumerable questions regarding the site. It is sad to record that Rolond Sauvaget, who worked on the site and was responsible for a considerable amount of excavation in Area A, died in 2001 — he added much to our understanding of the site and it was unfortunate that we were not able to call upon his extensive knowledge during the writing of this report. I would like to extent my thanks to Adrian Challands for his help in dealing with the question of early military burials found near to the main Lynch Farm 2 (LF2) excavation site; moreover, it was due to his prompt action after the site was first spotted that excavations were initiated. The gravel contractors ARC were most generous in permitting access to the site and in changing their working pattern to allow for excavations to take place, while the Peterborough Development Corporation and Peterborough City Council showed considerable understanding and forethought in both urging excavation to take place and changing the overall plans for the proposed country park to incorporate a preserved part of the site for long-term public display.

The officers and members of the Nene Valley Archaeological Research Committee, including the late George Dixon (Treasurer), the late Eric Standen (Secretary) and, more recently, John Hadman (present Secretary) and the late Donald Mackreth (Field Unit Director), all made the process of excavation very smooth. Volunteer workers at the site comprised members of the Peterborough Museum Society and the Middle Nene Archaeological Group, university students and interested people who came to work at the site as part of their holidays — and thanks are due to all. Thanks are also due to Mary Hawkins (now Fenton), Carolyn Dallas, John Manley, John Hadman, Stephen Upex and the late Rolond Sauvaget who all worked as site supervisors.

During the preparation of the archive for publication Louisa Gidney of Durham University made many useful comments on the possible 'lucet' (Fig. 70 no. 4 and Pl. 53) and drew my attention to references for similar objects. Dr Nick Garland of University College London was most helpful in discussions regarding the 'status' and potential importance of the site at Lynch Farm in the late Iron Age. Dr Rebecca Casa Hatton, Sarah Botfield and Dr Ben Robinson, formerly of the planning department of Peterborough City Council, were, as always, brilliantly helpful in allowing access to the Historic Environment Record (HER) and for their help with viewing the records of finds from the LF2 area. The specialist contributors within this volume who have either picked up and redrafted their own 'long forgotten' reports on this site or, in the case of the faunal report, edited an archived report that was not their own, are owed particular thanks. P.W. Fifield and Vicky Hughes, who produced the draft reports on the faunal and beetle remains, could not be traced and some editing of their original comments has been undertaken to make their work acceptable for publication, but their original input is duly acknowledged. Glynis Watts, Sarah Wilson, Julia Habershaw and Stuart Orme at Peterborough Museum gave both help and ready access to the pottery and other finds from the site which was invaluable.

Photographs are by G.B. Dannell, R. Sauvaget and J.P. Wild unless credited otherwise. Figures are drawn by Stephen G. Upex except Figure 65, no. 1, credited to Marion Cox; Figure 67, drawn by M.J. Snelgrove; Figure 78, credited to C. Bates and Figure 79, credited to Felicity Wild.

The impetus for this present report has come from the Nene Valley Archeological Trust, who have embarked on a long-term commitment to publishing the backlog of work from their past excavations. All thanks and credit are therefore due to them for pushing this site into print. Generous funding for publication came from the Roman Research Trust, the Earl Fitzwilliam Charitable Foundation, the Robert Kiln Trust, the Marc Fitch Fund and the Nene Valley Archeological Trust.

Geoffrey Dannell, John Peter Wild, John Hadman and Sylvia Upex read earlier drafts of the manuscript and made many sensible and grammatical suggestions that have added fluency to the text and improved the whole style of the document — their input has been invaluable. I am grateful also to Martin Millett for making many very useful comments and suggestions on the draft manuscript which have sharpened the view we now have of the site. Jenny Glazebrook and the staff at *East Anglian Archaeology* have dealt with the main editorial side of this monograph and their help has been brilliant. Any remaining errors are, however, all of my own making.

Summary

Excavations at the Lynch Farm 2 site were the second in a series of three major excavations carried out in a meander of the River Nene, to the west of Peterborough, during the early 1970s. The area within the meander showed aerial photographic evidence of extensive occupation during the prehistoric period and was demarcated in the Iron Age by a system of multiple ditches which may have marked the area out as that of a minor oppidum. Part of this ditched system was dug in 1973 by Adrian Challands and is now termed Lynch Farm 1; it remains unpublished. The extensive cropmarks also indicated Roman occupation, including parchmarks of a number of suspected Roman buildings. These cropmarked areas of the site were scheduled for preservation, although gravel working did encroach on one area which contained part of a late Roman cemetery; this was dug in 1972 by Rick Jones, is now termed Lynch Farm 3 and was published in 1975.

The peripheral areas within the meander were thought to lack archaeological significance and thus were deemed suitable for gravel extraction to provide aggregate for the expansion of Greater Peterborough. However, once gravel workings started on the eastern part of the meander, unknown Roman buildings began to be found and gravel extraction was partly halted while an archaeological rescue excavation was undertaken, now termed Lynch Farm 2. The archaeological work revealed a late Iron Age pit alignment, with one pit containing an adult burial. During the early Roman invasion period a fort was situated over the top of this earlier Iron Age occupation. The fort appeared to be of the same date as the fortress at Longthorpe, some 800m to the east. Once the military had abandoned the site the area within the Lynch Farm fort was immediately occupied by a small enclosure set within the south-west corner of the rampart. In the 2nd century an aisled building was constructed within which were furnaces used possibly for salt extraction. This building was later demolished and a larger aisled building was built on the same site, although with a different alignment. By the late 3rd/early 4th century ditches and pits were being dug for drainage purposes and other buildings constructed, including a small Romano-Celtic shrine. Two wells were also dug. Occupation at the site continued until the late 4th century, when the site underwent a demolition and clearance phase associated with late surfaces and site reorganisation.

The Roman occupation at Lynch Farm 2 forms what appears to be a small part of a much larger Roman settlement seen only on air photographs. This consists of scattered buildings arranged over an area 800m wide and is unlike most local villa or farmstead establishments, although a growing number of parallels for such settlements are now being added to the literature.

Résumé

Les fouilles désignées ici par le terme de Lynch Farm 2 furent les secondes d'une série de trois grandes fouilles qui furent entreprises dans un méandre de la rivière Nene, à l'ouest de Peterborough au début des années 70. Les photographies aériennes de cette zone du méandre révèlent l'existence d'une occupation extensive pendant la période préhistorique. Cette zone était délimitée à l'âge du fer par un système formé de multiples fossés qui dessinaient peut-être les limites d'un petit oppidum. Une partie de ce système de fossés a été creusée en 1973 par Adrian Challands et elle est maintenant désignée par le terme de Lynch Farm 1; ces fouilles ont fait l'objet d'une étude qui n'a pas été publiée. Ces indices d'une occupation extensive se présentent sous la forme d'une variation de couleurs des sols contenant plusieurs bâtiments qui pourraient correspondre à une occupation romaine. Les zones du site ainsi délimitées devaient être préservées, même si l'exploitation du gravier empiétait réellement sur l'une des zones qui contenait une partie d'un cimetière romain tardif. Cette zone fut fouillée en

1972 par Rick Jones. Elle est maintenant désignée par le terme de Lynch Farm 3 et elle a fait l'objet d'une publication en 1975.

En outre, on a considéré que les zones périphériques situées à l'intérieur du méandre étaient dépourvues d'intérêt archéologique et qu'elles convenaient par conséquent à l'extraction de gravier. Celui-ci devait fournir des agrégats destinés à l'extension du Greater Peterborough. Toutefois, après le début de l'extraction du gravier sur la partie est du méandre, on a commencé à mettre à jour des bâtiments romains inconnus, ce qui a entraîné une interruption partielle du chantier et le déclenchement de fouilles de sauvetage. Celles-ci ont révélé un alignement de fosses de la fin de l'âge du fer, l'une d'entre elles contenant une tombe adulte. Quand commença l'invasion romaine, un fort se trouvait au sommet de cette occupation qui remontait au début de l'âge de fer. Le fort semblait être de la même époque que la forteresse de Longthorpe qui se situe à environ 800 m à l'est. Une fois que les militaires eurent abandonné le site, la zone du fort de Lynch Farm fut immédiatement occupée par une petite enceinte située dans le coin sud-ouest du rempart. Au deuxième siècle, un bâtiment doté d'une aile fut construit; il contenait des fours qui étaient peut-être utilisés pour l'extraction du sel. Ce bâtiment fut démoli plus tard et un autre bâtiment, plus grand et doté d'une aile, fut construit sur le même site avec toutefois un alignement différent. À la fin du 3ème et au début du 4ème siècle, un ensemble de fossés et de fosses fut creusé à des fins de drainage et d'autres bâtiments furent construits, dont un petit temple romano-celtique. Deux puits furent également creusés. L'occupation du site continua jusqu'à la fin du 4ème siècle, période pendant laquelle le site passa par une phase de démolition et de déblaiement qui était associée avec une réorganisation tardive du site et des surfaces fouillées.

L'occupation romaine de Lynch Farm 2 correspond, semble-t-il, à une petite partie d'un établissement romain beaucoup plus large qui n'apparaît que sur les photographies aériennes. Lynch Farm 2 se compose de bâtiments éparpillés sur une surface de 800 mètres de large et elle diffère de la plupart des villas locales ou des implantations de fermes, même si un nombre grandissant d'études parallèles s'ajoute actuellement à la documentation existante.

(Traduction: Didier Don)

Zusammenfassung

Die hier unter dem Namen Lynch Farm 2 beschriebene Ausgrabung war die zweite von drei größeren Grabungen, die in einer Schleife des Flusses Nene westlich von Peterborough zu Beginn der 1970er Jahre durchgeführt wurden. Luftaufnahmen des Gebiets innerhalb der Flussschleife hatten Hinweise auf eine großflächige prähistorische Besiedlung ergeben. In der Eisenzeit wurde das Gebiet durch ein System von Gräben befestigt, die das Areal möglicherweise als kleines Oppidum abgrenzten. Ein Teil des Grabensystems wurde 1973 von Adrian Challands ausgegraben – es wird heute als Lynch Farm 1 bezeichnet; die zugehörigen Befunde wurden bislang nicht veröffentlicht. Zudem deuteten ausgedehnte Bewuchsmerkmale in Form von Verfärbungen über mehreren Gebäuden auf eine womöglich römische Besiedlung hin. Das Gebiet mit den Bewuchsmerkmalen wurde unter Schutz gestellt, allerdings drangen Kiesabbauarbeiten in einen Teil der Fläche vor, der Teile eines spätrömischen Gräberfelds enthielt. Dieses Gräberfeld wurde 1972 von Rick Jones ausgegraben und wird heute als Lynch Farm 3 bezeichnet; die zugehörigen Befunde wurden 1975 veröffentlicht.

Die Randbereiche innerhalb der Flussschleife wurden als archäologisch unbedeutend eingestuft und daher für den Kiesabbau freigegeben, um Aggregat für die Ausweitung von Greater Peterborough zu gewinnen. Als mit dem Kiesabbau begonnen wurde, stieß man jedoch im östlichen Teil der Flussschleife auf unbekannte römische Gebäude, woraufhin die Abbauarbeiten zum Teil unterbrochen wurden, um eine archäologische Rettungsgrabung zu ermöglichen. In deren Verlauf wurde eine späteisenzeitliche Grubenreihe entdeckt; in einer der Gruben war eine erwachsene Person bestattet. Zu Beginn der römischen Invasion wurde die eisenzeitliche Siedlung durch eine Festung überlagert, die aus derselben Zeit zu stammen scheint wie die Festung von Longthorpe etwa 800 Meter weiter östlich. Unmittelbar nachdem das Militär die Stätte aufgegeben hatte, wurde innerhalb der Festung von Lynch Farm eine kleine Grabenanlage in der Südwestecke des Festungswalls angelegt. Im 2. Jahrhundert wurde ein mehrschiffiges Bauwerk errichtet, das Siedeöfen enthielt, die womöglich der Salzgewinnung dienten. Das Gebäude wurde später abgerissen und durch ein größeres mehrschiffiges Gebäude an gleicher Stelle, allerdings mit anderer Ausrichtung, ersetzt. An der Wende vom 3. zum 4. Jahrhundert wurden mehrere Gräben und Gruben für Entwässerungszwecke angelegt und weitere Bauwerke errichtet, darunter ein kleiner römisch-keltischer Schrein. Außerdem wurden zwei Brunnen ausgehoben. Die Besiedlung hielt bis zum Ende des 4. Jahrhunderts an, als die Stätte im Zuge von Abriss- und Aufräumarbeiten umstrukturiert und dadurch die späten Oberflächen geschaffen wurden.

Die römische Besiedlung von Lynch Farm 2 bildete offenbar nur einen kleinen Teil einer weit größeren Römersiedlung, die lediglich auf Luftaufnahmen zu erkennen ist. Diese bestand aus Gebäuden, die über ein Gebiet von 800 Meter Breite verstreut waren. Die Siedlung unterschied sich von den meisten anderen römischen Landgütern oder Gehöften in der Gegend, auch wenn derzeit zunehmend mehr Parallelen für derartige Siedlungen in die Literatur Eingang finden.

(Übersetzung: Gerlinde Krug)

Chapter 1. Introduction

I. Introduction
(Fig. 1)

In 1969 the Royal Commission on Historic Monuments (RCHM) published a volume called *Peterborough New Town: A Survey of the Antiquities in the Area of Development* and for the first time drew together a series of aerial photographs of archaeological cropmarks at Lynch Farm, located within Orton Waterville, Orton Longueville and Alwalton parishes and contained within a meander of the river Nene to the west of Peterborough (Fig. 1) (RCHM 1969, 31–3, fig. 7, pl. 2). The RCHM publication was instigated in the mid-1960s by the proposed expansion of Peterborough and its designation as a 'New Town', with new townships planned and added onto the existing medieval and later footprint of the city. Although the villages of Orton Waterville and Orton Longueville were intended for extensive building and housing expansion the area containing the archaeological cropmarks within the loop of the Nene was outside the building plan, owing largely to its low-lying nature and the possibility of its flooding. However, the planners recognised that Peterborough's expansion would require vast amounts of aggregate and that the meanders of the Nene would be an ideal place from which to extract sand and gravel. It was also recognised that gravel extraction — and thus the creation of lakes — would provide an ideal location for later recreational facilities. Therefore, it was proposed that gravel be extracted from the areas which were thought to contain no, or only limited, archaeological remains and what was later called 'Ferry Meadows' be created as the centre of a larger designation of recreational land within what is now called the 'Nene Park', administered by the Nene Park Trust.

The Nene Valley (Archaeological) Research Committee (NVRC), responsible for archaeological work within the lower Nene valley, worked closely with the Peterborough Development Corporation (PDC) to limit any damage to the archaeological landscape during the years of gravel extraction at Lynch Farm. The intention was to incorporate any archaeological findings into an understanding of the broader historic landscapes of the area. This aim was especially important because the site at Lynch Farm was close to other major prehistoric and Roman centres which were of both regional and national importance.

Major prehistoric finds from the early Neolithic to the Iron Age were known from excavations at Fengate, to the east of Peterborough, carried out by George Wyman Abbott in the early 1900s (Wyman Abbott 1910) and

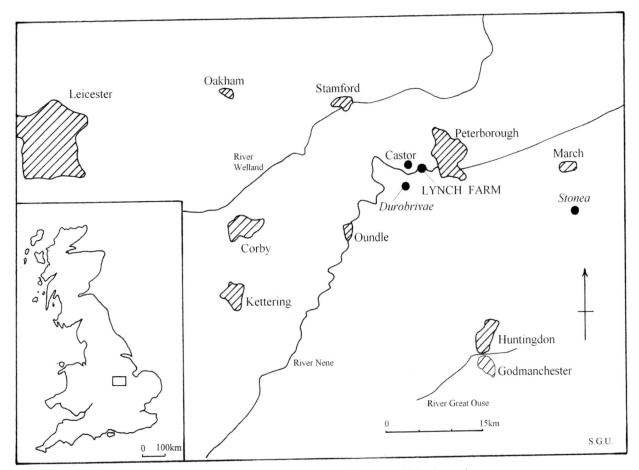

Figure 1 The site of Lynch Farm's location within the region

during the 1970s by Francis Pryor (1974; 1977; 1978; 1980; 1984). Several barrows of Bronze Age date survived along the flood plain of the river Nene. One, in Ailsworth parish, was recorded by the RCHM (1969, fig. 10, no. 8), while other barrows were recorded by David Hall and Paul Martin during a fieldwalking survey of the Soke of Peterborough in 1974 (Hall and Martin 1980, 13–14). These barrows were excavated in 1975 (O'Neil and Mackreth 1982; Mackreth forthcoming) and their significance discussed in 1988 (French and Wait 1988, 42–4). In addition, significant finds of later prehistoric metalwork were recovered from the river Nene in Orton Longueville parish and some 1km downstream from the Lynch Farm site (Stead 1984). The RCHM volume listed all of the known sites within the area of Peterborough's designated expansion and discussed the idea that the late prehistoric landscape was densely settled (RCHM 1969). Some sites, at places such as Werrington and Monument 97 in Orton Longueville, were excavated and the sequences of late prehistoric occupation were shown to continue through into the Roman period (Mackreth 1988; 2001).

Moreover, the wealth of Roman sites within the immediate area of Lynch Farm signified a region of outstanding importance during the Roman period. The foundation of the Roman town of *Durobrivae* (Fig. 2), with its sprawling industrial suburbs, and the development of a wealthy villa system based around this town seem to have been forged from early military origins (see Upex 2008a; 2014, 5–10). The discovery in 1961 of a Roman fortress at Longthorpe and its partial excavation between 1967 and 1973 (Frere and St Joseph 1974), and the much earlier discovery by Major Allen in 1930 of an auxiliary fort at Water Newton (Hawkes 1939; Upex 2014, 5–10),

indicated a significant military presence in the area. To the north-west of Peterborough town centre, Victorian and later development of the railway yards revealed extensive Roman remains of what may have been an additional urban area, although the finds records are poor and the exact nature of the site remains unclear. Few of the major civilian sites have been explored archaeologically since the time of Edmund Artis, who published a series of illustrations in 1828 as an account of his local excavations and findings (Artis 1828). Work was carried out between 1964 and 1975 on a Roman farmstead at Orton Hall Farm, in Orton Longueville parish, and other farmsteads were explored at Monument 97 (Orton Longueville) and in Werrington and Walton parishes within Greater Peterborough during the same period (Mackreth 1996b; 1988; 2001; Jones 1974). At Haddon a farmstead was partially excavated during 1989 (French 1994) and further excavations were undertaken during 1999 (Hinman 2003). During 2011 the discovery of a major villa complex at Walton was made by Oxford Archaeology East under the direction of Alex Pickstone (Pickstone 2012) and the publication of this site will add considerably to the understanding of villa development in the area.

II. The archaeological landscape of the Lynch Farm complex and the sites of Lynch Farm 1 and 3
(Figs 2–3; Pls 1 and 2)

The area which forms the focus of this report is within a meander of the river Nene (see Fig. 2) and now within the area of the Nene Park, a recreational area set aside for public use. The topography and geology of the immediate

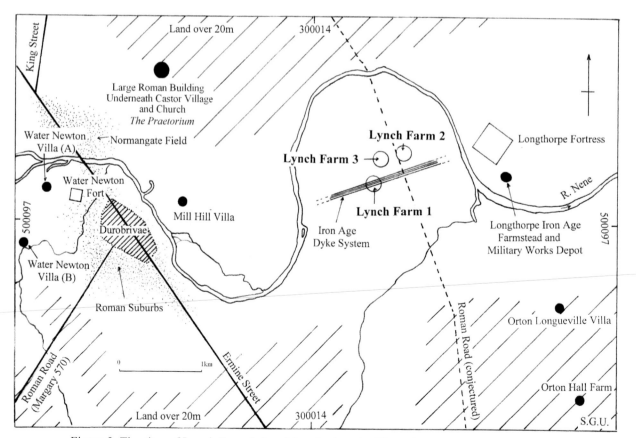

Figure 2 The sites of Lynch Farm 1, 2 and 3 and other significant local archaeological features

Plate 1 Air photograph of the Lynch Farm cropmarks looking north-west (some parts of the site bottom left and right have already been worked for gravel). *Stephen G. Upex (photograph part of a collection housed at Peterborough Museum)*

Plate 2 Air photograph of part of the Lynch Farm 1 site, showing the multiple ditch system under excavation and as a crop mark. *Stephen G. Upex (photograph part of a collection housed at Peterborough Museum)*

LYNCH FARM CROPMARKS
Sites 1, 2 & 3.

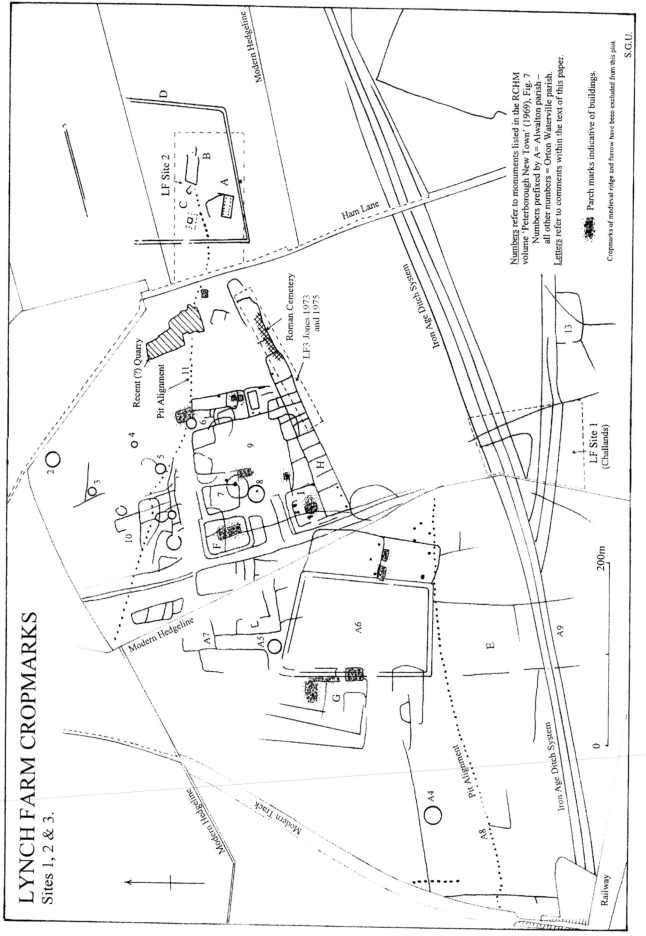

Numbers refer to monuments listed in the RCHM volume 'Peterborough New Town' (1969), Fig. 7
Numbers prefixed by A= Alwalton parish –
all other numbers = Orton Waterville parish.
Letters refer to comments within the text of this paper.

▨ Parch marks indicative of buildings.

Cropmarks of medieval ridge and furrow have been excluded from this plot.

S.G.U.

Figure 3 The Lynch Farm cropmark evidence

4

area is characterised by a low-lying gravel filled meander in which alluvium skirts the banks of the river Nene. The ground rises slightly within the central part of the meander to around 7m AOD, where the gravel from the first terrace is encountered (Geological Survey 1972; see also Hains and Horton 1969).

The archaeological landscape is largely known from air photographs taken by J.K.S. St Joseph and photographs lodged in the National Monuments Record which were used to form the first plot of the cropmarks in 1969 (RCHM 1969, fig. 7). Additional photographs of the area, taken between 1974 and 1980, are held by Peterborough Museum and are incorporated within the Historic Environment Record (HER) maintained by Peterborough City Council Planning Department.

The cropmarks (see Pl. 1), which run through the parishes of Orton Longueville, Orton Waterville and Alwalton, form a complex pattern which clearly includes both prehistoric and Roman features. The 1969 plot of the cropmarks drawn by the Royal Commission (RCHM 1969, fig. 7) shows a series of ring-ditches presumed to represent ploughed-out burial mounds of possible Bronze Age date and a series of single pits, pit alignments and enclosures of both prehistoric and Roman date. To the south of the main complex of cropmarks was a set of triple and quadruple ditches which appears to run across the neck of the river's meander and was thus possibly intended to demarcate an area of land contained within the loop of the meander itself.

The series of air photographs taken since the publication of the 1969 Royal Commission plan has added considerable new detail to the overall cropmark pattern of archaeological features and has necessitated a re-drawing of the plan of the site. This new plan is shown in Figure 3, which retains the RCHM features and numbering system alongside the addition of 'new' features seen on the more recent photographic surveys. The more recent photographs show a series of rectangular parchmarks which are likely to be the areas above stone-built (and -floored?) structures of probable Roman date. Some of these areas were observed in the grassland of the Nene Park by the writer during the dry summer of 2011 and were associated with fragments of Roman pottery. A major addition to the cropmarked features which appeared on the 1969 RCHM plan was observed to the east of Ham Lane and proved to be the outline of a Roman military installation (Fig. 3, 'D').

It is within this archaeological framework that excavations were undertaken at Lynch Farm between 1972 and 1974. The extensive programme of gravel extraction necessitated the excavation in 1972 of part of the area covered by cropmarks and work was therefore undertaken by Richard Jones to clear this area. These excavations, given the code Lynch Farm Site 3 (LF3 — see Figs 2 and 3), found pits and ditches which yielded evidence for 3rd- and 4th-century Roman occupation associated with what Jones termed a 'farmstead'. One of the enclosures found during these excavations contained a small cemetery of at least fifty inhumations and one cremation. Many of the burials had wooden coffins and two were in stone cists; there were few grave goods. Some of the grave plots had been reused several times, with one example having six adults and one child successively interred on virtually the same spot. This site has been fully published (Jones 1973; 1975).

During 1973 Adrian Challands carried out further work within the area termed Lynch Farm Site I (LF1 — see Figs 2 and 3) which was directed towards dating and interpreting the series of triple and quadruple ditches that were shown on the air photographs to run for over 900m (see Pl. 2). Sections across these ditches were cut by hand and there was seen to be a great variation in the profiles and fills of these features. The layers making up the top 0.30–0.50m appeared to be a deliberate filling and contained a significant amount' of 'Belgic style' Iron Age pottery. Mixed with this material was some 1st- and mid-2nd-century Roman pottery, suggesting that the ditches had been part-filled but were still partially open in the mid-2nd century.

Cut into the upper filling of each of the two central ditches were cremation burials within rectangular pits measuring 1.50×1.65m and approximately 0.25m deep. Pottery associated with these burials was of the same type and fabric as pottery made at the Roman military 'works depot' at Longthorpe and dated to AD 50–65. A fragment of a 'thistle brooch' recovered from the same context was of a similar date (Challands 1973, 22).

The lack of dating evidence from the lowest levels of the triple and quadruple ditch system prevented a firm construction date being determined. However, the discovery of an entrance through the ditched system showed that the terminal ends of the ditches, which formed this entrance, were slightly inturned (Challands 1973; 1974a; *Northamptonshire Archaeology* 1974a, 85).

In addition to the ditched system several oval pits produced well-stratified late Iron Age pottery and the presence of hearths and gullies indicated that the area contained hut circles, although plough damage had destroyed most of this evidence. Two Neolithic stone axes were also recovered from these excavations: one was a polished green stone axe and the other a stone flake that was initially interpreted as a 'polishing stone' for other axes, but later reinterpreted as an axe in its own right (Challands 1973, 23; Briggs 1979).

Work continued at LF1 through most of 1974, clearing the archaeology that was to be destroyed by gravel extraction and the creation of the recreational lake on the western side of the proposed Nene Park area. In this part of the site a large pit produced beaker pottery and flints, and to the west of this area an enclosure 29j×18m produced evidence from the Iron Age. Next to this enclosure ten pits from a pit alignment were also excavated. These were oval and varied between 2.5m and 3.0m in diameter, although they remained undated because of a lack of finds (*Northamptonshire Archaeology* 1975a, 149). All of this work remains unpublished.

III. Lynch Farm 2 (LF2)
(Pls 3–6)

In May 1972 the stone footings of Roman buildings and silt-filled drainage channels were unexpectedly uncovered at Lynch Farm during gravel extraction to the east of the LF3 site. This area lay to the east of Ham Lane, where the cropmark evidence was limited to a few indistinct linear ditches that, prior to the gravel extraction, were considered to be Roman field boundaries and thus peripheral to the main settlement area. Owing to the prompt action of Mr Adrian Challands, Peterborough Development Corporation's archaeologist, the kind

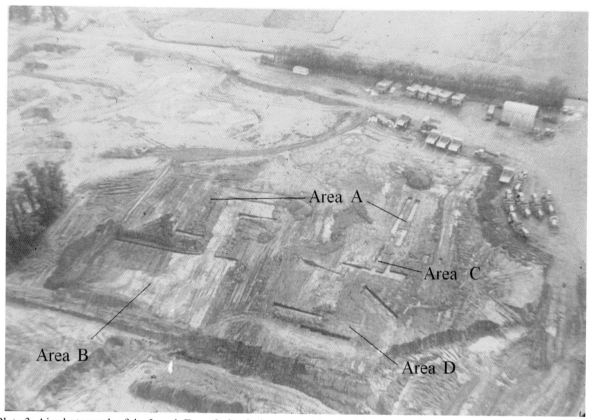

Plate 3 Air photograph of the Lynch Farm 2 site during excavation, looking west, with gravel contractor's depot in the upper part of the photograph. *Stephen G. Upex (photograph part of a collection housed at Peterborough Museum)*

co-operation of the contractors A.R.C. and the Development Corporation, an archaeological rescue excavation was set in place by the Nene Valley Research Committee. It soon became clear that several Roman buildings were present in the area of concern and thus it was agreed to change the gravel extraction plan and to permanently preserve the tongue of land on which these buildings were situated. The surrounding area, including land to the east of these Roman buildings that appeared to contain a complex of ditches, would, however, be destroyed after archaeological excavations had taken place (see Pl. 3).

Work commenced during the summer of 1972 with the intention of clearing the area that was to be taken for gravel extraction first so that this land could be released back to the contractors. It soon became clear that moving onto an area in which the contractors had already removed the topsoil posed considerable difficulties. The ground surface was left in a very churned-up state (see Pls 4 and 5) where machines weighing 20–30 tons, when fully laden with spoil, had manoeuvred. Consequently, several archaeological features were compressed, especially where they were located over soft fills of earlier ditches and pits. Stonework from surviving structures also appeared in some cases to have been 'shifted' sideways, in some instances for several metres, as heavy machines had moved across the area during the process of topsoil removal. At the edges of the area set aside for permanent preservation the gravel extraction process left a steep cliff some 2–5m high where aggregate had been removed and the intended banks of the new recreational lakes were being created. This newly created 'cliff' also produced a massive 'slice' through the site in which ditches and other features were seen; some attempt was therefore made to

recover dating evidence and record sections here (see Pl. 6).

Initial excavation work was also undertaken during 1972 on the site of a large Roman aisled building which was within the tongue of land intended for preservation. This work has been described in summary form (Wild 1973a, 20–21; see also NVRC 1972). Further work was carried out on this building and other features during the spring and summer of 1973, when excavations continued to uncover and clear the ditch complexes surrounding the aisled building and other Roman stone structures which lay to the east. One of these features — thought at the time to be a stone-lined pool, fed by a complex system of ditches and sluices — was initially interpreted as some form of pond for the breeding of fish (Wild 1973a, 20–21). Work also indicated the presence of earlier features, including part of a pit alignment which was thought to date to the late Iron Age and a double ditched system which was thought to be part of some form of 1st-century military installation (*Northamptonshire Archaeology* 1974**b**, 92–5).

Work continued into 1974 with the complete excavation of the pits within the pit alignment and the firm identification of both military ditches and pits. This last season of work was carried out with a much-reduced labour force (unpubl. typescript in Peterborough Museum collection 1974; *Northamptonshire Archaeology* 1975b, 158–61).

Thus three periods of work were carried out the site — a preliminary clearance operation during 1972, followed by two full summer seasons of work during 1973 and 1974. The work was directed by Geoffrey Dannell and John Peter Wild, with additional direction during the 1972 season from Adrian Challands and during 1974 from

Plate 4 Area C, looking north after the gravel contractor had withdrawn from the site and prior to excavation

Rolond Sauvaget. The digging team comprised local and regional volunteers, members of the recently formed Middle Nene Archaeological Group, members of the Peterborough Museum Society Archaeological Field Group and students from Manchester University, many of whom were accommodated at the Stibbington Outdoor Centre.

The work at Lynch Farm 2 was essentially a rescue and salvage excavation carried out by the NVRC in the knowledge that funds were not available at the time for post-excavation work or full publication. Given the degree of degradation and distortion of the stratigraphy caused by the machine stripping of the topsoil and the use of heavy machinery, the strategic objective was to try to record the principal structures and recover artefacts from the stratigraphy that remained in the hope that, at some later date, funds might become available for a fuller interpretation of the site.

Some scientific work was undertaken as the excavations were being carried out and graduate theses were produced on both the faunal remains and the Coleoptera from Well I (see Chapters 9 and 10). These go some way to increasing our understanding of the natural landscape of the area during the Roman period.

Not only was work at the site rushed and clearly of a rescue nature but, in an effort to record the maximum amount of information, shortcuts were taken which have left weaknesses within the excavation record and thus also in the archive which is held at Peterborough Museum. Levels of some features were not recorded and this has posed a number of problems for interpretation. At the time of the excavations the amount of overburden that was removed by the contractors was considered to have been so great that trying to record all features in detail with levels was thought to be somewhat pointless, and the focus

Plate 5 Area C, the southern wall of Building C2 (wall C1 in Fig. 52) after the gravel contractor had withdrawn from the site and prior to excavation

Plate 6 Clearing a section dug by the gravel contractor to recover details of Roman ditches in Area B

was thus on recovering the total plan of the site. For similar reasons, some records of the site were largely photographic and to this end more photographs have been offered for publication than would normally have been included.

The site was dug using imperial measurements which have, within the written report, been converted to metric. Most of the site photographs, such as Plates 20 and 21, also show imperial scales. However there are exceptions to this and Plate 15, for example, appears with metric scales. All of the small find photographs (Plates 51–59) have metric scales.

The publication of this work at Lynch Farm 2 is long overdue and has been made possible by the long-term programme of publications instigated by the Nene Valley Research Committee and the support of the Nene Valley Archaeological Trust.

Chapter 2. The excavation: Area A, I–VI

I. Introduction
(Fig. 4; Table 1).

The excavations at the site of Area A ran over three seasons of work from 1972 to 1974, although the initial season, when the site was first identified, consisted of a massive cleaning operation and an attempt to identify both the limits of the site and individual features. The machines used to extract the gravel from the surrounding area had run over the archaeological features, compressing some, physically shifting others and generally making the job of recovering an archaeological story very difficult. Areas of stonework, including some wall lines, could be identified in some parts of the site, while in other areas only the dark, organic fills of ditch-like features could be seen. Almost all of these features were covered in loose soil, gravel and material spread unintentionally by the gravel extraction company during the removal of the overburden from the gravel deposits. The site was archaeologically cleaned by hand and the excavators classed everything that came from this initial cleaning layer as + or 1+.

The archaeological site was divided up into Areas A, B, C and D (Fig. 4). Initially work in Area A concentrated on the recovery of the plan of an aisled building, which was fairly easy to identify as the prior machining had removed the topsoil to reveal the outline of pitched limestone walls. Some 40m to the north of this structure was a smaller building, again with pitched limestone walls laid in herringbone fashion, and 30m to the west of this second building a spread of limestone and some Roman tile indicated yet another structure. This last building was within the area where the contractors parked their machinery and off-limits for any archaeological work other than the recovery of surface material during a lull in machinery activity.

Stonework, walling lines and related ditches were also recorded from Areas C and D (Fig. 4), where the passage of machinery had been particularly destructive to the archaeological deposits. To the south of these two Areas a complex of ditches and large dark areas containing organic deposits was revealed in Area B.

After the start made during 1972, which concentrated on clearing and identifying features, during 1973 work focused on excavating and emptying parts of the ditch systems (which began to be revealed in all areas) and cleaning and interpreting the stonework and buildings in Areas A, C and D. The archaeological work was finished in Areas B, C and D by the end of the 1973 season and these areas were released back to the gravel contractors. The 1974 season concentrated solely on Area A, with work being extended from the three-week summer season during August to the beginning of October so that the excavation could be completed. Figure 4 shows the trench and area plan for the whole of the site and to some extent indicates the archaeological methods employed within each of the areas. Areas B, C and D were, in part, cleared using a JCB mechanical digger to remove the debris left by the gravel extraction traffic. In Area B this process was fairly easy, as there were very few stone features other than some stone-lined post-holes, and overlying debris was thus cleared down to the tops of the undisturbed ditch fills. In Areas C and D some clearance was made in the same way, but where stonework was encountered soil was removed by hand. Thus Area B had hand-cleared areas and sectional cuts that were mechanically cleared. The treatment of these Areas contrasted with that of Area A. Here the encounters with stonework and the less urgent need to clear an area already designated for preservation, saw hand-dug trenching as the main form of operation, with only a few machine-pulled trenches being required (for example, Trenches T45, T49 and T50). Most of these hand-dug trenches, which were predominantly set out to respect the lines of the site grid, were orientated north–south, although a few were set out to cut particular features at right angles, especially ditches, and thus had slightly differing orientations. In some cases trenches which were set out and excavated were later expanded and incorporated other nearby trenches, so that their final numbering comprised the amalgamation of several numbers.

This report sets out the findings in a chronological sequence for each Area in turn. Stratigraphic links between Areas were not possible, although the finds from the Areas, including pottery, did allow for sequential phases to be identified for the whole excavation — an aspect of the site which will be returned to in the Discussion (Chapter 11). In only one period, that represented by military activity, was it possible to trace a direct link between Areas and this consisted of a pair of parallel ditches that were located in Area A and ran through into Area B (see Fig. 4).

A general scatter of twenty-five prehistoric flints was recovered during the excavations; all were residual and many came from surface finds or the topsoil. A transverse arrowhead, leaf-shaped arrowhead and scrapers, along with the polished axe head (Challands 1973), indicated Neolithic occupation. This occupation seems to have continued into the Bronze Age, with a general scatter of flint flakes; both the Neolithic and Bronze Age assemblages are reported more fully below. The air photographs also indicate several ring-ditches (see Fig. 3) which probably represent ploughed-out Bronze Age round barrows. No archaeological features earlier than the Iron Age were encountered during the Lynch Farm 2 excavations.

Dating for the site was provided mainly by pottery, including some samian. Only forty-three coins were found, with only two dating to the period before c. AD 300, and only nineteen brooches were recovered. The limitations of the dating evidence from the site have caused some problems in dealing with the overall phasing of the excavations and in some cases the stratigraphical sequences were the only means of identifying earlier or later deposits. The main chronological periods into which the site has been divided are summarised in Table 1.

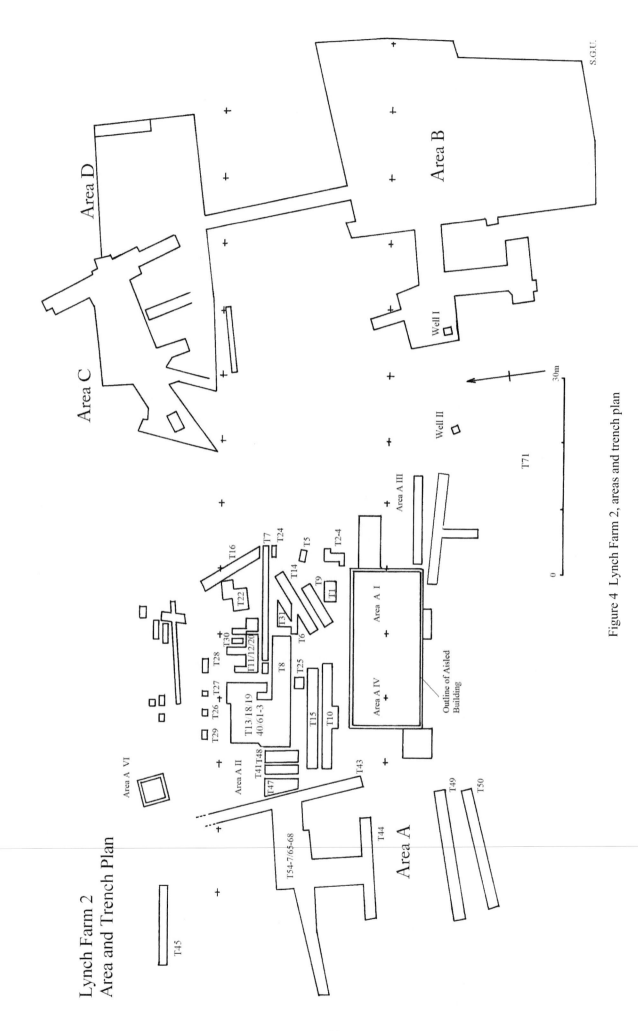

Lynch Farm 2
Area and Trench Plan

Area C

Area D

Area B

Area A

Figure 4 Lynch Farm 2, areas and trench plan

10

Period	Date	
	Neolithic and Bronze Age flint scatter	
1	Late Iron Age	Up to AD *c.* 44/45
2	Roman military phase	*c.* AD 44–45 to 60–65
3	Late 1st/early 2nd century	*c.* AD 60–65 to 130–150
4	Late 2nd century	
5	Early 3rd century	
6	Late 3rd/early 4th century	
7	Mid-4th century	
8	Late 4th/early 5th century	*c.* AD 375 onwards

Table 1 Summary of datable periods

	Section drawing showing this Pit	Figure number
A	S30	Fig. 7
B	S31	Fig. 7
C	S32	Fig. 7
D	S33	Fig. 7
E		
F	S28	Fig. 14
G	S28	Fig. 14
H	S36	Fig. 15
I	S38	Fig. 15
J	S37	Fig. 15
K	S39	Fig. 15
L	S35	Fig. 15
M		
N		
R	S49	Fig. 17
S		
T	S34	Fig. 7

Table 2 Pit alignment numbers and section drawings

II. Area A

Area A, which lay in the western part of the excavated area, was excavated largely by hand with a complex trenching pattern emerging after the end of the 1974 season, which is shown in Figs 4 and 5. The Area was subdivided still further into five smaller units numbered I, II, III, IV and VI — for some reason there was no area V!

Period 1. Iron Age Pit Alignment
(Figs 5–8; Pls 7–8; Table 2).
The earliest features encountered within Area A were a series of oval/sub-rectangular pits which ran in linear fashion across part of the site (Fig. 5; Pl. 7; Table 2). There were seventeen pits in total, labelled A to N and R to T in Figure 5. The break in the lettering system, O–Q, made allowances for three pits in the sequence, although there was no trace of these pits during work at the site. The line of pits ran roughly east–west and appeared to be a continuation of a pit alignment seen on air photographs and plotted in Figure 3. The pits within this alignment could thus be traced for approximately 500m, with the excavated examples being the easternmost section. Another pit alignment running for approximately 450m to the south west was also noted on the air photographs — this, again, is shown in Figure 3.

The pits were all roughly the same shape, being approximately 2.20m long by 1.30m wide, and most had a depth of 0.50m. The gaps between the pits varied from 1.6m (between Pits B and C) to 3.0m (between Pits K and L). There appeared to be a break in the line of pits between Pits N and R. This impression may have been due to later features cutting into the positions of these possible pits and destroying the evidence; however, during the excavation these pits were searched for unsuccessfully. It may simply be that these pits were never dug. If there was a gap in the line of the pits, then the reason for it remains unclear. No similar gaps have been recorded in the other pit alignments shown on the air photographs of the Lynch Farm complex.

Some pits were fully excavated and others sectioned in part and from these profiles composite plans and sections could be produced, which are shown in Figures 6 and 7. The pits were all dug into the underlying sand/gravel subsoil of the river terrace gravels and the fills of all those excavated consisted of mixed sand and gravel, with little indication of long-term silt deposits being allowed to build

up. The impression was that the pits had not been open for long before they were filled in. The fills of all illustrated sections are described in Appendix 2.

The finds from the pits were very limited. In Pit D a crouched adult male inhumation was found lying on its

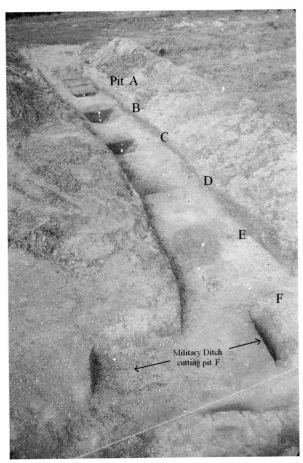

Plate 7 Pits A–F of the Iron Age pit alignment, looking west (Period 2)

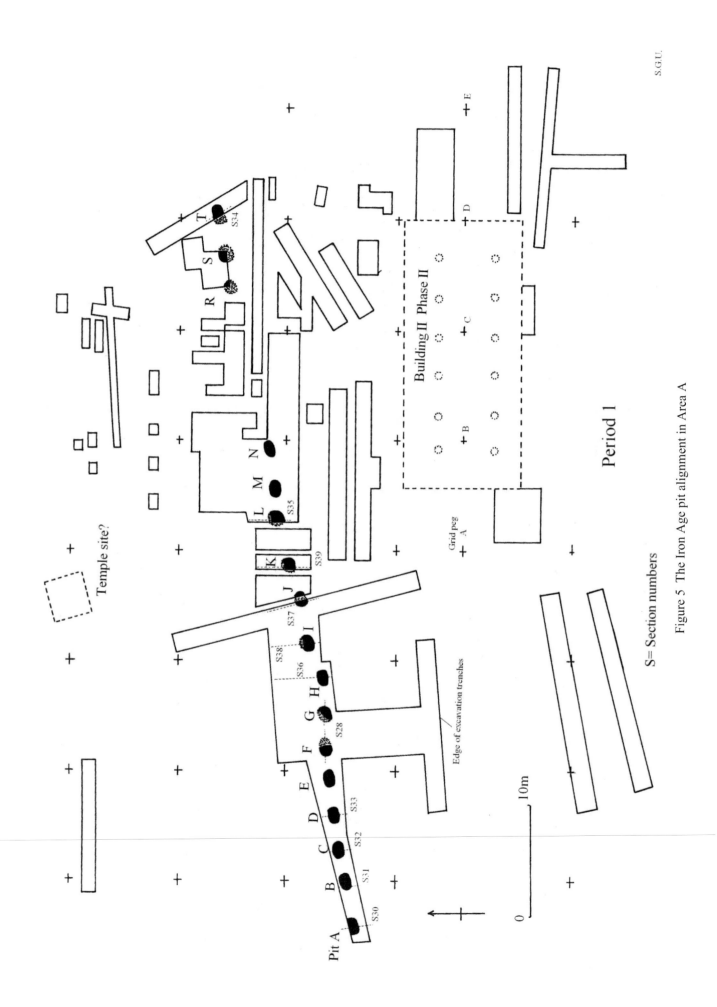

Figure 5 The Iron Age pit alignment in Area A

S = Section numbers

Period 1

Pit A

Temple site?

Building II Phase II

Grid peg

Edge of excavation trenches

10m

S.G.U.

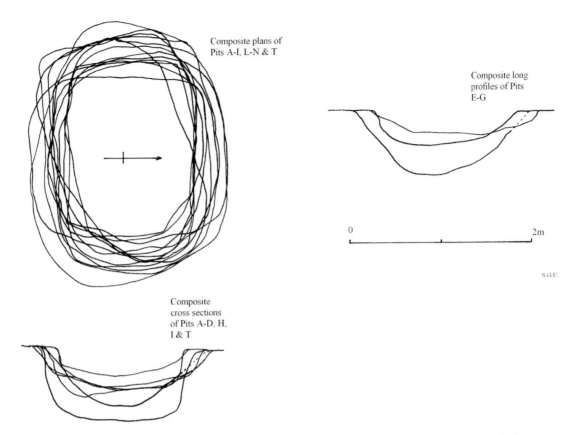

Composite plans of
Pits A-I, L-N & T

Composite long
profiles of Pits
E-G

Composite
cross sections
of Pits A-D, H,
I & T

0   2m

S.G.U.

Figure 6 The Iron Age pits: composite plans, and cross and long profiles of excavated pits

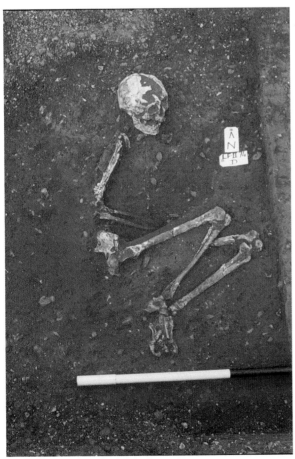

Plate 8 Burial within Pit D of the Iron Age pit
alignment (Period 2)

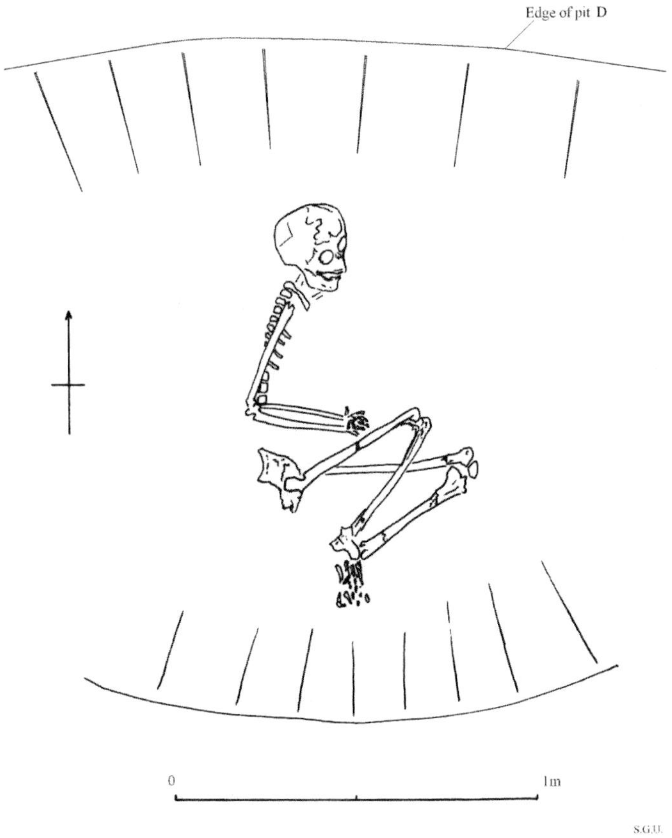

Edge of pit D

0   1m

S.G.U.

Figure 8 The burial from Iron Age pit D

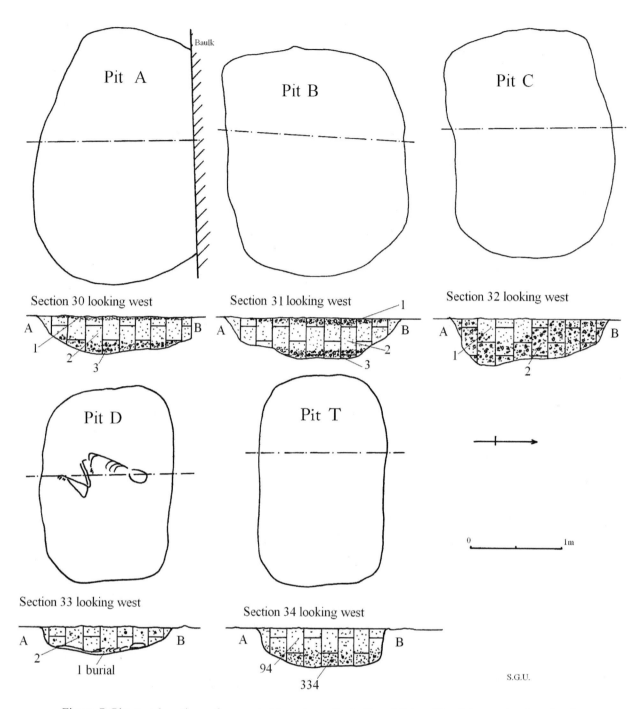

Figure 7 Plans and sections of excavated Iron Age pits A–D and T (see Fig. 5 for section locations)

side with the head facing to the east (Fig. 8 and Pl. 8). The bones were very badly preserved and crumbled into powder on excavation, and only part of the total skeletal assemblage survived. There were no accompanying grave goods or pottery and the body was laid directly onto the gravel floor of the pit (see Fig. 7 Pit D). Iron Age pottery was recovered, however, from Pits F, H, J and L (see Chapter 7 and Fig. 80, nos 1–4; these pits (H, J and L) are also shown in section in S35, S36 and S37: see Fig. 15 and Table 2). A total of eighty-three sherds of Iron Age pottery was recovered from the excavations, largely from Area A. Limited amounts of animal bone were also recovered from some of the pits and two fragments of triangular loom weights of probable Iron Age date also come from the area

associated with the pits (see Fig. 76). The Iron Age pit deposits also produced quantities of pot boilers formed from river cobbles (see Chapter 6, IX Quern stones, hone stones and other stone objects; Pl. 55)

The pit alignment was the only feature associated with late Iron Age occupation. There was no sign or indication of the types of settlement evidence, such as enclosure ditches or hut circles, that were encountered at other local sites, such as at Monument 97 or along the fen-edge at the Fengate sites on the outskirts of Peterborough (Mackreth 2001; Pryor 1974; 1978; 1980; 1984). However, the cropmark features to the east, and outside the excavated area, indicated considerable late pre-Roman occupation.

Period 2. Roman military occupation
(Figs 9–11)

The suggestion was put forward as early as 1972, based on two aerial photographs taken by J.K.S. St Joseph when the area was under crop, that a Roman military installation was located within the area of the LF2 site (NVRC 1973). These photographs showed, to the east of Ham Lane, two parallel ditches running approximately north–south which at their southern end then turned to the east, with a rounded corner forming the change of alignment; all these features are reminiscent of a Roman military installation. The air photographs also showed a similar parallel pair of ditches to the north and some 180m away from the ditches to the south, while another pair were recorded further to the east (see Fig. 3).

During the excavations it soon became clear that this rounded corner and parts of the parallel ditches were within the limits of Area A, and trenches were set out to examine these features. It was found that in part the ditches had cut into the earlier Iron Age pit alignment, as can be seen in Plate 7, where Pit F is truncated by the later military ditch. Figure 9 indicates the layout of these excavation trenches and shows the line of the Roman military ditches, as well as a series of pits which contained pottery associated with this military phase of the site. The pair of parallel ditches ran through Trenches 44, 45, 49, 50, 54 and 71, all in Area A, and were also seen in Area B (see Fig. 45 was 46 S125). Although it should be noted that in most of the sections dug across these ditches the actual depth and widths of the original features was obscured by the fact that the gravel extraction machinery had already stripped some of the upper levels away from the archaeological features, the sections (Fig. 10 S40–S44 and Fig. 45 was 46 S125) showed that the western/southern 'outer' ditch was the shallower and narrower of the pair. This ditch had a rounded profile, was 0.75–0.40m deep in the shallowest section and varied from 1.15m to 0.80m wide (see Fig. 10). The larger, 'inner' ditch varied between 0.90m and 0.60m deep and was from 2.0m to 1.80m wide. This ditch also differed from the outer ditch in that it was asymmetrical in profile, with a slightly steeper 'inner' face and a shallower outer face, while the outer ditch had a rounded profile. One section across the 'inner' ditch (Fig. 10 S42) revealed a narrow slot at the bottom which may have been dug to assist drainage.

The fills of the 'outer' ditch sections consisted of fairly clean gravel with occasional fragments of pottery and bone. In contrast, the fills of the 'inner' ditch were more varied; mixed clean sand and gravel were present but three sections (S41, S42 and S43) also produced a layer of reddish-brown clayey loam with a gravel mix. It may be that this material represents a possible demolition process at the site in which part of the rampart of the fort was thrown back into the ditch. Certainly none of the ditches had any primary silting that might indicate that they were open for any length of time, unless regular cleaning during the military occupation had removed all trace of such silt.

If the indications from the air photographs referred to above do represent the outline of a Roman fort then it would appear to have eastern and western sides of approximately 175m in length, with the southern side being approximately 150m long. This would give an internal area of approximately 2.8ha, or seven acres. The indications from the ditch profiles and the apparent corner noted above suggested that the central area of Area A was inside the circuit of the possible fort — to be precise, in the south-western corner of the fort — the original main area of which lay to the north-east.

Excavations within the area of Area A and away from what were presumed to be the defensive ditches of the fort also revealed five pits which all contained pottery and other finds of the same period. These pits were underneath and to the side of a later aisled building, the outline of which is marked in Figure 9. As with the outer defensive ditches, some levels that had formed the upper fills of these pits had been removed or compressed by modern gravel extraction machinery (see, for example, Pit 3, shown in section in Fig. 11). All these pits were oval in plan and ranged from 0.25m to 0.75m deep, although the shallowest of these pits had had its upper fills removed prior to archaeological excavation. It is also possible that they had been set out in two rows, one row consisting of Pits 3–5, with a parallel row of Pits 1 and 2. It was also seen that the fills of the pits varied between these two possible rows. The fills of Pits 3–5 were more sandy/gravelly when compared with those from Pits 1 and 2, which not only comprised more layers but contained a greater variety of material. The upper layers of the latter two pits had been capped with limestone fragments and gravel during a later period when the overlying aisled building was in use, and the soft fills of the pits were beginning to become compressed. Below this capping, however, many of the fills contained silty loam with green flecking which was possibly derived from sewage. It therefore seems likely that either or both of these pits were originally dug as latrine pits or they were being filled with sewage as a secondary and later use.

The pottery recovered from contexts within this military phase of the site contained many fragments which matched the pottery found at the site of the fortress and military works depot at Longthorpe, some 1km to the east (Frere and St Joseph 1974; Dannell and Wild 1987). The obvious implication is that the two sites functioned at much the same time and pottery produced at the works depot was used at the LF2 fort. Finds from the LF2 parallel ditches included two fragments of rotary quern stones (Fig. 73), one formed out of lava stone which came from the Rhineland (from Trench 49, II, 263 — Fig. 9; Fig. 10 S42) and the other, a coarse grit stone, whose provenance is uncertain (from Trench 44, II, 248 — Fig. 9; Fig. 10 S41). A complete iron axe head was also recovered from context 19 in Pit 1 (see Fig. 11 S45). The querns and axe head are typical finds on military sites and are discussed more fully below.

In addition to these finds from the LF2 excavations, Adrian Challands found cremation burials accompanied by pottery made in the Longthorpe military works depot kilns. There was also a fragment of a mid-1st-century brooch dated to *c*. AD 50–65 (Wild 1973a, 21; NVRC 1973; *Northamptonshire Archaeology* 1973, 8, 9). These cremations lay some 80m from the fort ditches and to the west of Ham Lane. One burial contained at least four vessels and the excavator commented that the 'burning around the edge of the burial pits echoed a mode of cremation practiced in the Roman Rhineland in the 1st century' (*Northamptonshire Archaeology* 1973, 9).

However, a note of caution should be added to this interpretation as a military site. Many examples of multiple-ditched sub-rectangular Iron Age or early Roman enclosure farmsteads are known within the area.

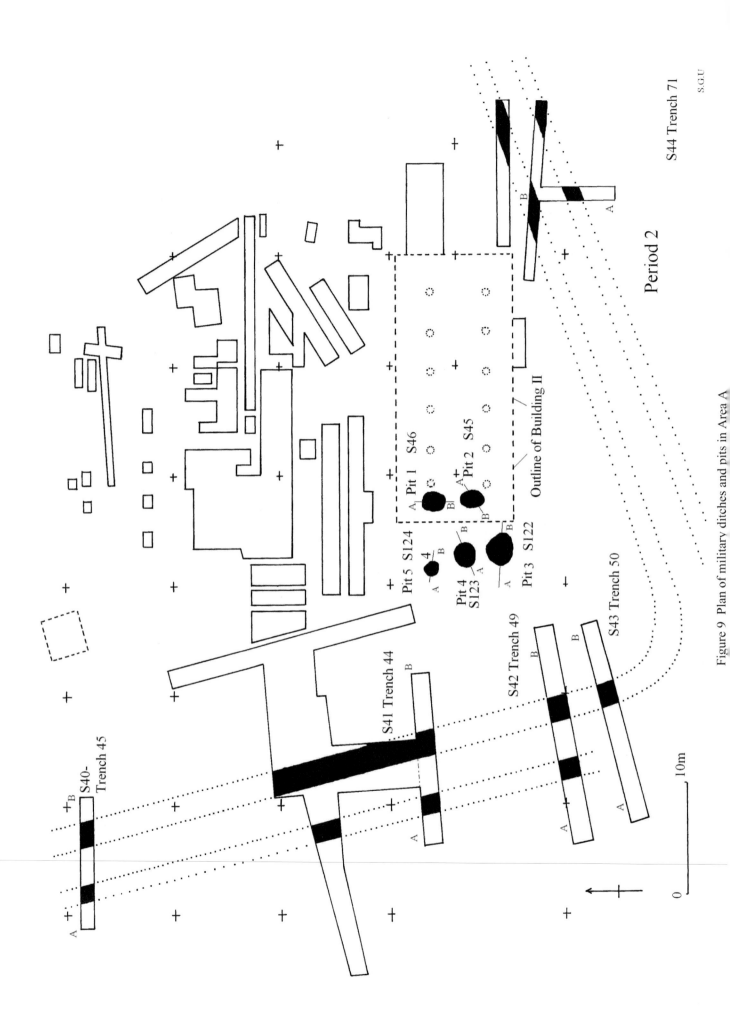

S.G.U

Period 2

S44 Trench 71

Outline of Building II

Pit 1 S46

Pit 2 S45

Pit 5 S124

Pit 4 S123

Pit 3 S122

S41 Trench 44

S40- Trench 45

S42 Trench 49

S43 Trench 50

10m

0

Figure 9 Plan of military ditches and pits in Area A

16

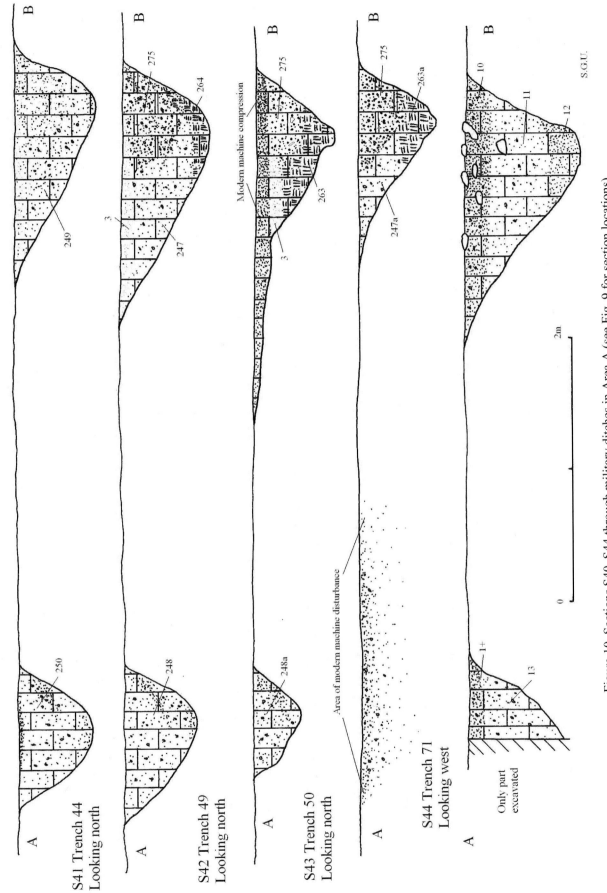

S40 Trench 45
Looking north

S41 Trench 44
Looking north

S42 Trench 49
Looking north

S43 Trench 50
Looking north

S44 Trench 71
Looking west

A

B

249

250

275

247

248

3

264

275

263

248a

Modern machine compression

3

Area of modern machine disturbance

275

247a

263a

10

11

12

1+

13

S.G.U.

Only part excavated

0

2m

Figure 10 Sections S40–S44 through military ditches in Area A (see Fig. 9 for section locations)

17

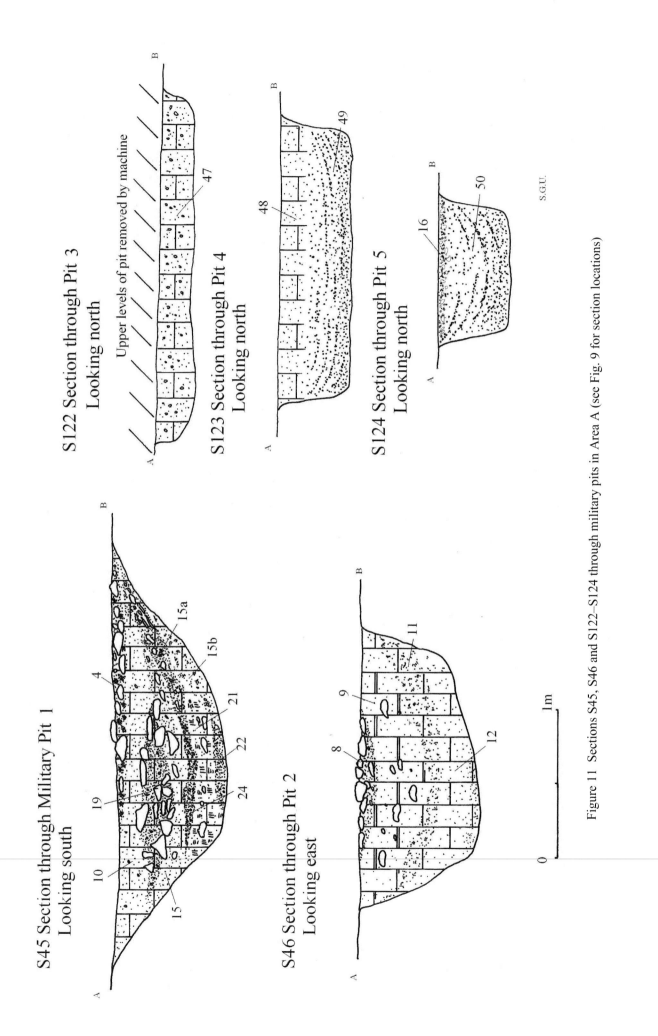

S45 Section through Military Pit 1
Looking south

S46 Section through Pit 2
Looking east

S122 Section through Pit 3
Looking north

Upper levels of pit removed by machine

S123 Section through Pit 4
Looking north

S124 Section through Pit 5
Looking north

S.G.U.

1m

Figure 11 Sections S45, S46 and S122–S124 through military pits in Area A (see Fig. 9 for section locations)

18

Deegan has outlined numerous examples from Northamptonshire, including large near-rectangular multiple-ditched enclosures and very regular enclosures laid out in a gridlike pattern (Deegan 2007, figs 6.10, 6.11 and 6.15). The two enclosures in Upton parish, some 4km to the west of Lynch Farm, were referred to as 'Roman' by the Royal Commission in 1969 (RCHM 1969, 34, fig. 14 and pl. 3) and labelled on Ordnance Survey maps as 'Roman camps' until their excavation in the 1980s showed one of them to be Neolithic and the other to be Iron Age (Adrian Challands pers. comm. — these excavations await publication). Thus it is possible that the ditches represent some form of non-military complex, although within this report the author has, on balance, taken the view that a military case can be argued.

Period 3. Late 1st/early 2nd century
(Figs 12–18; Pls 9 –12)
The lack of dating evidence makes it difficult to be certain when the military occupation of the site ceased, but the fills of the military ditches and the five pits contained no pottery or samian later than *c*. AD 65–70, which is also the proposed date for the abandonment of the fortress at Longthorpe (Frere and St Joseph 1974, 36–8). The best evidence, therefore, suggests that both military sites were abandoned at the same time, with the military personnel moving further north. The indication from the fills of the various features associated with the military occupation at LF2 is that the site was partly cleared and levelled, with the ramparts perhaps being thrown into the ditches.

Pits 6 and 7
However, very soon after this military abandonment, the site seems to have been taken over and two pits dug within the circuit of the Period 2 defensive ditches. The first pit, 6, was dug into the gravel (Fig. 12 and Fig. 13 S128) and backfilled fairly quickly; this was followed by a second, larger pit (Pit 7), which partly cut into the filling of the earlier pit. Why both pits were dug is unclear; they may have been dug for gravel, although where this was used is not known. It is equally possible that they may have been 'delvings' to obtain iron nodules for metalworking. The Nene valley gravels contain various amounts of iron which concretes into nodules and also forms 'pans' from which it is possible that iron could have been extracted. These two pits did contain a few sherds of early Roman pottery, but none matched the pottery from the military phase of the site and it was therefore thought that they were post-military in origin. These pits were also large (Pit 7 was approximately 4.0×2.8m) and comparatively deep (1.35m), and so it is difficult to see how they would have been used or would have fitted into any sort of arrangement within a fort. However, the finds from these pits were very limited and it is just possible that they belonged to the military phase.

Once dug into the backfill of Pit 6, Pit 7 in turn was soon backfilled with material that contained various fragments of mid–late 1st-century pottery. There was some evidence that during this backfilling process a small recut pit was dug (see Fig. 13 S128), but this in turn was filled in fairly quickly. Neither of the pits had any evidence of silts being allowed to build up.

Ditch 3
Once Pit 7 was part-filled the site was enclosed by three sides of what could be interpreted a ditched enclosure which followed the line of the partially filled-in military ditch from Period 2 on the western side (Fig. 12 Ditch 3). This ditch line also was seen in the sections through the 'inner' military ditch (Figure 10, S41, S42 and S43 (layer 275 in all section drawings)).

The north-western corner of the enclosure is also shown in Plates 9 and 10, where it can be seen cutting the part-backfilled line of the Period 2 inner military ditch and the even earlier Iron Age pits from Period 1. The stratigraphical relationship between the Iron Age pits, the inner military ditch and the mid–late 1st-century line of Ditch 3 is also shown in Figure 14, where in S28 and S29 (see Fig. 12 for the positions of these sections) the line of Ditch 3 is seen cutting into the earlier military ditch, which in turn cuts into Iron Age Pits F and G.

On the northern side of the enclosure Ditch 3 turned from the military ditch line and ran to the east for approximately 35m. This line is shown in Plates 11 and 12 and in section drawings S35–S39 (Fig. 15). The line of the ditch also cut over the top of the earlier Pits 6 and 7, where it was seen in S128 (Fig. 13). The laying out of Ditch 3 may have used the depressions of these part-filled-in pits as markers because Ditch 3, once it had rounded the area of these two pits, then turned to the south and ran for another 32m. This ditch line is shown in section drawings S60–S66 (Fig. 16).

Beyond this point the ditch line was not detected or excavated, but it is possible that it followed the southern side of the earlier military ditch line — as it had on its western side — and thus completed a circuit. The lack of available land for excavation (owing to gravel extraction) around what would have been the southern side of both the military ditch and the putative circuit formed by Ditch 3, made even partial interpretation impossible. However, if the hypothesis advanced above is valid, it would suggest that the enclosure formed by Ditch 3 was approximately 35m square. There was no indication of any entrance into the enclosure or any internal features other than a small kiln which produced pottery (see below). However, the time limits imposed by the requirements of the gravel extraction company and the extremely dry conditions during parts of the excavation limited the scope of the archaeological work and some features may have been overlooked.

At several points on the northern side of the line of Ditch 3 it was seen to have cut into the fills of the earlier Iron Age pit alignment. These cuts can be seen in Figure 14 S28–S29, and Figure 15 S35, S37–S39; they are also partly seen in Plates 9–12. For most of the rest of the circuit the line of Ditch 3 was masked by later features, especially those associated with the aisled buildings of later periods.

The fills and profile of Ditch 3 varied considerably along its total length (for descriptions of fills see Appendix 2). Along its northern length it was generally 1.0m wide and varied between 0.45m and 0.75m deep. Along its eastern length it varied similarly, but here, various sections along its line show that it was recut. For example there is a short length of a recut shown in Fig. 16 S61, and then it appears to have been recut for over twelve metres or more (see Fig. 16, S63–S66). These recuts were clearly made when the ditch was part-filled and there was some evidence for primary silting in S61 (layer 218a) and in the dark loamy fills shown in S64 (layer 67) and S65 (layer 85) (Fig. 16).

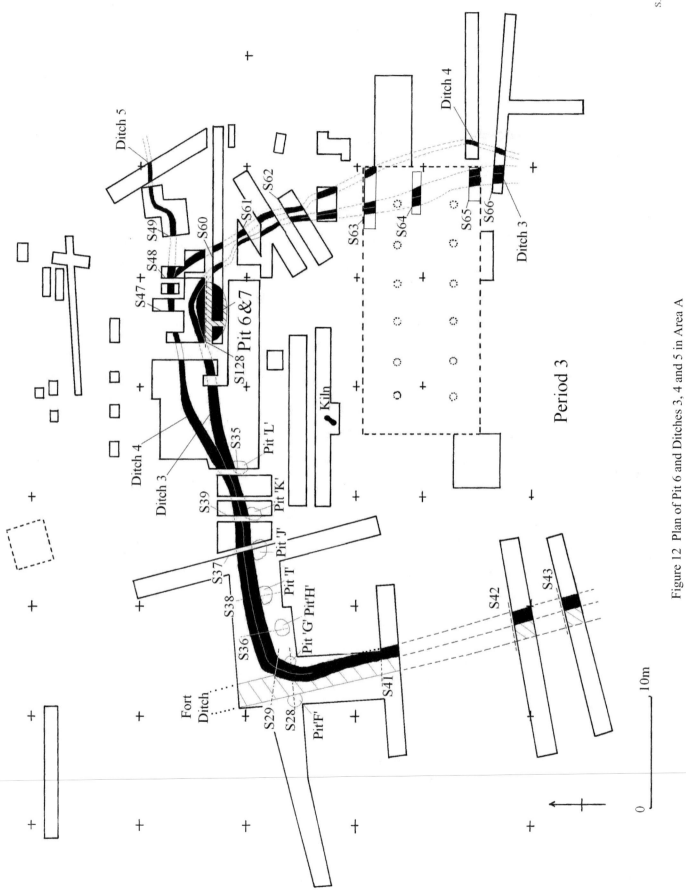

S.G.U

Ditch 5

Ditch 4

S62

S61

S60

S49
S48

S47

S128 Pit 6 & 7

Ditch 4

Ditch 3

S35

Pit 'L'

S39

Pit 'K'

Kiln

S37

Pit 'J'

Pit 'I'

S38

S36

Pit 'G' Pit 'H'

Fort
Ditch

S29

S28

Pit'F'

S41

S42

S43

S63

S64

S65

S66

Ditch 3

Period 3

10m

0

Figure 12 Plan of Pit 6 and Ditches 3, 4 and 5 in Area A

20

S128 Section of Pit 6 in Trench 11
Looking south

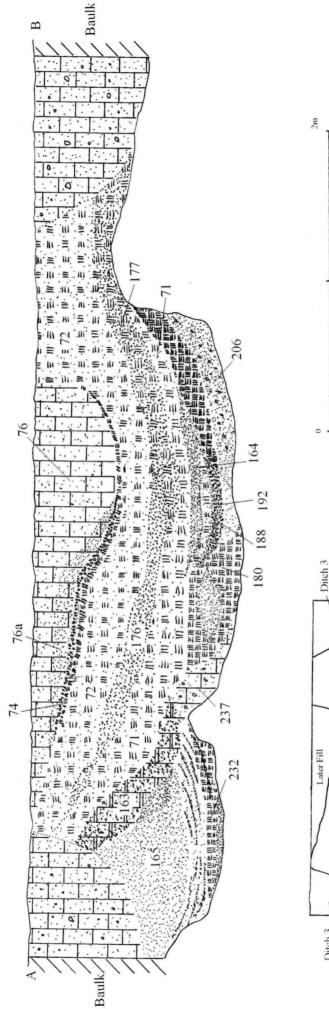

Figure 13   Section S128 through Pit 6 in Area A

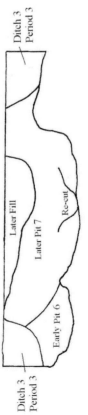

Interpretive view of main section

21

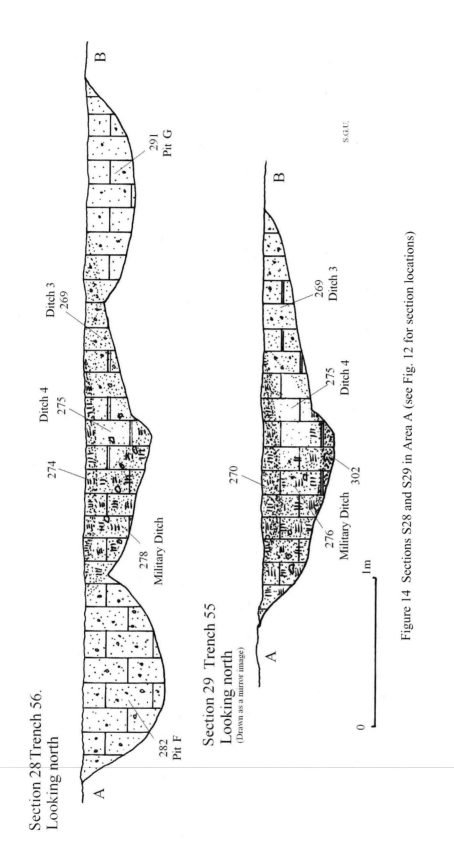

Section 28 Trench 56.
Looking north

Section 29 Trench 55
Looking north
(Drawn as a mirror image)

Figure 14 Sections S28 and S29 in Area A (see Fig. 12 for section locations)

22

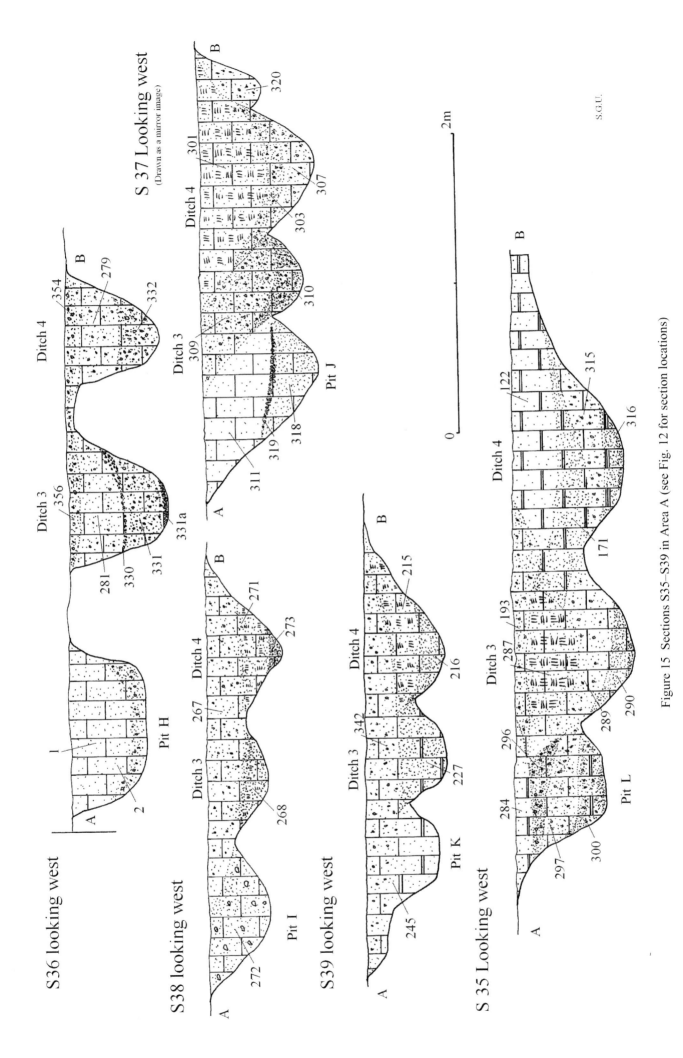

Figure 15 Sections S35–S39 in Area A (see Fig. 12 for section locations)

S36 looking west

Ditch 4

B
354
279
332

Ditch 3
356
281
330
331
331a

Pit H
A
2

S 37 Looking west
(Drawn as a mirror image)

B
320
301
307
303

Ditch 4

Ditch 3
309
310

Pit J
319
318
311
A

2m

0

S.G.U.

S38 looking west

B
271
273

Ditch 4
267

Ditch 3

268

Pit I
A
272

S39 looking west

B
215

Ditch 4
216

Ditch 3
342
227

Pit K
245
A

S 35 Looking west

B
122
315
316

Ditch 4
171

193
287

Ditch 3
296
289
290

Pit L
284
297
300
A

23

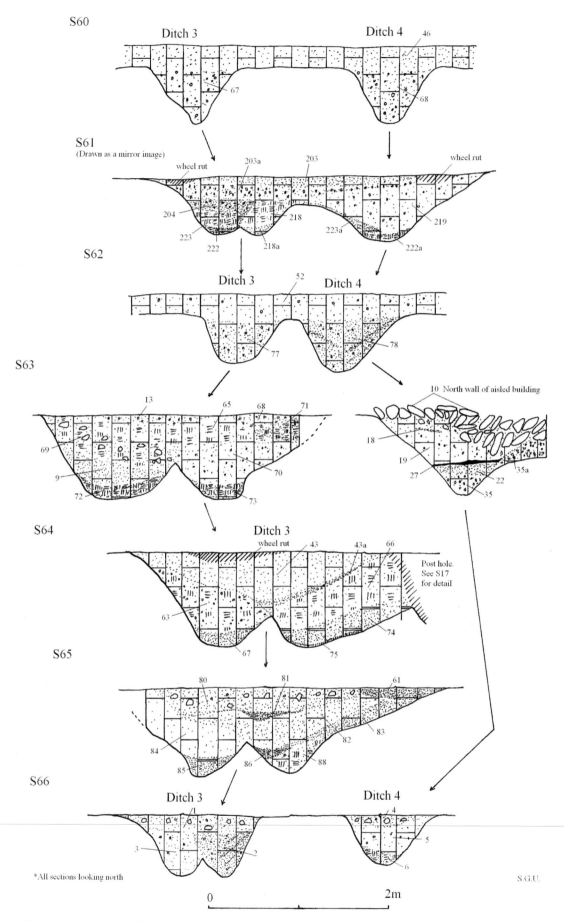

Figure 16 Sections S60–S66 in Area A (all sections looking north, see Fig. 12 for section locations)

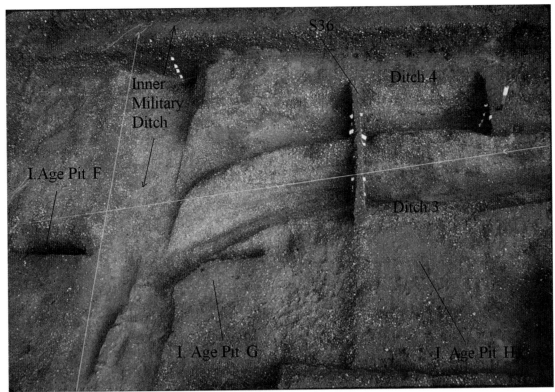

Plate 9 Area A, excavation of part of the Iron Age (Period 2) pit alignment (Pits F, G and H) cut by the fort ditch (Period 3), which in turn was cut by Ditches 3 and 4 (Period 3)

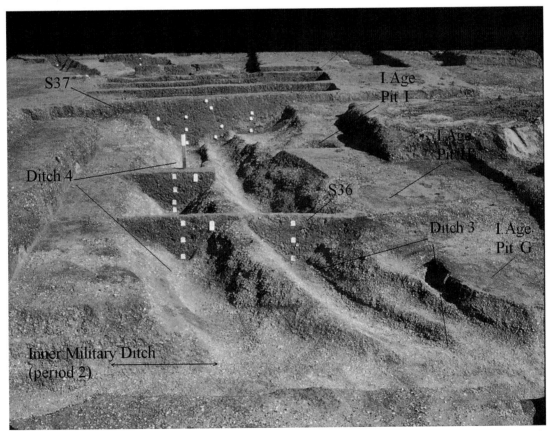

Plate 10 Area A, Iron Age pit alignment (Period 1) cut by fort ditch (Period 2), cut by Ditches 3 and 4 (Period 3)

Plate 12 Area A, looking east: Iron Age pit alignment (Pits I, J and L) (Period 2) cut by Ditches 3 and 4 (Period 3)

Plate 11 Area A, looking west: Ditches 3 and 4 under excavation (Period 3)

26

Ditch 4

The impression from the finds from Ditch 3 and the line of the slightly later Ditch 4 is that Ditch 3 was open for a limited amount of time, although admittedly long enough for some primary silting to occur and for short recuts to have been required to maintain the line of the ditch. However, at some point when the line of Ditch 3 was partly filled in, the line of the ditch was re-established by the cutting of Ditch 4. The line of Ditch 4 (shown in Fig. 12) follows the former line of Ditch 3 for 20m of its northern and western lengths and then heads slightly further north and breaks with the line of Ditch 3 (see Pls 11–12). It then turns south and runs roughly parallel with the former line of Ditch 3 until its line ran out of the area available for excavation. As has been suggested for Ditch 3, it is possible that Ditch 4 could have followed the southern line of the earlier military ditch. Certainly, it was seen to turn and cut into the line of Ditch 3 and the earlier military ditch in the north-western corner of the possible enclosure (see Fig. 12; Fig. 14 S28–S29; Pls 9–10). The implication here is that the ditch again followed the line of the original military ditch, maintaining the boundary which had been established in the middle of the 1st century.

In various sections cut through this ditch along its northern length it was seen to be slightly wider than Ditch 3 (see Fig. 15 S35–S39 and Fig. 17 S47), although where it turns to the south it becomes narrow and shallow (Fig. 16 S60–S66). The fills along its entire length are very similar to those found within Ditch 3, namely varied and mixed (see Appendix 2).

Ditch 5

At a date when at least the north-eastern corner of the line of Ditch 4 had been partly filled in, a small ditch, Ditch 5,

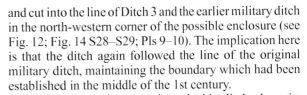
S47. Sections through Ditches 4 and 5

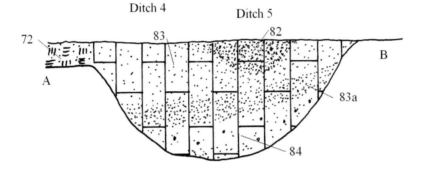

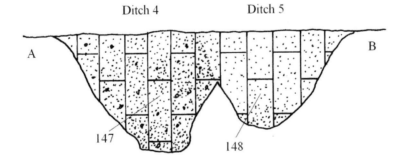
S48. Section through ditch junction - looking west

S49. Section through ditch extension to east and Iron Age Ditch R - looking west

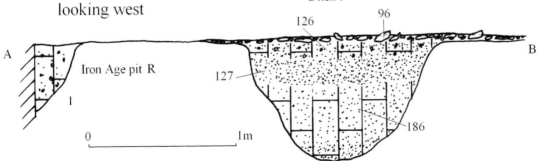

Figure 17 Sections S47–S49 in Area A (see Fig. 12 for section locations)

was cut into its upper fills and ran for some 10m to the east. The line of this ditch had a slight dog-leg along part of its length (Fig. 12; Fig. 17 S47–S49). This ditch appeared to increase in depth and width as it ran to the east. It was first seen in S47 as a slight upper recut (layer 82) into the top of Ditch 4 (layers 83/83a/84), but at the point where S48 was cut (see Fig. 12) the line of this feature was seen to be a separate ditch in its own right, and its width and depth were seen to increase further in S49 (Fig. 17). This ditch was also observed in Trench T16 (see Fig. 4 for trench plan), where it was 1.20m wide and 0.75m deep. Unfortunately it was not recorded to the east of T16, other than being observed within the bank of the lake when gravel extraction was underway.

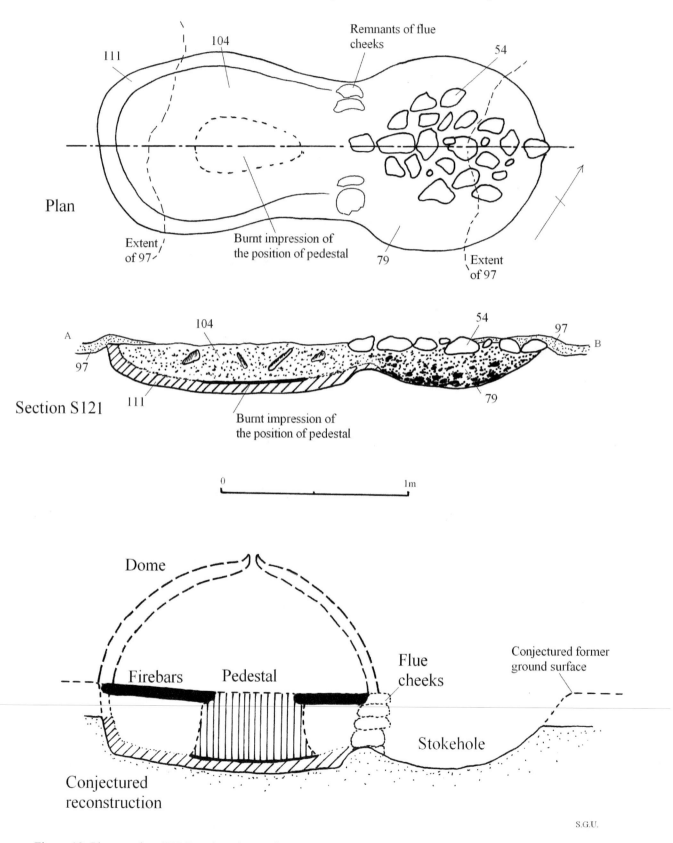

Figure 18 Plan, section (S121) and conjectured reconstruction of kiln (Period 3) (see Fig. 12 for kiln location)

28

The finds from all three of these ditches, especially the pottery, spanned the latter part of the 1st century and the first half of the 2nd century. Apart from the stratigraphical relationships between the three ditches there was little to separate the finds into distinct, datable groups, even though the material from Ditch 3 could well have been potentially 60–80 years earlier than the material from Ditch 5. The general impression was that Ditch 3 had been deliberately part-filled before Ditch 4 was dug and that the same was true of the relationship between Ditches 4 and 5. However, the pottery from all three contexts contained some sizable sherds, giving the impression that it had been discarded very shortly after being broken and was not residual in these features. Some contexts contained large sherd assemblages. For example, context LF2 II, 171 contained sixty-eight sherds weighing 1.390kg (see Fig. 15 S35) and seemed to represent a single deposit of recently broken pottery (see also Fig. 84 for part of this assemblage).

The pottery kiln
In what would have been the open area of the enclosure probably formed by Ditches 3 and 4 a surface-built pottery kiln was constructed. The kiln had a rounded firing chamber 1.25m long and 0.75m wide that at its south-western end had a small round stokehole 0.50m in diameter (for the position of this kiln see Fig. 12 and for detail see Fig. 18). The flue still retained some of its baked clay lining, in the bottom of which was the burnt impression of what was interpreted as the position of a small pedestal for supporting the fire bars and floor of the firing chamber. There was some evidence that at the junction between the firing chamber and the stokehole there had once been a limestone wall which would have formed the flue cheeks and through which a flue would have been formed, connecting the stokehole with the firing chamber. The stokehole contained charcoal and ash (Fig. 18 S121, layer 79) and the upper part was filled with burnt limestone packing, which could have come from the demolished flue cheeks. From this evidence it was possible to partly reconstruct the form and cross section of the kiln (Fig. 18).

The kiln appears to have been producing very early forms of lower Nene valley grey wares and must represent one of the earliest identifiable grey ware kilns in the lower Nene valley area. Within the fill of layer 104 (see Fig. 18 S121) were several fragments of grey ware vessels, including beakers and jars, two of which are illustrated (Fig. 83 no. 40 and Fig. 85 no. 70).

The kiln was probably active when either Ditches 4 or 5 were open. Part of a straight-sided bowl, which was probably a 'waster', was recovered from context 171 in Ditch 4 (Fig. 15 S35). This vessel was in an identical fabric to the vessels recovered from within the firing chamber of the kiln. Also recovered from Ditch 5 (context 186; Fig. 17 S49) were a collection of three fire bars and a fragment of a dome plate. The fire bars matched a fourth fire bar recovered from the chamber of the kiln. The fire bars and dome plate are reported below (see Chapter 6, XII Objects of burnt clay including briquetage and fire bars; and Pl. 59).

The kiln appears to have operated during either the very late 1st century or more probably the first half of the 2nd century, and was out of use by *c*. AD 150–60, when fragments of 'London' type ware were found within the sealing deposit (see context 97, Fig. 18 S121) over the already demolished firing chamber and stokehole. The style and construction of the kiln is unusual in that it is not a classic surface-built kiln — as noted at the military works depot at Longthorpe (Dannell and Wild 1987) — nor is it a kiln where the firing chamber and stokehole are dug into the ground, which is the more common later and certainly larger type of structure that one might expect in the mid-2nd to 4th centuries (see, for example, Hartley 1960; Hadman and Upex 1975a; Upex 2008b). The basic structure of the kiln is close to Wood's Type IC (Woods 1974, fig. 2) or Swan's 'Type iii', which she describes as a 'surface built kiln with an open-topped temporary superstructure' (Swan 1984, fig. II). It may be that this type of kiln, where the firing chamber is above ground, represents a local, transitional form of structure between the surface-built kilns of the 1st century and what came later.

Period 4. Late 2nd century
(Figs 19–24; Pls 13–18)
The ditched enclosure that had been created during Period 3 was eventually levelled by the middle of the 2nd century. The ditches were filled in with fairly clean material containing loams, sand and gravels. Such infilling actually continued for the next two centuries, as these ditches continually sagged and were then consolidated with residual material from the later occupation of the site. During the later part of the 2nd century the site appears to have been laid out anew with an aisled building and a section of ditch. This period of the site is shown in Figure 19.

Aisled Building I
Nearly all traces of this building, apart from its nave post-holes, had been swept away by later occupation, but enough survived to recover a plan of the structure and an associated lean-to on the north, which are shown in detail in Figure 20. The aisled structure was orientated roughly north–south and had overall dimensions of approximately 7.0×11.5m. However, the short axis walls were of different lengths (south 7.5m; north 6.5m), so the building was not perfectly rectangular. Eight posts were set in pairs to form a central nave and two side aisles. These posts were slightly splayed in their alignment, being 3.5m between centres at the northern end of the building, (Posts 1 and 2), and 3.95m between centres at the southern end, (Posts 7 and 8). One pair of posts was missing (Posts 3 and 4), having been destroyed by a later phase of building on the site. The posts were set in holes dug into the underlying gravel subsoil of the site, although Post 8 was dug into the top fills of the underlying ditch from Period 3 (see Fig. 21 S17 and Fig. 16 S64). The posts had been packed around the base with limestone and gravel and then the holes were backfilled to hold the post upright and fast (see Pls 13 and 14). The line of posts forming the nave also formed the inner edge of aisles that were a fairly standard width of 1.75m and extended around both the long and the short axis walls.

Nearly all traces of the surrounding walling of the structure appeared to have been either destroyed by later occupation or deliberately levelled during a second phase of construction. In the north-eastern corner of the building were the remains of much damaged limestone footings set within a gravel matrix. In addition, another possible fragment of pitched limestone footing survived along the southern part of the western long axis wall (see Fig. 20).

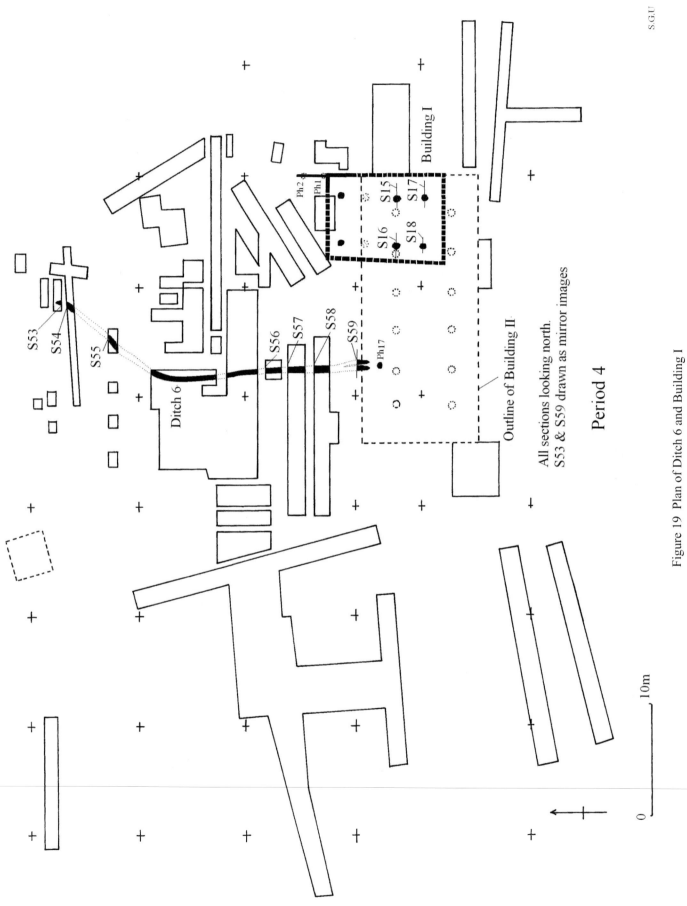

S.G.U

Building I

Ph2
Ph1

S15
S17
S16
S18

S53
S54
S55

Ditch 6

S56
S57
S58
S59

Ph17

Outline of Building II

All sections looking north.
S53 & S59 drawn as mirror images

Period 4

10m

0

Figure 19 Plan of Ditch 6 and Building I

30

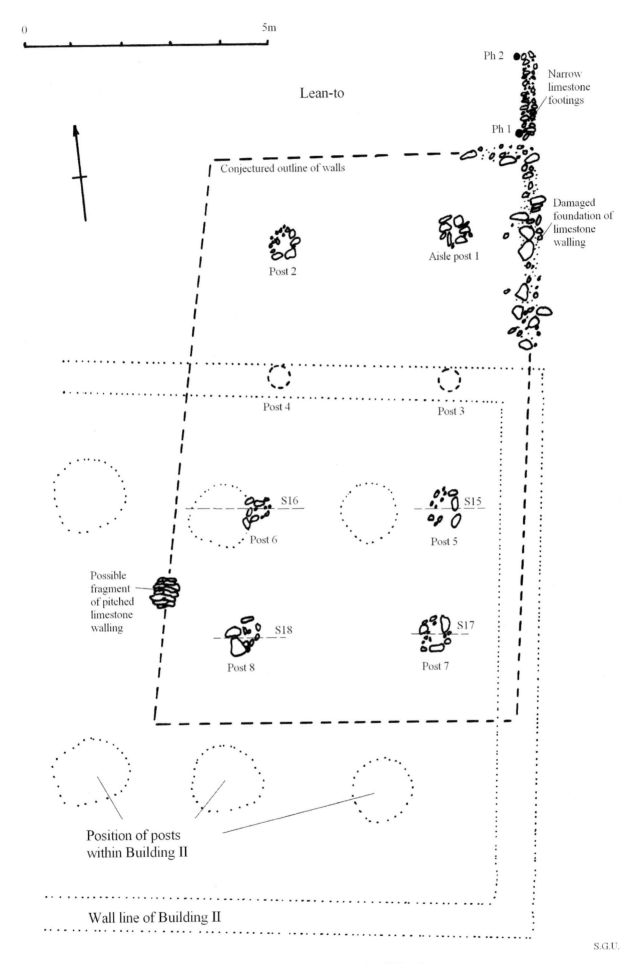

0   5m

Lean-to

Ph 2

Narrow
limestone
footings

Ph 1

Conjectured outline of walls

Damaged
foundation of
limestone
walling

Aisle post 1

Post 2

Post 4

Post 3

S16

S15

Post 6

Post 5

Possible
fragment
of pitched
limestone
walling

S18

S17

Post 8

Post 7

Position of posts
within Building II

Wall line of Building II

S.G.U.

Figure 20 Detailed plan of Building I

The surrounding limestone pitched walling probably represents a dwarf wall which would have been constructed as the foundation of a wooden superstructure, probably of overlapping weatherboard construction.

Furnaces

There was no evidence of any entrance into the structure and nothing survived to suggest any internal arrangements. However, six furnaces or ovens were located within the structure and appear to be contemporary with its use (Fig. 22). These features were positioned away from the bases of the aisle posts, presumably to reduce the risk of fire. Most had their flue ends to the south-east or east, apart from Furnace 5, which had its flue at its north-eastern end. These furnaces can be roughly divided into two groups: those which have stone linings and those which do not. Furnaces 1, 2, 3 and 7 were simple oval scoops in the underlying deposits or the gravel subsoil and contained ash and burnt material. Most had burnt limestone packing within their bowls. Furnace 2 appeared to have the end of its short flue also packed with limestone (see Fig. 23). Furnace 1 had an encircling heavily fired band of burnt sand which lined the bowl of the structure, while the flue end was less heavily burnt (see Pl. 15).

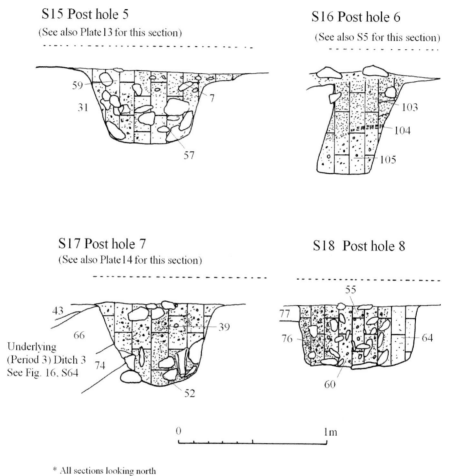

Figure 21 Sections (S15–S18) through post-holes of Building I (see Fig. 20 for section locations)

Plate 13 Area A, Post-hole 5, S15 from Building I
(see Fig. 20)

Plate 14 Area A, Post-hole 7, S17 from Building I
(see Fig. 20)

Of those features which had stone linings, Furnace 4 was very simple in its layout (see Fig. 23 S9, also Pl. 16). It consisted of heavily burned unworked limestone set in a rectangular form. There was little evidence of any stokehole area, but this was the case with all of the furnaces from this period. By contrast, Furnace 5 was more complex, with a recognisable division between the flue and the bowl of the feature (see Fig. 23 S10, Pl. 17). It was also the largest of the structures, measuring 2m along the flue and across the bowl, and was, again, built out of unworked limestone set in courses.

How these furnaces functioned and what their exact purpose was remains uncertain and more will be said of this in the Discussion (Chapter 11). However, there was no evidence of any significant amounts of metal residue in the form of slag or of the sorts of deposit, such as hammerscale, which would be associated with metalworking and metal fabrication processes. Furnaces found at Normangate Field at Castor, and at Ashton and Sacrewell all produced significant amounts of 'scale' and other metalworking debris, and the volumes of ash and 'rake out' at these sites was also large (Dannell 1974 and pers. comm.; Hadman

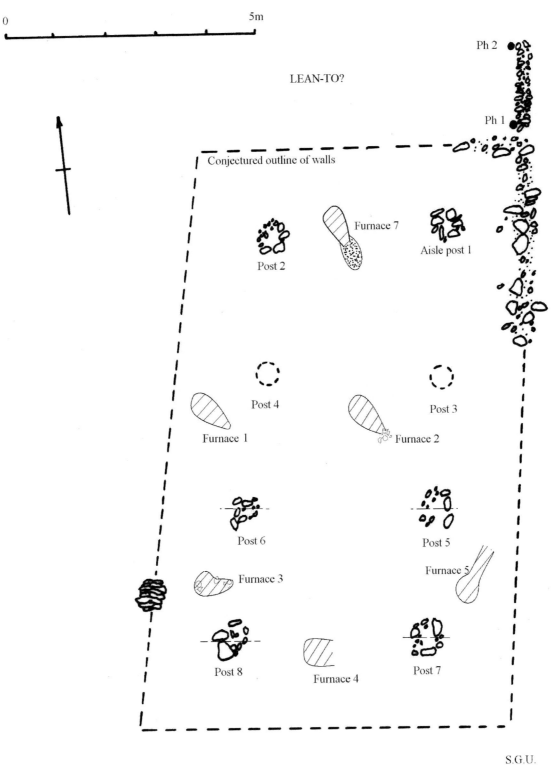

Figure 22 Plan of Furnaces 1–5 within Building I

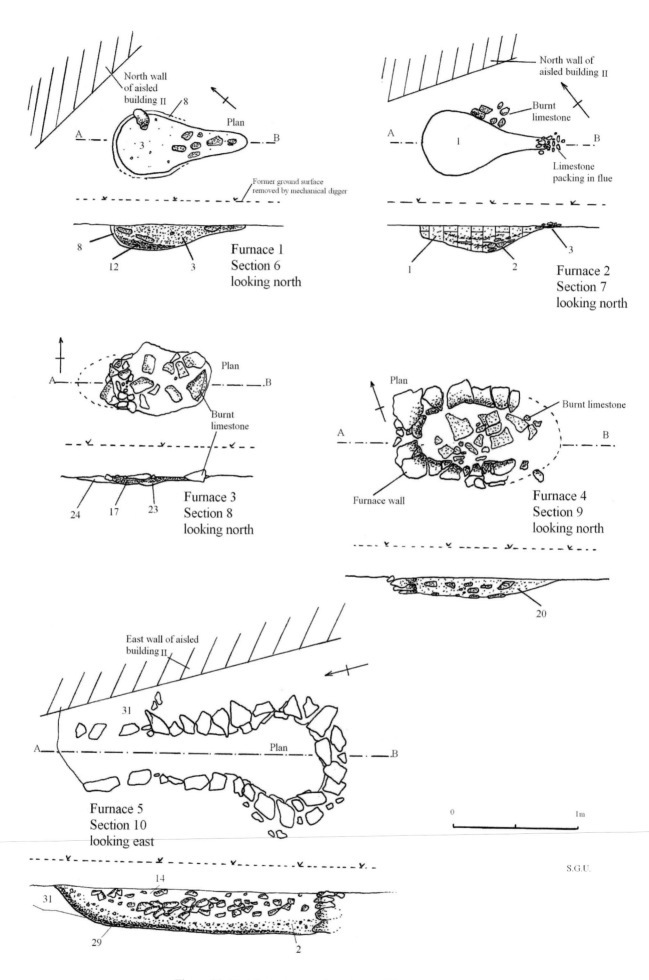

Figure 23 Detail of plans and sections of Furnaces 1–5

34

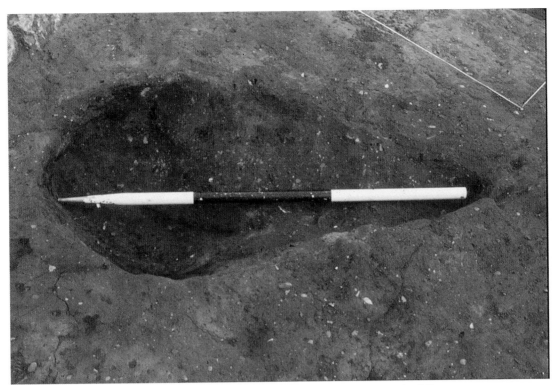

Plate 15 Furnace I in Building I from the west (see Fig. 23)

Plate 16 Furnace 4 in Building I from the south-east (see Fig. 23)

and Upex 1975b, 15; Challands 1974b). Nor was there any evidence that the features were used to fire pottery.

It is possible that the features were all rather utilitarian ovens for either baking or cooking, although the amount of heat generated to redden the 'linings' of the features was considerable. The other option is that they were being used for salt extraction by evaporation. Significant amounts of briquetage (see Chapter 6, XII Objects of burnt clay including briquetage and fire bars) were found in contemporary deposits and one small fragment came from within the fill (context 2; see Fig. 23 S10) of Furnace 5. Most of the other salt extraction sites within the local fenland seem to have been outside (Lane and Morris 2001), so if salt were being extracted within the aisled structure this would perhaps be unusual.

Plate 17 Furnace 2 in Building I from the north
(see Fig. 23)

Lean-to structure
To the north of this aisled building a short length of
limestone walling of a different character to that which
formed the outer walls of the main structure was also
excavated. Along this length of wall were two post-holes
(Ph 1 and Ph 2; see Fig. 20). There was also a very light
spread of limestone and gravel on this northern side of the
building which appeared to have been contained by this
short length of walling, as if it had been spread up to it. The
nature of these constructional and surfacing elements is
difficult to define owing to both later occupational activity
within this area and the destruction caused by the gravel
contractor's heavy machinery first stripping the area of
topsoil and the upper archaeological layers, and then
disturbing the area even further by using it as a
thoroughfare. However, the features may represent some
form of surfaced or floored lean-to arrangement on this
north side of the aisled building.

Ditch 6
Some 10m to the west was a ditch (Ditch 6) that ran
north–south for 20m and then turned to the north-east (see
Fig. 19 and Pl. 18 was 15). The ditch, which was roughly
contemporary with the construction of the aisled building,
had a rounded terminal end to the north-east, where it was
0.45m wide and 0.45m deep. To the south it appeared to
widen to 1.30m and deepen to 0.70m and at its extreme
southern end had been recut so that there were two
separate branches. These sections (Fig. 24) show that,
although the fills were varied, those of the earlier cut to the
south contained clays and limestone fragments, while the
later fill of the recut sections contained more loams and
silts. Part of the answer to the different fills of the two
southern ends of the ditch line is the date at which these
infillings occurred. The ditch is contemporary with the
construction of the aisled building, but the filling-in of the
first cut of this ditch had already started by the very early
3rd century (e.g. layer 69 in S58, Fig. 24). Once

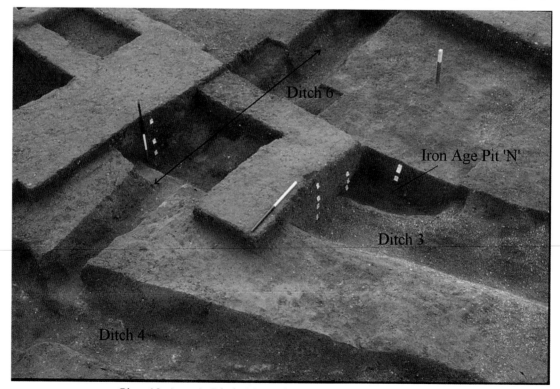

Plate 18 Area A, Ditch 6 (see Fig. 19) cutting Ditches 3 and 4

36

part-filled, this line was then re-established with the recutting of the ditch probably at the same time as the construction of the second aisled building on the site in Period 5. Any continuation of the line of this ditch was not explored during the excavations: the area that it might lie in was within the walls of the second aisled building mentioned above, and this building had both a demolition phase and a later building over this demolition material, thus limiting any work following the line of Ditch 6.

Sections of Ditch 6

S53. Trench 36

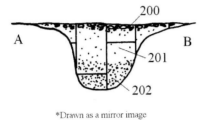

200
A   B
201
202

*Drawn as a mirror image

S54. Trench 32

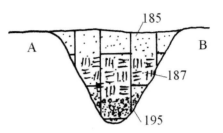

185
A   B
187
195

S55. Trench 28

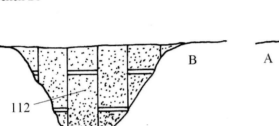

A   B
112

S 56. Trench 25

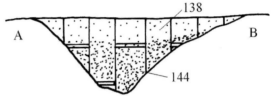

138
A   B
144

S 57. Trench 15

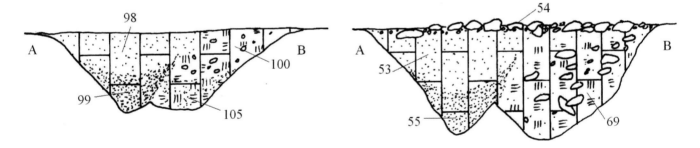

98
A   B
100
99
105

S58. Trench 10

54
A   B
53
55   69

S59. Trench within Aisled Building

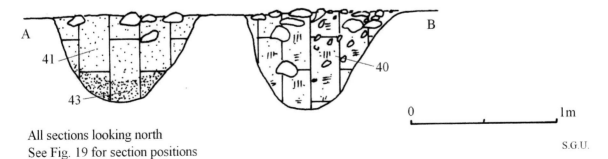

A   B
41
40
43

0   1m

All sections looking north
See Fig. 19 for section positions

S.G.U.

Figure 24 Sections S53–S59 through Ditch 6 (see Fig. 19 for section locations)

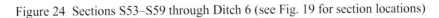

It is possible that Ditch 6 did carry on and formed a boundary to an enclosure that encircled the aisled building. The evidence for this is tenuous, but at the southern terminal end of Ditch 6 was a post-hole (Ph 17 on Fig 19) which could have formed part of a gateway or entrance feature giving access to the aisled building.

End of Period 4

There was little evidence to suggest a lifespan for Aisled Building I. None of the post-pits showed signs of the posts having been replaced — in fact, all of them appear to show considerable disturbance, as if the posts had been removed as part of some sort of demolition event, perhaps prior to the building of the later aisled building (Building II, below). The same can be said of the lean-to on the north side of Building I. The internal furnaces or ovens appear to have been systematically filled in and levelled, and several contained late 2nd-century pottery, but nothing later. The line of Ditch 6, however, was recut (see Fig. 24 S57–S59) after its initial infilling and seems to have carried on into Period 5, possibly associated with the construction of Building II.

Period 5. Early 3rd century
(Figs 25–27; Pls 19–22)

Aisled Building II, Phase I

Building I appears to have been demolished at some point, perhaps around AD 200 or the very beginning of the 3rd century, and a larger aisled structure built. Building I had been set out on a north–south orientation to give approximately 80 square metres of floor space — this new building provided 173 square metres of floor space in its first phase and was set out on a completely new alignment with the long axis of the building orientated east–west (see Figs 19, 25 and 26). The outer wall foundations, approximately 0.85m wide, were of partly pitched limestone masonry and uncoursed limestone rubble bonded with gravel and earth set within a very slight foundation trench. There was little indication of how high this wall stood but it presumably acted as a damp-proof barrier for a timber superstructure of posts covered with a wooden cladding, similar to that described for Building I (above). Along the south wall there were three post-holes set within the width of the wall (see Fig. 26) and these may represent the remnants of a wooden superstructure anchored into the foundation dwarf wall. Alternatively, the limestone foundation wall may have been used as the base for a sole plate or sill beam into which the timber framing was anchored; if this were the general construction technique used for the outer wall then the three posts along the south wall could represent some form of later repair, perhaps when the sill beam had rotted.

The builders were clearly aware of the underlying features from earlier periods, especially the soft fills of Ditches 3 and 4 from Period 3. Where the wall foundations of Building II crossed these ditches the foundations were, in part, continued down into the ditch lines in an attempt to stop the building sagging at these points. This is seen in Plate 19 and Figure 16 (S63), which show the foundation in the north-eastern corner of the building, where it is carried over Ditch 4 by two courses of herringbone masonry.

Internally the roof was held up by eight posts set in four pairs, so that the building was provided with a central nave area 5.5m wide and an aisled area 2.5m wide which ran all the way around the building within the outer wall. The nave posts must have been of some considerable size, as the post-pits that were dug to receive them were substantial. Three sections were taken across the post-pits for Posts 9, 11 and 14 (Figs 26 and 27 and Pls 20 and 21). The post-pits were up to 0.80m deep and up to 1.75m wide at the top, and most were flat-bottomed. There is evidence

Plate 19 North-east corner of Building II over the part-filled Ditch 4 from Period 3 (see S63 in Fig. 16 for this section)

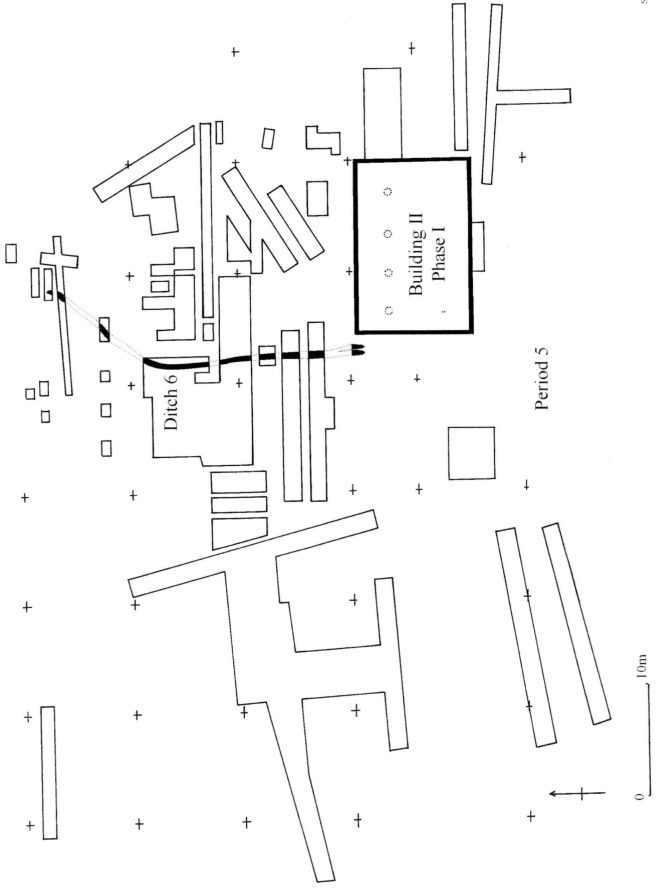

S.G.U

Ditch 6

Building II
Phase I

Period 5

0 _____ 10m

Figure 25 Plan of Building II (Phase I) and Ditch 6 (Period 5)

39

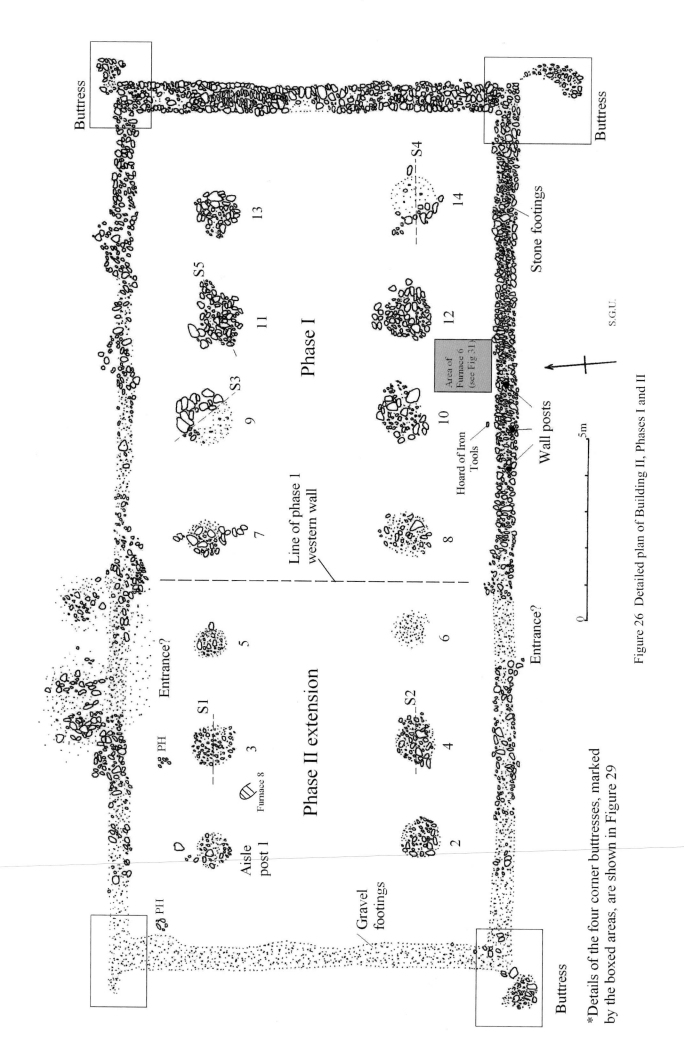

Buttress

Buttress

Phase I

S4

14

S5

13

11

S3

12

Stone footings

9

10

Area of
Furnace 6
(see Fig 31)

Line of phase 1
western wall

Hoard of Iron
Tools

Wall posts

7

8

S.G.U.

5m

Entrance?

0

Entrance?

PH

S1

Phase II extension

3

5

6

Furnace 8

Aisle
post 1

S2

4

2

PII

Gravel
footings

Buttress

Buttress

Figure 26 Detailed plan of Building II, Phases I and II

*Details of the four corner buttresses, marked
by the boxed areas, are shown in Figure 29

40

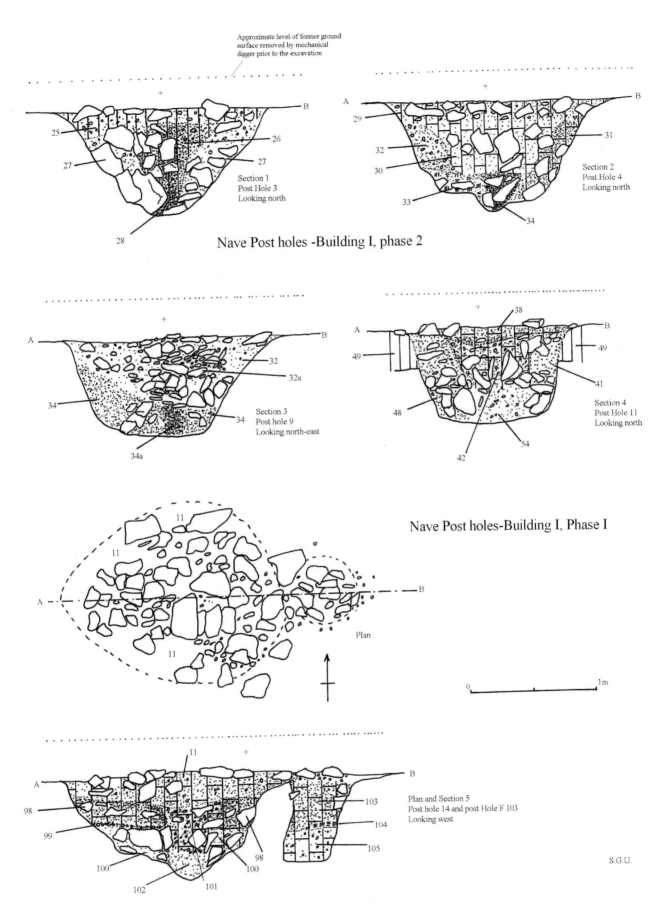

Nave Post holes -Building I, phase 2

Nave Post holes-Building I, Phase I

Figure 27 Sections S1–S5 of the post-holes related to Building II (see Fig. 26 for section locations)

Plate 20 Section of Post-hole 14 within Building II
(see Fig. 26 for position of section line and S4 shown in
Fig. 27)

Plate 22 Top limestone packing around the base of Post
12, within Building II
(see Fig. 26 for the position of this post)

Plate 21 Section of Post-hole 9 within Building II
(see Fig. 26 for position of section line and S3 shown in
Fig. 27)

that, once set into position, the posts were packed around with limestone and gravel which must have then been rammed down hard, making the posts secure. There also seemed to have been an attempt to pack limestone around the posts at the Roman floor level (see Pl. 22), perhaps to protect the post from any internal activities, particularly those involving fire.

How long these posts lasted is debatable and there was little sign that the posts were replaced — if they were, one might expect that the post-pits would have been cleared out so that the packing process around the base of the post could be repeated. Post 9 (see Fig. 27 S3 and Pl. 21) may have rotted *in situ*, as the section of this post-pit revealed what was thought to be the rotted impression of the timber (S3, context 34a) and the part-collapsed central packing around the former post.

In this period there was no indication of any entrance into the building, but entrances could be expected to have existed in both the long and the short axis walls (see Upex 2008a, 134–7). Nor was there any indication as to what the building was used for. The inner area of the building consisted of clean, sandy-gravelly subsoil that was near-indistinguishable from the undisturbed geology apart from slight spreads of burning, which were a residual feature from Building I.

Ditch 6

The dating evidence from Ditch 6 suggests that most of the length of this feature was redug in this period and that it perhaps continued to function as a drainage ditch for Building II. If this were the case the end of this ditch would have terminated close to the north-western corner of the building and would have allowed access around the building at this point (see Figs 19 and 25).

Period 6. Late 3rd century–early 4th century
(Figs 28–36; Pls 23–27)

Aisled Building II, Phase II

Building II was extended to the west in a second phase of construction at some point in the late 3rd or early 4th century by the addition of three extra pairs of posts, giving the aisled building seven pair of posts in total (see Figs 26 and 28 and Pl. 23). This provided for a building still 11.0m wide but now 22.75m long, compared with its former length during Phase I of approximately 12.75m. This extension was carried out with a different foundation arrangement for the encircling outer wall than that employed in Phase I of the building. This contrast between the Phase I and Phase II foundations was especially marked along the south wall of the building. The foundations in the second phase consisted of a shallow trench filled with gravel, although limestone was used as an additional material part-way along the south wall and again in parts of the northern extension wall. However, the western wall had a foundation entirely of gravel, which is particularly noticeable in Plate 23 (see also Fig. 26). Again, it was assumed that a wooden sill beam was set along this gravel/limestone foundation and that a wooden superstructure was set on this sill.

Internally the roof was supported on massive wooden posts set into pits. Two of these post-pits (for Posts 3 and 4) were sectioned (Fig. 27 S1 and S2). These post-pits were similar in shape and dimensions to those dug to accept the posts in Phase I of the building. The posts were again packed around with limestone and gravel to hold them fast in an upright position. The section (S1) through the post-pit for Post 3 suggested that the post had been left to rot *in situ* at the end of the life of the building, as the packing around what would have been the base of the post was still intact and the possible outline of the decayed post was also apparent.

42

Plate 23 Aisled Building II, looking east

It was unclear when the modifications and extension to the original end wall of the building were made and whether the builders had also repositioned Posts 7 and 8 of the first phase of the building. The distances between the post centres seem to be approximately 2.80m in both the first and the second phase. However, the distances between the centres of Posts 7 and 9 and of Posts 8 and 10 are both 3.25m, suggesting that there was some aspect of the rebuilding or reorganisation taking place here which was not fully explained during the excavations. The packing around the Phase II posts also consisted of greater amounts of gravel mixed in with smaller limestone fragments.

Along both the extended southern and northern walls of the Phase II building, changes in the character of the

Plate 24 The buttress at the south-east corner of Building II, from the south (see also Fig. 29)

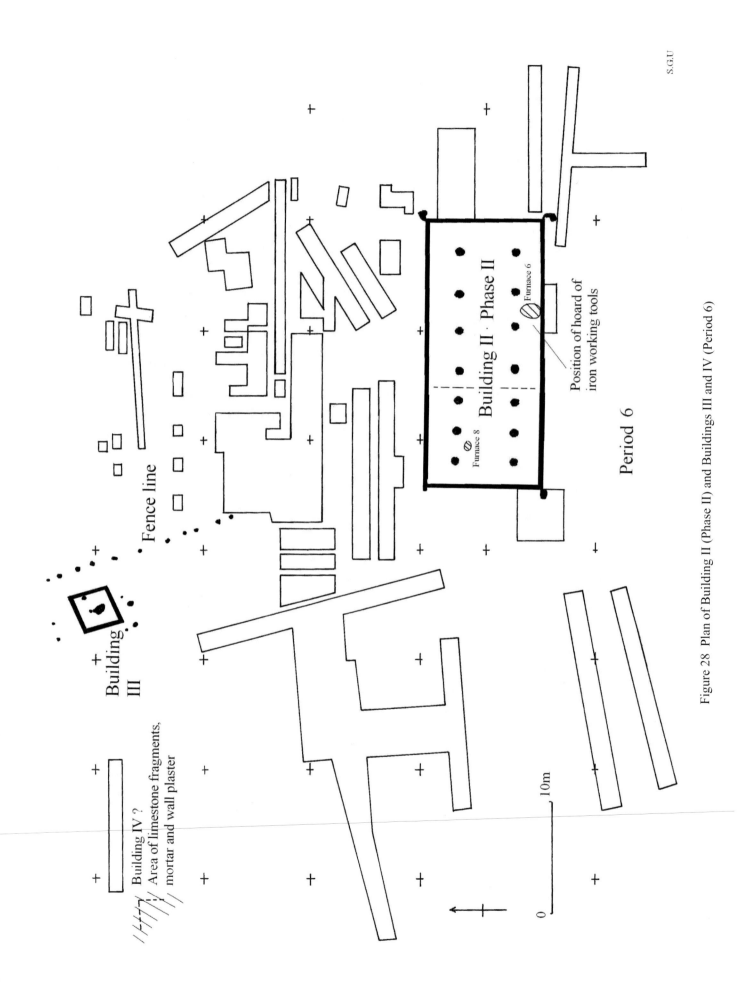

Building
III

Fence line

Building II · Phase II

Furnace 8

Furnace 6

Position of hoard of
iron working tools

Period 6

Building IV ?

Area of limestone fragments,
mortar and wall plaster

10m

0

S.G.U

Figure 28 Plan of Building II (Phase II) and Buildings III and IV (Period 6)

44

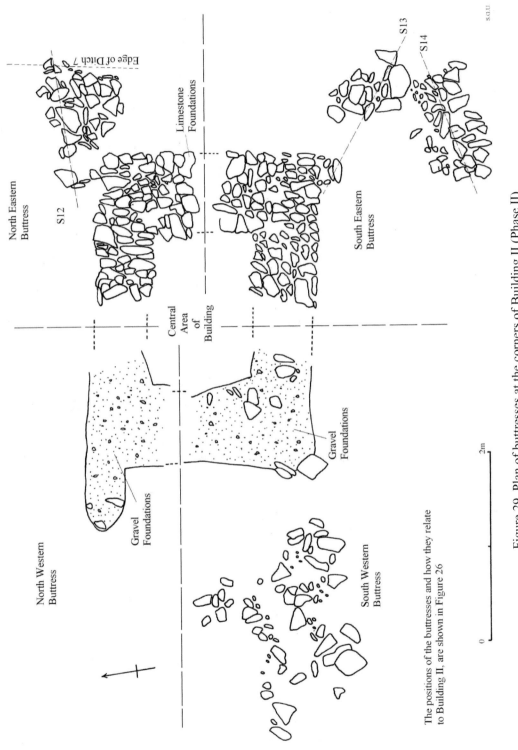

North Eastern
Buttress

Edge of Ditch 7

Limestone
Foundations

S12

S13

S14

S.G.U.

North Western
Buttress

Central
Area
of
Building

South Eastern
Buttress

Gravel
Foundations

Gravel
Foundations

Gravel
Foundations

South Western
Buttress

The positions of the buttresses and how they relate
to Building II, are shown in Figure 26

0   2m

Figure 29 Plan of buttresses at the corners of Building II (Phase II)

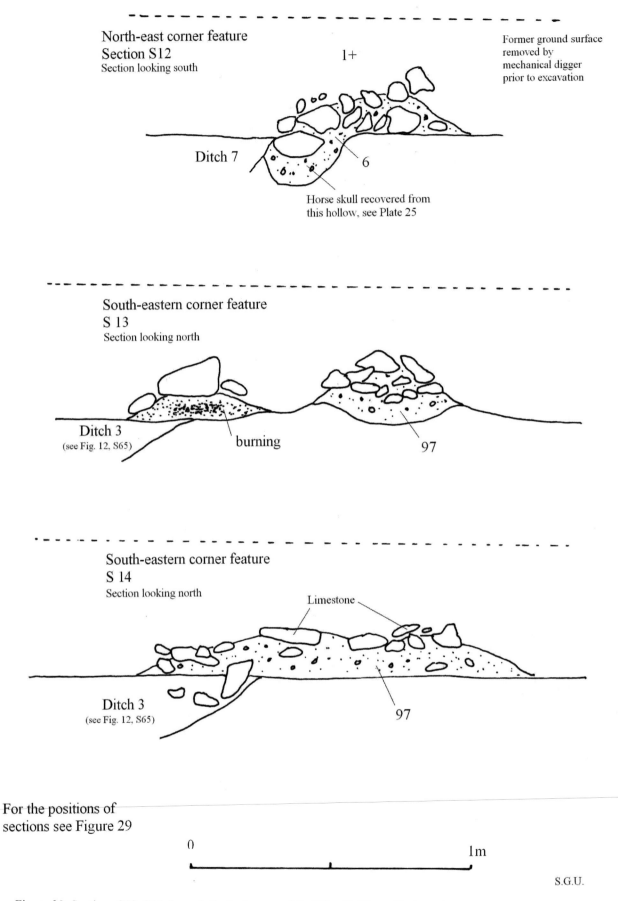

North-east corner feature
Section S12
Section looking south

1+

Former ground surface
removed by
mechanical digger
prior to excavation

Ditch 7

6

Horse skull recovered from
this hollow, see Plate 25

South-eastern corner feature
S 13
Section looking north

Ditch 3
(see Fig. 12, S65)

burning

97

South-eastern corner feature
S 14
Section looking north

Limestone

Ditch 3
(see Fig. 12, S65)

97

For the positions of
sections see Figure 29

0

1m

S.G.U.

Figure 30 Sections S12–S14 through the buttresses of Building II (Phase II) (see Fig. 29 for section locations)

foundations suggested that entrances into the building had been formed. Along the southern wall the small limestone aggregate used in the gravel foundation was absent for a length of 1.9m and this may represent an entrance (see Fig. 26). Along the northern wall a more complicated picture was recorded. Again the actual line of the wall for a length of 2.1m was comprised simply of gravel, but on the outside of the building and at the same point along the wall there was a considerable limestone spread, which may have been some form of surfaced apron leading up to an entrance.

Also added in this phase of the building were small packed limestone spreads associated with three of the four corners of the entire building — the fourth, north-west, corner had a slight gravel spread associated with it but nothing like the more substantial features associated with the other corners (see Fig. 29). Each of these three limestone features differed in shape and size and none seemed to be integral to the main walls of the structure (see Fig. 26). They are shown in detail in Figure 29 and in section in Figure 30. That at the south-eastern corner is shown in Plate 24.

These features may have been in some way structural, acting perhaps as buttresses for the corners of the building, although if this were the case it is unclear how they supported either the short axis or the long axis walls. It may be that they formed the base for a post or posts linked with supporting the wall corners but there is little evidence to show how such posts would have been fixed into the ground, unless they were supported on some form of post

Plate 25 The buttress at the north-east corner of Building II, from the north, with the part-excavated horse skull *in situ* (see also Fig. 30)

pad. An alternative view is that they acted as some form of emplacement, perhaps for barrels collecting water from the roof.

Underneath the feature at the north-eastern corner a section revealed the skull of an adult horse set within a shallow pit (see Pl. 25). Whether this was some form of votive offering linked with the construction of the corner feature is unclear, but the deposition of the skull and the corner construction seemed to be contemporary.

Aisled Building II, Phase II: internal features
There was nothing to show how the use of space within the second phase of Building I operated. No flooring surfaces were identifiable and it may be that the occupants simply used the natural gravel subsoil as a hard, dry surface on which to live and work.

There was no indication of any division along the length of the building suggesting perhaps a separation of activities and it is unclear what the main function of the structure was. In the north-western corner of the building were two post-holes that were both set 1.1m from the inner edge of the north wall (see Fig. 26) — these could have supported some internal feature, perhaps a rack or shelving of some sort that also utilised the wall.

Between Posts 1 and 3 and within the area of the central nave, a small oven or furnace had been constructed (Furnace 8; see Fig. 26), but this appeared to be a short-lived feature consisting of a shallow scoop out of the surface of the floor which had been severely damaged by later activity. It was unclear if this feature was for domestic use or had some industrial function.

A more substantial furnace (Furnace 6; Fig. 26) was found between Posts 10 and 12, set so that it backed onto the south wall of the building. This feature is shown in detail in Figure 31 and Pl. 26. It was constructed from undressed heavily burned limestone blocks (context 30 in Fig. 31) which were laid out to form a flue 1m long and 0.55m wide. The floor of this flue (context 44) was flagged with limestone and at the northern end — that is, set between Posts 10 and 12 and towards the central part of the nave of the building — was a shallow stokehole (context 45). At the southern end the flue appeared to open out and two large smoothed limestone flagstones (context 30a) were set at a slightly higher level to that of the flue lining (context 30), indicating that they perhaps gave access to the end of the flue and formed some sort of working surface. The area of the stokehole was part-filled with hammerscale and considerable amounts of ash and raked-out flue material were present, suggesting that the furnace was used for ironworking. Close by a hoard of three iron tools (hammer, mower's anvil and axe; see Figs 26 and 67) was found, perhaps linked with some aspect of metalworking at this furnace (Manning 1973, 28–30).

Building III
Some 30m north of Building II was another building, Building III, which was revealed as the gravel contractors scraped the topsoil from the site prior to digging the gravel. This structure and its associated post-holes are shown in Figure 28 and in detail in Figure 32 and Plate 27. The building was constructed in pitched limestone along part of its walled length, especially on the northern side; elsewhere the footings, which were damaged, consisted of limestone fragments in a matrix of gravel set in a shallow trench. Internally the building measured 2.5×2.75m and

Plate 26 Furnace 6 within Building II, looking to the south (see Fig. 31)

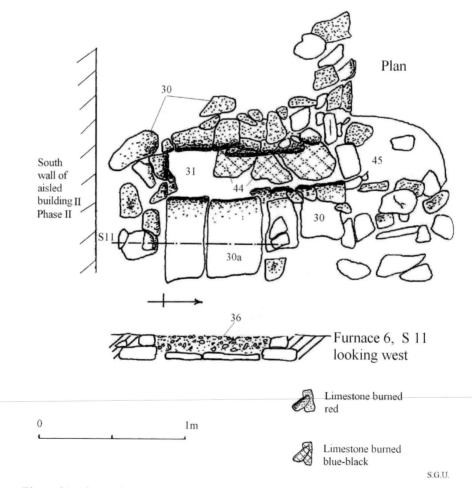

Plan

30

South
wall of
aisled
building II
Phase II

S11

31

44

45

30

30a

36

Furnace 6, S 11
looking west

Limestone burned
red

Limestone burned
blue-black

S.G.U.

0   1m

Figure 31 Plan and section S11 of Furnace 6 (see Fig. 26 for position of this furnace)

the walls were 0.75m wide. Within the structure was a shallow depression filled with limestone and gravel which may have formed the base or setting for an internal feature. The central limestone feature and the remnants of the surrounding wall on the eastern side of the structure are shown in cross section in Figure 33 (S19). Along the eastern wall and 0.80m from the corner with the northern wall was a post-hole (Ph 9) which may have formed part of a doorway into the building (see Fig. 33 S20). The structure seemed to have been set out on an earlier occupation layer containing gravel and sand but with flecks of daub, while the central depression was dug into gravelly material which contained both daub and fragments of white wall plaster.

Around this building there was also a series of post-holes which could have been part of the same structure. One post setting was just to the north of the north wall (Ph 15), while others — Ph 16, Ph 17 and Ph 20 — were along the western and southern sides. Outside the north wall and

some 2.30m away were two additional post positions (Ph 8 and Ph 14). Along the eastern side of Building III were four certain post-holes and possibly a fifth (Ph 10, Ph 11, Ph 12, Ph13 +1?). Sections of Post-holes 11, 12 and 17 are shown in Figure 34; Post-hole 11 (S22) was dug down to a depth of 0.53m. As such they would have received substantial posts, which were then packed around at the base with limestone fragments. All of these three post-holes contained evidence that the posts had probably been left to rot *in situ* (see contexts 11a, 12a and 17a in Fig. 34). There were other small spreads of limestone fragments which may have formed additional post-holes (see Fig. 32) but the damage to the site caused by heavy machinery was so great that it was difficult to be certain about these features.

Over the whole area of Building III were patches of broken and fragmented wall plaster and mortar. Wall plaster was found within the make-up of the brown sand and gravel used as a matrix within the outer wall,

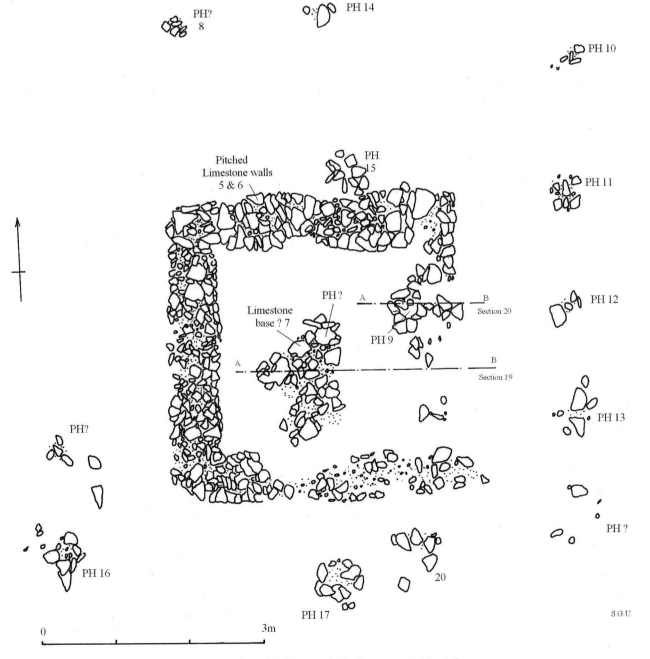

Figure 32 Plan of Building III, the Romano-Celtic shrine

49

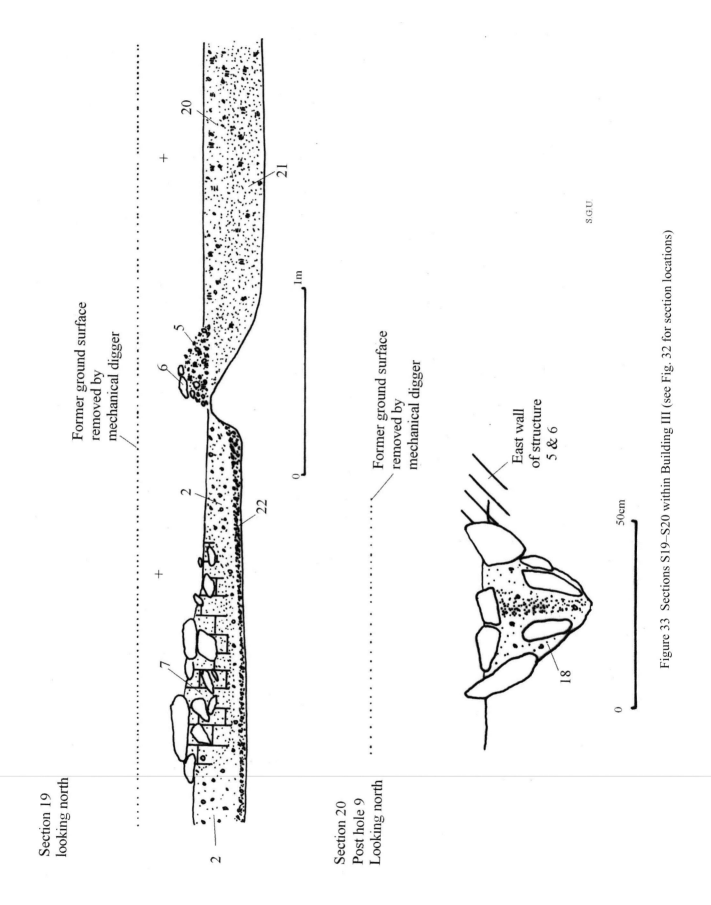

Section 19
looking north

Former ground surface
removed by
mechanical digger

Section 20
Post hole 9
Looking north

Former ground surface
removed by
mechanical digger

East wall
of structure
5 & 6

Figure 33 Sections S19–S20 within Building III (see Fig. 32 for section locations)

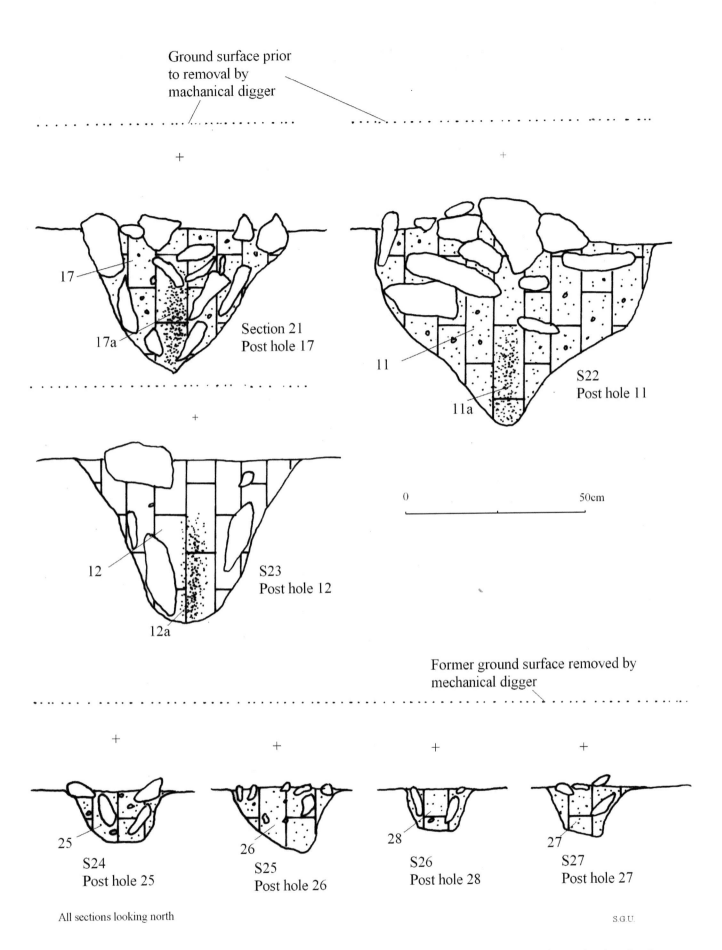

Ground surface prior to removal by machanical digger

17

17a

Section 21
Post hole 17

11

11a

S22
Post hole 11

0   50cm

12

12a

S23
Post hole 12

Former ground surface removed by mechanical digger

25

S24
Post hole 25

26

S25
Post hole 26

28

S26
Post hole 28

27

S27
Post hole 27

All sections looking north

S.G.U.

Figure 34 Sections S21–S27 of post-holes related to Building III and a fence line (see Fig. 36 for section locations)

especially on the western side of the structure (see Fig. 35 for the general distribution of wall plaster and context 5 for plaster within the wall). White plaster was also found in a large deposit within the north-western corner of the building and was associated with some of the post-holes around the structure (Ph 16, Ph 20 and Ph 8, see Fig. 35). Some of this wall plaster was mixed in with areas of sandy lime mortar, especially on the western and southern sides of the building. In no place was the wall plaster or the lime mortar found *in situ* and the 'general' spreads of material were difficult to interpret because the building was so badly damaged by modern heavy machinery. It may be that the spreads of mortar in the southern and western areas represent some form of outer flooring — perhaps a portico — around the central part of the structure.

There was little to indicate any painted scheme linked with this wall plaster. The colours were limited, with white the most common, but red and orange also present. One fragment had possibly come from a door or window jamb as the plaster was moulded at an angle. For a full description of the plaster from the site see Chapter 6, XI Wall plaster.

Fence line
Leading away from Building III was a row of post-holes that must originally have supported posts forming a fence line. This row of post-holes is shown in plan in Figures 28 and 36 and the sections of Posts 25, 26, 27 and 28 are shown in Figure 34. The post-holes which formed this fence line were different from the substantial post-holes associated with Building III, which were perhaps structural, in that

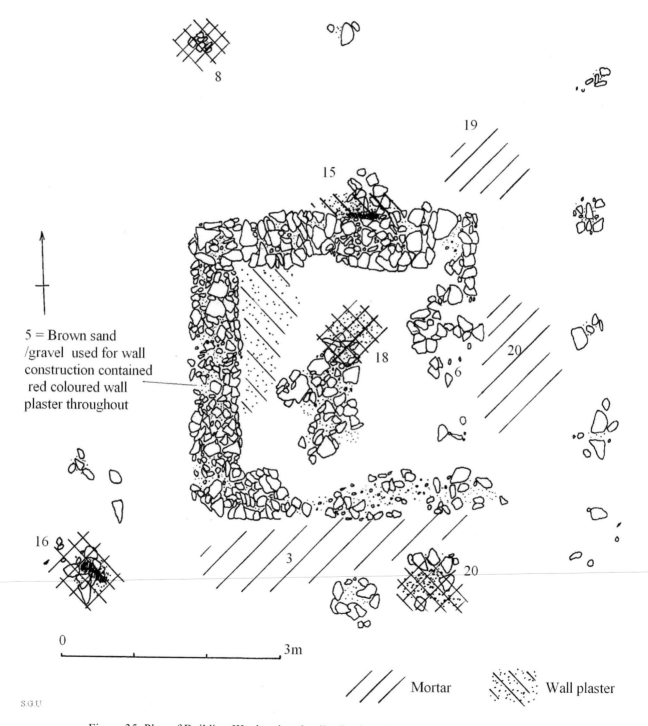

5 = Brown sand /gravel used for wall construction contained red coloured wall plaster throughout

0 _____ 3m

S.G.U

Figure 35 Plan of Building III, showing the distribution of mortar and painted wall plaster

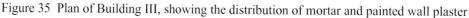

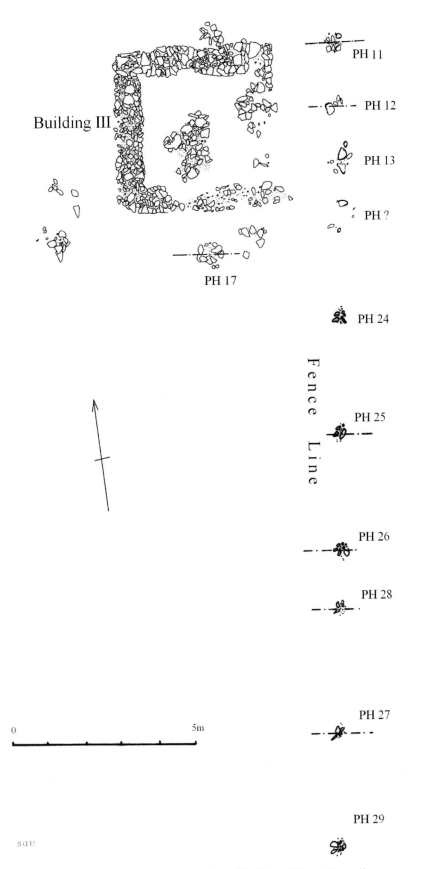

PH 10

PH 11

PH 12

PH 13

PH ?

PH 17

PH 24

Fence Line

PH 25

PH 26

PH 28

PH 27

PH 29

Building III

0   5m

Figure 36 Plan of Building III and fence line

they were small, shallow features, only some 0.20–0.30m deep. The best interpretation here is to see this fence line linking with existing 'structural' posts surrounding Building III, and following the line of the west wall of Building III. The southern end of the fence line may have extended as far as Building II (Phase II) (see Fig. 28), but posts were not recorded to the south of Ph 29 (see Fig. 36).

Building IV

The area containing Building IV was already heavily disturbed when excavations at the site began and most of the structure had already been destroyed (see Fig. 28). In addition, the area lay largely outside of the permitted excavation zone and within the area designated for the parking of the heavy machinery linked with gravel extraction. Thus almost nothing can be said about this structure except that a short fragment of very disturbed walling was recorded, which appeared to form the north-western corner of the building. The character of the remains suggested that originally the walls were at least partly of pitched limestone masonry and probably similar to the walls of Buildings II and III. There were fragments of both floor and roof tile and wall plaster recovered from the area of this building, suggesting that it had been somewhat more 'well appointed' than the other buildings examined. The wall plaster was in white, red, orange and black/blue, and one fragment (Pl. 57 no. 5) showed that a painting scheme had been followed in which a thin white line separated areas of red and black/blue.

Period 7. Mid-4th century
(Figs 37–38)

Ditch 7

At some point during the mid-4th century a ditch was dug that ran roughly north–south part-way along the east wall of Building II (Phase II). This ditch, Ditch 7 (see Fig. 37), was certainly dug after the limestone 'buttresses' had been constructed at the north-eastern corner of Phase II of Building II, because the ditch line removed part of the limestone of this feature. Ditch 7 was approximately 1.40m wide and 0.75m deep and was traced for 27m across Area A. Its northern length extended outside the available excavated area, while at its southern end it cut across Ditch 4 (see Fig. 12) but then seemed to peter out and could not be traced further south. The lower fills of this ditch (especially contexts 30 and 141; see Fig. 38) contained considerable amounts of charcoal, ash and some hammerscale — similar in character to the material associated with Furnace 6, context 45 (see Fig. 31). It may be that at least some of the rake-out from this furnace was dumped into the early fills of this ditch.

Certainly, part of the central/southern section of Ditch 7 was recut at some point — this can be clearly seen in section S52 (Fig. 38). However, the line of the ditch seems to have been taken out of use within a few decades of its construction and certainly by the late 4th century, when the central area of the line of the ditch was totally filled in and then covered with a spread of limestone and gravel forming a hard surface (context 7 in S52, Fig. 38) over the ditch and the surrounding area (Period 8).

Plate 27 Building III, the Romano-Celtic shrine, looking north (see Fig. 32)

54

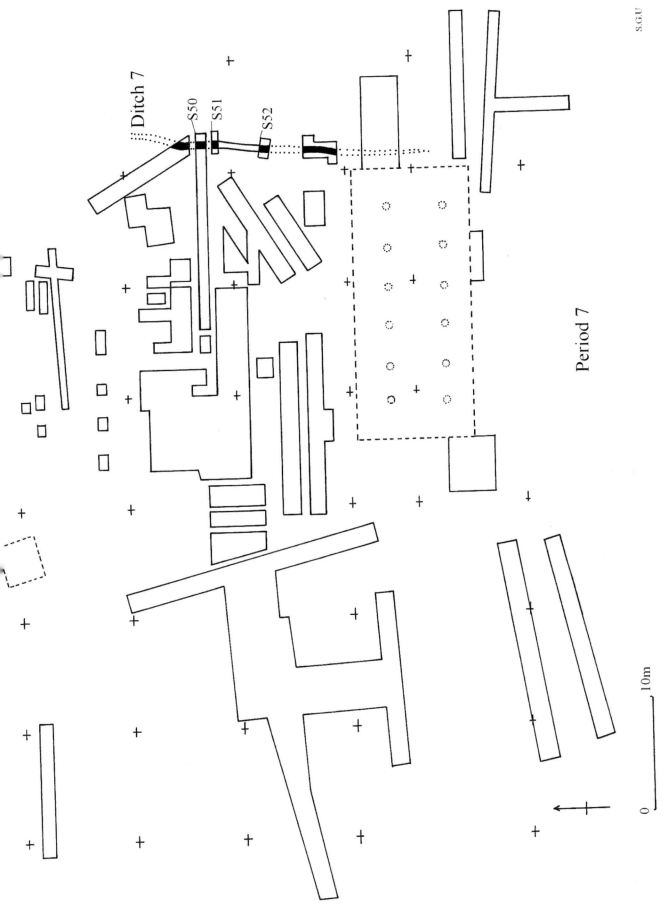

Ditch 7

S50
S51
S52

Period 7

Figure 37 Plan of Ditch 7 in Area A

S.G.U

0

10m

55

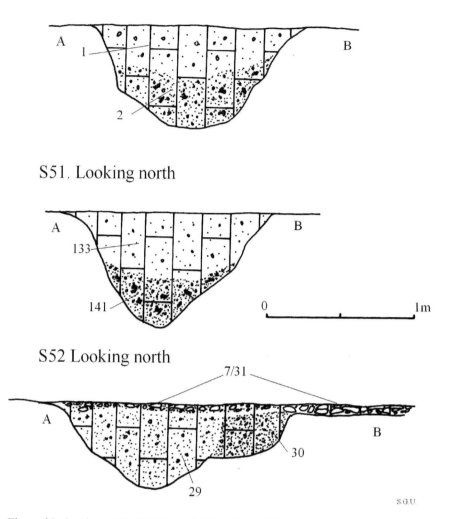

S50. Ditch A7 to east of
Aisled Building - looking north

S51. Looking north

S52 Looking north

Figure 38 Sections S50–S52 through Ditch 7 (see Fig. 37 for section locations)

Period 8. Late 4th century and early 5th century
(Fig. 39; Pl. 28)

Building II, Phase III
At some point at the end of the 4th century the whole of Building II was demolished. It is unclear whether all of the posts forming the nave of the building were left to rot *in situ*. This seems to have been the case with Post 3 (Fig. 27 S1), where the outline of the former post was detected in the section. Other posts may have been sawn off at ground level or pulled out, as there seemed to be some disturbances to the limestone packing around the bases of posts.

It is uncertain how much demolition of the wall lines occurred. There was little evidence of massive limestone spreads of material that could have derived from the walls being levelled and it may be that the walls were never carried up to any great height above the foundation level anyway. However, a considerable spread of limestone material (context 33, Fig. 39) mixed with patches of mortar and fragments of wall plaster was found within the central area of the building (see Pl. 28). The spread of this

material was confined by the line of the south wall and some of the upper surfaces of the spread showed signs of wear, as if the whole deposit had been used as some form of surfacing or floor. This spread of material also covered Furnace 6, which was completely packed with limestone and patches of mortar.

To the west of this spread of material was a linear setting of limestone 4.9m in length which may have formed a wall associated with this period of late occupation (context 51, Fig. 39). This wall was set out slightly askew to the outside walls of Building II and its internal posts and appeared to be built partly over the spread of limestone outlined above (context 33). It was thus considered to post-date Building II entirely.

A coin of the House of Theodosius and another uncertain issue of a similar late date (SF 232 and SF 240; see Chapter 6, II The Roman coins) came from the spread of material (context 33) which sealed Building II and on which the late wall (context 51) was constructed.

Exactly what this spread of material represented is uncertain and will be discussed at length below. However, it probably represents a late surfaced area which was

56

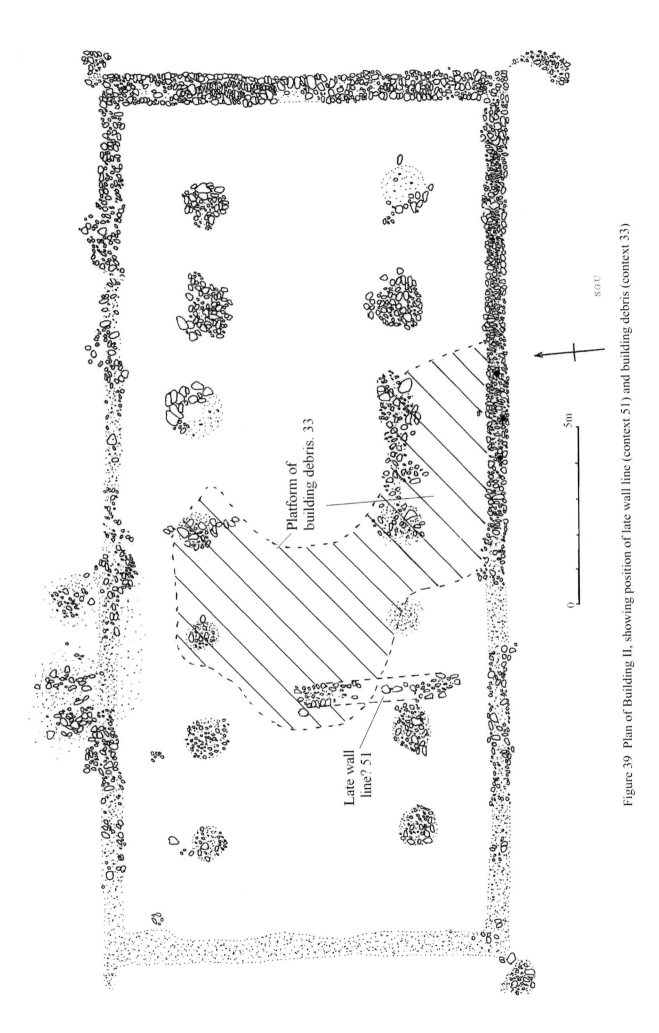

SGU

Platform of
building debris. 33

Late wall
line? 51

5m

0

Figure 39 Plan of Building II, showing position of late wall line (context 51) and building debris (context 33)

57

Plate 28 The platform of building debris (context 33) within Building II, looking south-east (see Fig. 39)

covered by a 'shed-like' structure and which may conceivably have used part of the south wall of Building II and the newly built wall (context 51) for at least some of its roof support. If this were the case, then there is no indication of how the remaining sides of this putative structure were supported or indeed what its function was.

Area A during Period 8
The whole area at this period seems to have been largely abandoned, apart from the activity taking place within the former area of Building II. The upper fills of Ditch 7 were capped in part with limestone and gravel which could have formed some sort of surface; certainly, this deposit (context 7/31, see Fig. 38 S52) contained late pottery, including fragments of imported Oxfordshire ware vessels and locally produced wares in a black fabric and finish (see Chapter 7).

Building III has no pottery associated with it later than the mid-4th century, but this structure was so badly damaged prior to excavation that most of its deposits had been destroyed; interpretation and dating here were therefore very problematic.

Some of the upper archaeological layers of Area A, and certainly all of the former plough soil, were also almost all removed by the gravel contractors and perhaps with them any late vestiges of post-Roman occupation. All of the pottery was screened by the original excavators before it was taken from the site for storage and later analysis, and large quantities of unwanted body sherds and small abraded sherds were discarded at this point; any small fragments of post-Roman/Saxon material may thus have been lost at this stage. However, within the remaining pottery assemblage there is nothing to suggest occupation extending at the site after the very late Roman period, which appears to have extended into the early 5th century.

Chapter 3. The wells

I. Introduction

Two wells were discovered during the excavations and both are shown on the general plan of the site (Fig. 4). Well I was found at the western edge of Area B and Well II was found some 24m to the west of Well I and 22m to the south-east of the south-east corner of Building II. Both wells were square and lined with coursed, dressed limestone blocks. Each was found to have been built on a wooded cradle, which the wet conditions at the site had preserved. Both wells had been dug so that they tapped the ground water within the gravel underlying the site and there was apparently no attempt in either construction to dig into deeper underlying deposits or to try to locate impermeable beds which would have restricted the penetration of ground water to any lower level (see Woodward and Thompson 1909; Woodland 1942). Both wells were located at approximately 6m AOD and some 600m to the west of the present course of the river Nene (see Fig. 2) which, since it flows in a distinctive meander, may have had its main channels in much the same position then as now.

The sediments from the base of Well I were analysed by V.C.E. Hughes and provided a reconstruction of the environment around the site based on the Coleoptera fauna (see Chapter 9).

II. Well I
(Fig. 40; Pls 29–32)

Well I was located within the western section of Area B. Its location is shown in detail in Figures 4 and 44 and it is shown in plan and section in Figure 40 and Plate 29. The top layers of the well's stonework had been removed by heavy machinery in the process of removing the topsoil layers over the underlying gravel beds, and it was thus impossible to say how deep the original well had been, but, assuming that approximately 1m of overburden had been taken away prior to excavation, the original depth may have been of the order of 2.0m. The well was 0.90m square and had been constructed out of coursed limestone blocks and set on a foundation raft of timber. The bottom profile of the well was rounded, perhaps the result of buckets scooping water from the bottom of the well.

The bottom fills of the well were dark brown silts (context 104), while the upper layers contained an ever increasing amount of gravel and limestone fragments, the limestone occurring in larger pieces as the upper levels were approached. The well contained amounts of pottery and bone and samples were taken for Coleoptera analysis, the results of which are outlined below (Chapter 10).

As this well was due to be totally destroyed by gravel extraction it was decided that, once excavation had been completed, the whole structure of the well should be dismantled and the timber frame which formed the foundation of the stone lining recovered. The timber frame

Plate 29 The fully excavated Well I, looking north-east (see Fig. 40)

Well I

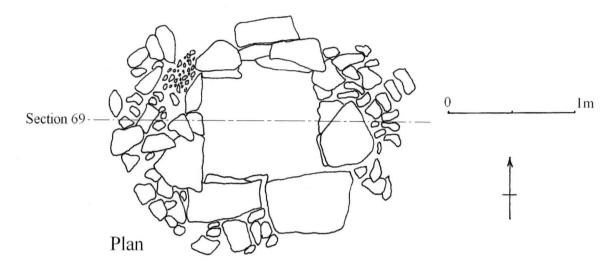

Section 69

Plan

0   1m

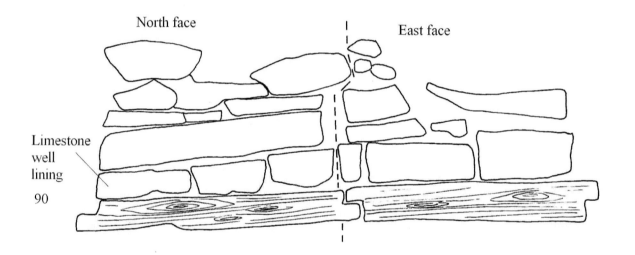

North face

East face

Limestone
well
lining

90

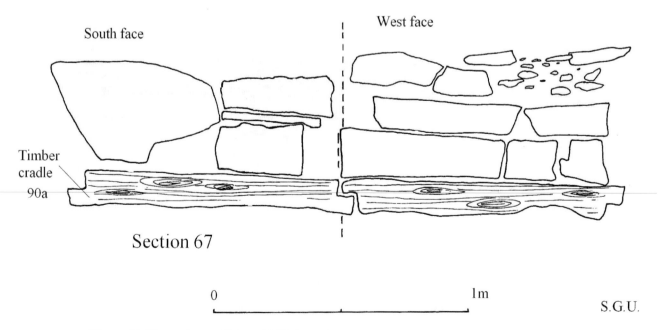

South face

West face

Timber
cradle

90a

Section 67

0   1m

S.G.U.

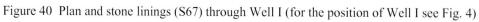

Figure 40 Plan and stone linings (S67) through Well I (for the position of Well I see Fig. 4)

Plate 30 The timber foundation raft at the base of Well I, looking south

is shown in Plate 30 where it can be seen that the timbers had clearly been reused, as there were cuts, saw marks and mortise holes. The frame itself measured 1.0m square internally and the timbers were approximately 0.25m square. Its corners had been 'lap jointed' together to hold them fast in a form that is fairly well known in the Nene valley from other sites, such as the pottery workshop site at Stibbington (Upex 2008b). Details of the corners of this frame are shown in Plates 31 and 32.

There was no staining on the sides of the stonework of the well shaft that might indicate water table levels when the well was open; in any case, such levels may have fluctuated during the time the well was in use.

III. Well II
(Figs 41–42; Pls 33–34)

Well II was of a remarkably similar design and construction to Well I (Figs 41 and 42; Pls 33 and 34). It was approximately 0.85m square and stone-lined to a depth of 1.70m with a rounded base which had probably been caused, like that of Well I, by the action of drawing water from the well. Again, what the original depth of the well would have been was not possible to compute owing to the removal of the uppermost archaeological horizons. However, it was thought that just the topsoil and probably the topmost course of stonework had been destroyed by the gravel contractor's machinery and that the original depth may have been approximately 2.70m. The

Plate 31 Detail of the north-eastern corner of the foundation raft from Well I, showing the saw marks, timber joint and the mortice hole from an earlier use

Plate 32 Detail of the south-western corner of the foundation raft from Well I, showing timber jointing

Well II

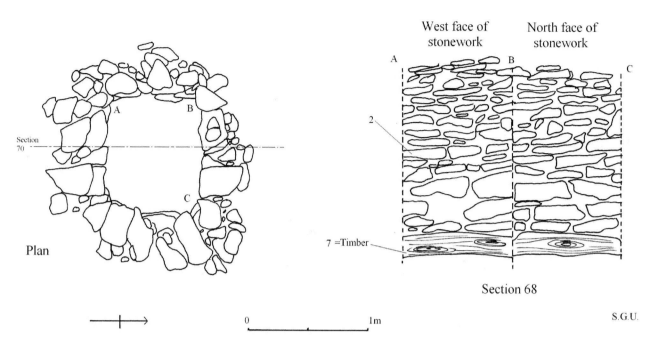

West face of stonework   North face of stonework

7 =Timber

Section 68

S.G.U.

0   1m

Figure 41   Plan and stone linings (S68) through Well II (for the position of Well II see Fig. 4)

stonework of this well was constructed of coursed limestone blocks that were slightly larger at the base of the well than at the top, a feature which may also have been seen in Well I, had a greater depth of that well survived. Again, the stonework of Well II sat directly on a cradle of timber, the exact lengths of which were not exposed but would probably have been of a similar length to the timbers used in Well I. Each of the timbers was approximately 0.20m square, and they were probably lap-jointed at the corners — again similar to the technique used in Well I. Well II was not totally dismantled, so precise details of the timbers were not recovered.

As with Well I, the fill of this well consisted of silts in the bottom horizons followed by upper fills of gravel and varying amounts of limestone. The top layer (context 3 in Fig. 42, Pl. 33) was in fact heavily packed with limestone and had been carefully consolidated.

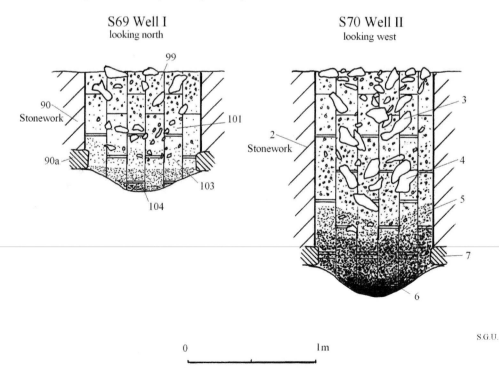

0   1m

Figure 42   Sections S69–S70 through Wells I and II

Plate 33 The late filling of Well II prior to excavation, looking north-west (see Fig. 41)

Plate 34 The fully excavated shaft of Well II, looking north

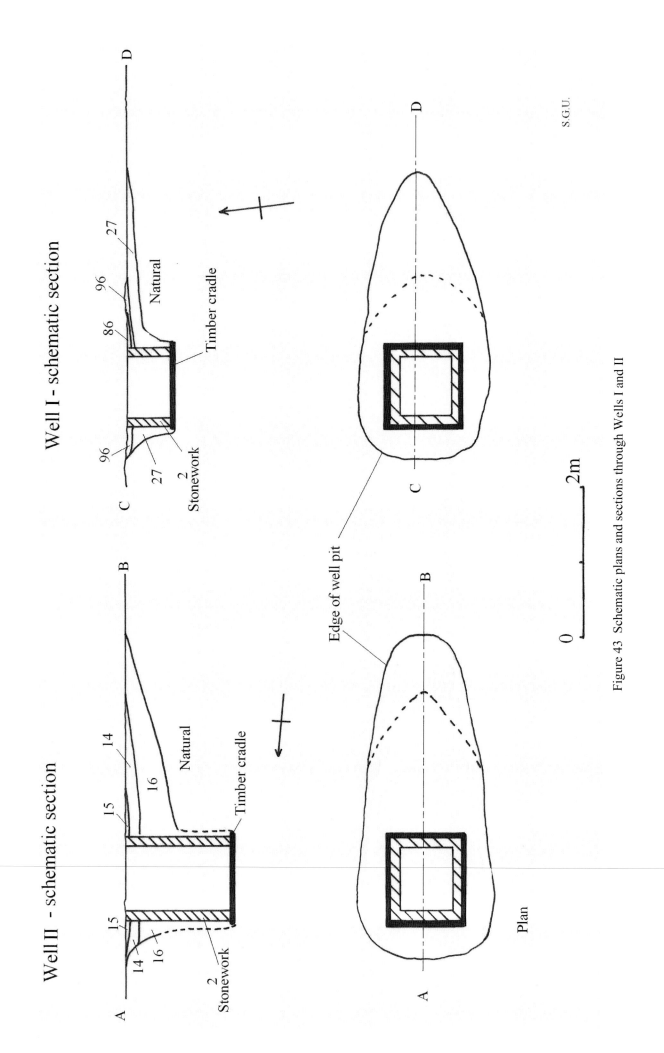

Well I - schematic section

Well II - schematic section

Natural

Timber cradle

Stonework

Natural

Timber cradle

Stonework

Edge of well pit

Plan

2m

0

S.G.U.

Figure 43 Schematic plans and sections through Wells I and II

64

IV. Well construction
(Fig. 43)

Both wells appeared to have been constructed in a similar way, with the excavation of a large oval pit with an asymmetrical vertical profile (schematic sections through both wells are shown in Fig. 43). Once this initial excavation had been completed the bottom section of the shafts were dug at the deepest part of the initial pit excavation, with the well diggers in all probability using the slope of the remaining part of the pit as a gentle gradient along which to carry the spoil from the shaft excavation. Once the required depth had been reached the timber frames would have been set in place and the stonework forming the shaft of the well would have been constructed. Any gap between the well pit and the back of the stonework forming the actual shaft was filled in with loose material (see context 16, Well II and context 27, Well I, Fig. 43). Various upper layers around the well possibly represent later consolidation layers added as the well packing around the shaft began to sag.

Also present around the top of both shafts were areas of blue and blue/black clay (context 15, Well II and context 96, Well I) which may have acted as a capping providing areas of 'waterproofing', which stopped spilt and dirty water from running back into the wells and thus contaminating the water supply.

V. Discussion and dating

Well I
All the timbers were of oak (*Quercus*) and were sent for dendrochronological analysis to the University of Sheffield, where Dr Ruth Morgan discovered that the felling dates ranged between AD 207 and AD 252 (Chapter 8). Thus, allowing for a first use of the timbers in a building, their reuse as a foundation raft for the well occurred at some point after this date. However, it was impossible to estimate from the timbers alone how long the gap between the first use of the timbers and their use in the well would have been. A coin of Theodora or Helena (AD 337–41) and three other coins probably minted between AD 206 and AD 402 (Chapter 6, II The Roman coins) came from the backfill surrounding the well shaft (context 27, Fig. 43), suggesting that construction of the stone lining took place some time after the middle of the 4th century. Thus the timbers might have been around 100 years old by the time they came to be reused as the foundation raft for the well. The latest pieces of pottery that were recovered from the fill of context 27 would also fit this date range, suggesting a construction date at some point in the middle of the 4th century. If this is the case

then the life of the well must have been fairly short, as the pottery which came from the filling of the well shaft was dated to the late 4th or very early 5th century (Period 8) (see sherd 154, shown in Figure 89 (below), which came from context 101, Fig. 42 S69). This dating for the well fits with a similar date range provided by new dating techniques that have been used to analyse the insect chitin from waterlogged samples recovered from the well (Panagiotakapulus *et al.* 2015, 27–8).

Well II
None of the timbers were removed from the foundation frame of Well II, so there was no chance for dendrochronological analysis; nor were there any coins to help with dating. To compound the problem of determining a construction date for this well, little pottery came from the well's construction pit. What can be said with some certainly is that the well appears to have been filled in at much the same time as Well I and in much the same way, with a mix of limestone and gravel and some occupation debris. All of the datable pottery from the contexts within the well shaft (contexts 2–6, Fig. 42 S70) suggest that a date in the late 4th or early 5th century would be sensible here (see, for example, sherds 159 and 160 from context 6).

Which of the two wells was the earlier is, on present evidence, difficult to say. Nor is it certain why two wells were constructed so close together, other than the obvious possibility that one may have replaced the other because of contamination. However, assuming that Well I was constructed at some point around the middle of the 4th century but had a very short life span, it may be that Well II was the earlier, although both wells were clearly filled in at much the same time in Period 8. Water table levels may also have played a part here. The general view is that the water table was gradually rising during the later Roman periods, and thus Well II, being the deeper, may be the earlier, as it tapped a lower water source.

It has to be assumed on present evidence that both wells served either Building II in its second or third phase (see above) or the buildings within Area C. However, the amount of damage caused by the gravel contractor's machinery to the area south of the two wells and the limited archaeological survey carried out in this area beforehand do not preclude the possibility that there were originally other buildings in this area which the wells may have served. In any case, the distance of both wells from Building II was not great (Well I = 22m and Well II = 36m) and the positioning of wells at such distance from buildings may have been in part a function of attempts to preserve the quality of the water by positioning them away from more general thoroughfares where the potential for contamination of the water may have been greater.

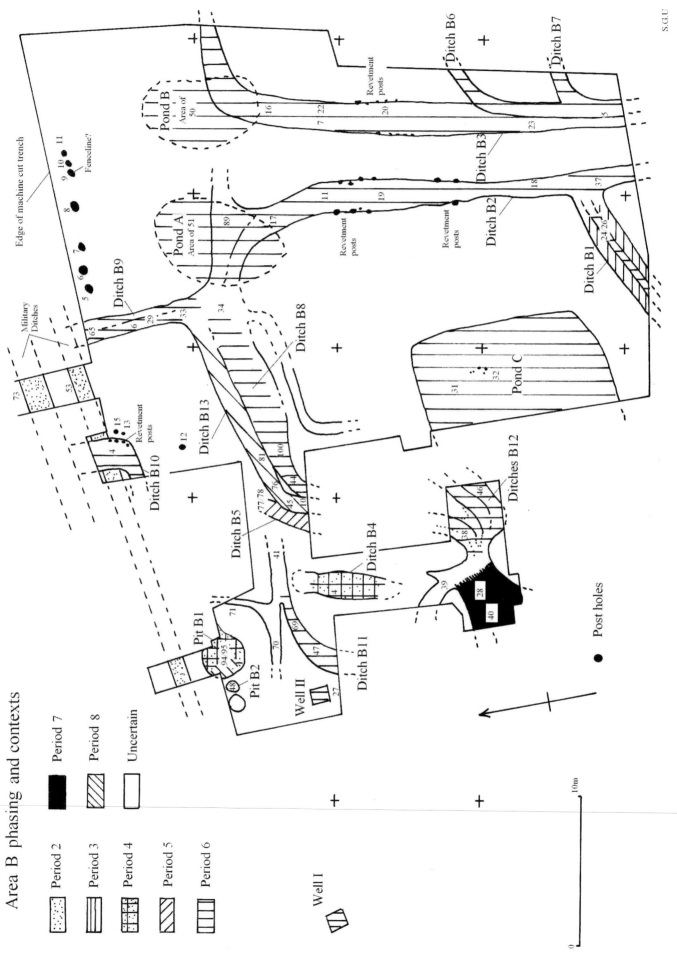

Area B phasing and contexts

Period 2
Period 3
Period 4
Period 5
Period 6
Period 7
Period 8
Uncertain

Edge of machine cut trench

Fenceline?

Military Ditches

Pond B
Area of 50

Pond A
Area of 51

Pond C

Revetment posts

Revetment posts

Revetment posts

Revetment posts

Ditch B6
Ditch B7
Ditch B3
Ditch B2
Ditch B1
Ditch B9
Ditch B8
Ditch B13
Ditch B5
Ditch B4
Ditch B10
Ditch B11
Ditches B12

Pit B1
Pit B2
Well I
Well II

Post holes

S.G.U

Figure 44 Area B, phasing plan and contexts

Chapter 4. The excavation of Area B

I. Introduction
(Fig. 44; Pl. 35)

To the south-east of Area A the contractor's machinery had disturbed evidence of a complex of archaeological features, including ditches and what appeared to be shallow ponded features (see Figs 4 and 44). By the time that any archaeological work was possible in this part of the site much of the detail of the Roman features had been destroyed by the stripping of topsoil and the 'over-burden to the gravel' prior to gravel extraction, making both dating and interpretation extremely difficult. the area that was made available for archaeological work was thus not only partly destroyed but the passage of heavy machinery over the area had left deep ruts compressed into the underlying natural gravels and subsoil. Part of the investigation that followed included much time spent wrestling with the problems of whether the ditch- and gully-like features were archaeological or modern wheel ruts.

After the contractor's heavy machinery had been withdrawn the area was cleaned up using a mechanical digger with a toothless ditching bucket and this process was then followed by hand cleaning. In general the area that was explored archaeologically was some 0.8m below the top of the former ground surface and in some cases the contractor's machinery had stripped away nearly 1m of material. Thus what remained consisted of the very bottoms of some of the ditches and other features and it was impossible to tell what else had been present and destroyed in the upper archaeological levels. For example, to the south of the area shown in Figure 44 (Area B) the contractor cut a section which revealed the full depth of Ditch B1 (for the position of Ditch(es) B1 within Area B, see Fig. 44). Here the full depth of this feature was recorded as being 1.30m deep (see Pl. 35), whereas within the excavated part of Area B the recorded depth of the feature, where the overlying layers had already been stripped away, was a mere 0.50m. Unfortunately records were not kept or details plotted with any accuracy of

Plate 35 A section through Ditch B1 cut by the contractor's machinery at the edge of Area B (see Fig. 44) prior to any excavation taking place at the site

features outside the areas that were allowed for archaeological excavation, but work and general observations showed what had been lost prior to any archaeological work starting on the site.

II. The excavations

Period 2. Roman military occupation
(Fig. 45)
The ditches of the military occupation of the site were cut at two points within the northern part of Area B and linked with what was known of the line of these defences which were first encountered in the excavations of Area A (see Figs 9 and 10). The interval between the centres of the two ditches was approximately 4.0m, whereas in Area A the interval was approximately 4.5m (see Fig. 45 was 46 S125). Apart from this, the character of the ditches' profiles was remarkably similar, although their fills were different. The fills from Area A were dominantly of gravels, mixed loam and clay, while the fills from Area B were more mixed and contained levels of humic material, including a black organic layer in the inner ditch (see Fig. 45 was 46 S125). This layer must have represented a flooding event or a period of waterlogging when the ditch had been part filled in and where settling or subsidence of the earlier fills had occurred. Pottery that belonged to the military phase of the site was recovered from both of these ditches and thus provided dating. One vessel came from the inner ditch (see Chapter 7 and Fig. 81, no. 14) and three vessels were recovered from the outer ditch (Fig. 81, nos 17, 22 and Fig. 82, no. 25). Apart from these ditches, no other military features were identified within Area B.

Period 3. Late 1st/early 2nd century
Only one small length of ditch (Ditch B1), located in the southern part of Area B, belonged to occupation during Period 3 (Fig. 44). Ditch B1 was 2.0m wide and 0.6m deep, and was filled with silty clay deposits which were later cut into by a narrow, shallow Period 6 recut (see Fig. 48 S112, context 24). The southern extent of the excavated length of this ditch ran into the baulk, while to the north-east the other end of the ditch joined the line of Ditch B2, which appeared to obliterate any further sign of the continuation of this ditch. Ditch B1 may have followed the line of Ditch B2, in which case the later ditch had been recut in such a way as to leave no trace of a predecessor.

Period 4. Late 2nd century
(Fig. 46)
Two shallow features were dug in Area B in this period. One, a roughly circular pit in the north-western part of the area filled by contexts 95 and 95a (see Figs 44, 46 was 45 and 49 S116, Pit B1), and the other a short ditch-like feature (Figs 44, 46 was 45 and 48 S115 Ditch B4) which was situated some 8m to the south-east.

Pit B1 was 0.5m deep and was filled with two layers, the lower consisting of black/blue silts (context 95a) and the upper layer (context 95) a grey silt, but with

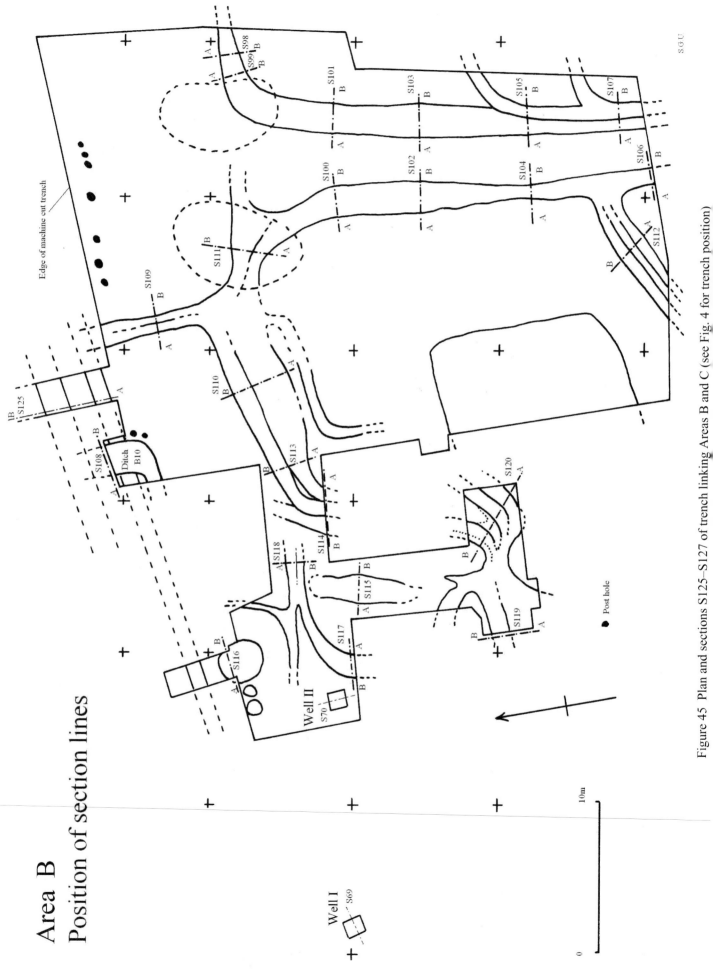

Area B
Position of section lines

Figure 45 Plan and sections S125–S127 of trench linking Areas B and C (see Fig. 4 for trench position)

68

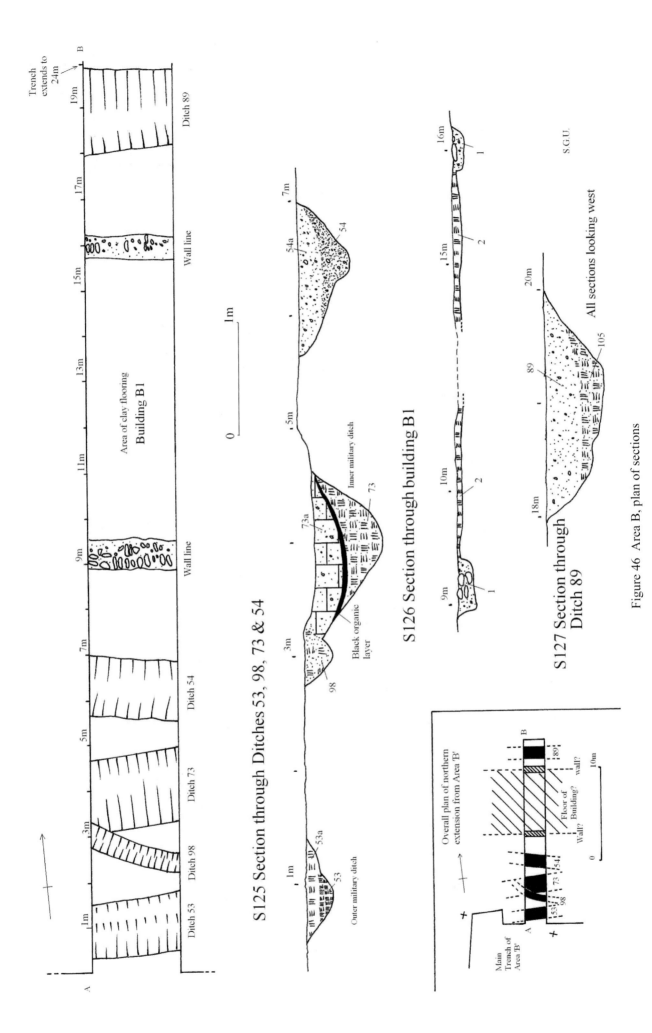

Trench extends to 24m

19m

Ditch 89

17m

Wall line

15m

Area of clay flooring
Building B1

13m

11m

9m

Wall line

7m

Ditch 54

5m

Ditch 73

3m

Ditch 98

1m

Ditch 53

A

S 125 Section through Ditches 53, 98, 73 & 54

0   1m

7m

54

54a

5m

73a

Inner military ditch

73

Black organic layer

98

3m

Outer military ditch

1m

53a

53

S 126 Section through building B1

16m

1

2

15m

10m

2

9m

1

S 127 Section through Ditch 89

20m

89

105

18m

All sections looking west

S.G.U.

Overall plan of northern extension from Area 'B'

B

89

Floor of Building?

wall?

Wall?

73   54

53   98

A

Main Trench of Area 'B'

0   10m

Figure 46   Area B, plan of sections

69

considerable iron staining within it. There appeared to be a shallow recutting into the top of these deposits on the western side of the pit during the 4th century. Ditch B4 ran for some 7m north–south and petered out at either end. Preservation in this part of the site was poor owing to the disturbances caused by the contractor's machinery and it is possible that the feature was originally more extensive. Of the remains that did survive the feature was 0.5m deep in its central area — although to the north and south it became shallow and eventually disappeared. Again, the fills were of silty grey clay. What these two features represent is uncertain. Neither contained any rubbish-like deposits and they both, like most features in Area B, seem to be (allowing for the problems caused by the total removal of the upper archaeological levels) shallow-cut features which were later filled with fluvially derived deposits.

Period 5. Early 3rd century
As in the previous period, there appeared to be few features of significance within this part of the site other than one shallow ditch, Ditch B5 (Figs 44, 46 was 45 and Fig. 48 S114). Again, preservation in this part of the site was poor and this ditch could only be traced for approximately 4.0m. It entered the baulk at its southern end and petered out at its northern end. This feature was later cut by part of another ditch system (S114, context 10).

Period 6. Late 3rd century–early 4th century
(Fig. 47–8; Pls 36–42)
Period 6 saw a considerable amount of activity within the area of Area B compared with the rather low-key and haphazard occupation of the earlier periods. A whole system of ditches was cut during this period in addition to the excavation of large shallow 'ponded' areas which were presumably intended to hold water. Some of these ditched features sat alone, in that they did not appear to form any part of a coherent system. This was true of Ditches B11 and B12 (see Figs 44, 46 was 45; Fig. 49 S117, S119 and S120), where the state of preservation was too poor or the area excavated was too small to recover any overall plan that allowed for a full interpretation of the features. In fact, the area around Ditch B12 appeared to show a very complicated set of intercutting ditches from this period of occupation that was never fully traced or interpreted. It is possible that the westernmost ditch of this group may have connected with Ditch B8 (see Fig. 44) to the north, but the lack of time during the excavation restricted the exploration of such possible links. Likewise, the extent of Ditch B10 could not be traced owing to the lack of time and the limitations of the trenches that were set out.

However, in the eastern part of Area B and within the main part of the trench system the plan of a more coherent ditched system was recovered. This consisted of Ditches B2 and B3, which ran parallel to one another in a north–south direction for some 28m (Pls 36 and 37). At the north end of the trench Ditch B3 curved to the east and ran into the baulk. Ditch B2, on the other hand, curved to the west and appeared to link to or form part of Ditch B8. A branch of this 'system' of ditches ran to the north at this point (Ditch B9: Pls 38 and 39). In addition, two further ditches (B6 and B7) branched off Ditch B3 and ran off into the baulk on the eastern side of the excavated area.

The profiles of these two sets of ditches are shown in Figure 47, with the section's positions shown in Figure 46 was 45. Most of the sections show fairly straightforward fills with little sign of any recutting. However, the profiles would suggest that recutting was fairly frequently done, as the bottoms of the ditches in almost all of the sections are very uneven in form. It is only in S105 and S107 that there was any suggestion of a secondary phase — here the line of Ditch B3 appears to reflect the entry of the two side ditches (B6 and B7) which join the main line of Ditch B3 in this area. Exactly why the profiles appear to suggest recutting but the actual fills show little sign of such activity is difficult to explain. However, the fills of these two ditches along most of their lengths were very similar, suggesting that, once abandoned, the water-filled ditches slowly filled with fluvially deposited silts and silty clays. It could be that the ditches were kept well scoured, both by being cleaned out regularly and by volumes of water washing sediments along the bottom of the ditches and thus helping to mix the sediments from early and late phases of the ditches' evolution. All that can be said with certainly is that the final profiles and fills show that the area was very wet for most of the functioning life of the ditches and that, once abandoned, they filled with water-derived material which was recorded during the excavation as black silts and silty clays (see Fig. 47 and Appendix 2 for section and fill descriptions; also Pl. 40). This same infilling of silt and silty clays within all the Area B ditches is also seen in the profile of Ditch B9 (Pl. 39).

In some areas, where the clearing of topsoil by the contractors had been less severe, post-holes survived following the lines of these ditches, apparently indicating that, at least in part, some of the ditch lengths had been revetted with timber planking. Some of these posts were set within holes packed with small stones, while the lines of other posts were visible as dark stains within the soil where the posts had rotted away. In a few cases the posts themselves were preserved owing to the wet conditions which prevailed on the site. Along the line of Ditch B2 there were five posts on the western side and six posts on the eastern side which survived, although they were not regularly spaced and survived in two groups (see Fig. 44). One group of posts survived along the line of Ditch B3, five posts on each side of the ditch. Also appearing to line the corner of Ditch B10, another group of four posts set into the side of the ditch showed merely as dark organic stains in the underlying natural (see Fig. 44 and Pl. 41).

Almost all of the planked revetting that appeared to have been placed behind these posts had rotted away. In some cases there was a dark organic stain lining the sides of the ditches, suggesting areas that had been revetted, but in most cases the ditch sides appeared to have been more rounded, as if revetting had never existed or that it had either been deliberately removed or rotted away naturally, leaving no trace. An alternative explanation is to see the areas of revetting as representing the areas along the ditch sides where there were formal crossing points, perhaps planked walkways. While there was no supporting evidence for this, it could explain why planked revetting was so intermittently found along these ditch lines.

Area B also had within it three large dark blue/grey silty spreads of material that were initially termed 'ponds'. These features are shown in Figure 44, where they are marked as Ponds A, B and C. Ponds A and B were oval spreads approximately 10×5m in the northern part of Area B.

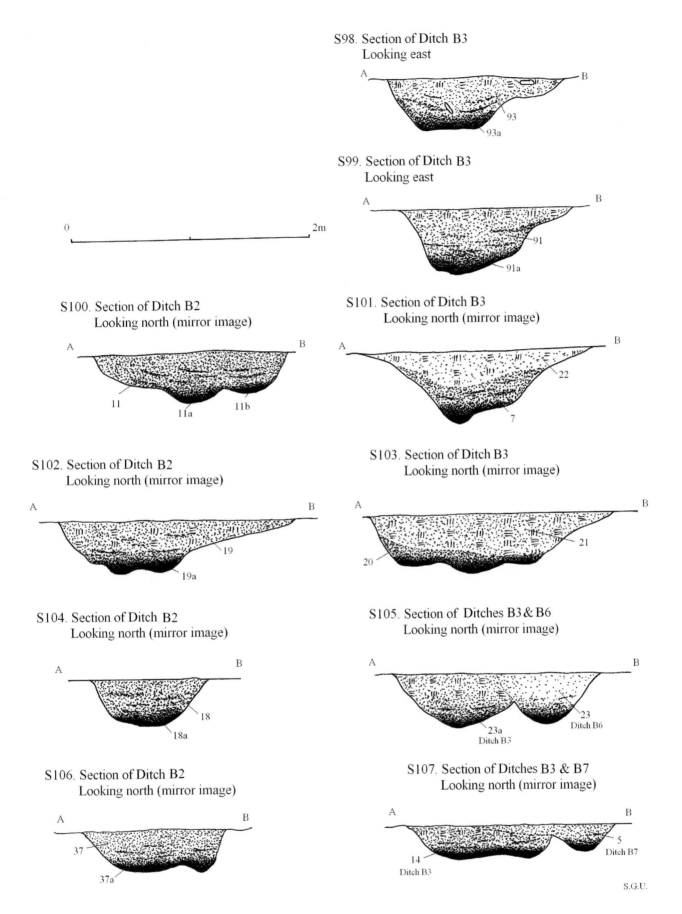

S98. Section of Ditch B3
Looking east

S99. Section of Ditch B3
Looking east

0   2m

S100. Section of Ditch B2
Looking north (mirror image)

S101. Section of Ditch B3
Looking north (mirror image)

S102. Section of Ditch B2
Looking north (mirror image)

S103. Section of Ditch B3
Looking north (mirror image)

S104. Section of Ditch B2
Looking north (mirror image)

S105. Section of Ditches B3 & B6
Looking north (mirror image)

S106. Section of Ditch B2
Looking north (mirror image)

S107. Section of Ditches B3 & B7
Looking north (mirror image)

S.G.U.

Figure 47 Sections S98–S107 through Ditches B2, B3, B6 and B7 in Area B (see Fig. 45 for section locations)

71

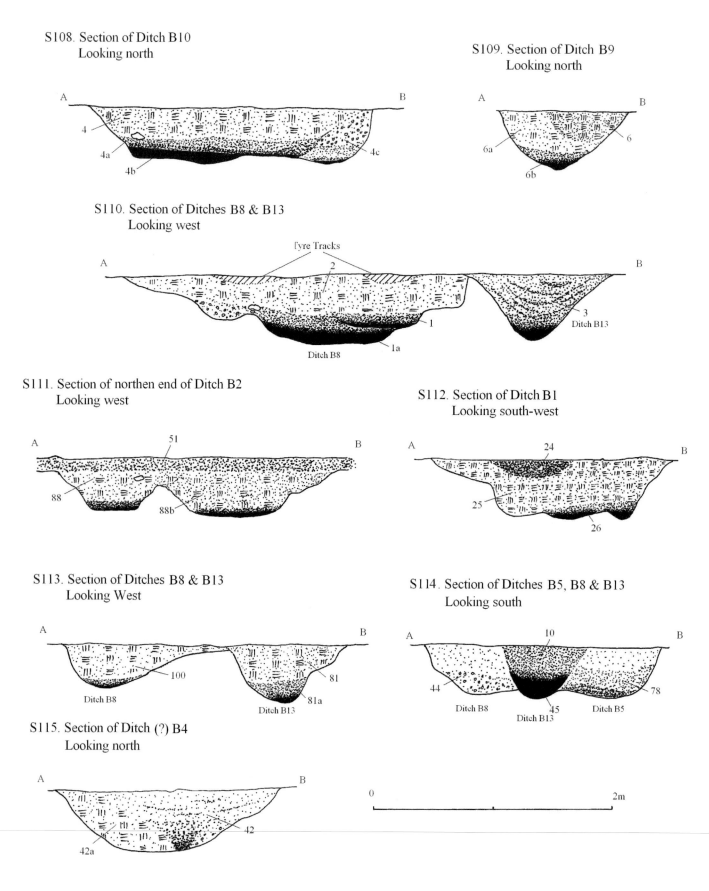

S108. Section of Ditch B10
Looking north

S109. Section of Ditch B9
Looking north

S110. Section of Ditches B8 & B13
Looking west

S111. Section of northen end of Ditch B2
Looking west

S112. Section of Ditch B1
Looking south-west

S113. Section of Ditches B8 & B13
Looking West

S114. Section of Ditches B5, B8 & B13
Looking south

S115. Section of Ditch (?) B4
Looking north

S.G.U.

Figure 48 Sections S108–S115 through ditches within Area B (see Fig. 45 for section locations)

Plate 36 Ditches B2 and B3 after an initial surface cleaning in the south-eastern corner of Area B. Section S107 has been part excavated (see Figs 44 and 45)

Plate 37 Ditch B3 under excavation in Area B with section S101 nearest the camera (see Fig. 45)

Plate 38 Ditch B9 under excavation in Area B, looking north (see Fig. 44). In the distance (left) the long trench connects areas B and C (see Fig. 46)

Plate 39 Ditches B2 and B3 after an initial surface cleaning in the south-eastern corner of Area B. Section S107 has been part excavated (see Figs 44 and 45)

Plate 40 Ditches B2 and B3 after an initial surface cleaning in the south-eastern corner of Area B. Section S107 has been part excavated (see Figs 44 and 45)

Pond C was more rectangular and the largest of the three features, measuring 12m long and 6.5m wide at the point where it was masked by the trench sides of the excavation. In all cases the term 'pond' may be misleading, as the features were very shallow. The area of Pond A, for example, was only 0.20m deep and consisted of a layer of dark blue silt (see Fig. 48 S111, context 51). Ponds A and B also partly sealed ditches of Period 6. Although the pottery derived from these ponded features could be ascribed to the late 3rd and early 4th century — the same

Plate 41 Detail of part of Ditch B10 in Area B, showing the positions marked by dark staining of posts forming part of the revetted side to this ditch. Post-hole 15 is shown **top left**

Plate 42 Part of section under excavation in Pit B2 (S116 in Figs 49 and 44)

date as the ditches they sealed — the ponded features were clearly at the end of this period of occupation and perhaps represent a time when the site was partly flooded. Thus they are best seen, perhaps, as representing the natural flooding of shallow or low areas within the complex of ditches found in Area B. Certainly, within the area of Pond C the silty deposit of context 32 covered five (undated) post positions set into the underlying natural. It is also important to note that any interpretation of all three features was hampered by the top layers having been

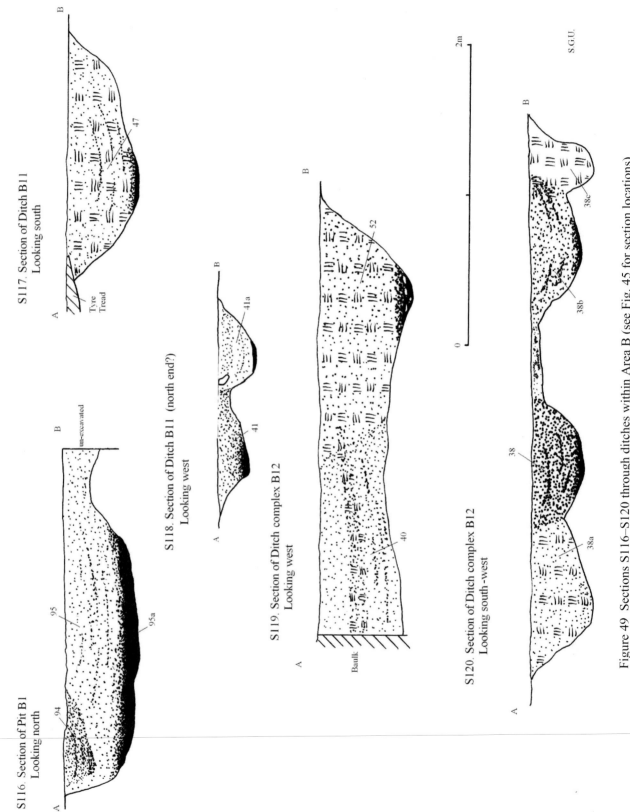

S116. Section of Pit B1
Looking north

S117. Section of Ditch B11
Looking south

S118. Section of Ditch B11 (north end?)
Looking west

S119. Section of Ditch complex B12
Looking west

S120. Section of Ditch complex B12
Looking south-west

Figure 49 Sections S116–S120 through ditches within Area B (see Fig. 45 for section locations)

76

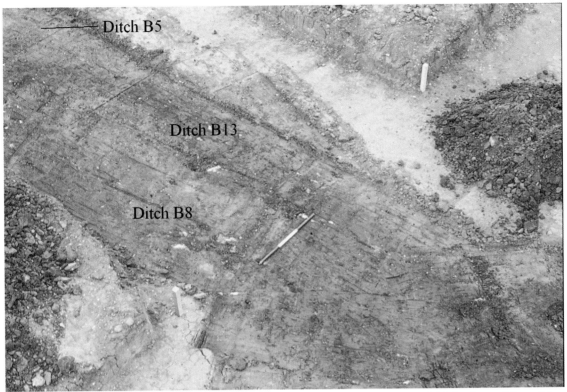

Ditch B5

Ditch B13

Ditch B8

Plate 43 Ditches B8 and B13 after cleaning and before excavation (see Figs 44 and 45 for the position of these ditches and S113, shown in Fig. 48)

Plate 44 Detail of Post-hole B15, showing stone packing (see Fig. 44)

stripped away by the contractor's machinery prior to any archaeological work taking place; therefore, a full assessment of the original depth of these features could not be made.

The only other feature which could be ascribed to this period was a small pit (Pit B2) in the north-western corner of Area B that was filled with dark blue/black/grey silt and amounts of limestone rubble (see Fig. 44 and Pl. 42). This pit was next to another slightly larger but shallower pit which lay immediately to the south-west which had a similar fill but lacked dating evidence. The function of these small pits is uncertain. Pit B2 contained only three sherds of 3rd- and 4th-century pottery and lacked any bone deposits, so it seems unlikely that the pits were dug for — or even used later for — rubbish disposal. Instead, the fills indicate that the process of infilling was rather slow, with silts washing into the pit, although the limestone rubble would have been added both periodically and regularly as it was present throughout the total depth of the feature.

Both wells, I and II, belong to this period and were discussed in Chapter 3.

Period 7. Mid-4th century
(Fig. 49)
The amount of activity within Area B declined after the major works of the previous period. It would appear that the flooding that occurred during the 3rd and 4th centuries and which had at least part-filled some of the features and perhaps caused the formation of the ponded areas had caused this part of the whole site to be abandoned. Only one small area produced pottery (twenty-eight sherds) that could be ascribed to the middle of the 4th century (see Chapter 7 nos 121, 126 and 134) and this came from a part-excavated feature in the south-western part of the site. This feature may have been a pit (contexts 28 and 52) dug over the top of a ditch complex (context 40) which produced no dating evidence at all. This area is shown in Figures 44 and 46, was 45 with a section (S119) shown in Figure 49.

Period 8. Late 4th century and early 5th century
(Pls 43–44)
Again, there was little activity within the area during this late period of occupation. A single length of ditch (Ditch B13) dug roughly east–west cut into the silted fill of Ditch B8 (Pl. 43). This ditch was traced for a length of 14m and can be seen in S110, S113 and S114 (shown in Fig. 48). A cut (context 94) was made into the top of the fill of Pit B1 (Fig. 49 S116). In both cases the features that were dug filled with dark silts and silty clays and had the appearance of having been deposited during a wet period, when the area was probably waterlogged.

A series of stone-packed post-holes was also found within Area B during the course of the excavation. These were located in two groups: first, a line of seven posts (Posts 5–11; see Fig. 44, Pl. 38) which ran parallel to the trench side in the northern part of the area; and second, a group of three posts set close to the edge of Ditch B10 (Posts 12, 13 and 15). Dating from these two sets of posts indicates that they belong to the late 4th century, with Posts 5–7 and 10 and 11 having fragments of pottery within their fills. Post 10 had sherds of black ware similar to those illustrated in the pottery report (Chapter 7) as nos 162–3 (see Fig. 90), which came from the fill of Ditch B13. It is possible that this row of posts represents some form of wooden structure, the rest of the structure lying under the baulk to the north. However, it is equally possible that the row represented a fence line limiting access from the north to the area to the south of this line, which best indications show was by this period very wet and probably waterlogged.

Of the other posts (Posts 12, 13 and 15; Fig. 44), little can be said with regard to dating, although the character of the fills was similar to those of Posts 5–11 (above), and thus may indicate a similar date. One post (Post 15) was set within a well-formed post-hole that was packed with limestone and was clearly intended to take a post of some size (see Pl. 44). However, again it was impossible to ascribe a function to this, or to the other posts in this group. These posts may, like the group 5–11, have been structural or could have divided the area from the wetter part of the site which lay within the south-eastern corner of Area B. Time limitations and the state of destruction in this part of the site made any further interpretation impossible.

Features excavated along the linking trench between Areas B and C/D
A trench linking Areas B and C/D was initially dug by machine and later cleaned and excavated by hand. It cut across several features. This trench can be seen in Plate 38 running to the north of Area B and is shown in plan and by section in Figure 45 was 46. Ditches 53 and 73 both relate to the military phase of the site and have been described above (Area B Period 2). Context 98, which cut 73a, was undatable, but appeared to be some form of small gully. However, the ditch filled by contexts 54a and 54 produced nine sherds of 2nd-century pottery (Period 4) and the upper fill of the ditch filled by layer 89 produced three sherds of pottery best described as belonging to Period 5. Little can be said with any confidence about the function of these ditches or whether they linked with any of the other ditches from any of the areas explored archaeologically. However, between the ditches filled by layers 54 and 89/105 were what appeared to be the foundation walls and clay floor of a structure, Building B1 (see Figure 45 was 46, plan and S126). The walls were very badly damaged and only the bottom of the foundations appeared to survive. These consisted of a shallow trench into which limestone rubble and gravel had been rammed. The form taken by the superstructure of this building was unclear but the best option, considering perhaps the narrowness of the wall foundations (c. 0.75m) is that it was of timber. There was no indication of any limestone or even clay/cob deposits to indicate other forms of walling. The clay floor, which was laid to a depth of 0.1m, was formed out of blue local clay and sat directly on the natural.

It appears most likely that the archaeological trench cut across the building at right angles with the width of the structure being approximately 7m wide to the centres of the walls. There was no indication of the length of the building, but other buildings within the Nene valley whose widths are similar to this often have a width to length ratio of approximately 2:1 (Upex 2008a, Chapters 5–6), which might indicate a structure 14m long. There was no indication of a date for this structure. The building did, however, follow the general trend of Ditches 54 and 89 in having an east–west alignment. Indeed, it is possible that these ditches were in some way connected to the building, perhaps to provide drainage around it. Little more can be said about this structure or any relationship it might have had to other surrounding features because of the lack of excavation within the area of this trench.

Chapter 5. The excavation of Areas C and D

I. Introduction
(Figs 50–52; Pl. 45)

Areas C and D lay to the north of Area B and to the east of Area A (Figs 4; Pl. 45). They were dug as two separate areas during the excavation for ease of recording but here are treated as a single unit (Figs 50–52). Like the other areas given over to archaeological work, these Areas had been severely damaged by the gravel contractor's machinery, which had compressed the soft fills of ditches and pits and left tyre ruts across the entire site that caused real problems in archaeological interpretation where they had compressed the topsoil or subsoil into areas of soft natural. In these Areas they were very difficult to distinguish from small gullies or ditches of proven archaeological significance. In addition, the Areas had considerable spreads of limestone rubble which appeared to fill earlier, softer features and act as some form of surfacing or hard standing. These, too, showed signs of modern damage and what must have been originally fairly flat surfaces of limestone were, on excavation, found to be very contorted and undulating where machinery had compressed the deposits. Some impression of the task facing the archaeological team as they arrived on the site can be gauged by viewing Plates 4 and 5, which show Area C prior to any cleaning and recording work.

Plate 45 General view of excavations within Areas C and D, looking east

Areas C and D contained a series of ditches and pits dug into the natural gravel subsoil that had filled with partly waterlogged material, causing the fills to retain a dark blue-grey colour. In addition, spreads of limestone rubble and wall lines indicated the presence of buildings. The demands of time during the archaeological work and the poor state of preservation resulted in a somewhat confused picture of both the chronological development of the site and the interpretation of the features.

II. The excavations

Periods 3 and 4. Late 1st to late 2nd century
(Figs 53–55)
There was clearly some activity within the two areas during the late 1st to late 2nd century, with the digging of several similarly dated but stratigraphically different pits, ditches and gullies. These features were concentrated in the north-western part of Area C. A short length of gully (context 56 in Fig. 50) was cut by another shallow but wider ditch, Ditch C11 (Fig. 50 and Fig. 54 S77), which in turn was cut by one of a pair of parallel narrow gullies, Ditches C1 and C2 (Fig. 50; Fig. 53 S72**S73** and Fig. 54 S78; for locations of sections see Fig. 51). These were very shallow features, only some 0.25m deep. Ditch C1 ran for a length of 12m across the site in a north–south direction, while Ditch C2 appeared to run further north and out of the area of excavation. The actual line of C2 was interrupted at its northern end by a similarly dated but again stratigraphically later pit (Pit C1), which cut across its line. Although of different phases, very little dating evidence was recovered from the fills of these features, but all appear to fall within Period 3 and 4. The latest feature from this group, Pit C1, is shown in Figure 54 (S74 and S75) as a shallow depression 0.50m deep which had filled with waterborne silts and silty clay deposits. A slightly deeper pit (Pit C2) lay some 8m to the south-west of Pit C1 and had a similar fill.

The remaining feature from this period was a 2m length of a shallow gully (context 52, shown in Fig. 50 and in section in Fig. 55 S79).

Little can be said about the purpose of any of these features. Ditches C1 and C2 were only 1m apart and can hardly represent any form of pathway, and at best the two pits Pits C1 and C2 could be interpreted as soakaways for surrounding areas, as their fills contained very few 'rubbish-like' deposits.

Period 5. Early 3rd century
A single short length of shallow ditch, Ditch C4 (Fig. 50; Fig. 55 S79 and S80), ran roughly north–south. Both ends of this feature ran into baulks and it was not traced for more than 5m within the excavated area, while another section of the feature was revealed in a slit trench to the south of the main area, making the total traceable length of the feature 8m. The slope of the feature along its length suggests that it was meant to drain to the south.

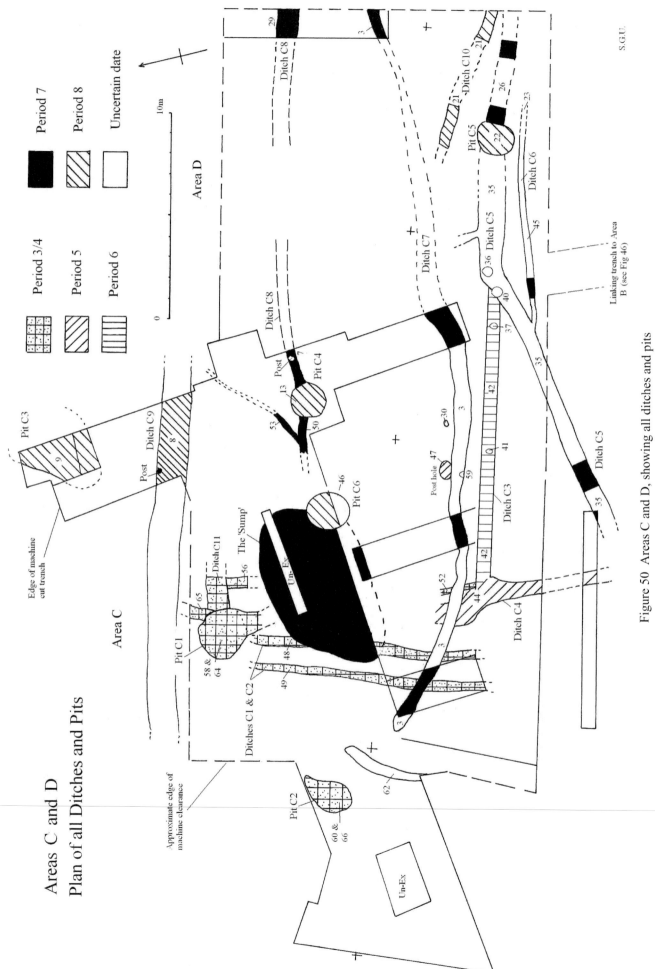

Areas C and D
Plan of all Ditches and Pits

Period 3/4 (dotted fill)
Period 5 (diagonal hatch fill)
Period 6 (vertical line fill)

Period 7 (black fill)
Period 8 (diagonal hatch fill)
Uncertain date (white)

0 — 10m

Area C

Area D

S.G.U.

Edge of machine cut trench

Approximate edge of machine clearance

Pit C3

Ditch C9

Post

9

8

Post

13

53

50

Pit C4

Ditch C8

Ditch C8

7

Ditch C7

30

3

3

Post hole 47

59

36 Ditch C5

40

37

42

42

41

Ditch C3

35

35

35

Ditch C5

Ditch C4

44

52

46

Pit C6

The 'Sump'

Un-Ex

Ditch C11

56

65

58 &
64

Pit C1

Ditches C1 & C2

48

49

3

3

Pit C2

60 &
66

62

Un-Ex

Pit C5

22

21

26

23

Ditch C10

21

21

Ditch C6

45

Linking trench to Area
B (see Fig 46)

29

3

Figure 50   Areas C and D, showing all ditches and pits

80

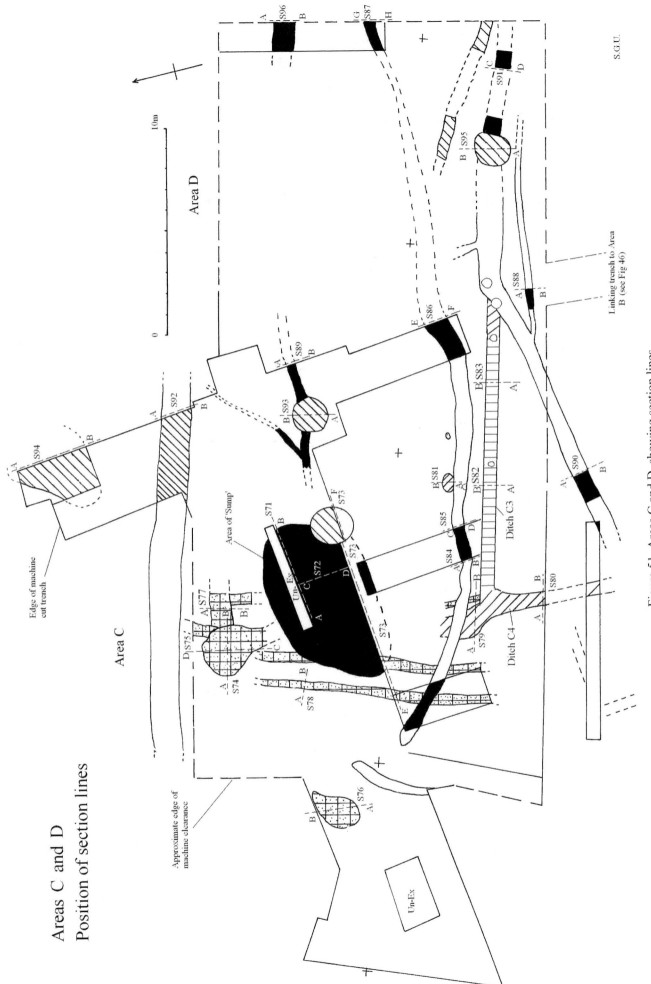

Areas C and D
Position of section lines

Figure 51   Areas C and D, showing section lines

81

Areas C and D
Period 8 features

Building D1

Corndrier

Area D

10m

0

Pit C3

9

8

Ditch C9

Edge of machine cut trench

Pit C5

22

Ditch C10

21

21

21V

21

Postholes

Linking trench to Area B (see Fig 46)

S.G.U.

Pit C4

13

Building C2

Area of 'Sump'

Pit C6

46

4

Area C

Line of modern land Drain

Wall C2

Un-Ex

Approximate edge of machine clearance

16

20

Wall C1

22

Trench VIII

Line of modern land drain

21

Un-Ex

23

Building C1

Figure 52 Areas C and D, showing Period 8 features

82

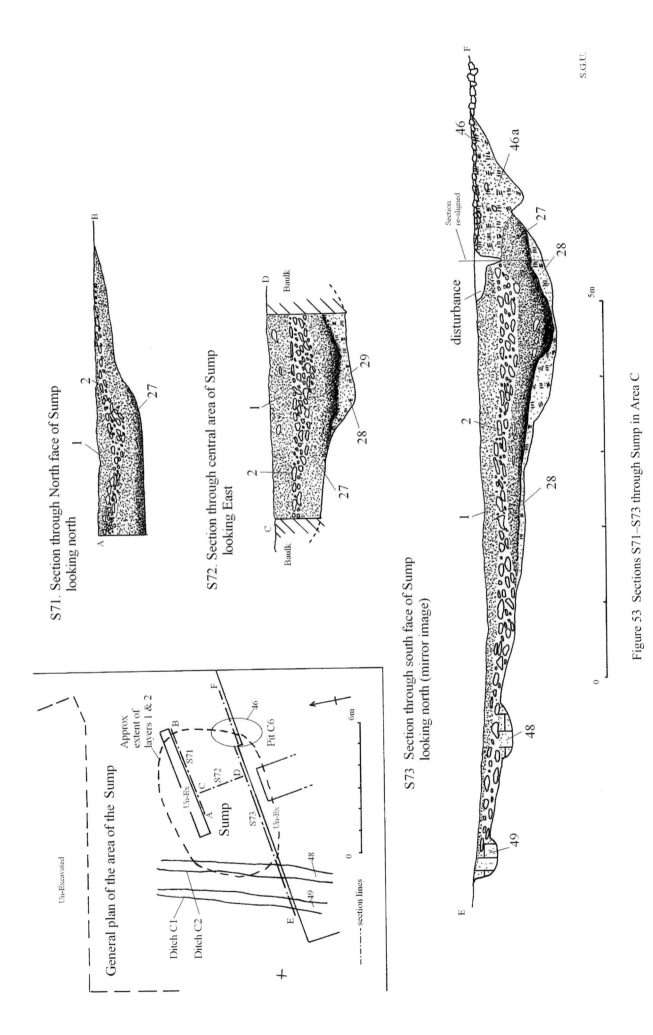

General plan of the area of the Sump

Un-Excavated

Approx extent of layers 1 & 2

Ditch C1

Ditch C2

Sump

Pit C6

Un-Ex

Un-Ex

------ section lines

S71

S72

S73

S71. Section through North face of Sump looking north

S72. Section through central area of Sump looking East

Baulk

Baulk

S73 Section through south face of Sump looking north (mirror image)

Section re-aligned

disturbance

S.G.U.

5m

Figure 53 Sections S71–S73 through Sump in Area C

83

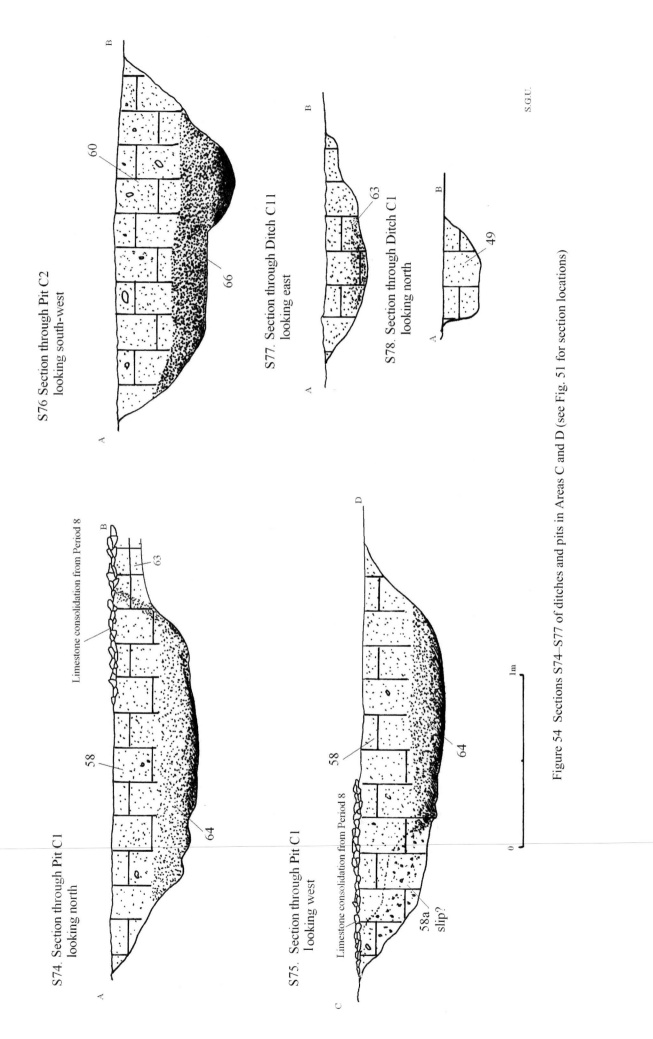

S76 Section through Pit C2
looking south-west

60

66

S77. Section through Ditch C11
looking east

63

S78. Section through Ditch C1
looking north

49

S.G.U.

S74. Section through Pit C1
looking north

Limestone consolidation from Period 8

63

58

64

S75. Section through Pit C1
looking west

Limestone consolidation from Period 8

58

64

58a
slip?

1m

0

Figure 54 Sections S74–S77 of ditches and pits in Areas C and D (see Fig. 51 for section locations)

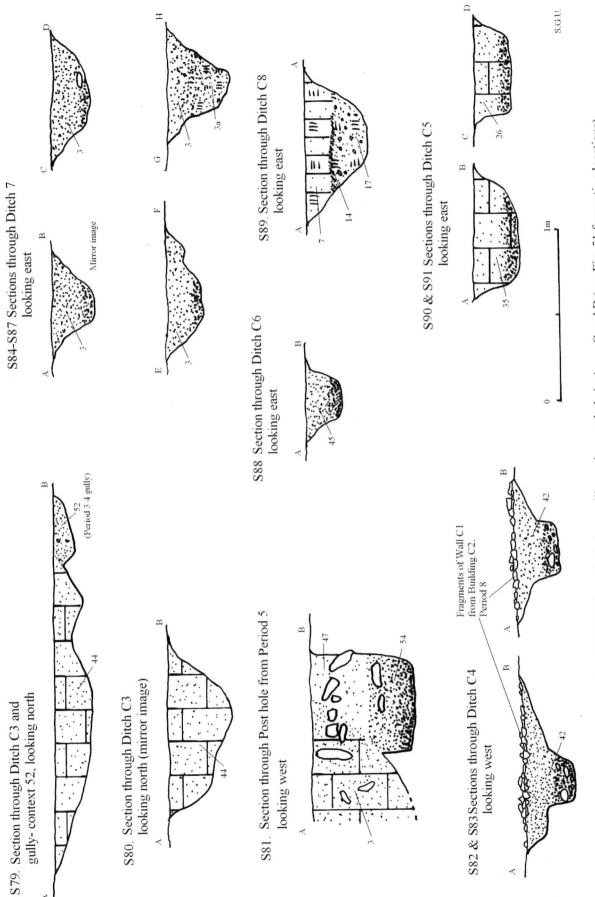

S79. Section through Ditch C3 and gully- context 52, looking north

S80. Section through Ditch C3 looking north (mirror image)

S81. Section through Post hole from Period 5 looking west

S82 & S83 Sections through Ditch C4 looking west

S84-S87 Sections through Ditch 7 looking east

S88 Section through Ditch C6 looking east

S89. Section through Ditch C8 looking east

S90 & S91 Sections through Ditch C5 looking east

Figure 55 Sections S79–S91 through ditches, gullies and a post-hole in Areas C and D (see Fig. 51 for section locations)

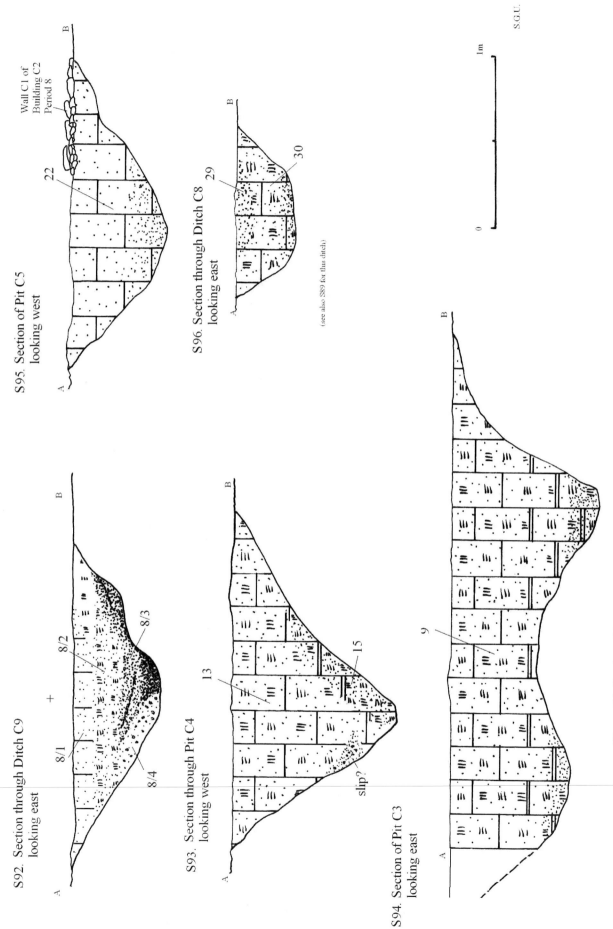

S95. Section of Pit C5
looking west

Wall C1 of
Building C2
Period 8

22

S96. Section through Ditch C8
looking east

29

30

(see also S89 for this ditch)

S92. Section through Ditch C9
looking east

8/1

8/2

8/3

8/4

S93. Section through Pit C4
looking west

13

15

slip?

S94. Section of Pit C3
looking east

9

1m

0

S.G.U.

Figure 56 Sections S92–S96 through ditches and pits in Areas C and D (see Fig. 51 for section locations)

The only other feature from this phase of the site's development was a post-hole some 0.6m across which was cut by Ditch C7 from Period 7 (see Fig. 55 S81). The post-hole (context 47) had limestone rubble in both of its fills and the general impression was that this fill was the disturbed packing around a post which had been removed at some point prior to the digging of the Period 7 ditch. What this post setting was used for is unclear.

Period 6. Late 3rd century–early 4th century

A single straight ditch 14.5m long that ran along the southern edge of the area, Ditch C3 (Fig. 50; Fig. 55 S82 and S83), was dug in this period. The fills from both sections which were cut into this feature were similar in that the bottom levels consisted of limestone fragments which were later covered with brown sandy silt and the profile of the feature was very symmetrical, with a flat base. Along the base of the ditch two posts were located (contexts 37 and 41, see Fig. 50) which gave rise to the suggestion that this feature was a foundation trench for a building. The western end of Ditch C3 butted against Ditch C4, while at the eastern end the feature was cut by a Period 7 ditch, Ditch C5.

It is difficult to see with what other structural elements this straight length of possible foundation trench could be linked. To the south the proximity of the excavation baulk masked any possible associated wall lines and to the north the area was so disturbed by later archaeological features and the general disturbances caused by contractor's machinery that nothing of similar character was found here either. Later, in Period 8, a wall with a limestone foundation (see Fig. 52 Wall C1) followed the same general alignment as Ditch C3, although set approximately 1m to the north. It is possible that this later stonework represents some form of rebuilding of an earlier timber structure.

Period 7. Mid-4th century
(Fig. 56; Pl. 46)

There appeared to be considerable activity within Areas C and D during this period, contrasting with the lack of activity which was found in Area B at the same time. Although few surveyed levels were taken during the excavation it became clear that Area B was slightly lower in height (above OD) than Areas C and D and whereas most of the activity in Area B had occurred during Period 6, with few features found during Period 7, the reverse was true on the slightly higher ground of Area C and D. Such a move in site activity must to some extent reveal the problems that the site's occupants were having with drainage and flooding over the whole area during the 3rd and 4th centuries.

Along the southern line of the trench, Ditch C5 (cut in part over the top of the earlier Ditch C3 of Period 6) was traced for 18m and then turned to the south-west and ran out of the area. Two sections cut across this feature (Figs 51 and 55 S90 and S91) showed it to be 0.35m deep and filled with silty loam with charcoal flecks. A much smaller and very shallow gully (Ditch C6) ran into this ditch line near the edge of the southern trench baulk (Fig. 55 S88).

Another length of ditch (Ditch C7) ran east–west for a total length of 35m across the central area of both Areas C and D, and terminated in a rounded butt end within the excavation area. Four sections were cut across this feature (Figs 51 and 55 S84–S87). The fill along most of the length of this ditch was of black silt and only in S87 (G–H), cut against the baulk where the ditch ran into the trench side, was there a lower fill of clay and silt. The general indications were that the ditch was meant to drain water from west to east and toward the lower ground and the river Nene.

The same drainage function may have been true of another ditch, Ditch C8, which ran further to the north of

Plate 46 Section through the sump in Area C (see also S73 Fig. 53)

Ditch C7. This entered the site in Area D against the baulk (see Fig. 50; Fig. 56 S96) and then appeared to run across the site to the west where it became narrower and shallower (Fig. 55 S89). It is not clear whether Ditch C8 linked with the large shallow 'sump' which formed a central feature of this period of the site's occupation — but it seems likely.

Another very narrow gully-like feature joined Ditch C8 from the north of the site (context 53) just prior to the suspected link with the 'sump'. Both these features were filled with similar material which was less silty and contained more loam than the fills of the other ditches so far described within the area.

The largest feature of this period within Area C was a large oval depression or 'sump' 9×5m in plan and 1.10m deep. The feature cut through some of the earlier ditches and pits of Periods 3 and 4. Sections cut through the 'sump' (Figs 51 and 53; Pl. 46) show that the feature was dug into the natural gravel and then partly lined with an orange-brown clay (Fig. 53 S72, S73 context 28), presumably to hold water. It is probable that the orange staining within this clay may have come from decaying vegetable matter that had partly oxidised and this may have been derived from a phase in the life of the 'sump' when reeds or other plants were growing in what would have been a shallow waterlogged depression. On top of this fill there had accumulated a deposit of black silt 0.50m deep (context 27) with a high organic content which again suggests a period of time when reeds and other aquatic or marginal plants were colonising the area. The remaining and upper levels of the 'sump' were filled with a large capping layer of limestone rubble (context 2) which was set down in Period 8, presumably in an attempt to provide a hard surfacing for the underlying softer fills of the 'sump' and to consolidate any 'settling' or compression in the area. On top of this limestone surfacing and during the

very last archaeological sequences on the site the soft fills of the 'sump' caused the limestone surfacing to consolidate still further and a depression clearly evolved in the area of the underlying feature which was filled with black silts along with some clay inclusions (Fig. 53 S71–S73 context 1). This fill contained late pottery sequences reported on below (Chapter 7).

What function the 'sump' served, other than the obvious comment that it was meant to hold water, is not known. It may have acted as a pond or watering hole for cattle or other stock, although the area was not only very low-lying — and therefore must have always been generally wet in the first place — but it was also close to the river Nene and as such the need for a water hole may have been superfluous. It has been suggested above that there was a narrow outlet (Ditch C8) from the eastern side of the 'sump', which may have acted as a drain or overflow from the feature, and this would perhaps have been essential during times of heavy rain.

Period 8. Late 4th century and early 5th century (Pl. 47)

Although there was some suggestion above that during Period 6 a short length of Ditch C6 may have been structural it is only during Period 8 that structures were confirmed within Areas C and D. It appears that during this period of the site's development there was some form of radical replanning of the area and all of the earlier ditches and pits were either filled deliberately or, from the looks of their fills, had silted up naturally, perhaps during a period of prolonged flooding or wet weather within the area. The sump outlined in Period 7 may well have been filled with largely fluvially derived material and the other ditches and pits seem to have suffered the same fate. It was over the top of all of these earlier features that three buildings — shown in Figure 55 as Buildings C1, C2 and

Plate 47 Detailed view of Area C under excavation, looking east. Building C1 in the foreground, Building C2 and the sump beyond

D1 — appear to have been constructed. All three buildings were in a poor state of preservation due to factors such as their natural subsidence into the softer fills of underlying features and, more significantly, because the contractor's heavy machinery had compressed this subsidence still further, literally moving and pushing some wall lines significantly away from their original line. This state of preservation not only made interpretation very difficult but also caused immense problems for the understanding of the chronological development of the site. Plates 4–5 show the state of the site when archaeological work began in the area of these buildings and Plates 45 and 47 illustrate the area after attempts to clean and cut sections into the deposits had been undertaken.

Building C1

This structure lay to the west of Area D and was severely damaged when archaeological work started. It appeared to be 5.0m wide and was traceable for 8.5m along its long axis but its eastern end was disturbed by the walls of Building C2, which appeared to be later in date. The wall lines of Building C1 were of limestone rubble and gravel laid in a narrow mason's trench. Some parts of the western short axis wall were 1.0m wide (Fig. 52 context 23), but the rest of the foundation was slightly narrower. The northern wall line was further complicated by the fact that a modern land drain had cut along much the same line. This drain was simply backfilled with soil, but its digging had disturbed still further this already disturbed feature. There was no indication of any internal features within the area of this structure, nor of whether the walls had been carried up to any height; it seems likely, however, that the building may have had, in keeping with many excavated Nene valley buildings of this type, a dwarf wall and timber superstructure. The pottery and dating evidence that could be ascribed to the building were all from the late Roman period. However, it is fair to say that the dating evidence from this part of the site was weak. There were no significant underlying features which the building cut other than an undated gully (see Fig. 50 context 62), so it may have related to a period earlier than Period 8, although at present the best indications are that it does belong to this period of occupation.

Building C2
(Pl. 48)

Building C2, which had also been severely damaged by heavy machinery, was approximately 29m long by 12.5m wide. Its walls were constructed in a similar way to those of Building C1 and Buildings II and III from Area A in that they were formed of limestone rubble and gravel laid in a shallow mason's trench. The walls varied in width between 0.9m and 0.5m but again preservation was very variable and one might assume that generally they were originally all approximately 0.9m wide. Some sections of walling, such as that along the south wall at its western end (see Fig. 52, wall C1), were well laid, with two courses of stonework. For the most part, however, the walls were of a single layer of limestone rubble foundation (see Pl. 48 for a section of the south wall). In one place along the north wall (Fig. 52, Wall C2), one short section survived which retained its foundation course and a first coursed layer of pitched stonework, suggesting that if it were ever taken higher it would have been of typical 'herringbone' construction. The southern wall line was badly affected by

the passage of heavy machinery and in some places the wall had been physically moved off line by up to 1.5m. This point was dramatically illustrated by the central section of the southern wall, where two 'northerly' curved lengths of wall were found to have been pushed off their original line by the passage of modern tyres some 2m across! Elsewhere the wall foundation appeared to sit, with little attempt at a foundation trench, over the top of an underlying ditch (Ditch C4: Fig. 55 S82 and S83).

The western short axis wall of Building C2 was again very variable in its preservation along its length. It survived well in the northern section but had all but been destroyed in its southern section. Similarly, the eastern short axis wall was very fragmentary, with a considerable amount more gravel in its make-up than the other walls. It is just possible that such a difference in foundation construction between the western and eastern ends of Building C2 suggests that it followed a similar developmental path to Building II in Area A, in that it underwent two phases of development, with an eastern extension added to an initial phase (see Figs 26 and 28). However, although this sequence cannot be ruled out the site was just too damaged to say that it positively took place.

Part-way along the southern wall two posts were set on the line of the wall. These may have been integral with the walling itself and formed part of the way the superstructure of the building was keyed into the foundation — perhaps by a series of posts set into the foundation to take timber uprights. It is equally possible that they represent an entrance into the building; there is no indication of any limestone foundation between the posts, thus suggesting clear access into the building at this point. However, preservation of the archaeological deposits was not good in this area and it would be wrong to read too much into the surviving evidence.

Whatever the sequential development of Building C2, it is clear that internally there was a serious attempt to cover the area of the underlying sump-like feature with limestone rubble. This may have acted as a base for some form of surfacing within the building — of which there was no indication — but perhaps more importantly, it acted as consolidation for the underlying soft fills of the sump (Figure 53 S71–73 context 2).

Most of this attempt to consolidate the floored area of the structure was related to the area of the former sump but an additional spread of limestone did extend over the top of features to the north-west of the sump that belonged to Periods 3 and 4. Thus the sections shown across Pit C1 (see Figs 50 and 54 S74 and S75) were capped in part with limestone from this spread of material within Building C2.

There is little to say about surviving features within Building C2. There was a suggestion of some form of inner walling to the south of the unexcavated baulk within the central area of the building (see Fig. 52), but this was at a different alignment to the outer walls and the impression of walling may just have been caused by the way that the rubble consolidation within the whole area was laid down.

Along the internal face of the south wall there was an area of limestone that could have been the foundation for some form of 'benching'. This was a spread of limestone 3.5m long which seemed to have been fairly well preserved and may have related to some form of internal feature set against the inner south wall. Along the external face of the north wall was a similar area of limestone that was set out and appeared to run parallel to the wall line. This spread of limestone may have been intended to form some type of 'seating' for a feature set against the outer wall of the building, but it is also worth pointing out that the area of this spread of limestone also overlay a section of ditch (Ditch C11: Fig. 50 context 63) and may have been consolidation for any settling that had occurred in this area of the site. However, to the west of this location, in an area without any underlying subsidence, there was another spread of limestone 0.75m long set apparently deliberately against the outer face of the wall. Whether this feature acted as some form of buttress for the main wall of the building at this point is difficult to say but the foundations along this part of the walling would have been very vulnerable to settling into the underlying soft deposits of earlier pits and ditches and some form of buttressing may have been required.

Clearly the major problem with the interpretation of Building C2 is the roofing arrangements, especially considering that the width of the building was 12.5m. This would be too wide to bridge with a single span of timber and various options present themselves, therefore. The building may have been an aisled structure similar to Building II in Area A. This building was 11.0m wide (wall centre to wall centre) and its roof was supported on a series of aisle posts set in two rows. Buildings of this type are known from many sites within the Nene valley and beyond (Upex 2008a, 130–37; Hadman 1978, 187–95); Orton Hall Farm Barn 1 and Haddon structure 2, for example, were both 11.0m wide (Mackreth 1996b, fig. 35; Hinman 2003, fig. 14). Thus the internal dimensions for Building

Plate 48 Part of the southern wall-line of Building C2 (Wall C1 in Fig. 52)

C2 in Area C fit well with other known structures apart from the absence of evidence for internal aisle posts. No rows of posts were found within the area of Building C2 during the excavations, even allowing for the poor state of preservation when the site was examined. The alternative here is to argue that the internal roof supports were set on post pads, of which no trace survived. Such pads, set on the floor of the structure to receive the post, could have been formed of limestone or wooden planking. However, neither of these options has been shown by evidence from the site to have been used and thus the problem of how such a building was spanned remains.

There remains the possibility of course that the building was never finished and remained roofless or that it was designed as a part-open walled space. The site was clearly very close to areas, like Area B, which were susceptible to flooding, and the builders may have miscalculated with regard to the firmness of the foundations and the area in general. This may have been especially true of the area around the sump, which clearly they did later pack with limestone in an attempt to make the area stable and usable. Whichever argument is favoured, the problem of the roofing of Building C2 remains and it may just be, once again, that significant evidence for the sites' full interpretation had been removed before any archaeological work could start. More will be said of this building and its interpretation below (Chapter 11).

To the south of Building C2 there appeared to be a spread of limestone rubble which was seen in Trench VIII (see Fig. 52). What this was intended for was unclear — it may have been an attempt to provide a hard surfacing to the area outside the building at this point or been part of another damaged structure. Limited time during the archaeological work restricted any further work in this area.

Building D1
(Figs 57–58; Pls 49–50)
To the east of the short axis wall of Building C2 lay another badly damaged structure, Building D1 (Fig. 52). This consisted of a south wall (Fig. 57 Wall D1) which was set on a foundation of limestone rubble with fragments of a first course layer of limestone surviving, and a very poorly preserved section of walling to the north constructed of limestone rubble but with no apparent foundation trench. The two walls were very different in character and were set on slightly different alignments, and it is unclear what the original layout of this structure was meant to be or if the walls were part of the same structure. Between the two walls was a structure that was interpreted as a corn drier (Fig. 57; Pls 49 and 50). It was constructed out of limestone rubble and consisted of a central flue floored with rough limestone flagging, on either side of which at the southern end were four courses of limestone rubble forming walls to line the flue. The flue was 0.9m long and 0.5m wide. At the southern end of the feature limestone was set in a rectangular 'platform', best seen in Pl. 50, while at the northern end a spread of limestone rubble extended from the flue toward the north wall of the building. This spread of material is best seen in Pl. 49. It may be that originally the northern wall was an integral part of the overall spread of limestone in this area and related more to the corn drier than it did to Building D1.

The flue of the feature contained heavily burned and reddened limestone flagging and evidence for burning extended up and along the limestone walls on either side of the flue and to a lesser extent along the flue end to the south. On its discovery the flue of the feature was found to be filled with black ashy material (see Fig. 58 S97) that had presumably derived from the last firing(s) of the feature. On top of this were burnt limestone rubble blocks which had possibly come from the partial demolition of the upper linings of the flue.

This feature has been interpreted as a corn drier although, as Mackreth (1996b, 77) points out, the word 'corn' is best dropped as such features were probably used for drying several kinds of agricultural products, not only corn, and also used for preparing malt for brewing and part-roasting for milling. Morris's survey (1979, 88–103) of driers of this kind produced ten basic types, most of which seemed to have had rectangular drying floors even though their flues were configured in a variety of ways; at Orton Hall Farm, for example, there were both T- and H-shaped flue settings (Mackreth 1996b, 75–80). Morris's 'driers' also varied in size tremendously, ranging from 20sqm down to very small heated areas. He also points out, however, that only 'gentle' heating was required for the operation of these driers. This gentle heat may be somewhat at odds with the heavy burning observed along the lining to the flue found within Building D1. However, continued use or even a change of use for the feature may have resulted in the blue/red colouration of the limestone. It is also difficult to understand how the feature functioned as a drier as none of the 'flooring' area suspected or surviving at other examples has been preserved in the Building D1 example. It may be that the flue led under a raised floor at the southern end of the feature and that this was the function of the 'platform'-like arrangement —to form the base for some type of raised or suspended floor.

Plate 49 Area D, the corn drier looking south

Plate 50 Area D, detail of southern end of the corn drier

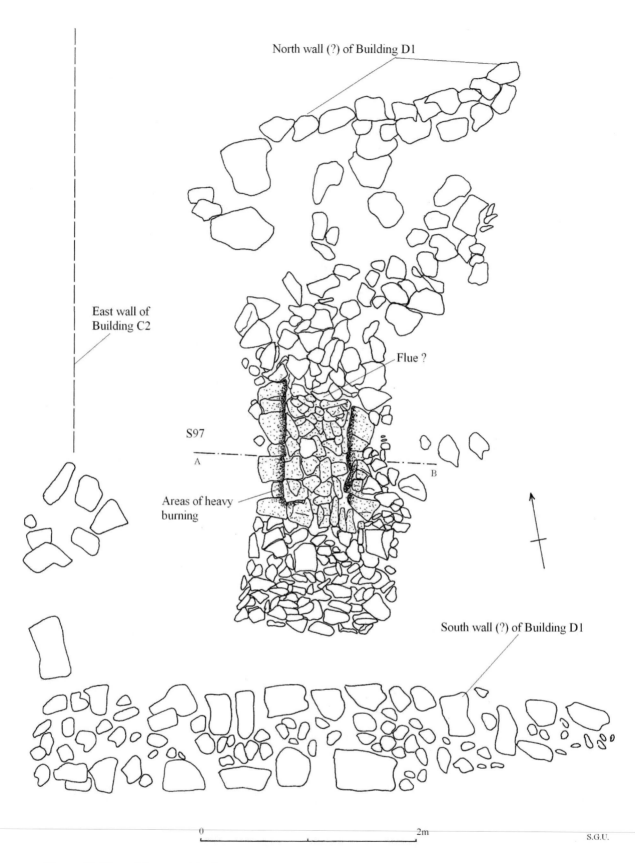

North wall (?) of Building D1

East wall of
Building C2

Flue ?

S97

A

B

Areas of heavy
burning

South wall (?) of Building D1

0   2m

S.G.U.

Figure 57 Plan of the corn drier in Area D (see Fig. 52 for the location of this feature within Building D1)

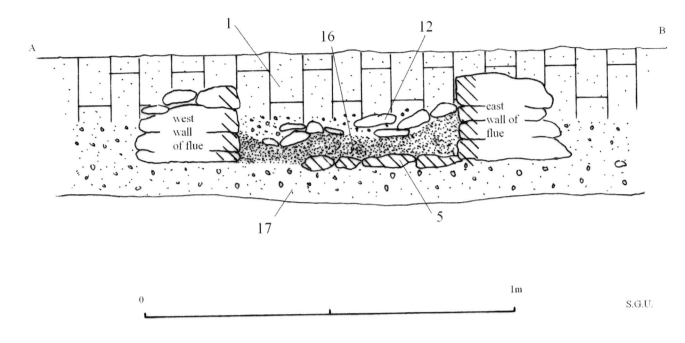

S97. Section through Corn Drier
Looking north

Figure 58 Section S97 through the corn drier (see Fig. 57 for the location of this section)

Ditches and pits

Four pits were dug at this period. One large pit (Pit C3) was located against the northernmost part of the excavated area within Area C and was filled largely with a light brown/grey clay which became progressively more silty toward its base (see Figs 52 and 56 S94). This feature was 0.9m deep with an undulating base, and its full extent was not recovered as part of it lay outside of the excavation trench.

The remaining three pits were all, by comparison, small and cut into earlier features. Pit C4 (see Fig. 52) was 1.0m deep and cut Ditch C8 from Period 7. It was steep-sided and filled with clays and loam. Pit C5 cut Ditch C5, also from Period 7, and after this pit was filled in part of the wall line from Building C2 was laid over it. This sequence can be seen in Fig. 56 S95. The remaining pit, Pit C6, was cut into deposits (Fig. 53 S73 context 1) which had accumulated over the top of the limestone surfacing within Building C2 and thus was probably the latest feature within this area of the excavation. It formed a near-oval cut into the softer material of the underlying fills and through the limestone layer which had formerly acted as perhaps surfacing or flooring for Building C2. This pit was filled with a single fill of grey clay and silt which was, in turn, capped with limestone (see Fig. 53 S73 context 46).

Of the two ditches relating to this period, Ditch C9 was 1.6m wide and 0.5m deep and filled with silts capped by a clay deposit and it was traced for 19m along the northern side of Area C. In contrast, Ditch C10 was a narrow and

shallow gully filled with clays and loam which was traced for only a short length (7.5m) before it entered the trench side.

One can only assume that both of these ditches were dug to help drain the site. The larger of the two ditches, Ditch C9, appears to run parallel with the northern long axis of Building C2 and thus would have drained the site on this side and stopped surface water from running too close to the base of the wall of the building. The space between the base of the wall and the edge of the ditch was 2.3m wide, which would have allowed for access along a pathway by the side of the wall, but this path would have presumably been along the line of any eaves drip gully. It is possible that Ditch C9 may have been intended to act both as an eaves drip gully and also double up as a substantial drainage ditch, but if this were the case then it would imply a very large roof overhang along this wall line. Precisely which, if any, of these options was adopted during Period 8 is unclear.

In contrast, Ditch C10 was a small gully-like feature that ran away from the junction of Buildings C2 and D1. It was presumably intended to drain water away from these buildings to the south-east.

All of the pits and ditches from this period of the site's history seem to have fills different from those of the pits and ditches of earlier periods. The fills from Period 8 contained more clay and loam than the siltier fills of preceding periods, and this may indicate a slightly drier phase at the site. Only Ditch C9 had lower fills of silt overlain by clay.

Chapter 6. The small finds

In the catalogues that follow, the entry for each find contains a site context code and a small finds (SF) number, both of which relate to the details given within the text and to the site archive.

I. Prehistoric flint objects

Twenty-five prehistoric flints were recovered from the excavated areas, of which eighteen were flakes, some with evidence of retouching or working. Two objects (nos 1 and 2 below) are illustrated in Figure 59. The total sample from which to make a detailed analysis of prehistoric occupation within the area is comparatively small, but the finding of a Neolithic axe head (no. 7) and both a transverse (no. 1) and a leaf-shaped arrowhead (no. 6) clearly indicate Neolithic occupation close to the excavated areas. There is also a general scatter of later material which shows that occupation certainly continued into the Bronze Age. This phase of the site's history may be connected with the ring-ditches of probable Bronze Age date shown in Figure 3.

This material is paralleled by the recovery of a second Neolithic polished axe head and an axe polishing stone from the area to the west of the excavations undertaken at

Lynch Farm 2 (see Challands 1973). No early prehistoric features were excavated during 1972–74 — the pit alignment excavated in 1974 was Iron Age in date.

Figure 59 nos 1–2
1. Transverse arrowhead, bifacial. LF2 72, B, 27. SF 146
2. Projectile point/scraper, worked on one side only. LF2 72, IV, +. SF 183

Unillustrated
3. Scraper, worked on one side only. LF2–74, T8, 288. SF 360
4. Blade, bifacially retouched, tip broken. LF2 72, B, 27. SF 165
5. Thumbnail scraper. LF2 72, central area, +. SF 43
6. Leaf-shaped arrowhead. LF2 72, Central area, +. SF 77
7. Polished Neolithic axe head. LF2 72, Central area, +. SF 45
8–25. Flint flakes

II. The Roman coins by Philippa Walton

Introduction
(Table 3)
The excavations at Lynch Farm 2, Orton Longueville, produced a small assemblage of forty-three coins. The preservation of the coins was poor, but it was still possible to date the coins with relative accuracy and thirty-three

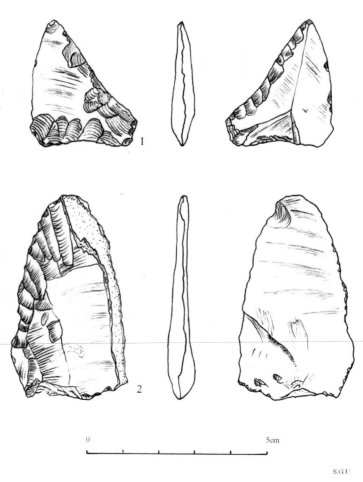

Figure 59 Flint implements from the Lynch Farm 2 site, nos 1–2

SF No.	Area and layer	Denomination	Emperor	Date	Reverse	Mint	Reference
3	FI +	Nummus	Valens	AD 367–75	SECVRITAS REI PVBLICAE	Lyon	LRBC p. 52, no. 363
8	F1 +	Nummus	Arcadius or Honorius	AD 388–402	SALVS REI PVBLICAE		
9	F10 +	Nummus	House of Theodosius	AD 388–402	SALVS REI PVBLICAE		
10	F1 +	Nummus	House of Constantine	AD 335–341	GLORIA EXERCITVS		
35	Stonework NW of aisled barn	Nummus	House of Theodosius	AD 378–388	VICTORIA AVGGG		
66	F2 +	Nummus	Uncertain	AD 306–402	illegible		
108	I +	Nummus	Uncertain	AD 306–402			
110	I +	Nummus	Constans	AD 335–341	GLORIA EXERCITVS	Trier	
117	B10	Nummus	Uncertain	AD 306–402	illegible		
135	B27	Nummus	Uncertain	AD 306–402	illegible		
149	B27	Nummus	Uncertain	AD 306–402	illegible		
154	B27	Nummus	Theodora or Helena	AD 337–341	illegible		
156	B76	Nummus	House of Constantine	AD 330–335	GLORIA EXERCITVS		
157	I +	Nummus	Uncertain	AD 330–402	illegible		
159	B76	Nummus	House of Constantine	AD 330–335	GLORIA EXERCITVS		
164	B27	Nummus	AD 306–402	AD 306–402	illegible		
168	II +	Nummus	Constantius II	AD 355–361	SPES REI PVBLICE		
172	I I +	Nummus	House of Theodosius	AD 378–388	VICTORIA AVGGG		
177	IV +	Nummus	Constantius II (copy)	AD 355–361	FEL TEMP REPARATIO	Trier	
181	IV +	Nummus	Constantius II (copy)	AD 355–61	FEL TEMP REPARATIO		
184	IV +	Nummus	Uncertain	AD 330–402	illegible		
189	IV +	Nummus	House of Theodosius	AD 378–388	VICTORIA AVGGG		
192	IV +	Nummus	House of Theodosius	AD 388–402	SALVS REI PVBLICAE		Either a contemporary copy of AD 395–402 Rome or Aquileia
194	IV +	Nummus	House of Theodosius	AD 378–388	VICTORIA AVGGG		
196	C1	Nummus	Constantius II	AD 355–361	FEL TEMP REPARATIO		
206	IV +	Nummus	House of Valentinian	AD 364–378	SECVRITAS REI PVBLICAE		
207	I I +	Nummus	Valens	AD 364–378	SECVRITAS REI PVBLICAE	Style of Lyon	Cf. LRBC p. 50, no. 280 passim
211	C23	Nummus	House of Constantine	AD 364–378	SECVRITAS REI PVBLICAE	Trier	
217	C10	Nummus	House of Valentinian	AD 364–378	SECVRITAS REI PVBLICAE		
218	C23	Nummus	House of Valentinian	AD 364–378	SECVRITAS REI PVBLICAE	Lyon	cf. LRBC p. 52, no. 352
231	B +	Nummus	Valens	AD 367–78	SECVRITAS REI PVBLICAE	Rome	LRBC, p. 61, no. 724 passim
232	I 33	Nummus	Uncertain	AD 306–402	illegible		
240	I 33	Nummus	House of Theodosius		VICTORIA AVGGG		
253	IV 13	Nummus	Constantius II	AD 348–351	FEL TEMP REPARATIO		
300	+	Sestertius	Trajan	AD 98–117	illegible	Rome	
301	I +	Nummus	Constantius II (copy)	AD 355–361	FEL TEMP REPARATIO		
307	II 16	Sestertius	Antoninus Pius	AD 150–151	[TR POT XIIII COS IIII MON] AVG SC	Rome	RIC III, p. 135, no. 872
321	II 87	Nummus	House of Valentinian	AD 364–378	SECVRITAS REI PVBLICAE		
325	II 91	Nummus	Constans	AD 335–341	GLORIA EXERCITVS		
329	II +	Nummus	Constantine I	AD 323–324	SARMATIA DEVICTA		RIC VII, p. 202, no. 435
343	II 133	Nummus	Theodora	AD 337–341	PIETAS ROMANA		
u/s	u/s	Nummus	Constans	AD 347–348	VICTORIAE DD AVGG Q NN	Trier	RIC VII, p. 152, no. 193

Table 3 Summary catalogue of coins from Lynch Farm 2

could be assigned to Reece periods, while the remaining ten issues could be dated more broadly to the 4th century AD. Although the earliest coin recovered was a *sestertius* of Trajan (AD 98–117), the assemblage is dominated by late 4th-century *nummi*, particularly from the period AD 348–402. A summary catalogue of the coins is presented as Table 3.

An interpretation of the assemblage
(Fig. 60; Table 4)

The coins from Lynch Farm 2 represent the standard range of issues one would expect from a site occupied during the 4th century AD. However, of individual numismatic interest are SF 168 and SF 192. SF 168 is a SPES REI PVBLICE issue of Constantius II, and is of a type not commonly found in Britain. Although the mintmark is not legible, it is quite possibly the product of an eastern mint. SF 192 is either a copy of a SALVS REI PVBLICAE issue of the House of Theodosius or an official issue dating to the period AD 395–402. Either way, the coin is an unusual find on a Romano-British site.

Analysis of the coins using Applied Numismatic methods is far more informative. The framework of chronological periods developed by Richard Reece has been adopted to enable comparison of the assemblage from Lynch Farm with the background of coin supply to Britain represented by Reece's 'British Mean' (Reece 1995). All datable coins have therefore been assigned to Reece periods and the total number of coins for each Reece period converted to a 'coins per thousand' (per mill) value. This data is summarised in Table 4 and displayed graphically in Figure 60.

As the assemblage is very small there is a danger of over-interpreting the resulting per mill profile. However, Figure 60 clearly illustrates a chronology for coin use at the site. Coin issues range in date from the 2nd century through to the early 5th century AD, the two earliest issues recovered from the excavations being a *sestertius* of Trajan (SF 300) and a *sestertius* of Antoninus Pius (SF 307). Due to the longevity of circulation of coinage, their presence at Lynch Farm need not necessarily indicate 2nd-century activity. Indeed, evidence from hoards found throughout Britain indicates that 1st- and 2nd-century *sestertii* frequently remained in circulation until at least

Reece period	Total coins	Lynch Farm	Reece's British Mean
1 (pre AD 41)	0	0	6.47
2 (AD 41–54)	0	0	11.73
3 (AD 54–68)	0	0	5.9
4 (AD 69–76)	0	0	30.85
5 (96–117)	1	31.25	19.9
6 (AD 117–138)	0	0	15.79
7 (AD 138–161)	1	31.25	18.67
8 (AD 161–180)	0	0	11.52
9 (AD 180–193)	0	0	4.66
10 (AD 193–222)	0	0	15.18
11 (AD 222–238)	0	0	7.29
12 (AD 238–260)	0	0	8.08
13 (AD 260–275)	0	0	144.3
14 (AD 275–296)	0	0	121.24
15 (AD 296–317)	1	31.25	17.49
16 (AD 317–330)	1	31.25	44.13
17 (AD 330–348)	7	187.5	245.54
18 (AD 348–364)	5	156.25	98.22
19 (AD 364–378)	8	250	118
20 (AD 378–388)	3	69.76744186	4.8
21 (AD 388–402)	6	281.25	50.25

Table 4 Coins from Lynch Farm 2 by Reece period

the second decade of the 3rd century AD (Robertson 2000, 107, 109 and 113).

With the exception of these two coins, all other issues date to the 4th or early 5th century AD (see Table 3 was 4). This in itself is unusual. Although prolific 4th-century Roman coin loss is a common feature of Romano-British site assemblages, particularly those with a rural emphasis (Reece 1972), such sites usually exhibit at least some coin loss in the late 3rd century AD. The lack of *radiates*, barbarous or otherwise, from Lynch Farm is therefore somewhat surprising. It indicates either a lack of activity at the site in the period AD 260–296 or, more plausibly, a lack of coin use. This may have implications for our understanding of the site's function.

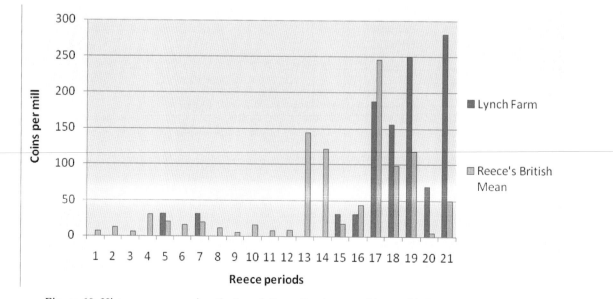

Figure 60 Histogram comparing the Lynch Farm 2 coin assemblage with Reece's British Mean

Coin loss continues until the end of the Roman period at Lynch Farm, with above average per mill values throughout the late 4th century AD. Of particular note is the value for Period 21 (AD 388–402), which at 281.25 per mill is nearly six times that of Reece's British Mean. While other sites in Cambridgeshire do have assemblages with some Theodosian coinage (e.g. Wimpole (Horton *et al.* 1994); Great Staughton (Carson 1994); Water Newton (Reece 1991)) such high values are hard to parallel in the region. Elsewhere in Britain assemblages with above average Period 21 coin loss are associated with sites on the major road networks and at nodal points in the landscape, such as crossroads (Walton 2012, 109). It is possible that

the continued use of coinage at such sites indicates an association with the late Roman administration and, particularly, with the collection of taxation (Walton 2012).

III. Objects of copper alloy

Brooches
Nineteen brooches or parts of brooches were recovered from the excavations, four from unstratified contexts. Five of the brooches were very fragmentary and have not been illustrated.

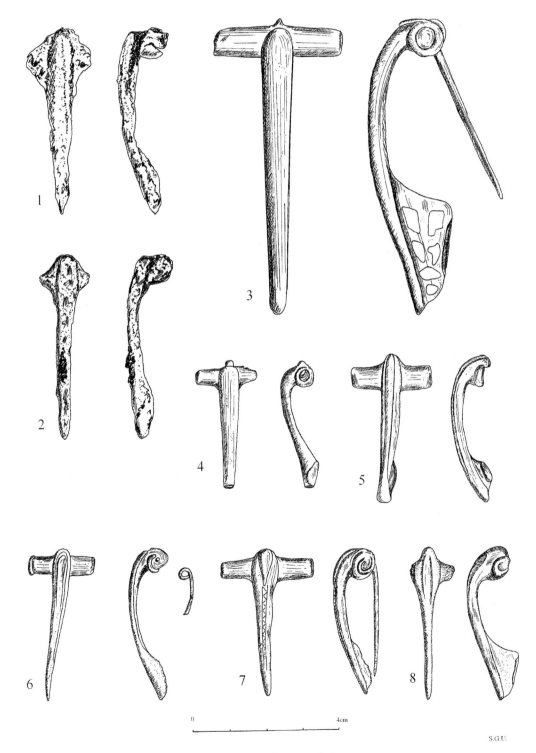

0   4cm

S.G.U.

Figure 61 Brooches, nos 1–8

Figure 61 nos 1–8

1. Iron brooch 50mm long and very corroded but probably falls into the 'Colchester Derivative' class and thus is within the range described by Mackreth (2011, I, 87–8) and can probably be dated to the second half of the 1st century AD (Hattatt 1982, 44) although Mackreth (1981, 135) suggests that such brooches are common only in the first twenty years of the Roman occupation and 'are to be expected in pre-conquest times' (see also Goodburn 1974, fig. 23 no. 3 for an iron brooch from Longthorpe). Period 3 (LF2 73. II, 122. SF 339)

2. Iron brooch 49mm long and similar to no. 1 above with the same date range. Period 3 (LF2 73. II, 122. SF 341)

3. Colchester Derivative. Large brooch, 79mm long with the pin intact. The catchplate is pierced in six places and the bow of the brooch is plain. Mid 1st century–first quarter of the 2nd century AD (Hattatt 1982, 64–70; Mackreth 2011, I, 72–3). Period 4/5 (LF2 72. II, 1. SF 250)

4. Colchester Derivative. Brooch 34mm long with the pin missing; small catchplate. Dating as for no. 3 above (Hattatt 1982, 64–70;

Mackreth 2011, I, 72: and II, no. 1882). Period 3 (LF2 73. B 2. SF 103)

5. Colchester Derivative. Brooch 40mm long, pin missing, narrow catchplate; has a rib running along the entire length of the bow. Dating as for no. 3 above (Hattatt 1982, 64–70; Mackreth 2011, I, 72). Period 6 (LF2 73. C, 10. SF 222)

6. Colchester Derivative. Brooch 40mm long, ribbed along bow and with a narrow catchplate, although this area of the brooch is heavily corroded. Part of the pin was recovered with this brooch, although detached. Similar in form to no. 5 above. Dating as for no. 3 above (Hattatt 1982, 64–70; Mackreth 2011, I, 72). Period 5/6 (LF2 73. II 126. SF 352)

7. Colchester Derivative. Brooch 38mm long with the bow decorated with chevron design. The pin remains intact but the catchplate is very corroded. Dating as for no. 3 above (Hattatt 1982, 64–70; Mackreth 2011, I, 72–3). Period 5 (LF2 73 II 96. SF 342)

8. Colchester Derivative. Brooch 41mm long; the head of the brooch has a slight ridge but the wings are very corroded. Dating as for no. 3 above (Hattatt 1982, 64–70; Mackreth 2011, I, 72–3). Period 5/6 (LF2 73. II 200. SF 348)

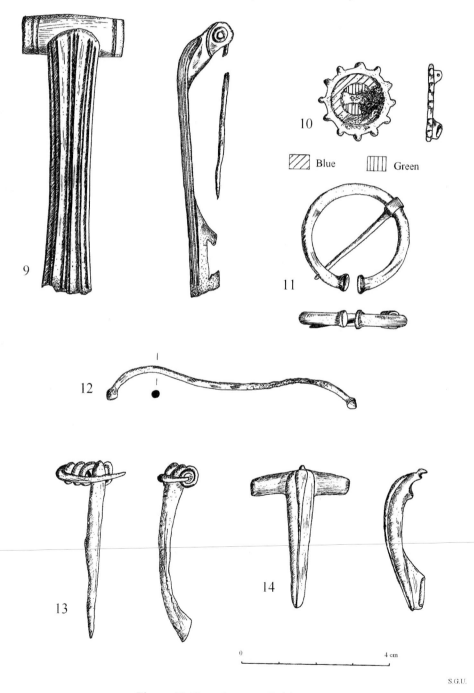

Blue

Green

Figure 62 Brooches, nos 9–14

Figure 62 nos 9–14

9. Langton Down. Brooch 74mm long with part of the pin still intact and part of the rest surviving with the brooch. The bow of the brooch is slightly waisted along the length of the bow and the junction of the bow with the head is rounded. The bow is ridged to form the decoration. Second/third quarter of the 1st century (Hattatt 1982, 80–82; Mackreth 2011, I, 33–4; Stead 1986, nos 87–95). Period 3 (LF2 74. T8 288. SF 359)

10. Disc brooch 20mm in diameter with twelve lugs set around the edge. The central part of the brooch is divided into zones with inset blue enamel on the outer concentric zone and green enamel on an inner zone. The central part of the brooch consists of a bar of metal with concave edges. The pin is missing but was fixed into a simple casting on the back of the disc and was clipped under a similar cast catchplate. Mid 1st to late 2nd century AD (See Hattatt 1982, fig. 58, no. 122; Mackreth 2011, I, 157–8; see especially II, pl. 106, nos 10784, 10771 and 10766). Period 6 (LF2 72. IV 1. SF 230)

11. Pennanular brooch 29mm in diameter with the circumference of the brooch being cast with a circular profile. The terminal ends are formed by knobs with a flattened inner surface. The pin survives and is formed by a flattened loop of metal set around the circumference of the brooch which changes to a circular profile to form the main part of the pin. Probably 2nd century (Mackreth 2011, I, 212. II, pl. 145; see especially no. 3441). Period 3 (LF2 74. T59 284. SF 367)

12. Pennanular brooch which has been partly straightened out to form a strand of metal 750mm long. The terminal ends to the brooch are formed by rounded knobs (see Hattatt 1982, fig. 55, A). The pin is missing (Mackreth 2011, I 212. II, pl. 145; see 3422). (LF2 72. F2 surface find. SF 15)

13. Colchester brooch which has been much damaged. The brooch is 48mm long and part of the spring and chord still survive. The catchplate is very abraded. Middle to third quarter of the 1st century (Hattatt 1982, 60–61; Mackreth 2011, I 36–49. II, pls 22–25). (LF2 73. Surface find. SF 103)

14. Colchester Derivative. Brooch 38mm long with a ridge running down the back of the bow. The catchplate is formed by a simple roll-over casting; pin is missing. A near identical brooch comes from the excavations at Stonea (see Mackreth 1996a, fig. 95, no. 26). Mid–late 1st century (Hattatt 1982, 64–70; Mackreth 2011, I, 72–3. II, pl. 46). (LF2 73. Surface find. SF 6)

Any analysis or discussion of the brooches from Lynch Farm is limited by the small size of the total assemblage. However, a possibly significant aspect of the collection is the bias toward brooches from the 1st and the early part of the 2nd century. The iron brooches, the Colchester type brooches and the single example of a Langton Down type brooch (see Hattatt 1982, 80–82) may possibly have been associated with the site in either a phase of military occupation or the period when it was being reorganised in the post-military phase, Period 3 (see Fig. 12).

Bracelets

Figure 63 nos 1–10

1. A complete bracelet made from a single piece of copper alloy 1mm thick. The overall internal size is 62×49mm, and the piece was presumably shaped to fit the wrist of the wearer. The outer edge is 'castellated', with the areas contained by the 'hollows' having four cut ridges. Such ridges were presumably hand cut, as the very last hollow, against one terminal, has only three cut ridges where the workman had to 'fit' the design to the available remaining space. The terminals each have holes which could have held a rivet to close the bracelet. An identical bracelet from Orton Hall Farm (Mackreth 1996b, 97, no. 52) could have come from the same workshop, while a similar design is reported from Gadebridge Park (Neal and Butcher 1974, fig. 60, no. 159). A late 4th-century bracelet from Leicester has a solid terminal, without the rivet holes (Kenyon 1948, fig. 83, no. 3), while an example from Great Chesterford (Liversidge 1968, fig. 54, no. c) has rivet holes and is identical to the Lynch Farm example. That from Lankhills has a rivet securing the terminals (Clarke 1979, 305, figs 37 and 99). The style seems to belong to the 4th century (Clarke 1979, 305), although a late 3rd-century bracelet of similar design is shown by Brodribb *et al.* (1971, 114, fig. 49 104). Swift terms these bracelets 'cogwheel type', and gives their distribution as almost exclusively confined to

Britain (Swift 2000, figs 24 and 25). Period 7 (LF2 72, IV, 4. SF 174)

2. A half of a bracelet which has a surviving diameter of 48mm. The design consists of ribbed areas divided by regularly spaced raised areas which have a lozenge shape. The overall effect may have been intended to imitate stone beads threaded onto a metal chain. The remaining terminal has a 'hook and eye' arrangement. Unstratified, but this style appears to date to after *c.* AD 350 (see Goodburn 1984, 33, fig. 10, 65–7). (LF2 72, F2, +. SF 39)

3. Bracelet fragment with a surviving length of 52mm. The design consists of sets of ribbed bands interspersed with flattened areas. The style is similar to that on a bracelet from Lydney Park, Gloucestershire, shown by Swift (2000, fig. 6). Period 7 (LF2 72, B, 27. SF 150)

4. A half of a bracelet which has a surviving diameter of 39mm. The design has irregularly spaced groupings of ribbed areas interspersed with smoothed areas. The section of the bracelet is 'D'-shaped. The ribbed areas also vary in how many ribs each contains, implying that the object is hand-made, rather than cast from a mould. The surviving terminal has part of the remaining rivet hole surviving. The style is close to that on a bracelet from Lankhills (Clarke 1979, 306, no. 163, fig. 37), where it is dated to the mid–late 4th century. Period 7 (LF2 72, B, 27. SF 147)

5. Part of a broad, flat, slightly 'D'-shaped sectioned bracelet some 62mm long. The decoration consists of a circle set within a lozenge-shaped area near the terminal, then follows a short ribbed section followed by a central linear feature flanked by 'V'-shaped chip carving, more ribbing and, last, a circle. The terminal consists of a hole to receive a rivet set within a facetted surround. Similar designs are found on bracelets from Verulamium (Waugh and Goodburn 1972, fig. 32, nos 32–4), Gadebridge Park (Neal and Butcher 1974, fig. 60, 154–5) and Orton Hall Farm (Mackreth 1996b, fig. 62, no. 54), and are shown by Swift to have a distribution in the south-east of England and between the Loire and the Rhine (Swift 2000, figs 26–27). In terms of date they are best seen as belonging to the late 4th century (see Clarke 1979, 307–9, fig. 37, nos 502, 525, 605). Period 8, see Fig. 55 was 56 S95 (LF2 72, C, 22. SF 212)

6. Part of a bracelet 85mm long formed from two twisted, slightly elliptical strands of copper alloy. One terminal survives, in the form of a simple hook. Twisted wire bracelets seem fairly common on Roman sites and examples come from Gadebridge Park (Neal and Butcher 1974, fig. 61, nos 164–170). Period 8, see Fig. 53 S71, S72 and S73 (LF2 72, C, 1. SF 155)

7. Part of a bracelet 38mm long formed from three strands of twisted copper alloy. This form of bracelet made from three twisted strands of wire is very common on rural Roman sites, especially in later Roman contexts, with an identical bracelet recovered from Stanground (Dannell *et al.* 1993, fig. 13, no. 2). Period 8, see Fig. 48 S114 (LF2 72, B, 10. SF 118)

8. Part of a bracelet 39mm long formed from three twisted strands of copper alloy. One end appears to be 'frayed' but this may be the terminal end, which originally had a simple hook arrangement. See also no. 7 above. Period 6 (LF2 72, B, 85. SF 161) Unillustrated

9. Part of a copper-alloy bracelet 55mm long which has been cut and rolled into a ring with a diameter of approximately 12mm. The original bracelet decoration is very worn and abraded but is similar in design and conception to no. 5 above, with chip cut and stamped marking. Period 6 (LF2 72, C, 23. SF 215)

10. A very abraded and damaged copper-alloy bracelet in two parts with a total length of approximately 160mm. Any decoration that was originally on the outer surface of the object has been corroded away, one end suggests that the bracelet originally had a simple hook and eye terminal. Period 6, see Fig. 47 S100 (LF2 72, B, 11. SF 119)

Needles, pins, ligula and a ring

Figure 64 nos 1–8

1. A 106mm-long section of a copper-alloy needle with a slightly oval section. The top and the beginning of the eye is broken and the original length may have been of the order of 120mm. Needles of this form appear to have a very wide date range, from the 1st to the 4th centuries (see Jackson 1996a, fig. 108, nos 32–37; Neal and Butcher 1974, fig. 64, nos 229–232). (LF2 72, II, 1+. SF 225)

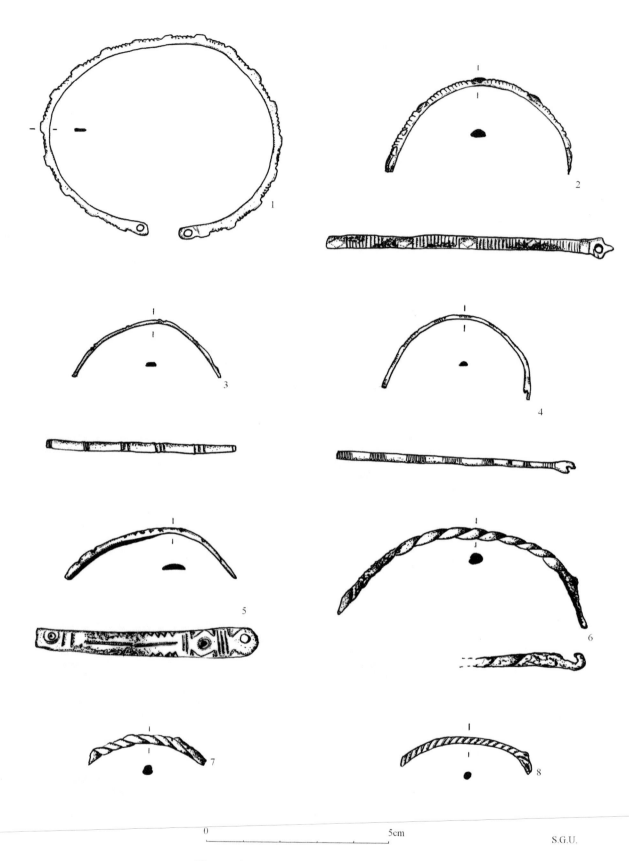

Figure 63 Copper alloy bracelets, nos 1–8

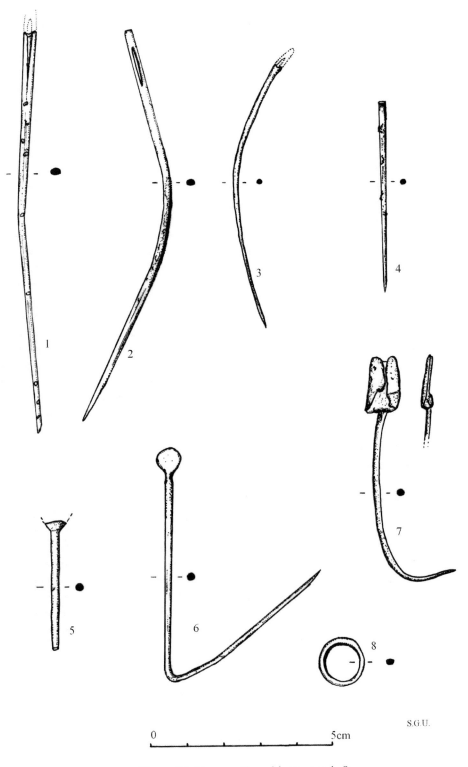

Figure 64 Copper alloy objects, nos 1–8

2. A complete needle 110mm long with an eye 10mm long. Period 7/8, see Fig. 13 S128 (LF2–73, II, 76. SF 319)

3. A needle, broken at the beginning of the eye, which may have had an original length of perhaps 100mm. Period 3, see Fig. 16 S63 (LF-73, II, 35. SF 306)

4. Pin or possible needle 60mm long. The blunt end is broken. Period 6 (LF2 72, C, 4. SF 197)

5. Fragment of a cosmetic scoop or ligula 35mm long. Period 8 (LF-72, F10. SF 11)

6. Complete cosmetic scoop or ligula 110mm long. One end is tapered to a point and the other end is flattened into a discoidal plate 6mm in diameter. The object is well preserved and the flat plate shows evidence of having been 'finished' with a file during manufacture.

Such scoops are common items on Roman sites and date from the 1st to the 4th centuries, although the later ones may be residual (Jackson 1996a, fig. 109, nos 46–52; Neal and Butcher 1974, fig. 63, nos 200–209). (LF2 72, IV, 1+. SF 227)

7. Near-complete but much damaged spoon with a tapering handle approximately 90mm long and with the bowl folded in on itself. The bowl part of the spoon could have originally been approximately 25mm in diameter. Spoons with tapering handles and either pear-shaped or round bowls tend to belong to the 1st or 2nd centuries (Jackson 1996a, fig. 113, 105; Waugh and Goodburn 1972, fig. 35, 74; Cunliffe 1971, fig. 47, nos 120–121). Period 7 (LF2 72, F2, 1. SF 5)

8. Ring with internal diameter of 13mm and rounded but rectangular section (see Neal and Butcher 1974, fig. 60, nos 121–128). Period 8, see Fig. 42 S69 (LF2 72, B, 101. SF 201)

Copper-alloy toilet instruments

Figure 65 nos 1–2

1. Copper-alloy toilet instrument/nail cleaner. This object has already been reported in full by Sonia Chadwick-Hawkes (1976), who dates the object to the late Roman period and describes the peacock decoration as having links with Christian symbolism (see also Thomas 1993, 92–3). (LF2 72, IV, +. SF 175)

2. Toilet instrument of similar function to no. 1 above, but without any elaborate decoration. The simple strip of metal is notched at one end and folded over at the other so it could be attached to a chain or belt, perhaps with other toilet instruments. A similar item comes from Haddon, although here the belt attachment is formed by a drilled hole into a slight swelling at the terminal (Fraser 1994, fig. 73, no. 9). (LF2 72, Unstrat. SF 76)

Chain and bead

Plate 51

1. A 53mm length of copper-alloy chain with a green/blue glass bead at one end. The chain is made up of double links 3mm in diameter but the bead is threaded into a single stand of copper wire and fixed to the chain by a simple loop in the style of the beads on a chain found at Gadebridge Park (Neal and Butcher 1974, fig. 58, no. 75). Period 6, see Fig. 48 S113 (LF2 72, B, 81. SF 179)

IV. Iron objects

Ninety-six iron objects were recovered from the excavations at Lynch Farm 2 during the 1972–4 excavations. The vast majority of these were from sealed deposits, with six finds coming from unstratified contexts. A large proportion of these finds were nails, almost all of rectangular or square section and ranging in size from 25mm up to 120mm (not illustrated). Among the most notable finds were a small group of tools (Figure 67 nos 10–12) comprising a mower's anvil, a smith's cross-pane hammer and an axe. These three objects have already been published by Manning (1973), who provided a full description. All three objects were found within the aisled building and just below the plough soil in a cleaning or 1+ context.

Figure 66 nos 1–8

1. Large iron hook 175mm long, with a loop at one end and a rectangular section below the loop. The hook end has a slight swelling at the terminal. May be a large bucket handle (cf. Jackson 1996b, fig. 119, no. 30); alternatively, it could be a cauldron hook. Period 3, see Fig. 10 S44 (LF2 72, IV, 13. SF 252)

2. Drill bit/probe? 150mm long with square section, slightly thicker at one end.. (LF2 72, I, +. SF 114)

3. Iron spike with both ends tapering from a central thicker rectangular section. Period 2 (LF2–73, II, 191. SF 347)

4. Tapering metal object 100mm long with rectangular section. May have been part of a file or tool? Period 4 (LF2–73, IV, 26. SF 310)

5. Flesh hook, 90mm long with square section and two hooks. This object has the characteristic double pronged arrangement with part of the handle surviving. They occur frequently with a looped handle plate (see Manning 1985, 35, pl. 51, no. 105). A similar flesh hook comes from Stonea and was dated to the mid-3rd century (Jackson 1996b, fig. 119, no. 27). Period 5 (LF2 72, F2, 1. SF 7)

6. Small knife blade 90mm long with remains of the tang at one end. The blade is slightly tapered. Blades of this form are fairly common and this example matches a complete example from Silchester (Boon 1974, fig. 34, 15) and a late 3rd-/4th-century example from Stonea (Jackson 1996b, fig. 119, no. 24). Period 6 (LF2–73, IV, 47. SF 355)

7. Possibly a small chisel blade with part of the tang remaining; 50mm long with a blade 10mm wide. The blade tapers to a sharp edge above which the section becomes rectangular (cf. Neal and Butcher 1974, fig. 77, nos 610 and 622). Period 5 (LF2 72, F2. SF 29)

8. Tool or implement (chisel?) with a blade 30mm wide at one end and a rounded socket at the other to take some form of handle. Period 8, See Fig. 39 (LF2–72, I, 33. SF 229)

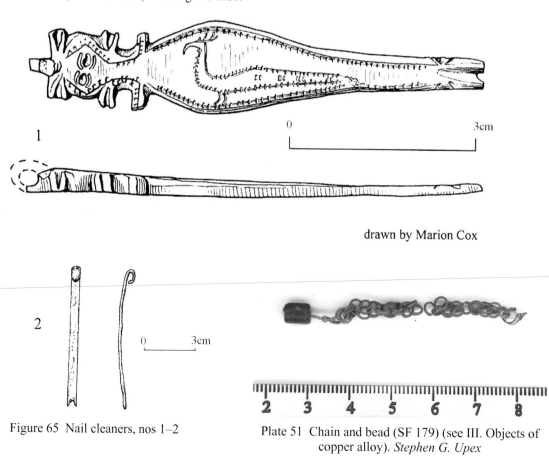

drawn by Marion Cox

Figure 65 Nail cleaners, nos 1–2

Plate 51 Chain and bead (SF 179) (see III. Objects of copper alloy). *Stephen G. Upex*

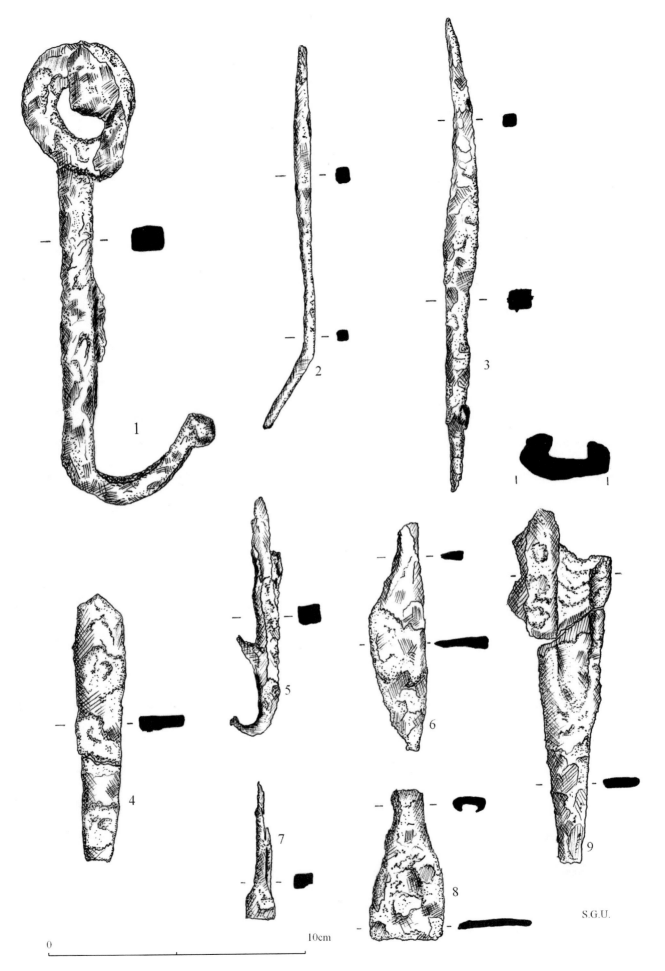

0   10cm

S.G.U.

Figure 66 Iron objects, nos 1–9

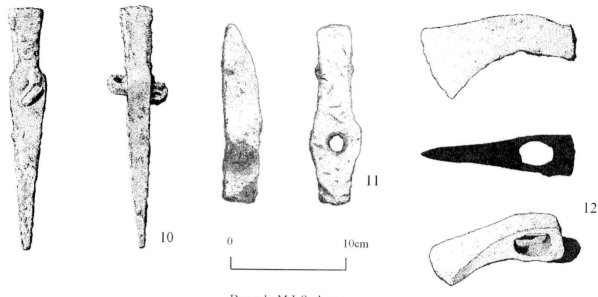

Drawn by M.J. Snelgrove

Figure 67 Iron objects, nos 10–12

9. Implement with a rounded socket at one end and a tapering rectangular sectioned blade at the other. It may be part of a knife, although the blade is perhaps rather narrow (cf. Jackson 1996b, fig. 118, no. 17). (LF2 72, C, +. SF 228)

Figure 67 nos 10–12
For the find spot of this group of objects see Fig. 26; for a full account and description of these objects see Manning 1973. Although all objects come from a 1+ context the fact that they were found together suggests that they were from a hoard and probably relate to Period 8.

10. Mower's anvil. (LF2 72, I+. SF 113)
11. Hammer. (LF2 72, I+. SF 112)
12. Axe. (LF2 72, I+. SF 111)

Figure 68 No. 13 and Plate 52
13. Axe head with a blade 110mm wide and an overall length of 185mm long. The handle was fitted into a socket with an irregular shape. This axe comes from a pit linked with the early military phase of the site. Period 2, see Fig. 11 S45 (LF2 72, IV, 19. SF 384).

Plate 52 Axe head (SF 384) (see IV. Iron objects and Figure 68 no. 13). *Stephen G. Upex*

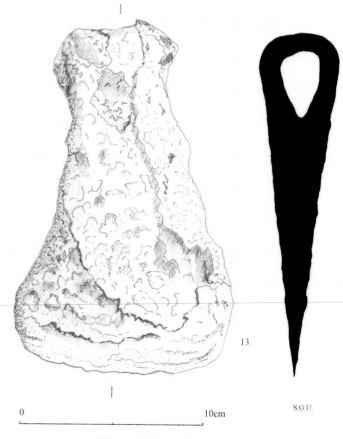

Figure 68 Iron object, no. 13

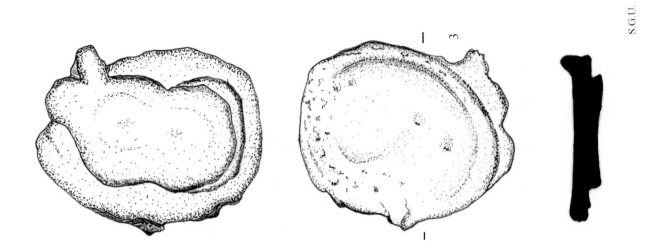

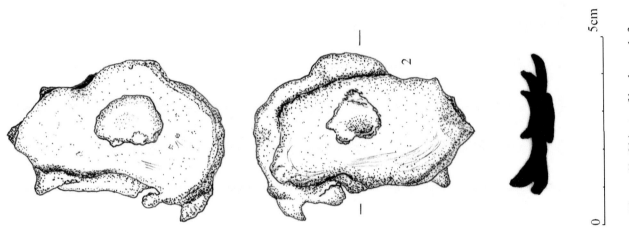

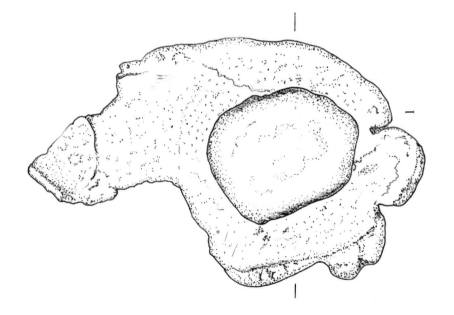

S.G.U.

5cm

0

Figure 69 Objects of lead, nos 1–3

105

V. Objects of lead

Figure 69 nos 1–3

1. A large piece of lead formed from a once molten pool, the underside of which is rough and uneven where the molten lead has been poured onto a rough and uneven surface. The upper surface of the piece is smooth and gives the impression of being air cooled. Onto this lower pool of lead a second pool of lead has been poured, presumably when the first pool had cooled. This additional lead is also smooth and must have cooled in contact with the air. Weight 220g. Period 8, see Fig. 42 S69 (LF2 72, B, 101. SF 198)

2. Lead base with a repair patch? An irregular piece of lead with rounded edges, concave in section on one face and flat on the other face. Roughly central to this piece there appears to be a patch or repair rivet which has filled an aperture in the main part of the object. One side of this rivet or repair is smoothed and rounded and the other side is roughly finished. It is difficult to be certain what this lead fragment was used for; it may have formed a weight within some piece of sculpture or even a pottery or bronze vessel where it acted to balance the encasing object. The later repair patch or rivet clearly fills a hole in the earlier lead feature. Weight 95g. (LF2 72, I, 1+. SF 152)

3. Lead repair patch? An oval repair patch which could have been run into an oval hole, perhaps in the base of a pottery vessel. Similar repair patches are published at Stonea (Jackson 1996a, fig. 123, nos 67–69). Weight 165g. (LF2 72, IV, +. SF 176)

Unillustrated

4. Lead fragment part cut away by machining during excavation. Upper surface smooth and air cooled while the lower surface is rough, uneven and concave. Has part of a circular hole remaining on one side of the fragment. Weight 105g. (LF2–73, +. SF 346)

VI. Glass

Thirty-seven fragments of glass came from the excavations, of which ten appeared to be plain green window glass fragments. The remaining fragments were all from vessels. One 'collection' of glass (LF2 72, F17) formed approximately half a glass vessel (unillustrated); the remaining fragments were small rim fragments and body sherds. No further reporting of this glass assemblage from the site has been possible.

VII. Bone and antler objects

Figure 70 nos 1–4; Pl. 53

1. Bone pin 70mm long. The head is 4mm in diameter and domed. Pins with similar heads come from Orton Hall Farm (Mackreth 1996b, fig. 63 nos 66–68) and Stonea (Greep 1996, fig. 194, 526–7). Greep (1995, 1113–21) suggests that those pins with swelling stems, which this pin exhibits, are generally later within the Roman period. The pin falls within Crummy's Type 2, with 1–3 transverse grooves beneath a conical head (Crummy 1979, 157 and fig. 1) and although this type has a broad date range (1st–4th centuries) they are most common in the 3rd and 4th centuries. Period 6 (LF2 72, II, 89. SF 328)

2. Part of a bone bracelet 90mm long and approximately 5mm wide, with a flat inner side and a rounded outer surface. One end has two grooves cut across the outer face and another groove was cut at the other end, along which the break occurred. Seven fragments of bone bracelets were found at Orton Hall Farm, of which six were ascribed to the period after AD 300 (Mackreth 1996b, 96). Similarly, of the forty-two bone bracelets from Lankhills, thirty-eight were dated to the period between AD 310 and 370 (Clarke 1979, 313–14). (LF2–73, II, +. SF 312)

3. Part of a toothed segment from a bone comb. The seven teeth on one side are larger than the eleven teeth on the other side and the fragment has a central half circle which formed the rivet hole by which the comb was clamped together by a central rib. Double-sided Roman combs are not common finds on Nene valley Roman sites and the best parallels come from cemetery sites (Crummy 1983, 56–7; Clarke 1979, fig. 31). Part of a comb, dated to the mid–late 3rd–early 4th century, does come from Orton Hall

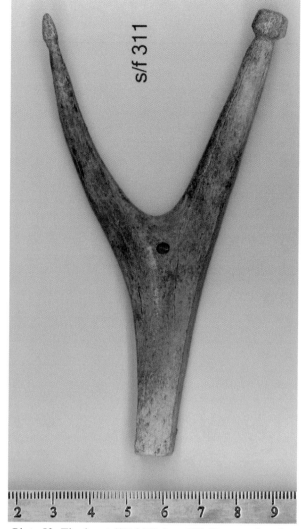

Plate 53 The lucet (SF 311) (see VII. Bone and antler objects and Fig. 70, no. 4). *Stephen G. Upex*

Farm (Mackreth 1996b, fig. 64, 94). The LF2 find comes from an unstratified level and it would be equally possible to see the object as Saxon or later, where there are countless examples known from local sites. (LF2 72, I+. SF 136)

4. A 'lucet' cut from the end of an antler, with a drilled hole just below the junction of the two forks; the lower part has a square cut end. The two 'tines' or forks of the antler are of different sizes and diameters and each has a differently shaped finial. The larger tine has a flatter, rectangular finial while the smaller tine has a more elongated and rounded finial. Lucets were used to produce cord by means of a basic 'French knitting' technique and produced a square, tightly knotted cord that was extremely strong and did not stretch — points of considerable importance when tying and lacing were concerned. A thread was configured around the two tines and then 'knitted' (either by using the fingers or by means of a pin or needle) over each tine in turn, producing a woven cord which was then threaded through the hole between the junction of the tines so that the weaver's thumb could apply some tension to the length of cord (Groves 1973, 93 and fig. 10).

    Made of antler, this object is broadly similar to the Anglo-Scandinavian example from York (MacGregor *et al.* 1999, 1994–5). The interpretation of such objects as lucets is still contested (Walton Rogers 1997, 1790). This example is more convincing as a possible lucet than the York example in that both arms are of comparable length. The difference in the thickness of the arms is a result of the smaller arm being shaped from a tine and the larger arm from the beam of the antler. The hole in the main shaft of the object is characteristic of larger, wooden, handled type

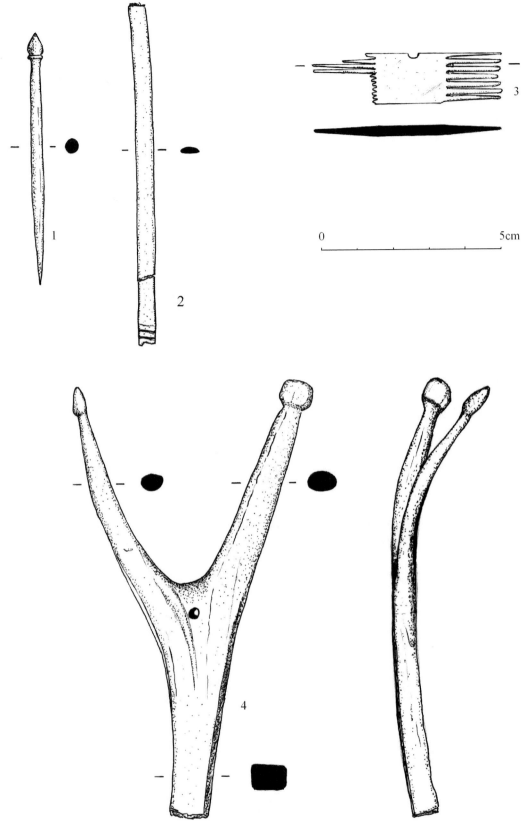

Figure 70 Objects of bone and antler, nos 1–4

S.G.U.

lucets of similar overall size to this example. The knobs on the ends of the two prongs could appear to be a disadvantage in terms of the ease of slipping the stitch off the end. However, similar, though detachable, ends can be fitted to modern lucets to stop the work in progress from slipping off the prongs when not in use. Whatever the function of such objects, there does appear to be an association with textile crafts. The object comes from a sealed Period 2 deposit and thus is likely to have been linked with the military phase of the site's development.

Identification as a lucet makes this example possibly the earliest known example from Britain and continental Europe, and indicates that cord was being produced in the Roman world, a fact that does not appear within the literature so far (J.P. Wild pers. comm.). One might presume that cord would have been used for all manner of tying and securing functions on clothing, bags and other woven or leather accessories. Whether the Roman army used cord for such functions and even for securing items of harness or even tent fastenings is at present unknown, and more research is clearly required into such topic areas before more definitive comments can be made. Lucets were still being used to produce cord in Georgian and Victorian England and well into the 20th century (Groves 1973, 94 and pl. 153). Fingers were often employed to slip the thread over the lucet tines to produce cord, but long pins or needles could also have been used for the same purpose and are certainly supplied with modern examples which can be bought in craft shops. This poses the question as to whether wooden, bone or antler pins/awls (or similar classes of object) which occur on early sites, especially Roman sites, were used in conjunction with lucets. For example, the series of crude pins from Stonea (Greep 1996, fig. 194, 3–13) described as hairpins or the similar pins and an awl from Gadebridge Park (Neal and Butcher 1974, fig. 67, 302–5 and 333) could all have served to 'knit' thread on a lucet. Period 2, see Fig. 11 S124; Pl. 53 (LF2–73, II, 50. SF 311)

Unillustrated

5. Fragment of the pointed end of a bone pin 55mm long. (LF2–73, II, +. No SF number)

VIII. Objects of shale, jet and a glass bead

Figure 71 nos 1–3

1. Shale spindle whorl 40mm in diameter. Shale objects are fairly common on Romano-British settlement sites (see, for example, Lawson 1976, 247–52), although few have been published from the Nene valley. A shale bracelet comes from Haddon (Fraser 1994, fig. 73, no. 1) and two shale bracelets were found at Orton Hall Farm (Mackreth 1996b, fig. 62, nos 55–56). Shale was traded from Kimmeridge in Dorset and its distribution extends far to the north. However, specific trade routes may have limited its spread in eastern England (Davis 1936, 200–213; Allen *et al.* 2007, 167–91). A similar piece comes from Verulamium (Waugh and Goodburn 1972, fig. 57, 227) (LF2 72, B, +. SF 101)

2. Jet bead with two flat sides through which holes for threading have been drilled, the remaining sides are slightly curved. Part broken on one side; 15×13mm. The bead appears to have been initially turned as one face has a slight central 'lathe' indentation (Johns 1996, 101–3). Beads of this form are probably made in Yorkshire from the jet deposits at Whitby. Blocks of jet were found at York and workshops must have existed there (RCHM 1962, 141–4, Allason-Jones 1996; 2002). Jet is an uncommon find on Nene valley settlement sites. For an identical bead see Fairless 2009, fig. D11 99, no. 16. Period 4, see Fig. 16 S66 (LF2 72, F2, 1. SF 6)

3. Green glass bead, 6mm diameter. Period 8, see Fig. 53 S71, S72, S73 (LF2 72, C, 2. SF 187)

Unillustrated

4. Green glass bead, 5mm diameter. (LF2 72, F2, +. SF 65)

IX. Quern stones, hone stones and other stone objects

Quern stones

A total of nine quern stone fragments were recovered from the excavations, of which six are illustrated within this report. With the exception of stones nos 1, 5 and 6, all of the stones are of fine to medium coarse-grained millstone grit and probably come from the area of the north Derbyshire area of the Pennines. This is the dominant geological type for Roman querns from the lower Nene valley and the east midlands generally (see, for example, Shaffery 2009a, 254–5) The exception to this geological source is no. 1 (below), which is of a fine-grained sandstone. The source for this is uncertain and in fact the stone could be a reworked glacial erratic boulder. This stone, typologically, would seem to be much earlier than the remaining assemblage and probably dates to the early prehistoric period. The remaining stones are Iron Age or Roman. Two stones (nos 5 and 6) come from the military ditches of the Roman fort and belong to this phase of occupation.

Figure 72 nos 1–4

1. Part of a saddle quern with an upper surface *c.*210×220mm and 120mm thick. The stone has a smoothed, shallow, trough-like

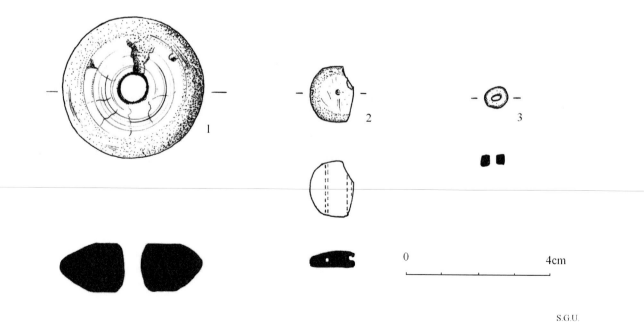

S.G.U.

Figure 71 Objects of shale, jet and glass, nos 1–3

depression which has parallel striations indicative of the wear pattern caused by a smaller 'rider' stone. The underside is rough and unworked. The stone is of fine sandstone grit with some larger granules up to 1mm in diameter, and shows signs of reddening suggestive of it having been burned at some point. Saddle querns are uncommon on local prehistoric and Roman sites and the quern from Lynch Farm 2 must represent either a residual stone or the reuse of an earlier stone during the later prehistoric or even Roman period. There are no indications that the stone was used as a sharpening stone. Weight 5.85kg. Period 6 (LF2 72. I 32. SF 210)

2. Lower stone from a mill. The stone is *c*.180×280mm and is 46mm at its thickest point. The upper surface is roughly dressed and shows worn concentric grooves. The underside is rough and shows a series of circular peck marks where the stone has been trimmed to a level surface. One part of the stone is bevelled over and would have formed the outer edge of the stone; the projected diameter is thus approximately 1.20m. The stone is formed out of a medium coarse-grained millstone grit. This is clearly the lower stone from a mill rather than a hand quern. While large hand querns are known, the Lynch Farm 2 fragment is best seen as being used in a geared Vitruvian style mill operated by hand (Moritz 1958, 122). A stone

from Longthorpe with a diameter of 800mm (Wild 1987b, 97–8) and other stones from Orton Hall Farm with diameters ranging from 0.89–1.00m (Spain 1996, 105–13) show that hand-powered rotary mills were extensively used in the Roman Nene valley. Weight 3.75kg. Period 3/4, see Fig. 16 S66 (LF2 72, IV 2, SF 209)

3. Lower stone from a rotary quern 180×230mm and 75mm at its thickest point. The stone has a very worn upper surface but still has concentric striations and evidence of a grooved surface; the underside is unworked and rough. Geologically it is similar to no. 2 above and shows some signs of burning. The inclination on the grinding face increases towards the centre of the quern. The stone has a projected diameter of approximately 380mm. Weight 2.61kg. Period 3/4, see Fig. 54 S74 (LF2 72, C 64, SF 263)

4. Upper stone from a beehive quern. The undersurface is worn smooth and flat while the upper, rounded surface shows circular peck marks where the stone has been worked into shape. To the lower edge of the upper surface there is a worn groove which was perhaps formed where the upper stone rubbed against the outer edge of a lower stone. The quern is of medium/coarse millstone grit from the north to mid Pennine region, north Derbyshire being the most likely source. There was a wide-ranging trade in grit stones

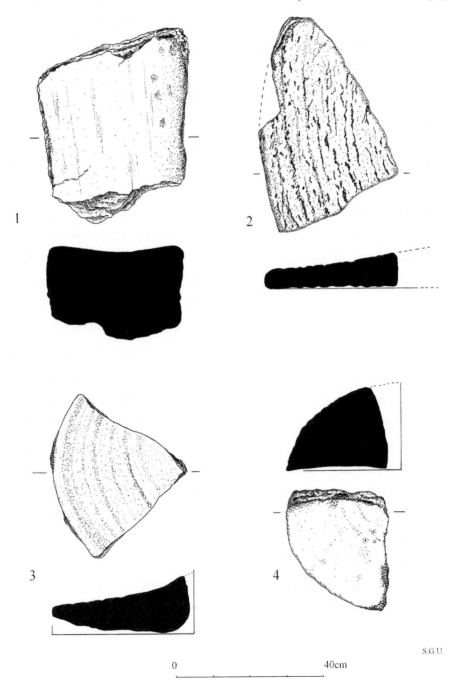

S.G.U.

0   40cm

Figure 72 Millstones, nos 1–4

from the Pennines into the lower Nene valley area and elsewhere in the east midlands. Beehive querns are often associated with the Iron Age (Mackreth 2001, 43, nos 2 and 4) and this quern may fall into this original dating framework. Weight 3.25kg. (LF2 72, B+, SF 153)

Figure 73 nos 5–6 and Plate 54

5. Lower stone from a rotary quern, broken. The stone is made from very coarse mill stone grit (provenance uncertain) and has a central hole some 20mm wide on the upper surface, widening to 35mm on the underside. The stone has part of the outer edge still surviving,

giving a radius of 173mm. The stone comes from the outer ditch of the military fort (Trench 44). Weight 2.529kg. Period 2, see Fig. 10 S41 (LF2 73, II, 248. No SF number)

6. Fragment of (Niedermendig ?) lava quern. The stone is 55mm thick at its outer edge and tapers to 18mm. The upper surface, which is very abraded and worn, appears to have a slight stepping, as if it originally had a ledge. Lava querns are a common find on military sites, where in the 1st and 2nd centuries they are often the dominant type of quern (Shaffery 2009b, 887). This stone comes from the inner ditch of the military fort (Trench 49). Weight 0.580kg. Period 2, see Fig. 10 S42 (LF2 73, II 263. No SF number)

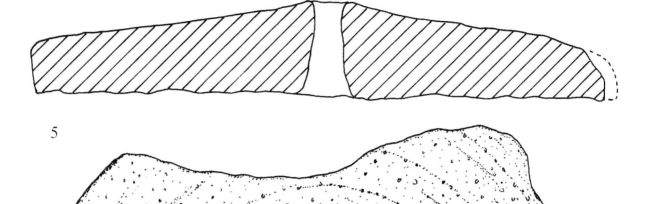

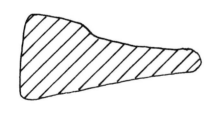

5

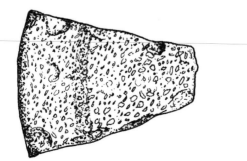

6

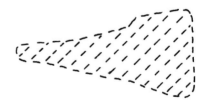

Figure 73 Millstones, nos 5–6

110

Plate 54 Two quern stone fragments from military contexts; the lava quern fragment is on the right (see IX. Quern stones, hone stones and other stone objects and Fig. 73 nos 5 and 6)

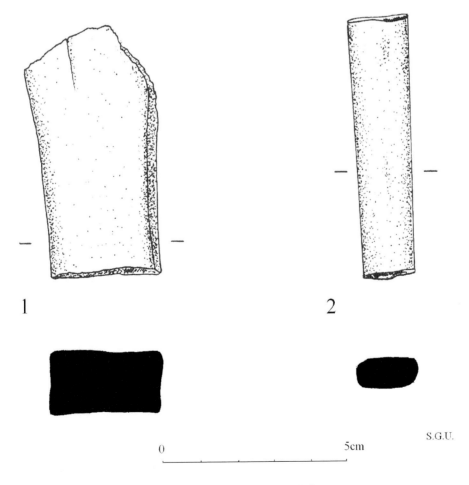

1

2

S.G.U.

0 _____ 5cm

Figure 74 Stone objects, nos 1–2

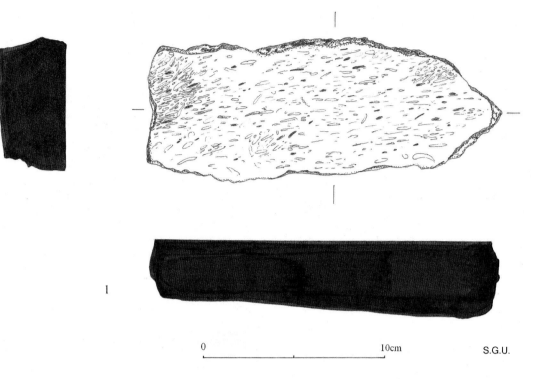

Figure 75 Fragment of 'Alwalton Marble'

Unillustrated

7. Lower stone from a rotary quern. The upper surface has concentric striations and is worn nearly smooth. The underside is rough and unworked. The stone would have had an original diameter of approximately 0.84m. Geologically the stone is similar to no. 4 above. Weight 1.35kg. Period 8 (LF2 72, D 6, SF 221)

8. Part of a saddle quern that may have been later modified and used as a hone stone. The stone is of fine sandstone grit with some larger granules up to 1mm in diameter. Weight 2.225kg. (LF2 73 II, +. SF 305)

9. Fragment of quern formed from coarse millstone grit. Weight 0.650kg. (LF2 73, B +. No SF number)

Hone stones

Figure 74 nos 1–2

1. Whetstone made from a reddish-pink, fine-grained sandstone. The fragment is 65mm long and has a rectangular section which is slightly tapered along the length of the stone from 33×30mm to 30×15mm. All sides are slightly concave and indicate use. (LF2 F1, +. SF 4)

2. Whetstone made from a white fine-grained sandstone; 65mm long with oval section. Both ends appear to have been broken. Period 5 (LF2 72, I, 42. SF 246)

Polished fragment of 'Alwalton Marble'

Figure 75 no. 1

1. Fragment of 'Alwalton Marble' 180mm long by 70mm wide and 42mm thick. The upper face has been polished to a fine and flat surface with no indication of bevelling or any wear depression which might have been expected if the stone had been used as a whetstone. Alwalton Marble is the name given to a highly fossiliferous limestone outcrop close to the village of Alwalton in northern Cambridgeshire, some 2km from the site at Lynch Farm 2. The quarries were active during the medieval period and growing evidence suggests their use during the Roman period (Lott and Smith 2001, 94; Ashurst and Dimes 1990, 109; RCHM 1969, 19; Alexander 1995, 118–22; Tomlin and Hassall 2001, 388). Two fragments of Alwalton Marble veneer come from the Roman site at Castor *Praetorium* (Rollo 1981, 2; I am grateful to Dr Ben Robinson of English Heritage for drawing the second piece of veneer to my attention). Both fragments are *c.*10mm thick and are

smoothly polished on one surface, but it is unclear whether the pieces were used as flooring or as wall veneer — both pieces are probably too large to have been used as furniture veneer (Upex 2011a, 71). Artis clearly found evidence of Alwalton Marble veneers being used in some of the buildings of *Durobrivae* and he shows a schematic view of how they were applied to walls (Artis 1828, pl. XXVI).

The fragment from Lynch Farm comes from the topsoil and may conceivably be medieval; however, if it is Roman it is perhaps too thick to have been used as wall veneer and most probably comes from a paved internal (?) floor. (LF2 72 1+ SF 243)

Pot boilers
Plate 55

A total of 127 heavily burned and reddened cobbles were found during the excavations which were identified as pot boilers. They vary in size from 60mm to 140mm and in weight from 0.20kg to 0.80kg. The average weight was 0.31kg. All of the pot boilers were of smooth cobbles taken, presumably, from the local gravels; geologically, all were imports into the region made during a past fluvio-glacial period. Almost all these items were recovered from the series of Iron Age pits forming the alignment shown in Figure 5, with nineteen pot boilers coming from Pit N and fourteen from Pit B. Only three post-Iron Age contexts (Area AII 369, 376 and 380) contained pot boilers and all of these contexts were datable to Period 2 and 3 of the site's development. This could imply that the pot boilers from these three Roman contexts were either residual or that their use continued into the early Roman period.

Pot boilers are not common on both prehistoric and Roman sites within the area, although a lack of recognition may have limited the reporting of such finds. Iron Age and Roman examples are known from Bardyke Field at Maxey, where three are reported (May 1985, 262), and earlier Bronze Age examples come from fen-edge pits associated with barrows (Downes 1993, 23). The numbers found at Lynch Farm 2 compared with other excavated local sites spanning a similar date range (cf. the Iron Age and Roman enclosure at Werrington where no pot boilers were reported: Mackreth 1988), is therefore of interest and may be linked with either aspects of cooking which were peculiar to the site or some other aspect of the site, such as salt production (discussed below).

X. Clay building materials
Plate 56

Clay building materials (CBM) totalling eighty-seven fragments came from thirty separate contexts across the site, and included *imbrex* and *tegular* roof tiles; *pedalis* and *bipedalis*, which may have been more commonly used in flooring, walls and heating systems; and *tubulus* (box tiles; see Pl. 56), also used in heating systems (Brodribb 1987, *passim*). Most of the contexts contained single fragments of CBM, but one (LF2 72, A VI 3) contained twelve pieces weighing a total of 2.5kg. However, much of this total assemblage was recovered from the 1+ and + layers of the site — for example, context LF2 72 A, VI + produced fifty fragments weighing 5.4kg. The overall distribution of CBM across the site was interesting in the sense that it was concentrated largely within Area A (see Fig. 4), in the 'cleaning' layer over the centre of Building II. This area was cleaned by hand during the initial phase of the excavation and the material kept separately within a '+ layer' context. The area of this cleaning lay immediately over context LF2 72, A, IV 33 (shown in Fig. 39), which was an area of limestone rubble with some CBM fragments. This appeared to consist of demolition material, either from Building II or from some other local demolished building which formed a hard standing or surface during the last phase of the site's occupation (Period 8).

Elsewhere on the site fragments of tile and brick were found in small quantities — often single pieces — within the fills of ditches and pits; all came from late contexts (Periods 7 and 8) across Areas A, B, C and D.

It seems unlikely that any of the CBM related to any of the excavated buildings on the site. There was no indication that any of these tiles and bricks had been used either initially or in any secondary usage within any of the structures. Their function on site simply seems to be that of forming rubble spreads during the latest period of the site's history, with some fragments finding their way into ditch fills. The only instance of the packing of earlier features with limestone rubble was found within the 'sump' of Area C (see Figs 52 and 53), and this packing contained no tile or brick fragments.

One can only assume that the CBM was brought onto the site in the late Roman period from other and as yet undiscovered building(s) which were close by. This importation of material from a more substantial local building which had heating would also explain the fragments of *opus signinum*, which were also found within the late rubble platform (LF2 72, A, IV, 33) shown in Figure 39, along with small quantities of red and white wall plaster.

The suggestion that this was imported rubble may also account for the roofing tile on the site. There was no indication that any of the excavated buildings had tiled roofs — again, all the contexts from which tile was recovered were either from late phases of the buildings or post-dated their demolition.

Plate 55 Pot boilers from various contexts (see IX. Quern stones, hone stones and other stone objects).
Stephen G. Upex

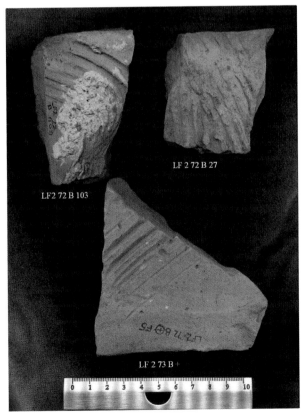

LF2 72 B 27

LF2 72 B 103

LF 2 73 B +

Plate 56 Three fragments of box tile from contexts B+, B27 and B103 (see X. Clay building materials).
Stephen G. Upex

Plate 57 Fragments of painted wall plaster from the Romano-Celtic shrine (Building III) (see Fig. 35 for the distribution of plaster within and around Building III). *Stephen G. Upex*

XI. Painted plaster
Plate 57

Wall plaster was recovered from limited areas of the excavation, with the main deposits being within the aisled building (Building II), where three spreads of plaster were found. In each case the plaster appeared to be mixed with building rubble (Phase II of this building — Period 8, see Fig. 39), pottery and general make-up layers in the demolition phase of the structure (LF2 72 A, IV, 33). In no case was plaster found adhering to the walls of any of the excavated structures, including the aisled buildings, and this material appeared to have been imported onto the site from other, as yet unidentified, buildings. Only two colours were identified, white (LF2–73, VI, +. SF 354) and a terracotta red (LF2–73, VI, 5. SF 335).

White, red and orange wall plaster was also recovered from Building III. The distribution of this material is shown in Figure 35. Here, patches of wall plaster were found both scattered across the area of Building III, but also seemed to be mixed in with the matrix of gravel which formed the core of the wall.

Wall plaster in red, white and brown/black was also recovered from an area associated with a limestone scatter (Building IV) in the north-western section of Area A (see Fig. 28). Recovered from this disturbed area was a fragment of plaster with a painted scheme with red, white and black zones on it (see Pl. 57 no. 5). However, this building was poorly preserved when archaeological work began and lay outside the area set aside for excavation, so that little can be said of this building other than it may have provided some of the material that was later imported as rubble in the area of Building II (see above).

XII. Objects of burnt clay including briquetage and fire bars

Loom weights, spindle whorl

Figure 76 no. 1

1. Fragment of a triangular loom weight 54mm wide and originally approximately 90mm high. The remnants of one diagonally pierced hole remains and the remaining corner angle is bevelled inwards to take cords from the loom. The piece has been crudely fired to give a light pink/red exterior finish; the core of the loom weight is fired grey to charcoal. The triangular form of the weight suggests an Iron Age date (Wild 1970, fig. 16) and similar weights from Maxey all come from Iron Age or early Roman contexts (Pryor *et al.* 1985, figs 119–123), with other examples from Longthorpe and Orton Longueville of Claudio-Neronian date (Wild 1987a, fig. 30, nos 171–174; Mackreth 2001, fig. 23, no. 21). Period 8, see Fig. 13 S128 (LF2–73, II, 76. SF 318)

Unillustrated

2. Part of a triangular loom weight in two pieces. The weight is 53mm wide with the remains of a diagonally pierced hole cutting across what would have been one of the angular corners, which is bevelled inwards to take the cord from the loom. In all other respects the weight is similar to no. 1 above. Period 1 (LF2–73, II, 90. SF 330)

3. Fragment of spindle whorl, 37mm in diameter, made from poorly fired clay. Period 3, see Fig. 15 S35 (LF2–73, T 63, 316. SF 368)

4. Oval baked clay object, 54mm long and 40mm wide, made from crude fired clay with impressions of vegetable matter within the clay. Purpose unknown. Period 1/2, see Fig. 15 S35 (LF2–74, T-59, 284. SF 362)

Briquetage

Twenty contexts produced fragments of briquetage. One context within Area B (context B10: see Fig. 44, Fig. 48 Ditch B13 and S114) was dated to Period 8 and two contexts within Area C, contexts C48 (see Fig. 50) and C64 (Fig. 54 S74, S75; Figs 50 and 51; see also Fig. 77 no. 2) were dated to Periods 3/4. All of the remaining eighteen

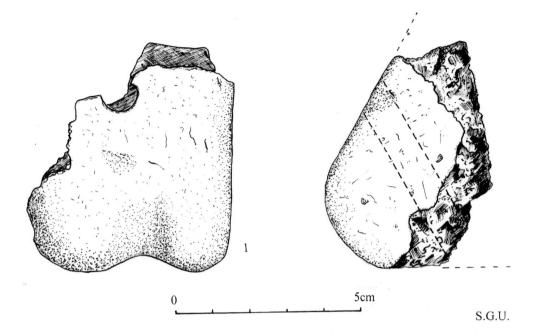

0   5cm

S.G.U.

Figure 76 Loom weight, no. 1

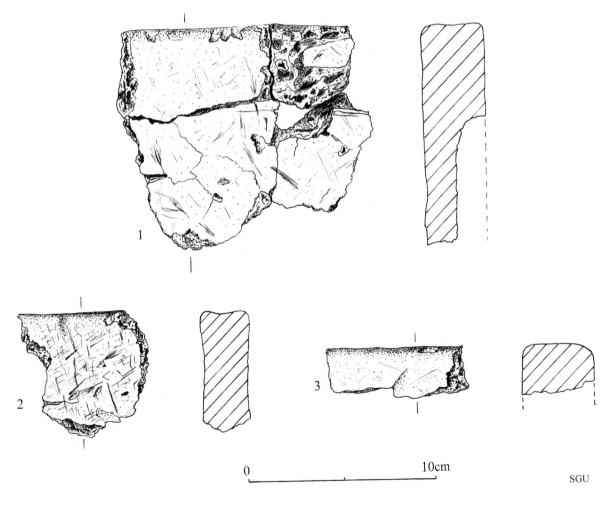

0   10cm

SGU

Figure 77 Objects of fired clay, nos 1–3

Plate 58 Fragment of briquetage (SF 256) (see XII. Objects of burnt clay including briquetage and fire bars).
Stephen G. Upex

Plate 59 Kiln fire bars and a fragment of dome plate (see XII. Objects of burnt clay including briquetage and fire
bars). *Stephen G. Upex*

116

contexts came from Area A and were dated within Periods 2 and 3. For example, fragments of briquetage from Period 2 came from context AI, 19, which is shown in Figure 11 (S45), while three fragments (AI, 2) came from the base of Furnace 5, which is shown in plan and section in Figure 23 and was dated to Period 4. Other similar fragments were also associated with the furnaces which were found in Building I (see Fig. 22) and it may be that these furnaces were associated with the use of briquetage vessels and salt production. The types of briquetage found at Lynch Farm 2 are very reminiscent of similar material found at other fen-edge sites that have been linked with salt production (see Malim 2005, 173–6). A whole repertoire of vessels and vessel supports made out of very poorly fired vegetable- and shell-tempered clays are known for example from Parson Drove (Every 2006, 35–7) and from March (Morris 2008, 93–102), where there were also hearths which closely matched the furnaces from Lynch Farm 2. A typical fragment of such vegetable-tempered fabric from LF2 is shown in Plate 58 and described below.

Figure 77 nos 1–3

1. Four fragments forming a slab of very poorly fired briquetage approximately 125×110mm. The fragments probably come from the straight-sided wall (30mm thick) of a vat-like container for salt extraction. The exterior and interior walls show that the fabric contains vegetable, seed and grass impressions as well as coarse to medium sand grains and larger ironstone and other stone fragments up to 16mm in size. This fabric form may match a similar fabric type from Cedar Close, Cambridge (Morris 2008, 95, V2G). Period 2 (LF2 72, IV, 7. SF 256)

2. Single fragment of briquetage approximately 75×60mm and 28mm thick. The section has a slightly concave profile, as does the rim. The fabric and surface finish contained much vegetable matter, which is evident as voids within the clay. Period 3 (LF2 72, C, 64. No SF no.)

3. Fragment of a rim (or part of a fire bar) 73×25mm and 34mm thick in a heavy briquetage fabric with small stone and grit inclusions. The rim has a rounded profile. Not enough of this object remains to be certain how it was used. The lack of vegetable grog or significant grit inclusion may indicate that it was part of a fire bar rather than a vat or container for salt production. It may have been used as a 'support' for briquetage containers in salt production (see Morris 2001, fig. 19, 28; Crosby 2001, fig. 34, 36). Period 3 (LF2 73, A II, 93. SF 340)

Plate 58

1. Fragment of briquetage with a wall 34mm thick, with inclusions of shell and vegetable matter. Period 3 (LF2 72, A IV 7. SF 256)

Fire bars and a fragment of a kiln dome plate

Four fragments of fire bars came from two areas within the excavations of Area A. Three fragments were recovered from context 186, which formed the fill of Ditch A5 (Fig. 12; Fig. 17 S49). The remaining fire bar and part of a dome plate (Pl. 59, nos 4 and 5) came from the fill (context 104) of a small surface-built kiln shown in Figures 12 and 18. The fabrics of the fire bars and their size suggested that they were all from small kiln-like structure(s) and may in fact have all been originally used within the excavated kiln from within the Period 3 enclosure shown in Figure 12. This kiln may have been used to produce very early forms of Nene valley grey ware; fragments of pottery were recovered from context 104 (see Chapter 7 no. 72 in the illustrated catalogue). Enough of this kiln survived, together with the dome plate and fire bar, to partly reconstruct the layout and section of the whole feature (Fig. 18).

Plate 59 nos 1–5

1. Broken length of fire bar 80mm long with a moulded and rounded profile with a terminal end that has been rounded. The fabric contains shell and vegetable matter. Period 3 (LF2 A II, 186. No SF no.)

2. Length of fire bar 80mm long with a rectangular section 23×26mm. The fabric is much coarser than no. 1 above, with a greater amount of vegetable matter included. Period 3 (LF2 A II, 186. No SF no.)

3. Broken length of fire bar 140mm long with an irregular section along the surviving length of the object but which was probably intended to be roughly rectangular. The fabric is as for no. 2 above. Period 3 (LF2 A II, 186. No SF no.)

4. Short 60mm long piece of fire bar with a roughly rectangular section some 20×24mm. One end of the bar is broken but the other widens slightly to end in a flat, rectangular terminal. The fabric is of a fine grey fired clay with shell and some vegetable matter. Period 3, see Fig. 16 S12 (LF2 73, A II 104. No SF no.)

5. Fragment of a curved kiln dome plate in the same fabric as no. 4 above. Period 3, see Fig. 16 S12 (LF2 73, A II 104. No SF no.)

XIII. Wooden objects (excluding the wooden foundation rafts of both wells)

Various wooden posts and sections of planking were found during the excavations, which had been preserved in the wet conditions encountered on the site. These formed three groups. isolated posts; groups of wooden posts often associated with the remnants of wooden planks set along the edges of the ditches and which had formed revetted sides to those ditches; and a line of posts which formed a fence.

In Area B there were four sets of posts which appeared to be associated with revetted sections of ditches and some of these wooden posts survived. Along the length of Ditches B2 and B3 were sets of preserved posts with remnants of horizontal planking set along the edges of the ditches, which must have been intended as a revetted edge. The positions of these sets of posts are shown in Figure 44. Another set of posts occurred at the bend in Ditch B10, where four posts were set along the edge of the line of the ditch. These posts were poorly preserved with only fragments of timber surviving, although the part-decayed post had left a dark impression within the soil (see Pl. 41). Any sign of preserved horizontal planking was also absent but slight staining within the soil suggested that this area may also have been revetted.

A single isolated post (context B12) was found in Area B to the north of Ditch B13. Two other isolated post ends, both 0.35m long and identified on site as oak, were recovered from Area C (Fig. 50; photographs of these posts are retained within the site archive). One post was set within the line of Ditch C8 and the other within the line of Ditch C9. In both cases the post ends had been cut to form a point, probably with an axe or adze type tool. The functions of these isolated posts are uncertain and they may have originally formed part(s) of a more extensive post group which made up fence lines/racking for farm produce (hay?), or had some other function.

A row of part-preserved posts possibly forming a fence line was also encountered along the northern edge of Area B. Some of these posts had rotted away completely and were only detectable by either the staining which was left within the soil or the limestone packing which had been set around them. Other posts (nos 7, 9 and 10; Fig. 44) were partly preserved with their ends sharpened to a point, perhaps by an axe or adze.

Of the ten posts that were recovered and recorded within the small finds system (SF 124–129, 140–141, 234–5 and 237), eight appeared to have been identified on site as oak; the remaining two were of ash. None of the posts was sufficiently well preserved or with sufficient thickness or bark to warrant their being considered for dendrochronology.

The preserved wooden foundations of the two wells from the site have already been outlined (see Figs 40 and 43) and a report on the dendrochronology of these timbers is found below (Chapter 8).

XIV. Leather objects
(Fig. 78)

A number of leather fragments were recovered from the waterlogged deposit at the base of Well I, including two shoes (Fig. 78) and two fragments from shoes (SF 2002–3, 224 and 226). One of the shoes was especially interesting in that it had been made for a child. A report on this material has already been published by June Swan and Alison Metcalf (1975, 2–25) and further publication is not therefore made here.

XV. Slag and a crucible fragment

The evidence for ironworking at the site was poor. The only substantial indication that iron was being fabricated

came from Furnace 6 (see Fig. 31) within Building II, Phase II and dated to Period 6 (see above). The furnaces that were found in Building I (see Figs 22 and 23) and dated to Period 4 had no slag, hammerscale or other associated material that might have linked them with ironworking. However, iron slag was recovered from six contexts within Area A, II and three contexts within Area B, where one fragment of slag from Ditch B5 weighed 0.4kg (see Fig. 47 S107). All of the slag was recovered from either ditch fills, such as those of Ditches A3 and A4 (see Fig. 16 S63, 73 and S66, 6) or Ditch B3 (Fig. 47 S107, 5), or as a single collection of material from one of the large and shallow 'ponded' features in Area B (see Pond C, Fig. 44). In total, the amount of slag from the whole site amounted to 2.34kg and the contexts were confined to Periods 3 and 6.

One fragment of a small crucible, some 60mm in diameter, that may have been used for bronze working, was found from the 'general' area of the site prior to archaeological work commencing (LF2 72 +, SF 80), but this was the only indication for any metalworking other than of iron.

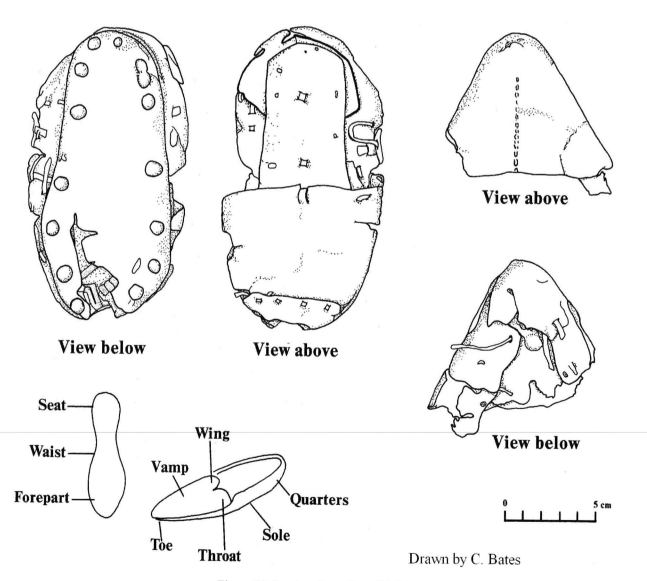

View below   View above   View above

Seat   Waist   Forepart

Vamp   Wing   Quarters   Toe   Throat   Sole

View below

0   5 cm

Drawn by C. Bates

Figure 78 Leather shoes from Well I

118

Chapter 7. The pottery

I. The samian
by Felicity C. Wild
(Table 5)

The excavations produced 188 sherds of samian ware from about 109 vessels. Of these, thirty-eight (35%) were South Gaulish, sixty-eight (62%) Central Gaulish and three (3%) East Gaulish. Of the Central Gaulish vessels, three were in the fabric of Les Martres-de-Veyre, two of form 18/31 and one of form Curle 15. The assemblage is too small for statistics necessarily to be reliable, a fact which should be borne in mind in considering the comments below. Excluding scraps of uncertain form, the forms are listed by origin in Table 5.

It seems likely that the site had seen a degree of disturbance during the Roman period. Not only were the sherds in small pieces, but joins were detectable between sherds from different contexts. Sherds from the largest of the decorated bowls, D5, came from no fewer than six contexts. Many of the South Gaulish sherds were pre-Flavian and likely to have arrived on site during the military phase, Period 2, though the amount stratified in Period 2 contexts was small (see below). Thirteen of the sixteen decorated bowls were South Gaulish, 37% of the South Gaulish ware as a whole and suggesting high status, as one would expect of a site with military connections (Willis 2011, 198–201).

Whether all the South Gaulish ware arrived during the lifetime of the fortress at Longthorpe, however, is doubtful. Some of the pieces, including three examples of form 37 (D4, D5 and D7) are of undoubtedly Flavian or Flavian–Trajanic date, but these are comparatively few. Also worthy of note is the almost complete absence of wares from Les Martres-de-Veyre, suggesting that, whatever the status of the site at the end of the 1st and beginning of the 2nd century AD, consumption of samian ware was minimal.

The import of samian ware on a larger scale, from Lezoux, appears to have restarted shortly before the middle of the 2nd century AD, peaking in the second half of the century. The Hadrianic–early Antonine forms 27, 18/31 and 18/31R are present, but heavily outnumbered by the later forms 33, 31, 31R, 79 and 80. Decorated ware, which in any case became less common towards the end of the 2nd century, is almost entirely absent. The general assemblage is typical of a low-status rural settlement.

The decorated ware and stamps are listed below, together with a catalogue of the samian from Periods 2–3/4. Potter and die numbers are those used in Hartley and Dickinson 2008–12. Figure types are quoted from Oswald 1936–37 (O).

Decorated ware
Figure 79 D1–D7

Phase 2

D1. Form 29, South Gaulish. In the upper zone are festoons with three rosettes in one lower concavity and part of a pronged terminal in the other. Insufficient remains to identify the type (a bird?) in the festoon. Similar triple rosettes appear on work in the style of Crestio from Mainz (Knorr 1952, Taf. 17B) and at Kingsholm (Wild 1985, fig. 21, 1), though in both cases at the end of a corner tendril on form 30 rather than on form 29. The lower zone shows panels with a chevron medallion and a saltire, but again, too little survives to identify the type in the medallion and the triple bud (?) at the top of the saltire is damaged. The large beads along the central cordon suggest a Claudio-Neronian date, probably c. AD 50–70. (LF2 III (1))

D2. Form 29, South Gaulish, showing a winding scroll in the upper zone, with rosette and probably a five-pronged terminal, a very common type of decoration in the pre-Flavian period. An identical sherd in both shape and decoration is illustrated in the Longthorpe Fortress report (Hartley 1974, fig. 49, 14), possibly a case of accidental confusion by the artist of similar sherds from two nearby and contemporary excavations. Hartley's note lists a Longthorpe provenance for no. 14, which also showed a winding scroll, whereas the present sherd is clearly marked with a Lynch Farm code. A date of c. AD 45–60 seems probable, as for the Longthorpe sherd. (LF2 73 T44 (249))

Period 3/4

D3. Form 29, South Gaulish. Sherd of upper zone showing panels with leaf tips and the lion (O.1447). The lion was used by Vespasianic potters such as Censor i, Coelus and Mommo. A number of bowls of form 29 by Mommo in the Pompeii Hoard show a similar arrangement of leaf tip panels and animal types in the upper zone (Atkinson 1914, 5–9, 13), though not with the lion. c. AD 60–85. (LF2 72 IV (21))

D4. Form 37, South Gaulish. Small scrap showing a panel with a leg probably of the cupid (O.390A). The type was in use at La

Form	SG	CG	EG	Total
29	6			6
30	4			4
37	3	2		5
30 or 37		1		1
27	4	5		9
33		11	1	12
15/17	2			2
15/17 or 18	3			3
18	5			5
18 or 18/31	1			1
18/31		3		3
18/31 or 31		4		4
31		7	1	8
18R	2			2
18/31R		2		2
18/31R or 31R		2		2
31R		6		6
18/31, 31 or R		2		2
35	2	1		3
36	1	1		2
42		1		1
79		2		2
80		1		1
Ritt 12	1			1
Curle 15		2		2
Bowl	1	2		3
Total	**35**	**58**	**2**	**95**

Table 5 Samian forms, by origin

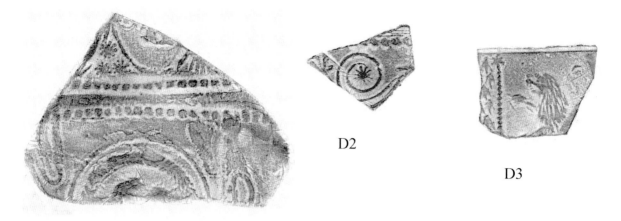

D2

D3

D1

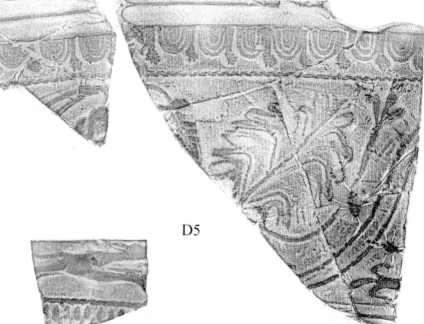

D4

D5

D6

D7

S1

S2

S3

S4

S5

S6

0   5cm

Figure 79 Illustrated samian, D1–7 and S1–6 (by Felicity Wild)

120

Graufesenque from Claudian times, but if this is indeed form 37, as it appears to be from its curvature, it will not be earlier than the Flavian period. *c.* AD 70–100. (LF2 73 II (9))

D5. Form 30, South Gaulish. Seventeen sherds in all, from the same bowl, showing an ovolo with tongue slightly angled to the left, ending in a damaged rosette (Dannell *et al.* 1998, CH) and leaf-scroll decoration. The ovolo and large leaf occur together on a bowl of form 37 from La Graufesenque (Mees 1995, Taf. 161, 1) showing a similar scroll, with the cursive signature PAS inscribed in the mould below the decoration, presumably by the mould-maker. Little is known of the potter Pas-, or even his complete name, though his connections and general style suggest a date in the Flavian–Trajanic period. Another bowl, with similar signature (Mees 1995, Taf. 160, 5), shows a leaf of similar shape to the smaller one here, though possibly slightly smaller. *c.* AD 80–110. (SF 357; T65 (321) SF 370; T58 (279) SF 372; T66 (348) SF 375; II (6); II (+))

D6. Form 37, Central Gaulish. Scrap, showing part of the ovolo, bead row and the edge of a festoon. Insufficient survives for a reliable identification, but the large beads suggest the work of potters such as Doeccus i. What remains of the ovolo fits his (Rogers 1974, B160) for size and there are examples in his work of the vertical bead row running up into the ovolo, as here (Rogers 1999, pl. 40, 8). The piece is certainly Antonine, and if by Doeccus, *c.* AD 165–200. (LF2 72 B (26))

Period 5/6

D7. Form 37, South Gaulish, with hound (O.1925), used by a number of Flavian potters, over a panel of leaf tips. A bowl by M. Crestio (Mees 1995, Taf. 37, 5) is a fairly close parallel, with hound and similar leaf tip panel. *c.* AD 80–100. (LF2 72 IV (23))

The samian stamps
Figure 79 S1–S6

S1. Form 33, East Gaulish. Four joining sherds showing a stamp of Firmus iv of Rheinzabern, almost certainly die 5a, read as FIRMVSFC, rather than die 3a, FIRMVSFE. Although his stamps have also been found at other East Gaulish manufacturing centres, Hartley and Dickinson (2008–12) consider that he almost certainly operated only at Rheinzabern and the fabric of the present piece is quite consistent with manufacture there. *c.* AD 165–220? (Period 4/5: LF2 72 T44 (247) SF 356)

S2. Form 80, Central Gaulish, stamped HABILISM, die 1a of the potter Habilis of Lezoux. Habilis was at work during the mid-2nd century, making form 27 as well as the later Antonine forms 79 and 80. The present base, although not entirely flat, has traces of a step between wall and base and is more likely to be form 80 than form 27. *c.* AD 150–80. (Period 4/5: LF2 72, AII (28) SF 304)

S3. Form 18R, South Gaulish. Four joining sherds from two different contexts, stamped [OF].LABIONIS, die 1a of Labio of La Graufesenque. Labio was a mainly pre-Flavian potter, but his work also occurs on military sites founded during the early Flavian period. This is one of his more common dies, occurring widely on sites in Britain, including Chester, Carlisle and the York fortress. *c.* AD 45–75. (Period 2: LF2 B (53), Period 3/4: LF2 72 IV (22))

S4. Form 15/17, South Gaulish. Two joining sherds showing a poorly impressed and abraded stamp, possibly one of the many dies used by Primus iii of La Graufesenque. The reading is uncertain, but could be OF.PRM or OF.PRIM. Primus was primarily a Claudio-Neronian potter, though there is evidence that he was still at work in the AD 70s, suggesting a date range of *c.* AD 40–80, if this is indeed by him. (Period 3/4: LF2 72 IV (19))

S5. Form 33, Central Gaulish, stamped VESPONI by Vespo of Lezoux. The die (1a) occurs in the Castleford Pottery Shop of the early AD 140s (Dickinson and Hartley 2000, 61, fig. 30, 974–82). His recorded forms include the Hadrianic–early Antonine forms 27 and 18/31, though he also produced the later Antonine form 79. The rather large form 33 here is typical of the early Antonine period. *c.* AD 140–70. (LF2 72 (+) SF 64)

S6. Form 27g, South Gaulish, with an illiterate stamp. Probably Flavian. (Period 4/5: LF2 AII (9) SF 302)

Catalogue

Period 2
Ritt. 12, South Gaulish. Nine joining sherds. Pre-Flavian. (I (12))
Form 22, South Gaulish (**D1**). *c.* AD 50–70. (III (1))
Form 29, South Gaulish (**D2**). *c.* AD 45–60. (T44 (249))
Form 27, South Gaulish. Three sherds, probably Claudian. (T71 (11))
Form 18R, South Gaulish. Two joining sherds of dish with stamp of Labio (**S3**), *c.* AD 45–75. (B (53))
Form 18/31–31, Central Gaulish. Hadrianic–Antonine. (B (53) upper levels)

Period 2/3
Form 29, South Gaulish. Rim scrap. Pre- or early Flavian. (II (90))

Period 2/4
Form 15/17 or 18, South Gaulish, burnt. Probably pre-Flavian. (IV (47))

Period 3
Form 30, South Gaulish. Rim scrap. Neronian or Flavian. (IV (9))
Form 33, Central Gaulish. Two joining sherds. Probably Antonine. (IV (9))
Uncertain scrap, Central Gaulish. Probably Antonine. (VI (3))

Period 3/4
Form 30, South Gaulish (**D5**). *c.* AD 80–110. (T58 (321), T66 (348))
Form 27, South Gaulish, slightly burnt. Probably pre-Flavian. (II (8))
Form 37, South Gaulish (**D4**). *c.* AD 70–100. (II (9))
Form 18/31 or 31 (R?), Central Gaulish. Hadrianic or Antonine. (II (9))
Form 35, South Gaulish. 1st century. (II (72))
4 sherds of form 18/31 or 31, rim sherd, probably from form 18/31R and footring scrap from bowl, all Central Gaulish and Hadrianic or Antonine (II (74))
Another group of Central Gaulish origin and Hadrianic or Antonine date comprising three scraps, one possibly from form 27. (II (194))
Form 79, Central Gaulish. *c.* AD 150–200. (IV (4))
Form 36, South Gaulish. Two joining sherds, probably Flavian or Trajanic. (IV (7))
A South Gaulish, probably pre-Flavian, group comprising form 15/17 with uncertain stamp, possibly Primus (**S3**), form 29 rim and form 18. (IV (19))
Another South Gaulish, pre-Flavian group, comprising form 29 (**D3**), 27g and 18. (IV (21))
A South Gaulish, pre-Flavian group, comprising form 30 rim, two more sherds of the form 18R of Labio (**S3**) and sherds from at least two dishes of form 18. (IV (22))
Form 37, Central Gaulish (**D6**). *c.* AD 165–200. (B (26))
Form 30 rim, South Gaulish. Probably pre-Flavian.

II. The coarse pottery
by Stephen G. Upex

Introduction
(Tables 6–10)
The coarse pottery from Lynch Farm 2 consisted of 8,648 sherds weighing a total of 143.308kg. This represents only part of the total assemblage recovered from the excavations, as the excavators sorted the material on site and discarded unwanted sherds back into finished trenches. The pottery from the site is thus difficult to quantify other than in a very basic way and the report therefore has limitations in the scope it could achieve. As such, it was decided to restrict the way the pottery was described and analysed. Pottery quantification has been given only in terms of weight and the numbers of sherds, and although estimated vessel equivalents (EVEs) were taken for the initial indexing of the assemblage it was decided to include only weights and numbers in this report.

The analysis is also open to criticism concerning the validity of the statistical methods employed. Making comparisons of various forms of pottery groups between

Area	Total weight in kg	Total no. of sherds	Average sherd weight in g	Total no. of contexts
AI	6.932	268	25.86	97
AII	49.169	2592	18.96	394
AIII	2.425	21	115.47	27
AIV	21.066	1272	16.56	53
AVI	8.175	319	25.62	23
B	25.304	1074	23.56	108
C	27.857	2983	9.33	81
D	2.380	119	20.00	26
Totals	**143.308**	**8648**	**16.57**	**809**

Table 6 Sherd numbers and weight of coarse pottery by area

Period	Sherd nos	Sherd nos as %	Weight in kg	Weight as %
1	83	0.959	0.790	0.005
2	120	1.387	1.34	0.935
3	639	7.388	9.39	6.552
4	531	6.140	6.78	4.731
5	239	2.76	3.1	2.162
6	2460	28.445	49.162	34.304
7	1036	11.979	11.48	8.010
8	2110	24.398	42.59	29.718
Unstra/+	1430	16.535	19.46	13.578
Total	**8648**	**99.99**	**143.31**	**99.996**

Table 7 Sherd numbers and weight by period

Fabric	Period 1	Period 2	Period 3	Period 4	Period 5	Period 6	Period 7	Period 8	Total
LIASGW	62								62
LIA/RGTW	21	8	2						31
RSGW		20	301	211	54	458	109	216	1369
RVTW		1							1
LNVRW			61	12	8				81
LNVGW			233	186	59	891	283	647	2299
LNVCCW				98	99	1091	617	1171	3004
LNVCWW				9	13	61	9	20	112
LW				5					5
NVPIRP								26	26
OXRW						25	13	26	64
OXMO						3	4		7
HADOX						3	1	4	8
BB1		2							2
Fabric 1		3	3	1					7
Fabric 2		7							7
Fabric 2a		4							4
Fabric 3		9							9
Fabric 4		1	8	2					11
Fabric 5		1	6	1					8
Fabric 6		11	9	3					23
Fabric 7		1	2						3
Fabric 8		6	8	3					17
Fabric 9		4	6						10
Fabric 10		2							2
Fabric 11		5							5
Fabric 12		16							16
Fabric 13		10							10
Fabric 14		6							6
Fabric 15		3			6				9
Totals	**83**	**120**	**639**	**531**	**239**	**2460**	**1036**	**2100**	**7218**

Table 8 Fabric by period (excluding samian and amphorae and unstratified pottery)

periods is beset with problems concerning actual vessel numbers and the volumes of material from period-based contexts. The volume of soil from Iron Age contexts, for example, was substantial, yet the actual number of sherds was minimal when compared with, say, later contexts.

The excavation was divided into eight discrete areas which produced a total of 809 contexts, of which 488 contained pottery (see Table 6). The amount of pottery from each context varied both in weight and the numbers of sherds (see Table 7). In Area AII, for example, context 81 contained sixty sherds from the same vessel weighing a total of 3.950kg; in Area B, context 27 contained 210 sherds from numerous vessels with a total weight of 3.20kg. At the other end of the range, many contexts produced single sherds of pottery, some weighing a mere 0.01kg.

Fabric	Period 1	Period 2	Period 3	Period 4	Period 5	Period 6	Period 7	Period 8	Total
LIASGW	62								62
%	100.								100%
LIA/RGTW	21	8	2						31
%	67.74	25.80	6.45						99.99%
RSGW		20	301	211	54	458	109	216	1369
%		1.46	21.98	15.41	3.94	33.45	7.96	15.77	99.97%
RVTW		1							1
%		100.							100%
LNVRW			61	12	8				81
%			75.30	14.81	9.8				99.91%
LNVGW			233	186	59	891	283	647	2299
%			10.13	8.90	2.5	38.75	12.30	28.14	100%
LNVCCW				98	99	1091	617	1171	3004
%				3.26	3.29	36.31	20.53	38.98	100%
LNVCWW				9	13	61	9	20	112
%				8.03	11.60	54.46	8.03	17.85	99.97%
LW				5					5
%				100.					100%
NVPIRP								26	26
%								100.	100%
OXRW						25	13	26	64
%						39.06	20.31	40.62	99.99%
OXMO						3	4		7
%						42.85	57.14		99.99%
HADOX						3	1	4	8
%						37.5	12.5	50.0	100%

Table 9 Fabrics by percentage and period

The pottery was divided into fabric groups (see Table 8), and fabric and surface colours were matched with those of the 'Munsell Soil Colour Chart' (1971 edn). The assemblage was assessed in line with the guidelines set out by the Study Group for Roman Pottery (Webster 1975; Young 1980; Darling 2004; Willis 2004). The total assemblage was scanned and a preliminary catalogue prepared. The sherds were examined using a hand lens (×20 magnification) and then the assemblage was divided into fabric groups based on broad criteria such as the presence/absence of inclusions visible to the naked eye; or estimates of fabric coarseness/fineness where the suites of inclusions were similar; or of a particular firing property of the clays used in manufacture. The resulting categories probably each contain products from more than one source, but without any formal fabric analysis programme and using only a visual inspection, the groupings could not hope to be definitive. Within the time frame for producing this report it was not possible to analyse fabric types and the forms of vessels from those fabric groupings.

Fabric codes are descriptive and, within the catalogue and this report, are abbreviated to the main letters of the title — thus Roman Shell Gritted Ware becomes RSGW. Spot dates were assigned to each context and sherd types were also recorded. Sherds from each context were weighed and counted by fabric group and comment was made on any decorated, unusual, abraded or residual sherds. Samian and amphorae were excluded from this analysis and are dealt with in separate sections.

Table 8 shows the thirty fabric groups distributed across the eight periods. Period 1 produced eighty-three sherds of either LIASGW or LIA/RGTW. Period 2 produced 120 sherds which ranged over twenty different fabric groups, representing the broadest range of fabrics by period within the whole assemblage; RSGW dominated with twenty sherds but significant groups also appeared in Fabric Groups 6, 12 and 13. Fabric Group 6 contained a series of platters (see nos 12–17 in the illustrated catalogue below); Fabric Group 12 contained a series of beakers and jars (see nos 12, 8–9, 11–17 in the illustrated catalogue below); while Fabric Group 13 contained jars and bowls (see nos 6, 10, 21 and 23 in the illustrated catalogue below). The fabrics of some vessels are clearly similar to vessels made at the Longthorpe potteries. For example the Longthorpe wares in creams, pinks and buffs (Dannell and Wild 1987, table VII), all match the range of variations within LF2 Fabrics 12 and 13 and the assumption is that many of the LF2 vessels were indeed made in the Longthorpe military kilns excavated between 1970 and 1975. It may be that several of the other LF2 fabrics were also made at Longthorpe military kilns yet to be excavated or at other local kilns related to the military base at Lynch Farm 2. That many of the fabrics within Period 2 are from a military context is suggested by the fact that many of the fabrics within Period 2 do not carry through into Period 3, suggesting perhaps that the military potters had either moved on or that military pottery production had ceased. However, Fabric 6, which is represented within the military period (Period 2), is found in Period 3 contexts (six sherds), although the possibility that such sherds are residual in Period 3 is distinctly possible. What is clear is that the

Vessel type	Period 1	Period 2	Period 3	Period 4	Period 5	Period 6	Period 7	Period 8	Total	Total as %
Cups/beakers	5	12	6	4	2	1	0	0	30	3.147
As % of group	14.28	40	20	13.33	6.66	3.33	0	0	97.6%	
Dishes	0	3	2	3	2	25	68	71	174	18.258
As % of group	0	1.72	1.14	1.72	1.14	14.36	39.08	40.80	99.96%	
Bowls	8	1	5	16	7	39	82	81	239	24.973
As % of group	3.36	0	2.10	6.72	2.94	16.38	34.45	34.03	99.98%	
Plates	0	12	0	0	0	0	0	0	12	1.259
As % of group	0	100	0	0	0	0	0	0	100%	
Jars	12	19	69	52	16	46	71	74	371	38.929
As % of group	3.23	5.12	18.59	14.01	4.31	12.39	19.13	19.94	96.72%	
Mortaria	0	0	2	6	1	13	16	18	56	5.876
As % of group	0	0	3.57	10.71	1.78	23.21	28.57	32.14	99.98%	
Flagons	0	1	2	1	0	2	1	2	9	0.944
lin0As % of group	0	11.11	22.22	11.11	0	22.22	11.11	22.22	99.99%	
Castor boxes	0	0	0	0	1	4	6	8	19	1.993
As % of group	0	0	0	0	5.25	21.04	31.57	42.10	99.96%	
Colanders	0	0	3	1	0	2	1	0	7	0.734
As % of group	0	0	42.85	14.28	0	28.57	14.28	0	99.98%	
Cheese press	0	0	1	1	0	3	1	6	12	1.259
As % of group	0	0	8.33	8.33	0	25.00	8.33	50.00	99.99%	
Lids	1	1	2	1	1	3	3	7	19	1.888
As % of group	5.55	0	11.11	5.55	5.55	16.66	16.66	38.88	99.96%	
Others	0	0	1	2	1	2	0	1	7	0.734
As % of group	0	0	14.28	28.57	14.28	28.57	0	14.28	99.98%	
Vessel totals	26	49	93	87	31	140	249	268	955	
As a %	.027	4.93	9.75	9.12	3.25	14.69	26.12	28.12	96.00	

Table 10 Vessel types by period (excluding all unstratified and topsoil material)

range of fabrics becomes ever more limited through time and by Period 5 only ten sherds from five fabric groups are represented, and again these are likely to be residual. By Period 3 it is apparent that what one might loosely term the Nene valley pottery industry had been established, with LNVGW and LNVRW dominating the assemblage. Such fabrics are broadened by Period 4 with the introduction of LNVCCW products which come to dominate by Periods 6, 7 and 8.

This gradual move from the foundations of the local pottery industry with many identifiable fabrics to the later periods, where a few fabrics dominate, is expressed in Table 9, where figures are given both as sherd numbers for each fabric group and period but also as percentages for the total number of sherds within specific fabric groups. Thus for LNVCCW for example the figures show that Period 4 represented only 3.26% of the total colour coated ware within the whole assemblage. This figure rises to 36.31% by Period 6 and 38.98% by Period 8. This rise in the production of colour coated ware products is matched by a decline in the quantities of grey ware products found at the site: Period 3 represented 10.13% of grey ware which then increases to 38.75% by Period 6 but falls away to 28.14% by Period 8.

Equally interesting is the rise of late pottery sequences within the assemblage. The imports from both the Oxford kilns and those from Hadham begin during the late 3rd century and continue until the end of the ceramic life of the site. Of especial interest is the production/manufacture of NVPIRP which is found exclusively in Period 8. This type of pottery is now being recognised as the latest to be produced within the area of the lower Nene valley, normally represented by basic Romanised forms, such as dishes and flanged bowls, but in debased fabrics.

Table 10 provides a basic analysis of the variety of vessels present at Lynch Farm 2 through the site's eight periods of occupation. This shows that the use of cups and beakers reaches a peak during the military phase, Period 2, with twelve vessels (40% of the total number of vessels within this category). This figure then declines through Period 3 (six vessels, or 20% of the total) and by Period 7 cups and beakers are not represented at all on the site. Such a decline in a 'basic' vessel type must indicate that alternative forms of receptacles were being used, perhaps made from glass, wood, metal or horn. There is little comparative evidence from other sites related to vessel numbers and forms. However, at Orton Hall Farm Perrin has provided data related to the forms of vessels against periods and shows that beakers are present throughout all of the occupation periods, reaching a peak in the late 3rd century (Perrin *et al.* 1996, table 76).

Dishes and bowls clearly increase in use through time at LF2, representing 18.2% and 24.9% of the total pottery assemblage respectively, with similar figures for these two groups of vessels at Orton Hall Farm. By contrast, plates, which are not represented at Orton Hall Farm, appear to have been used only during the military phase of Period 2 at LF2. It may be that the functions of plates during the later periods were taken over by shallow dishes. Jars seem to have been fairly ubiquitous throughout all periods, representing 38.9% of the total assemblage, but apparently slightly more common during the later periods. There has been no attempt, within the timescale allocated for the analysis of the pottery, to distinguish the great variation in jar sizes or the form of jars. Lid seated jars appear in increased numbers during the middle and later periods while jars with simple decorative bands around their girths are earlier and end by Period 4. Thereafter, the decoration on jars seems to have been confined to their shoulders and very occasionally their rims.

Specialist vessels such as cheese presses appear to increase in numbers over time, but their overall appearance within the collection is small (1.25% of the overall assemblage) and thus little can be said about them with confidence. On the other hand, Castor boxes do appear to increase from their first appearance during Period 5 to reach 42% of the total number of vessels represented at the site by Period 8. Similarly, lids, which are found in all periods except Period 2, also appear to increase in numbers — although again these numbers are small in actual terms.

For any of the periods represented at the site there would have been wooden, glass and metal vessels of all kinds which are not represented within the surviving evidence. Lids used either for covering food or to retain heat during cooking are found at the site (eighteen in number, representing 1.88% of the total assemblage) but the estimated numbers of jars with lid seating suggests that the eighteen surviving pottery lids were probably supplemented by many more lids made from wood, stone or cut-down broken pottery bases.

However, even though there was some selection of pottery for archiving during the excavation that may have skewed the pottery data somewhat, it may still be possible to pick out some general trends within the groupings of vessels and to speculate on possible diet, fashion or culinary changes. In general terms there seems to have been a trend towards the increased use of bowls and dishes during the later periods and this runs parallel with the rise of both mortaria and Castor boxes on the site. It could be suggested that food preparation and consumption was moving toward a greater emphasis on stews and casseroles where the pounding or mixing of ingredients was a prelude to their being cooked together in a single vessel and then served into dishes or bowls. Castor boxes are known from other sites at much earlier periods but the general trend is for them to increase in size during the later periods (Perrin 1999, 99–100) — perhaps another indication of the growing consumption of casserole-type meals. Such food consumption, indicated by Castor boxes, could contrast with the use of plates during Period 2, which would have allowed slightly drier food to have been eaten without the need for the 'dish like rim' required by wetter foods.

Variations in cooking methods are also worthy of consideration in terms of the way they may have influenced the ceramic assemblage. Thus Castor boxes may have been used to heat food within ovens while jars and other vessels may have been used over tripods or griddles to keep food hot or to simmer the contents (Perrin 1996, 179). The sooting on many of the vessels, including lids, clearly indicates that they came into contact with fires, but most of the actual cooking over fires would have been done in metal vessels, of which no evidence has survived.

The variations over time of the appearance of vessels from the LF2 site may indicate either changing fashions in food preparation and table dining or changes in the food supply. Of course, food fashion may have influenced food production but it is more likely that local agriculture simply produced what the environmental conditions allowed.

How perceptible changes in the ceramic assemblages and their links to food preparation, cooking and consumption at LF2 reflect broader aspects of the changing local geography and economy is beyond the scope of this present discussion. However, the local environment from which almost all the food would have been derived would have changed over the time of the site's occupation. We know of climatic variations during the Roman period which seem to have influenced the ways in which the nearby fenland and presumably the land along the line of the river Nene was managed from the 1st and 2nd centuries, when the area was drier, to the 3rd and 4th centuries, when it became wetter. Such variations in average weather conditions would have caused the local populations to respond in a variety of ways and, in simple terms, this can be seen in the breakdown of the numbers and management of stock and the quantities and extents of cropping and their relationship to soil types (see, for example, Jones 1996; Grove 1988; Dark 1996; Blackford and Chambers 1991; Potter 1981; 1989; 1996; Potter and Potter 1984; Phillips 1970, *passim*). Thus the overall analysis of the ceramic assemblage and the variation through time in the ways that differing forms of vessels are used on sites could reflect much broader environmental changes which have moulded the local and regional economies. Future work on the pottery collections from Nene valley sites and any connections between pottery and the geographical situations in which those sites are located might begin to fill in these gaps in our knowledge.

Although the range of pottery from LF2 is broad, both in the date range it spans and the repertoire of vessel types, there are some noticeable gaps in the forms of vessels which one might expect. For example, the limited presence of colour coated cups and beakers (thirty in total) has been already noted (in Table 5) — these forms of vessel appear to be absent from Period 7 onwards and are present only in small numbers in Periods 4–6. There are no plain rimmed beakers and only two fragments of cornice rimmed beakers from Period 5 and only one fragment of a folded beaker from Period 6. There are no scaled beakers or beakers with decorative, over-painted designs and certainly no fragments of 'hunt cups'. Such absences are to some extent odd and may reinforce the impression of a 'low-status rural settlement' which the samian suggests (see above). However, other low-status sites, such as that at Barnwell, produced a range of painted and scaled beakers (Upex forthcoming a, fig. 49), while at Orton Hall Farm Perrin (1996, 114–90) also describes a range of colour coated beakers with various forms of decoration.

The catalogue of pottery

The catalogue of pottery is organised into the chronological periods which are represented within the assemblage. The fabric of the vessel is given first (see the fabrics list below), followed by the colour of the vessels, which are matched with those of the 'Munsell Soil Colour Charts' (1971 edn) and are given in a 'range' form because the colour of many vessels' fabric and surfaces was rarely uniform and often had considerable variation (see colour range below). The colours below are given in numerical form prefixed by the letters CR and are listed below. Each entry has a site code (given within a bracket) which gives the area and context number. Where possible, the context of each sherd is given by reference to an illustrated section (e.g. S15) and Figure number. Then follows a description and any comparative detail.

Colour ranges

1	weak red	10R4/4, 2.5YR4/2
2	red	10R4/6, 2.5YR5/6, 2.5YR5/8
3	light red	10R6/6, 2.5YR6/6, 2.5YR6/8
4	reddish yellow	5YR5/6, 5YR6/6, 5YR6/8, 5YR7/6;
	yellowish red	5YR7/8, 7.5YR6/8, 7.5YR7.6, 7.5YR7/8, 7.5YR8/6
5	pink	5YR7/4, 5YR8/4, 7.5YR7/4, 7.5YR8/4
6	pinkish white	5YR8/2, 7.5YR8/2
7	pinkish grey	5YR6/2, 5YR7.2, 7.5YR6/2, 7.5YR7/2
8	reddish brown	2.5YR4/4, 2.5YR5/4, 5YR4/3, 5YR4/4, 5YR5/3, 5YR5/4
9	light reddish brown	2.5YR6/4, 5YR6/4
10	light brown	7.5YR6/4
11	brown	2.5YR5/2, 7.5YR5/2, 7.5YR5/3, 7.5YR5/4, 10YR5/3
12	dark brown	7.5YR3/2, 10YR4/3
13	dark reddish brown	5YR2.5/2, 5YR3/1
14	very pale brown	10YR7/3, 10YR7/4, 10YR8/3, 10YR8/4
15	light brownish grey	2.5YR6/2, 10YR6/2
16	greyish brown	10YR5/2, 2.5Y5/2
17	dark/very dark greyish brown	10YR3/2, 10YR4/2, 2.5Y3/2, 2.5Y4/2
18	light grey	5YR7/1, 7.5YR7/0, 10YR7/1, 10YR7/2, 2.5Y7/2, N7
19	light grey/grey	5YR6/1, 10YR6/1, N6, 5Y6/1
20	grey	10YR5/1, 5Y5/1, N5
21	dark grey	10YR4/1, 5Y4/1, N4
22	very dark grey	5YR3/1, 10YR3/1
23	light olive grey	5Y6/2
24	light blue grey	5B7/1
25	dark greenish grey	5BG4/1
26	white	5YR8/1, 7.5YR7/0, 10YR8/1, 10YR8/2, 2.5Y8/2
27	yellow	10YR7/6, 10YR8/6
28	black/reddish black	10R.2.5/1, 2.5YRN2.5/0, 5YR2.5/1, 10YR2.5/1, 2.5YN2.5/0, 5Y2.5/1, 5Y2.5/2

Notation

1. Where a number of different colours occur arbitrarily on the same vessel, the ranges are linked with a plus sign (e.g. 10+24).
2. Where the core varies from the surface the colours are separated by a solidus (e.g. 18/14/18). In these cases, the internal surface colour is given first, then the core, then the external surface. The colours of the surfaces can vary (e.g. 18/14/22).
3. Where there is a 'sandwich' core, the colour(s) of this are separated from the surface by a double solidus (e.g. 21//11/19/11//21).
4. Where the colour of a vessel is uniform except for just one surface, an en rule is used (e.g. 3–14). Sooting is not treated as a colour.
5. If the surface of a vessel has different coloured zones or areas, these are distinguished by a comma followed by text (e.g. 18/5/18,21 patches).
6. Colour ranges are not given for non-local wares which are described separately or adequately elsewhere.

Fabrics

LIASGW = Late Iron Age shell-gritted ware
LIA/RGTW = Late Iron Age/Roman grog-tempered ware
RSGW = Roman shell-gritted ware
RVTW = Roman vegetable-tempered ware
LNVRW = Lower Nene valley reduced ware; general dark grey/black finish produced in a reducing kiln atmosphere and not technically LNVGW but with a lower Nene valley fabric
LNVGW = lower Nene valley grey ware

LNVCCW = lower Nene valley colour coated ware
LNVCWW = lower Nene valley cream/white wares
LW = London ware
NVPIRP = Nene valley post-industrial Roman pottery
SAMIAN = samian
AMPH = amphorae
OXRW = Oxford red ware
OXMO = Oxford white ware
HADOX = Hadham red slipped ware
BB1 = Black burnished ware

Fabric 1. Fired black/grey with smooth finish. Some fine quartz sand inclusion

Fabric 2. Cream or cream/pink fired finish, with fine sand inclusion. Very hard finish with slightly abrasive exterior

Fabric 2a. As 2 above but with pink finish

Fabric 3. Fired red/orange brown with a slightly soapy but sandy feel. Rounded quartz sand inclusion

Fabric 4. Fired brown/grey with some oxidisation on outer surfaces. Very fine sandy inclusion

Fabric 5. Hard brittle surface fired grey/black with orange core. Fine sand inclusion giving slightly abrasive surface

Fabric 6. Grey/brown exterior surfaces with slightly greyer core. Very fine sand inclusion and slightly sandy feel to inner and outer surfaces. Hard fired

Fabric 7. Hard fired, grey exterior with lighter and slightly brown core. Very fine shell and sand inclusion

Fabric 8. Hard fired, grey exteriors with slightly brown/grey core. Soapy to touch although has very fine sand inclusion

Fabric 9. Very hard fired grey and abrasive surfaces. Sand inclusion

Fabric 10. Fired red/brown with grey core and medium sand inclusion

Fabric 11. Black/grey fired surfaces and core with considerable vegetable matter inclusions and soapy feel

Fabric 12. Crisp, hard fired pink/orange surfaces with either pink or grey core. Hard sand finish

Fabric 13. Smooth light brown/grey finish and black/grey core with slightly soapy feel

Fabric 14. Grey/brown exterior finish with grey core and open slightly soapy interior surfaces. Shell and sand inclusions

Fabric 15. Hard fired cream surfaces and core. Surfaces can have slightly brown/pink colouration

* Fabrics for mortaria are those given by Hartley 1996, 199

Iron Age pottery

Period I
Figure 80 nos 1–4
Eighty-three sherds of Iron Age pottery came from the site. These were divided into two fabric groups, consisting of shell-gritted wares (sixty-two sherds) and grog-tempered wares (twenty-one sherds). Most of the assemblage appeared to consist of hand-made vessels (sixty-two sherds representing 74.7% of the total). Hand-made sherds dominated at the site at Bretton Way, Peterborough (Upex 2011b), with a similar range of fabrics and forms to the Lynch Farm 2 material. As a collection, the LF2 material is limited by the small quantity of Iron Age sherds and vessels represented. However, the forms of the vessels appear to be similar to those from other local sites (Perrin 1988; 1996; Rollo and Wild 2001; Pryor 1984) and there is nothing to suggest that they are not all from local production sites. Most vessels appear to have been wiped when the surfaces were still wet and one vessel has decoration (no. 4 in the illustrated catalogue) in the form of a series of latticework lines drawn over the surface of the vessel, forming slightly burnished lines. The whole assemblage is best seen as falling into the period immediately prior to the Roman

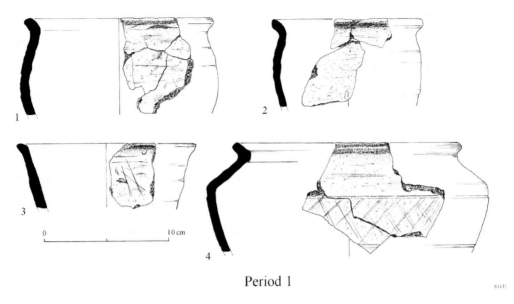

Period 1

Figure 80 Iron Age pottery, nos 1–4

invasion, although precise dating has been difficult and some sherds could easily be residual from much earlier in the Iron Age.

1. LIASGW. CR17–16 (LF2 73, II 282) Hand-made jar with shell tempering; exterior surfaces wiped. From Iron Age Pit F (see Pl. 7 and Fig. 14, S28).

2. LIASGW. CR17/16 (LF2 73, AII, 2) Hand-made jar with shell tempering; exterior surfaces wiped. From I/A Pit H (see Fig. 15, S36)

3. LIASGW. CR15+18/15+18 (LF2 73, II 300) Hand-made jar with shell tempering and some vegetable inclusion; exterior surfaces wiped. From I/A Pit L (see Fig. 15, S35)

4. LIASGW. CR21–21 (LF2 73, II 318) Wheel-thrown jar with shell inclusion. The rim is angular and appears to be lid seated; the wall of the jar has burnished, latticed decoration below the carination. From I/A Pit J (see Fig. 15, S37)

Roman pottery

Period 2
Figures 81 and 82 nos 5–34
The pottery from Period 2 contexts formed a mere 0.935% of the weight (1.34kg) of the total assemblage from the site, with 120 sherds, but makes up a significant group of early military pottery from the lower Nene valley. The material comes from either the defensive ditches of a fort or military camp or a series of pits found within this installation. Roman shell-gritted wares (RSGW) formed a single large fabric group (twenty sherds) and the rest of the assemblage consisted of another eighteen fabric groups, with sherd counts ranging from one to six sherds in each. The range of vessel forms was limited to cups and beakers, dishes, plates, jars and a single flagon. No detailed scientific analysis was carried out but most of the vessels seem to have been made at the Longthorpe military works depot, close to the Longthorpe fortress (Dannell and Wild 1987), where some of the styles, forms and fabrics of vessels are paralleled.

The LF2 bowls or beakers (see nos 5–6) are matched by nos 40 (a and b), 41 and 43 from Longthorpe (Dannell 1987, fig. 40). Some of the LF2 vessels have native forms; nos 8 and 22, for example, are matched by similar forms at Longthorpe. Further native forms include butt and girth beakers (no. 23), which, again, are matched at Longthorpe (Dannell 1987, fig. 39, 15, and 16a) and were also found within the Longthorpe fortress itself (Wilson 1974, fig. 52, 39–47)

The range of plates at LF2 is interesting. Twelve plates came from Period 2, four of which are illustrated (nos 14–17). All of the plate fragments are in Fabric Group 12, with an orange/red coating, again matching the finishes and fabric ranges from the Longthorpe kilns (see Dannell 1987, table VII), where the forms are identical (Dannell 1987, fig. 39, nos 29b–37). That the vessel illustrated here as no. 14 is identical to a vessel from Longthorpe (Dannell 1987, fig. 39 no. 33) is uncanny and clearly shows that the source of the two assemblages is the same. The majority of the plates find their origins in samian forms and must be an attempt by the potters to produce vessels that would sit on the same table as imported wares.

The remaining vessels are mostly jars in shell-gritted fabrics and are all considered to be of local manufacture, again matching the fabrics from the Longthorpe military depot site (Dannell and Wild 1987). Some of the jars have external scored ring decoration on the shoulders (see nos 30, 33 and 34), which again can be matched both at the depot site (Dannell 1987, fig. 42, nos 68a, 71a and 74) and at the fortress (Wilson 1974, fig. 53, nos 82, 87, 93 and 95). Some jars have lid seated rims (no. 31) and a single lid was also present (no. 12).

The collection of vessels from Period 2 (shown in Table 10) represents a fairly broad set of table and cooking wares. Only three dishes and one bowl (no. 13) are recognisable, compared with the greater number of both forms of vessels found at the Longthorpe Depot site. However, making such a comparison between the two assemblages is hardly statistically valid because of the small size of the LF2 collection. The collection does indicate, on the other hand, that a fairly broad range of both cooking and table wares was being used at the site and may suggest that the military installation in which they were found was something more than just a temporary camp.

As to dating the LF2 military phase, the assemblage matches so well the collections from both the Longthorpe fortress and the military depot site that the date ranges must be very similar: that is, within the period *c.* AD 44–62 (Frere and St Joseph 1974, 36–8).

5. Fabric 12. CR9/18/9 (LF2 72, IV 12). From Military Pit 2 (see Fig. 11 S46)

6. Fabric 13. CR9/20/10 (LF2, IV 49). From Military Pit 4 (see Fig. 11 S123

7. Fabric 3. CR9/18/9 (LF2 73, IV 47). From Military Pit 3 (see Fig. 11 S123

8. Fabric 12. CR 9/18/9 (LF2 72, Tr 71 12). From military inner defensive ditch (see Fig. 10 S44)

9. Fabric 12. CR9/18/9 (LF2 72, IV 50). From Military Pit 5 (see Fig. 11 S124)

10. Fabric 13. CR9/18/9 (LF2 72, IV 22). From Military Pit 1 (see Fig. 11 S45)

11. Fabric 12. CR9/18/9 (LF2 72, Tr 71 12). From military inner defensive ditch (see Fig. 10 S44)

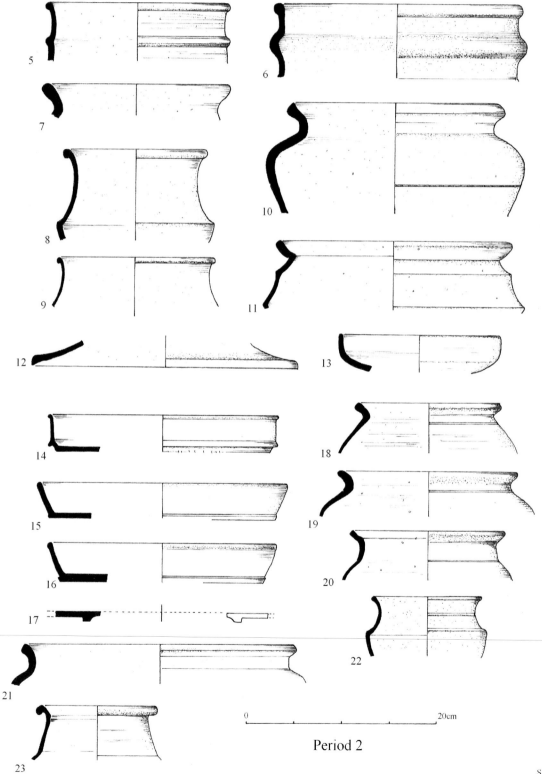

Period 2

0   20cm

S.G.U.

Figure 81 Roman pottery, nos 5–23, Period 2

12. Fabric 12. CR6/5/7 (LF2 72, II 263). From military inner defensive ditch (see Fig. 10 S42)

13. Fabric 12. CR6/5/7 (LF2 72, II 249). From military outer defensive ditch (see Fig. 10 S40)

14. Fabric 12. CR6/18/6 with a red finish or colour coat (LF2 72, B 73). From military inner defensive ditch (see Fig. 45 was 46 S125)

15. Fabric 12. CR6/18/6 with a red finish or colour coat (LF2 72, II 263). From military inner defensive ditch (see Fig. 10 S42)

16. Fabric 12. CR6/18/6 with a red finish or colour coat (LF2 72, V 47). From Military Pit 1 (see Fig. 11 S122)

17. Fabric 12. CR6/26/18 with an inner red finish of colour coat, the outer (lower) surface is in grey (LF2 72, B 53). From military outer defensive ditch (see Fig. 45 was 46 S125)

18. Fabric 6. CR23/21/23 (LF2 72, II 263). From military inner defensive ditch (see Fig. 10 S42)

19. Fabric 6. CR24/24/24 (LF2 72, I 22). From Military Pit 1 (see Fig. 11 S45)

20. Fabric 6. CR24/24/24 (LF2 72, II 248). Possible waster? From military outer defensive ditch (see Fig. 10 S41)

21. Fabric 13. CR3/20/16+18 (LF2 72, IV 22). From Military Pit 1 (see Fig. 11 S45)

22. Fabric 9. CR19/18/19 (LF2 72, B 53). From military outer defensive ditch (see Fig. 45 was 46 S125)

23. Fabric 13. CR14/18/14 slightly burnished finish (LF2 72, I 22). From Military Pit 1 (see Fig. 11 S45)

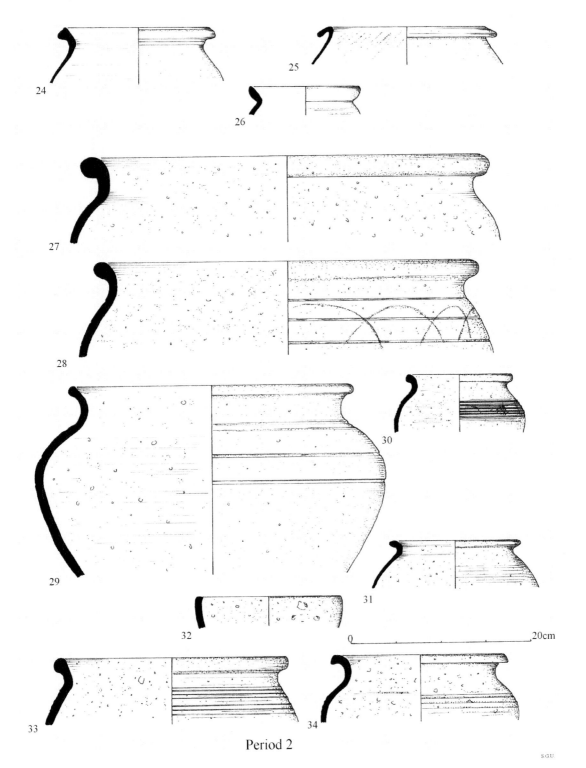

Period 2

Figure 82 Roman pottery, nos 24–34, Period 2

129

24. Fabric 14. CR14/15/14 slight burnishing on outer surface (LF2 73, IV 49). From Military Pit 4 (see Fig. 11 S123)

25. Fabric 14. CR14/15/14 slightly soapy feel (LF2 72, B 53). From military outer defensive ditch (see Fig. 45 was 46 S125)

26. BB1(?) CR22/21/21 external burnishing (LF2 73, IV 49). From Military Pit 4 (see Fig. 11 S123)

27. RSGW CR3/19/3 heavy shell inclusion up to 5mm (LF2 73, IV 22). From Military Pit 1 (see Fig. 11 S45)

28. RSGW CR9+15/1/3 heavy shell inclusion with some angular limestone fragments up to 5mm (LF2 73, IV 19). From Military Pit 1 (see Fig. 11 S45)

29. Fabric 14 CR 15+1+18/21/15+1+18 slight burnishing on rim and shoulder (LF2 73, IV 22). From Military Pit 1 (see Fig. 11 S45)

30. RSGW CR28/1/21 fine shell inclusion with some quartz sand grains up to 1mm (LF2 73, II 50). From Military Pit 5 (see Fig. 11 S124)

31. RSGW CR 10/18/17+18+16 (LF2 72, IV 22). From Military Pit 1 (see Fig. 11 S45)

32. RVTW (?) CR17/18/28 voids within fabric (LF2 72, B 53). From military outer defensive ditch (see Fig. 11 S125)

33. RSGW CR15/20/22+16 (LF2 73, IV 49). From Military Pit 4 (see Fig. 11 S123)

34. RSGW CR7/16/18+21 (LF2 72, IV 11). From Military Pit 2 (see Fig. 11 S46)

Period 3
Figures 83–85 nos 35–84

The pottery from Period 3 consists of 639 sherds weighing a total of 7.388kg. Most of this material comes from ditches which show evidence of recutting or realignment over a very short space of time and in part were cut into the former ditches of the military installation on the site. The collection shows the beginnings of the local grey ware industry, with some of the earliest grey ware forms known from the lower Nene valley. Grey ware represents one-third of the sherds from this period, the rest comprising shell-gritted ware (301 sherds), lower Nene valley reduced wares (sixty-one sherds) and seven other fabric groupings, all represented by very small sherd numbers (see Table 8).

Jars seem to dominate the material within this period with sixty-nine examples identified within the assemblage; cup and beakers come next with six examples and the rest of the identifiable forms consist of small numbers of bowls, colanders, mortaria, dishes, flagons, lids, and a single example of a cheese press.

The group is best paralleled by vessels from Monument 97 at Orton Longueville (Rollo and Wild 2001), Orton Hall Farm (Perrin 1996) and Haddon (Rollo 1994, 89–131), where jars again seem to have dominated. Several vessel forms from LF2 are early forms of beakers in grey ware. Some, such as no. 56, occur in a fabric that harks back to Period 2 type fabrics but are fired so as to produce a 'grey ware' and possibly represent the beginnings of the grey ware industry in the lower Nene valley. There are also 'girth type' beaker forms (nos 40–41) fired as grey ware products. Such vessels clearly bring an earlier tradition of vessel types, fired previously in oxidised atmospheres, into a period when grey ware production was becoming more common and fashionable.

Early jar forms with external decoration (see no. 35) are present within the group and must be very early forms of the vessels which appear commonly in the 2nd century (see Perrin 1999, fig. 56 nos 3–10). Wide-mouthed jars in grey ware are common, while jars with a wide mouth and angular profile (nos 49–51) in either grey ware or grey sandy fabrics are also common and are paralleled at Monument 97 and Orton Hall Farm (Rollo and Wild 2001, 65–8; Perrin *et al.* 1996 figs 84–85); the jars with a more angular profile (nos 48 and 52), although less common, are also present (see Potter and Potter 1982, 55, fig. 24, 106). Certain jars have been produced with narrow mouths (see no. 69) which perhaps shows an earlier beaker type form indicating a possible 'Belgic' origin.

Shell-gritted wares tend to be reserved for the larger vessels and these consist of jars of various sizes (nos 79–80 and 82), dishes (no. 81) and large bowls (no. 83). One 'base' in shell-gritted ware (no. 84) is difficult to interpret and may be the lower part of a jar or beaker, but could equally be a vessel in its own right and may have formed a holder or base to support some other vessel (possibly of glass?). Number 74 may be a plate or dish and thus similar to one from Monument 97 (Rollo and Wild 2001, fig. 35, no. 53) but the form is hard to assign, although it seems diagnostically to belong to the Flavian period (see Corder 1961, 44, 15, 39).

Vessels 56–67 all come from a single fill of Ditch 4 (Area II, layer 171, see Fig. 12 and Fig. 15 S35) that produced sixty-eight sherds, weighing 1.39kg. Many of the fragments were large and the deposit must represent material deposited very shortly after its breakage. Like the rest of the pottery from this period of the site's history, the repertoire from layer 171 contains beakers, jars and bowls, including a decorated wide-mouthed jar (no. 65 — Fabric Group 1) and the base of another jar or bowl with a burnished decorated lower body (no. 68).

Vessel no. 67 is a 'waster' and an early attempt at producing a form of what later became the standard Nene valley 'dog dish'. There are several other waster fragments (not illustrated). From this period that appear to be related to the kiln located within the area of the encircling ditched enclosure (see Fig. 18 plan, S121) — two other vessels which came from the bowl of this kiln are illustrated as nos 40 and 72. This kiln is sealed by layer 97 (see Fig. 18 S121) which contained sherds of 'London ware'-type pottery (not illustrated) and could indicate a kiln date within the late Flavian period or perhaps slightly later — thus making it one of the earliest post-military kilns known from the Nene valley.

The Period 3 assemblage does not contain any examples of the grey ware jars with slashed cordons dated to the second quarter of the 2nd century (see Perrin 1999, 80; Hadman and Upex 1975a, 16–18), nor are there any colour coated wares, which may indicate that this industry had yet to start when the final deposits were being made in Period 3. The best parallels for the group as a whole come from Monument 97 in Orton Longueville, where they are dated to before *c.* AD 125, and from Orton Hall Farm, where the dating is less tight (mid-1st century–*c.* AD 175) and colour coated products are present within the range of vessels. The dating of the deposits from LF2 is best viewed as running from *c.* AD 60–65 to *c.* AD 120–30.

Figure 83 nos 35–55

35. LNVGR CR 19/18/19 (LF2 73, II 126). From upper fill of Ditch 5 (see Fig. 17, S49)

36. LNVGW CR19/19/19 (LF2 73, II 6). From Ditch 4 **Same context as 68 in S60** (see Fig. 16)

37. LNVGW CR19/18/19 (LF2 73, II 216). From Ditch 4 (see Fig. 15, S39)

38. Fabric 5 CR 16/18/22 (LF2 73, II 122). From upper fill of Ditch 4 (see Fig. 15, S35)

39. LNVGW CR 19/19/19 (LF2 72, I 18). From upper fill of Ditch 4 (see Fig. 16 S63)

40. LNVGW CR20/20/19 (LF2 73, II 104). From within firing chamber of kiln (see Fig. 18, S121)

41. LNVGW CR20/18/22/18/20 (LF2 73, II 76). From bottom fill of Ditch 4

42. LNVGW CR19/19/19 (LF2 73, II 50). From fill of Ditch 4. (see Fig. 16 S62)

43. LNVGW CR19/18/19 (LF2 73, II 50). From fill of Ditch 4. (see Fig. 16 S62)

44. LNVGW CR21/20/21 (LF2 73, II 6). From lower fill of Ditch 4

45. LNVRW CR22/18/21/18/22 (LF2 73, II 219). From Ditch 4 (see Fig. 16 S61)

46. LNVRW CR20/20/20 (LF2 72, II 8). Lower fill of Ditch 3

47. Fabric 13 CR9/21/9 (LF2 73, II, 213). From lower fill of Ditch 4

48. LNVRW CR22/21/22 (LF2 73, II 171). Mid-fill of Ditch 4 (see Fig. 15 S35)

49. Fabric 9 CR16/20/16 (LF2 73 II 188). Lower fill of pit in Trench 11 (see Fig. 13 S128)

50. Fabric 6 CR15/16/15 fired with a grey ware finish (LF2 73, II 171). From fill of Ditch 4 (see Fig. 15 S35)

51. LNVGW CR19/21/19 (LF2 72, II 180). Lower fill of pit in Trench 11 (see Fig. 13 S128)

52. Fabric 5/LNVRW CR22/9/20/9/22 (LF2 73, II 77) Lower fill of Ditch 3 (see Fig. 16 S62)

53. Fabric 5 CR 22/20/9/20/22 (LF2 73, II 331). Lower fill of Ditch 3 (see Fig. 15 S36)

54. Fabric 4 CR18/22/15+20 (LF2 73, II 50). From Ditch 3 **Same context as 77 in S62** (see Fig. 16)

55. Fabric 4 CR 16/19/16 (LF2 73, II 71). Lower fill of pit in Trench 11 (see Fig. 13 S128)

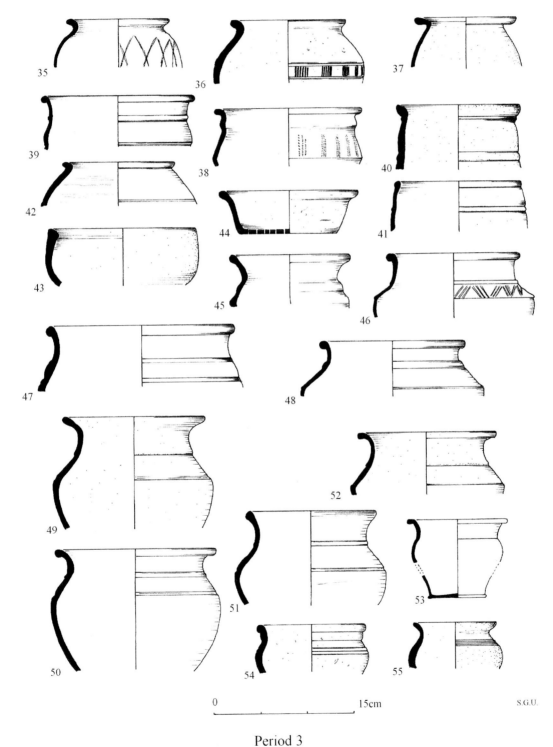

0   15cm   S.G.U.

Period 3

Figure 83 Roman pottery, nos 35–55, Period 3

131

56. Fabric 7, CR20/18/20 fired as grey ware (LF2 73, II 171). From middle fill of Ditch 4 (see Fig. 12 and Fig. 15 S35)

57. RSGW CR17/21/21 (LF2 73, II 171). From middle fill of Ditch 4 (see Fig. 12 and Fig. 15 S35)

58. RSGW CR17/22/14+18 (LF2 73, II 171). From middle fill of Ditch 4 (see Fig. 12 and Fig. 15 S35)

59. RSGW CR10/16/18+16 (LF2 73, II 171). From middle fill of Ditch 4 (see Fig. 12 and Fig. 15 S35)

60. RSGW CR16/20/9 (LF2 73, II 171). From middle fill of Ditch 4 (see Fig. 12 and Fig. 15 S35)

61. Fabric 6 CR15/19/15 fired as grey ware (LF2 73, II 171). From middle fill of Ditch 4 (see Fig. 12 and Fig. 15 S35)

62. Fabric 6 CR15/19/15 fired as grey ware (LF2 73, II 171). From middle fill of Ditch 4 (see Fig. 12 and Fig. 15 S35)

63. LNVGW CR20/18/20 (LF2 73, II 171). From middle fill of Ditch 4 (see Fig. 12 and Fig. 15 S35)

64. LNVGW CR20/18/20 (LF2 73, II 171). From middle fill of Ditch 4 (see Fig. 12 and Fig. 15 S35)

65. Fabric 1 CR28/20/28 (LF2 73, II 171). From middle fill of Ditch 4 (see Fig. 12 and Fig. 15 S35)

66. Fabric 8 CR19/19/19 (LF2 73, II 171). From middle fill of Ditch 4 (see Fig. 12 and Fig. 15 S35)

67. LNVGW CR 20/19/21 waster; early attempt at a dog dish? (LF2 73, II 171). From middle fill of Ditch 4 (see Fig. 12 and Fig. 15 S35)

68. LNVSGW CR17/21/22 slight burnishing on exterior (LF2 73, II 171). From middle fill of Ditch 4 (see Fig. 12 and Fig. 15 S35)

69. Fabric 6 CR15/19/15 fired as grey ware (LF2 73, II 171). From middle fill of Ditch 4 (see Fig. 15 S35)

70. LNVGW CR18/18/18 (LF2 73, II 171). From middle fill of Ditch 4 (see Fig. 15 S35)

71. LNVGW (?) CR16/10/16 (LF2 72, II 70). Fill of Ditch 3 (see Fig. 16 S63)

72. LNVGW CR18/18/20 (LF2 73, II 104). From firing chamber of kiln (see Fig. 18 S121)

73. LNVGW CR20/20/21 (LF2 72, I 22). From Ditch 4 (see Fig. 16 S63)

74. Fabric 6 CR16/19/16 (LF2 73, II 90). From Ditch 4

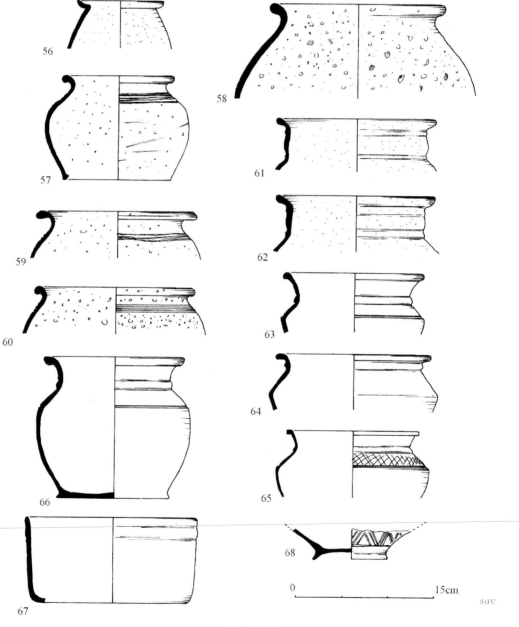

Period 3
Context II, 171

Figure 84 Roman pottery, nos 56–68, Period 3, context II, 171

75. RSGW CR21/21/22 very fine 0.5mm shell inclusion (LF2 72, I 19). From fill of Ditch 4 (see Fig. 16 S63)

76. RSGW CR22/21/22 (LF2 73, II 120). Upper fill of Ditch 4

77. RSGW CR13+20/19/19+3 (LF2 73, II 197). Lower fill of Ditch 4

78. RSGW CR1/1/1 (LF2 72 II 180). Lower fill of pit in Trench 11 (see Fig. 13 S128)

79. RSGW CR13/16/14+20 (LF2 73, II 75). Middle fill of Ditch 4

80. RSGW CR16/20/20 (LF2 73, II 171). Middle fill of Ditch 4 (see Fig. 15 S35)

81. RSGW CR10/21/10+3 (LF2 73, II 2). From the middle fill of Ditch 4 (see Fig. 16 S66)

82. RSGW CR8/18/8 (LF2 72 I 18). Upper fill of Ditch 4 (see Fig. 16 S63)

83. RSGW CR14/20/5+21 inclusion of flint and limestone up to 3mm (LF2 73, II 187). Same context as II 219, from fill of Ditch 4 (see Fig. 16 S61 context 219)

84. RSGW CR 10+9/21/10+9 (LF2 73, II 192). From lower fill of large pit (see Fig. 13 S128)

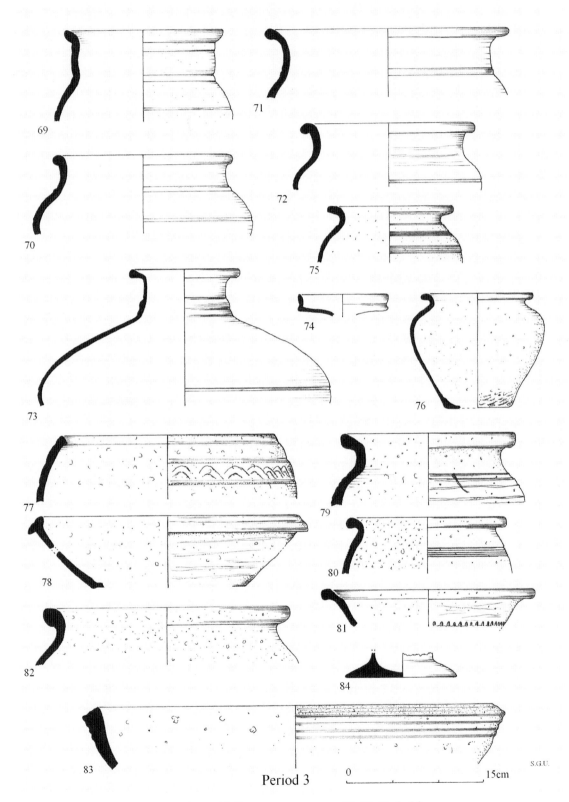

Figure 85 Roman pottery, nos 69–84, Period 3

133

Period 4

Figure 86 nos 85–96

The pottery from contexts related to Period 4 deposits consisted of 531 sherds weighing 6.78kg. The collection was dominated by shell-gritted wares (211 sherds) and grey wares (186 sherds), with the introduction of colour coated wares (ninety-eight sherds) and cream wares (nine sherds) seen at the site for the first time. In addition, there were five other fabric groups present (see Tables 8 and 9) and five sherds of London-type ware. Of the identifiable vessels (see Table 10), jars dominate, followed by bowls (sixteen) and mortaria (six), which were introduced to the site's assemblage in Period 3.

There are five fragments of London ware, all from bowls and all appearing to imitate samian form 30 vessels. The two illustrated sherds (nos 85 and 86), although described as London Ware, are probably local products and both in fabric and motif are similar to vessels from Chesterton, Ashton and Normangate Field (Castor — all as yet unpublished). The fabrics could easily fit into either the LNVGW or the LNVRW categories used within this report.

The LNVCCW beakers (nos 89 and 90) may represent products from the beginning of the colour coated industry in the lower Nene valley, while the appearance of a candle (or rush) holder (no. 93) is a rare find (see Perrin 1999, fig. 67, nos 364 and 365 for other candle holders).

This group of pottery is best dated to the mid–late 2nd century. London ware products are poorly understood at present but probably fall within the range *c.* AD 140–200 (Perrin 1999, 106–8), with some vessels from Stanground being produced into the early 3rd century (Dannell 1973; Dannell *et al.* 1993).

85. LW CR20/20/20 (LF2 72, IV 4). Late 2nd-century packing over Military Pit 1 (see Fig. 11 S45)

86. LW CR21/20/21 (LF2 73, II 235). Fill of Ditch 6 (see Fig. 19) (same context as 144; shown in Fig. 24 S56)

87. LNVGW CR18/18/18 (LF2 73, II 72). Upper fill of large pit (see Fig. 13 S128)

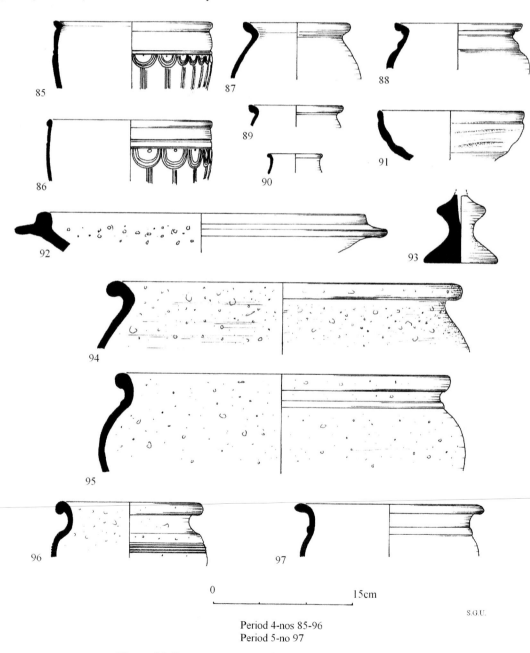

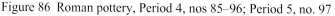

0   15cm

S.G.U.

Period 4-nos 85–96
Period 5-no 97

Figure 86 Roman pottery, Period 4, nos 85–96; Period 5, no. 97

134

88. LNVGW CR18/19/18 (LF2 73 C 52). Fill of gully 52 (see Fig. 51 and Fig. 54 was 55 S79)

89. LNVCCW CR10/9/10 (LF2 73, II 99). Fill of ditch C2 (see Fig. 24 S57)

90. LNVCCW CR17/26/17 (LF2 73, II 59). Top filling of Ditch 4

91. LNVGW CR18/18/18 (LF2 73, II 72). Upper fill of large pit (see Fig. 13 S128)

92. LNVCWW (?) CR5+6/26/7/5+6+26 (LF2 73, II 74). Upper fill of large pit (see Fig. 13 S128)

93. RSGW CR14/16/14+18 (LF2 73, II 76). A candle stick? Upper fill of large pit (see Fig. 13 S128)

94. RSGW CR11/20/3 slightly burnished exterior (LF2 73, II 72). Upper/middle fill of large pit (see Fig. 13 S128)

95. RSGW CR8/21/22+2 (LF2 72, C 16). Fill of ditch C2 (see Fig. 50)

96. RSGW CR8/21/22+2 (LF2 73, II 72). Upper/middle fill of large pit (see Fig. 13 S128)

Period 5
Fig. 86. No. 97
Period 5 contexts produced limited quantities of pottery (239 sherds weighing 2.76kg) compared with the earlier periods of the site and the range of fabric types was also reduced in number, with colour coated wares providing the most sherds (ninety-nine) (see Table 8). The assemblage of individual vessels which can be identified from this period is probably too small to make any viable comment, but jars and bowls dominate. This material is dated to the early 3rd century.

97. LNVCWW CR26/18/26 (LF2 72, C 44) (see Fig. 54 was 55 S79/S80)

Period 6
Figure 87 nos 98–120
This period provides the most pottery of any period by sherd count (2,460) and by weight (49.162kg), representing 28.44% of the site's sherd count and 34.30% of the total weight of pottery at the site. Much of this material came from the extensive range of ditches in the eastern part of the site which were being gradually filled during the late 3rd and early 4th centuries. LNVCCW dominated at this period, with 1,091 sherds, followed by LNVGW (891) and RSGW (458). Imports into the area from the Oxfordshire kilns (nos 99 and 118) and from Hadham (no. 120) also appear for the first time and match the situation on other local sites where imports from these two centres occur during the late 3rd and early 4th centuries (see, for example, pottery from Chesterton, Barnwell and Orton Hall Farm: Perrin 1999, 126–7; Upex forthcoming a, fig. 55; Perrin 1996).

The forms of the vessels from this period (see Table 10) are also of interest, with jars (nos 109–114), bowls (nos 99–100) and dishes dominating. The period also sees a rise in mortaria (nos 117–118) and Castor boxes (no. 103). All of these forms of vessel may indicate a change from previous periods in the format of table dining or food preparation, with casseroles and stews becoming more common.

All of the pottery from contexts of this period is matched by vessels from other dated sites. LNVCCW products, some with over-painted designs (see, for example, no. 100, which is matched at Chesterton: see Perrin 1999, fig. 63, no. 246), are in forms that range from the illustrated mortarium (no. 117) to flanged bowls (nos 105–108), and all are represented within other dated groups from Ashton, Chesterton, Orton Hall Farm, Barnwell and the Normangate Field excavations (1962–3 and 1968–74) at Castor (Ashton and Normangate Field,

Castor (1968–74) remain unpublished; Perrin 1999; 1996; Upex forthcoming a; Perrin and Webster 1990).

98. LNVGW CR16/20/20 (LF2 72, C 34). From Ditch C3, shown in Fig. 50 (same as context 42 see Fig. 54 S82/S83)

99. OXRW CR2/2/2 (LF2 72, B 18). From upper fill of ditch B2 (see Figs 44 and 47 S104)

100. LNVCCW CR14/26/14 with over-painted decoration in white slip (LF2 72, B 18). From upper fill of ditch B2 (see Figs 44 and 47 S104)

101. LNVGW CR20/21/20 (LF2 72 B 6). Fill of ditch B9 (see Figs 44 and 48 S109)

102. LNVCCW CR15/27/10 (LF2 72, B 94). From upper fill of B1 (see Figs 44 and 49 S116)

103. LNVCCW CR12/16/12 (LF2 72, II 29). Fill of ditch 7 (see Figs 37 and 38 S52)

104. LNVCCW CR19/20/20+16+12 (LF2 72, C 23). From underneath wall to W of Area C (see Fig. 52)

105. LNVCCW CR11/18/22 (LF2 72, B 46). From ditch complex B12. See Fig. 46 was 45 (same fill as context B 38 shown in Fig. 49 S120)

106. LNVCCW CR17/18/17 (LF2 72, B 27). From packing around Well I (see schematic section Fig. 43)

107. LNVCCW CR21/13/21 (LF2 72, B 27). From packing around Well I (see schematic section Fig. 43)

108. LNVCCW CR9/18/9 (LF2 72, B 38). Fill of ditch B12 (see Figs 44 and 49 S120)

109. RSGW CR12+20/21/12+20 (LF2 72, B 78). Fill of Ditch (see Figs 46 was 45 and 48 S114)

110. LNVCCW CR24/26/24 (LF2 72, B 27). From packing around Well I (see schematic section Fig. 43)

111. LNVCCW CR14/26/14 (LF2 72, B 27). From packing around Well I (see schematic section Fig. 43)

112. LNVCCW CR24/16/24 (LF2 72, B 4). Upper fill of Ditch B4 (see Figs 44 and 48 S108)

113. LNVCCW CR24/18/24 (LF2 72, B 94). Upper fill from B1 (see Figs 44 and 49 S116)

114. LNVCCW CR14/26/14 (LF2 72, B 20). Lower fill of ditch B3 (see Figs 44 and 47 S103)

115. LNVCWW CR26/26/26+28 (LF2 72, B 77). Fill of Ditch B13 (context as B78; see Figs 46 was 45 and 48 S114)

116. LNVCWW CR26/26/26 mortarium; no trituration grit present but a local product and similar to a vessel from Barnwell dated to the late 4th century (Upex forthcoming a, fig. 53, 94). Hartley Fabric 1 (LF2 72, B 94) upper fill from Pit B1 (see Figs 44 and 49 S166)

117. LNVCWW CR26/26/26 Hartley Fabric 1 (LF2 72, B 18) fill of Ditch B2 (see Figs 44 and 47, S104). Mortarium, local black trituration grit. For a similar vessel see Hartley and Perrin 1999, fig. 78, no M48; Upex forthcoming a, fig. 53, 96. Both these vessels were dated to the 4th century.

118. OXMO CR26/26/26 with slight wash of CR16 over finish; red/pink and grey angular trituration grit (LF2 72, II 1). From Ditch 7 (see Figs 37 and 38 S50)

119. LNVCCW CR 22/2/22 with over-painted white design (LF2 73, II 187). Mid fill of Ditch 6 (see Figs 19 and 24 S54)

120. HAD OX CR10/20/10 embossed decoration (LF2 73, II 28). From floor area of aisled building above sag in Ditch 3. For a similar vessel see Stead and Rigby 1986, fig. 155, no. 749 dated to the late 4th century

Period 7
Figure 88 nos 121–137
The mid-4th-century deposits of Period 7 represent only 11.97% of the total assemblage by sherd count and 8.0% by weight. However, the proportion of LNVCCW, which forms the largest fabric group (617 sherds), is considerable. LNVGW has only 283 sherds present and RSGW accounts for only 109 sherds of this period's assemblage. The numbers of bowls exceeds jars for the first time and dishes are also present in increased numbers, while mortaria and Castor boxes also appear to increase in popularity. The contexts from which this material is mainly derived consists of the series of ditches within the eastern part of the site.

All of the pottery can be dated by comparison with other datable groups from local sites such as Chesterton, Orton Hall Farm, Barnwell, Normangate Field Castor (1962–3 excavations) Ashton (unpublished) and Normangate Field, Castor (1968–74 excavations, unpublished) (Perrin 1999; 1996; Upex forthcoming a; Perrin and Webster 1990).

121. LNVCCW CR11/18/11 (LF2 72, B 28). Fill of Ditch complex B12 (same as context B 52 shown in Fig. 49 S119)

122. LNVCCW CR10/18/10 (LF2 72, C 3). Fill of Ditch C7 (see Figs 50 and 54 was 55 S84–87)

123. LNVCCW CR 21/20/16 (LF2 72, C 3). Fill of Ditch C7 (see Figs 50 and 54 was 55 S84–87)

124. LNVCCW CR9/3/9 slight 'glazing' on inner surfaces (LF2 73, III 9). From upper layers within Ditch 7 (same as 1 and 133 in S50 and S51; see Fig. 38)

125. LNVCWW CR7/18/7 with over-painted brown (CR10) decoration on rim (LF2 73, II 87). From upper layers within Ditch 7 (same as 1 in S50; see Fig. 38)

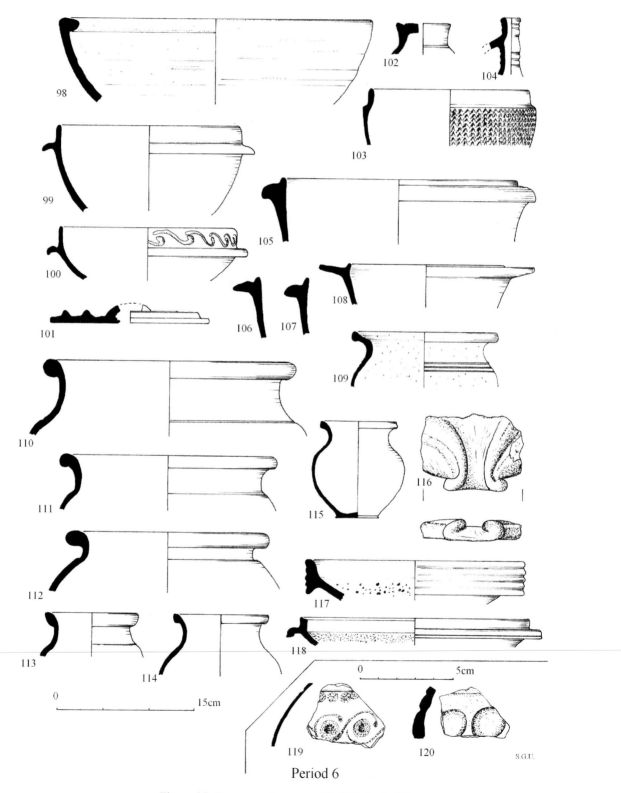

Period 6

Figure 87 Roman pottery, nos 98–120, Period 6

126. LNVGW CR21/21/21 slightly sandy feel (LF2 72, B 28). From Ditch complex B12 (same as context B 52 shown in Fig. 49 S119)

127. LNVGW (?) CR24/21/24 (LF2 73, II 87). From upper layers within Ditch 7 (same as 1 in S50; see Fig. 38)

128. LNVCCW CR15//3/4/3/15 (LF2 72, C 3). Fill of Ditch C7 (see Figs 51 and 54 was 55 S84–87)

129. LNVCCW CR21/2 (LF2 72, C 3). Fill of Ditch C7 (see Figs 51 and 54 was 55 S84–87)

130. LNVCCW CR21/26/21+9 (LF2 73, II 45). From fill of Ditch A7 (same as II 133, shown in Fig. 38 S51)

131. LNVGW CR20/18/20 (LF2 73, II 87). From upper fill of Ditch A7 (same as II 1, shown in Fig. 38 S50)

132. LNVGW CR21/26/21 (LF2 72, C 28). From bottom of 'sump' (see Fig. 53 S72 and S73)

133. LNVGW CR21/22/21 slightly sandy finish (LF2 72, C 5). From within 'sump' (same as context C 2 in Fig. 53 S71)

134. LNVCCW CR 9/9/17 (LF2 72, B 28). From Ditch complex B12 (same as context B 52 shown in Fig. 49 S119)

135. LNVCCW CR 13/18/13 (LF2 73, II 23). From fill of Ditch A7 (as II 29 in Fig. 38 S52)

136. LNVGW CR 18/20/18 (LF2 73, II 87). From upper layers within Ditch A7 (same as 1 in Fig. 38 S50)

137. RSGW CR13/20/13+18 (LF2 72, D 23). Fill of Ditch C8 (same as context C 30 shown in Figs 51 and 56 S96)

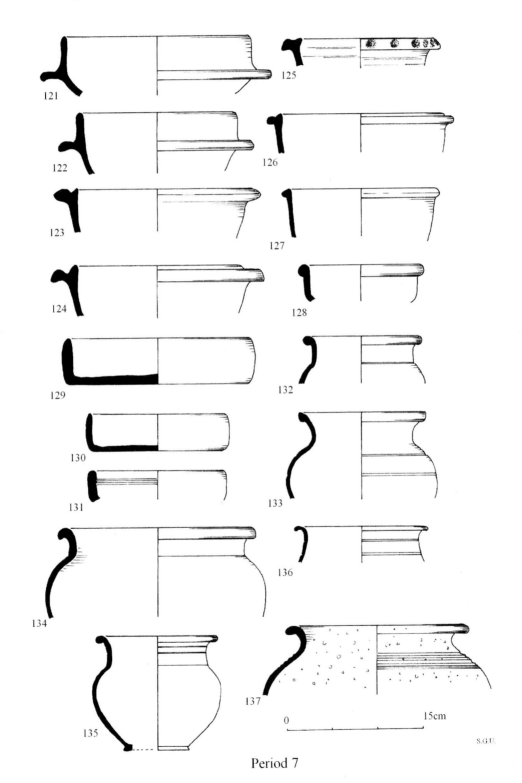

Period 7

Figure 88 Roman pottery, nos 121–137, Period 7

S.G.U.

Period 8
Figures 89 and 90 nos 138–171
The pottery from Period 8 contexts forms the second largest grouping from the LF2 site, with 24.39% of sherds and 29.7% of total pottery weight. As in Periods 6 and 7, the contexts from which this material is derived consist of the fills of the series of ditches located within the eastern part of the site, the fills from the 'sump' in Area C and the two wells. LNVCCW again dominates at this period by sherd count with 1,171 sherds, which is about half as much again as the second largest fabric group consisting of LNVGW products (647 sherds). Oxford and Hadham products are found in very small numbers and the appearance of NVPIRP is exclusive to this last period of the site's occupation (see Table 8).

Bowls (eighty-one examples), dishes (seventy-one) and jars (seventy-four) are found in roughly equal numbers, while mortaria (eighteen examples) and Castor boxes (eight examples) are ever-present. Cheese presses, which first appeared in Period 3 contexts (see Table 10) with a single example, are now represented by six examples (see also no. 101 for an example from Period 6) and could imply a growing liking for cheese products, a change in agricultural production practices or simply that the vessels in pottery forms were replacing similar wooden examples. Lids are present in their highest numbers during this period (seven examples) although the bases of broken vessels (which are present within the assemblage) and, again, wooden examples could also have served similar functions.

The dating of the group can be linked to some of the latest dated sites within the Nene valley. The range of bowls and dishes, including the large repertoire of flanged bowls, some so well fired that the surface of the vessels had a sheen on them, matches the material from the pottery production site at Stibbington, which dated to the late 4th and early 5th centuries (Perrin 2008, fig. 19, nos 42–49). The mortaria from LF2 may well be, in part, Stibbington products (compare for example LF2 nos 155–156 with Perrin 2008, fig. 24, nos 128–129). Similarly, vessels 146–147 from LF2 with an exaggerated curved shoulder are identical to vessels from the Stibbington kilns (see Perrin 2008, fig. 22, nos 109–112).

The range of LNVCCW with over-painting (nos 154 and 157) is also diagnostic of late Nene valley production (cf. Perrin 2008, fig. 25, nos 149, 157; fig. 26, nos 158–166 and fig. 28, no. 182), especially on flasks and shallow dishes. Some of these vessels and others within the date range at LF2 are also comparable with the latest sequences from Great Casterton, which are dated *c.* AD 375 or 'perhaps considerably later' (Corder 1951, 24–40; Perrin 1981). A series of vessels similar to no. 154 from LF2 certainly occurs at Haddon in contexts dated to the period after *c.* AD 380 (Upex 1993; the pottery remains unpublished at present).

Various forms of grey wares are present, some from contexts that are unstratified but which are presumed to be late. No. 178 for example is paralleled at Haddon by a similar vessel from a late context (Evans 2003, fig. 40, no. R11/15).

Imports from the Oxford kilns are still present. No. 176 has a stamped rouletted decoration and probably imitates a samian form 29 (see Young 1977). In all, twenty-six OXRW sherds came from Period 8 deposits — a similar proportion, when seen against the whole assemblage, to that from the site at Barnwell (Upex forthcoming a), showing that Oxford products were being imported into the lower Nene valley until the very end of the Roman occupation. A much smaller proportion of material was also present at LF2 from the Hadham kilns, of which three sherds are illustrated (nos 177, 179 and 180). No. 179, in a light reddish brown fabric and finish (CR9) with a decoration in relief, is probably a Hadham product intended to imitate a samian form 36. A vessel with a similar (but painted) decoration and form but in a colour coated fabric comes from the Great Casterton 'destruction layer' dated to after *c.* AD 375 (Corder 1951, fig. 10, no. 46) and a similar vessel in LNVCCW comes from Normangate Field (Perrin and Webster 1990, fig. 13, no. 219), although here the date is given as 'mid 3rd century'. It is probable that no. 179 from LF2 is an imported Hadham vessel, but local Nene valley potters were clearly making vessels with identical forms and decoration.

Of the remaining vessels from this period which are worthy of note, nos 161–170 are all reduced wares with black/dark grey finishes and with a fabric which has a quartz inclusion. Most have some burnishing to the exterior surfaces, a few (no. 168) having both internal and exterior burnishing. Such vessels have been referred to as NVPIRP (Upex forthcoming b) and appear on sites with very late occupation levels, possibly running into the 5th century (Upex 1993).

138. LNVCCW CR 9/18/9 (LF2 72, C 1). Top fill of 'sump' in Area C (see Fig. 53 S71/S72/S73)
139. LNVCCW CR9/18/9 (LF2 72, B 10). Fill of Ditch B8 (see Fig. 44 S114)
140. LNVCCW CR 17/20/17 (LF2 72, C 1). Top fill of 'sump' in Area C (see Fig. 53 S71/S72/S73)
141. LNVCCW CR9/7/9 (LF2 72, C 1). Top fill of 'sump' in Area C (see Fig. 53 S71/S72/S73)
142. RGTW CR15/21/22 (LF2 72, C 1). Top fill of 'sump' in Area C (see Fig. 53 S71/S72/S73)
143. LNVCCW CR15/7/15 (LF2 72, C 13). Fill of Pit C4 (see Figs 51 and 56 S93)
144. LNVCCW CR16/6/16 (LF2 72, C 1). Top fill of 'sump' in Area C (see Fig. 53 S71/S72/S73)
145. RVTW (?) CR13/15/9 open coarse fabric (LF2 72, C 1). Top fill of 'sump' in Area C (see Fig. 53 S71/S72/S73)
146. LNVCCW CR24/6/24 (LF2 72, B 10). Fill of Ditch B8 (see Figs 44 and 48 S114)
147. LNVCCW CR9/6/9 (LF2 72, C1). Top fill of 'sump' in Area C (see Fig. 53 S71/S72/S73)
148. LNVCCW CR9/6/14 (LF2 72, C 1). Top fill of 'sump' in Area C (see Fig. 53 S71/S72/S73)
149. LNVCCW CR20/21/20 sandy finish (LF2 72, C 8/2). Fill of Ditch C9 to north of 'sump' area (see Figs 51 and 56 S92)
150. LNVGW CR 19/18/19 (LF2 72, C 13). Fill of Pit C4 (see Figs 51 and 56 S93)
151. LNVGW CR19/18/19 (LF2 72, B 45). Fill of Ditch B13 (see Figs 44 and 48 S114)
152. RSGW CR16/21/8 (LF2 72, C 1). Top fill of 'sump' in Area C (see Fig. 53 S71/S72/S73)
153. LNVCCW CR9/20/13 (LF2 72, B 81). From fill of Ditch B13 (see Figs 44 and 48 S113)
154. LNVCCW CR17/26/17 (LF2 72, B 101). With over-painted white slip; from fill of Well I (see Fig. 42 S69)
155. LNVCWW CR6/26/5 Mortarium (Hartley N/V Fabric 1) local black trituration grit (LF2 72, I 33). From the general spread of debris/floor? over the aisled building (see plan shown in Fig. 39)
156. LNVCWW CR 7/18/7 Mortarium (Hartley N/V Fabric 1) local black trituration grit (LF2 72, C 1). Top fill of 'sump' in Area C (see Fig. 53 S71/S72/S73)

157. LNVCCW CR9/8/24 with pink/white (CR6) over-painted decoration (LF2 72, B 19). From Ditch B2 (see Figs 44 and 47 S102)

158. LNVCWW CR26 over-painted with bands (CR9) of colour (LF2 72, III 6). Fill of Well II (see Fig. 42 S70)

159. LNVCWW CR26 over-painted with bands (CR9) of colour (LF2 72, III 6). Fill of Well II (see Fig. 42 S70)

160. LNVCCW CR25/18/25 (LF2 72, III 6). Fill of Well II (see Fig. 42 S70)

161. NVPIRP CR28 (LF2 72, B 10). Fill of Ditch B13 (see Fig. 44, and 48 S114)

162. NVPIRP CR28 slight exterior burnishing (LF2 72, B 10). Fill of ditch (see Fig. 44 and 48 S114)

163. NVPIRP CR28 slight exterior burnishing (LF2 72, B 10). Fill of ditch (see Fig. 44 and 48 S114)

164. NVPIRP CR22//14/20/14//10 slight exterior burnishing (LF2 72, C 1). Top fill of 'sump' in Area C (see Fig. 53 S71/S72/S73)

165. NVPIRP CR22/21/22 shell inclusion; slight exterior burnishing (LF2 72, C 1). Top fill of 'sump' in Area C (see Fig. 53 S71/S72/S73)

166. NVPIRP CR28 slight exterior burnishing (LF2 72, IV 4). Uppermost fill of Military Pit 1 (see Figs 9 and 11 S45)

167. NVPIRP CR28 slight exterior and interior burnishing (LF2 72, IV 4). Uppermost fill of Military Pit 1 (see Figs 9 and 11 S45)

168. NVPIRP CR2872, slight exterior and interior burnishing (LF2 72, B 10). Fill of Ditch B13 (see Figs 44 and 48 S114)

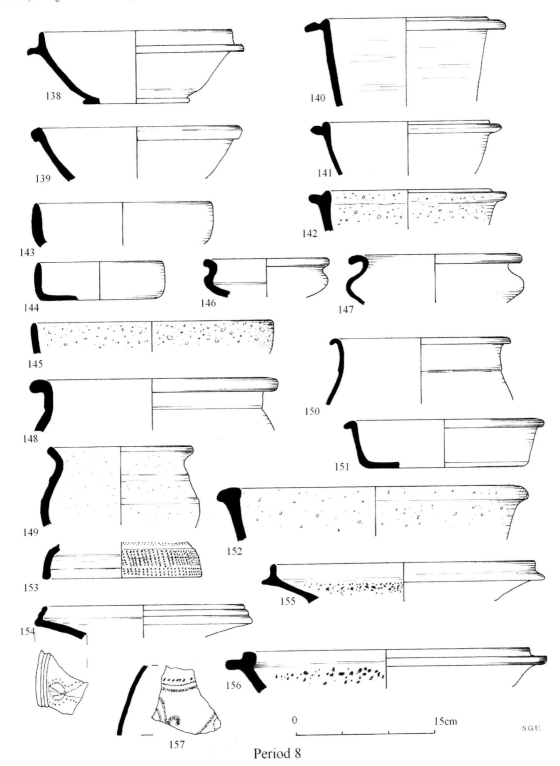

Period 8

Figure 89 Roman pottery, nos 138–157, Period 8

139

169. NVPIRP CR28 (LF2 72, B 76). As context B 10 (see Figs 44 and 48 S114)

170. NVPIRP CR28 (LF2 72, B 76). As context B 10 (see Figs 44 and 48 S114)

171. LNVGW (?) CR 21/18/21 (LF2 72, B 5). From Ditch B10 (same as B 4 in Fig. 48 S108)

172. RSGW CR13/21/13 (with sooting) (LF2 73, III 1+)

173. RSGW CR10/21/22 (LF2 72, IV 1+)

174. LNVGW CR19/18/19 (LF2 72, III +)

175. LNVGW CR21/20/21 (LF2 72, C 20+). From spread over context 20 (see Fig. 52)

176. OXRW (LF2 72, B 103). From fill of Well I (see Fig. 42 S69)

177. HAD OX fine mica inclusion (LF2 72, C 21). From fill of land drain shown in Fig. 52; treated as +

178. LNVGW CR18/19/18 sandy finish (LF2 72, I +)

179. HAD OX (?) CR9 (LF2 72, C 1). Top fill of 'sump' in Area C (see Fig. 53 S71/S72/S73)

180. HAD/OX (?) CR9 probably from the Hadham kilns; the half rosette decoration is similar to that on a vessel from Baldock (Rigby 1986, 248 no. 6) (LF2 72, C 8/2). From Ditch 8 Area C (see Figs 50 and 56 S92)

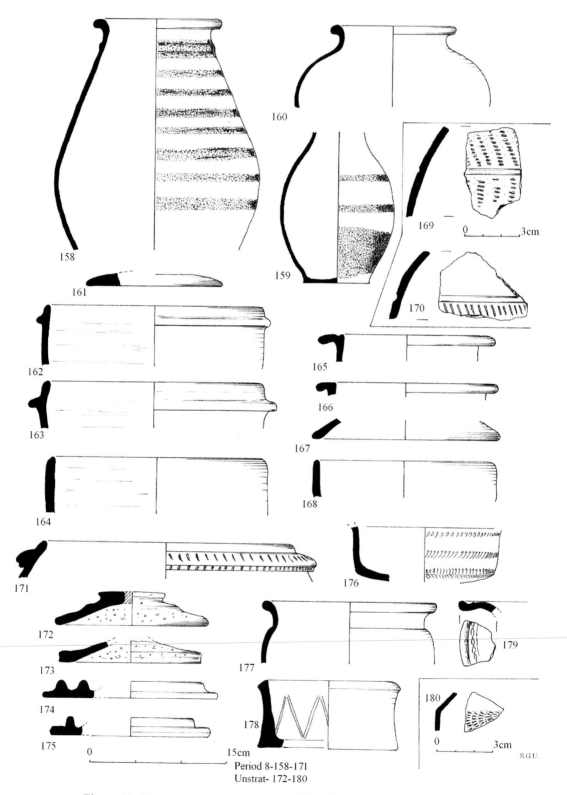

Period 8-158-171
Unstrat- 172-180

Figure 90 Roman pottery, Period 8, nos 158–171, unstratified, nos 172–180

140

III. The mortarium stamps

by Kay Hartley

Three fragments of stamped mortaria were recovered from the site. Fabrics were examined with a hand lens at ×20 magnification. Unless stated otherwise, stamps are impressed at right angles, across the flange. 'Right facing' and 'left facing', when applied to stamps, indicates the relation of the stamp to the spout when looking at the mortarium from the outside.

1. Flange and bead fragment from a mortarium (60g). Fabric: hard, white fabric fired to buff near parts of the surface. All surfaces are pale brown and there is some indication of a darker brown near the inside fracture. Inclusions: moderate, ill-sorted, tiny to small, mostly quartz (transparent and pinkish), with some opaque red-brown and rare black material. Trituration grit: no inside surface survives, but two or three grits which have strayed on to the bead are of hard, black material.

   The retrograde stamp, which can be assumed to be the left-facing, reads right to left: LO[....] and from the bead outwards across the flange; the L has a bar at the top as well as at the bottom. When complete this stamp reads LOCCI·PROB retrograde, presumably for Loccius Probus. The initial L in most of his stamps has two bars, but a few have only the normal single bar at the bottom. This lower bar often has a slight tip upwards at the end and this stamp from Lynch Farm differs from all others because the tip upwards is continued in a regular curve to join the adjacent letter O. The three versions of the L are probably the result of changes relating to cleaning or trimming during the life of the die. If this is true, then this stamp would be late in the production of Loccius Probus.

   Eleven of his mortaria are now recorded from Scotland and thirty-one from occupation sites in England, while several were found on the kiln site outside *Manduessedum*, where he worked. Loccius Probus was one of three potters working in the Mancetter-Hartshill (Warks) potteries who are linked by having the same name, Loccius, in common: Loccius Probus, Loccius Vibo and Iunius Loccius. We may reasonably assume that they were related in some way. Loccius Probus worked at some time with Iunius Loccius, as one mortarium, from Alcester, Warks (unpublished), carries the stamps of both potters. Fewer mortaria of Iunius Loccius than of the other two potters are known, but his rim profiles show markedly later traits than theirs and his work has not been recorded in Antonine Scotland, while Loccius Probus and Loccius Vibo are well represented there. The optimum production period for Loccius Probus is AD 140–65. The changed character of the letter L in this stamp suggests a late date in this period.

   Visually the fabric of this sherd is not unlike that of SF 83, which can be attributed to an origin in the lower Nene valley, but there is no other evidence to suggest that Loccius Probus ever worked outside the Warwickshire potteries. (LF2 72 LC2 +. SF 73)

2. Diameter 310mm 14% (weight 165g). Fabric: cream fabric; inclusions: fairly frequent, mostly transparent quartz with some tiny red-brown and rare black material. Trituration grit: few survive on the fragment; black slag with one quartz grit.

   The broken impression is part of a severely contracted stamp which at first sight reads SMLSLE from left to right when complete: reversed S, IMI ligatured, followed by *lambda* L for LI ligatured, reversed S and F written as Ii (i.e. a vertical stroke followed by a short upright) followed by E, for Similis *fecit*. This example, reading from the outside of the flange, preserves the second downstroke of the 'M' with the beginning of its diagonal stroke, followed by *lambda* L and reversed S; the bottom of the final E also survives.

   This potter is known as Similis 2 in order to distinguish his very characteristic stamps from another series reading Similis that is attributed to Similis 1 (Monaghan 1997, 932, no. 3372). We do not know whether both sets of mortaria were produced by a single potter or firm, but it is likely, as Similis 1 was always based in the Mancetter-Hartshill potteries and at least the initial work of Similis 2 can be attributed to the same source. The mortaria associated with Similis 1 date from within the decade AD 130–40 and his work is well represented in Antonine Scotland, while Similis 2 mortaria are completely absent. Some of the profiles used by Similis 1 date as early as AD 130–40 and no obviously late forms are associated with him. Some unusually late forms (e.g. Lynch Farm; Mill Hill, March; and Castor) are associated with the dies of Similis 2. The initial production of Similis 2 can be attributed to the Mancetter-Hartshill potteries, although only one stamp is recorded from *Manduessedum* (unpublished; Birmingham Museum). His Leicester mortaria stamped with die A are typical products for these workshops and they are not only in its prime marketing area but are outside the marketing areas of his other workshops.

   Twenty-eight mortaria are now recorded for Similis 2. The stamps are from four dies, A–D (A and B are so similar in type and size that it is not always possible to determine the die from fragmentary stamps or from drawings).

   Die A Leicester (St Nicholas St); Leicester (Connor and Buckley 1999, fig. 59, M9 and p.109); Leicester (298K probably die A); Manduessedum; Lincoln (St Mark's); Legsby, Lincs.; South Kyme, Lincs. (Hartley and Healey 1987, 44–5); Spalding; Stirtlow, near Buckden, Hunts (not seen, information E.E. Birley); Whitemoor Haye, Staffs.; Wroxeter (Bushe-Fox 1913, fig. 16, nos 12–13, probably stamps from the same mortarium; no. 13 is now missing). Water Newton (Oakham Museum, no other information); Lynch Farm 2; Mill Hill, March. Very fragmentary stamps: Chesterton (Kate's Cabin, CH7315 M117); Water Newton (WA/58/201+); Water Newton (WA 301+).

   Die B Carlisle (McCarthy 1990, fig. 195, no. 16, 262–3); Maryport; Tullie House Museum, Carlisle (provenance unknown).

   Mortaria with stamps from dies A or B which have not been examined: Kirkby Thore (not seen); Meering, Notts. (not seen) Meols, Cheshire (not seen); Northwich (not seen); provenance unknown (not seen; drawing from W.P. Richards, Newcastle under Lyme).

   Die C Castor (Normangate Field).

   Die D Whittlebury (The Gullet), Northants; Hertford. (Bengeo).

   The mortaria stamped with dies of Similis 2 are associated with at least three different fabrics: the normal cream fabric produced in the Mancetter-Hartshill potteries; a red-brown fabric which has so far appeared only in the Carlisle area and can be attributed to that area (it differs from an early 2nd-century red-brown fabric produced at Mancetter (Manduessdum)); and a white/cream fabric undoubtedly produced in the lower Nene valley. It can sometimes be difficult to distinguish by macroscopic examination, fabrics which have some superficial similarity, for example Mancetter-Hartshill fabric, that produced in the lower Nene valley in the 2nd century and fabric produced at Lincoln. The trituration grit may differ if one is fortunate enough to have it. One feature sometimes used on the Similis 2 mortaria in the Antonine period in the lower Nene valley is a brown slip. This was never used in the Warwickshire potteries. The profiles used for the Castor, Mill Hill and Lynch Farm mortaria are also quite distinct from profiles used in the Mancetter-Hartshill potteries. There is no positive identification of any manufacture at Lincoln by Similis 2, but the fabric of some mortaria in Lincolnshire could qualify on macroscopic examination; only analysis could identify this source.

   Die A is associated with production in the potteries at Mancetter-Hartshill and almost certainly with production in the lower Nene valley; die B with production in the Carlisle area; die C with the lower Nene valley; and die D perhaps with the lower Nene valley.

   The distribution pattern for the mortaria in cream fabric would be unusual for a solely Mancetter-Hartshill potter, but fits with activity in the two sources. It would also fit if any production at Lincoln were involved. On present evidence this is purely speculative because of some variations in fabric, especially of mortaria in Lincolnshire, but it cannot be entirely discounted without analysis and further examination.

   Similis 2 was certainly active in at least three areas: Mancetter-Hartshill, the lower Nene valley and the Carlisle area. While it would not be impossible for him to have moved around from one area to another, it is more likely that he was following the practice of the far more important Mancetter-Hartshill potter, Sarrius, of being active in subsidiary workshops while continuing in production at his main production centre at Mancetter-Hartshill. There is now no question that this occurred in the case of Sarrius, although it is not known how far the activity in the three subsidiary workshops was simultaneous or consecutive. His involvement in the workshop at Rossington Bridge, near Doncaster (Buckland *et al.* 2001, 42–7), at Bearsden on the Antonine Wall and at another, unlocated site in the north-east (Breeze 2016), is beyond question. These subsidiary workshops were short-lived and we do not know if the productions were intended to be short-lived or how far changes in military plans simply made them redundant. There is no reasonable doubt that Sarrius's production in Warwickshire

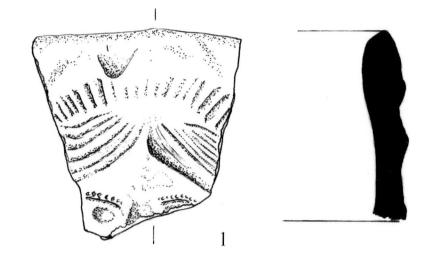

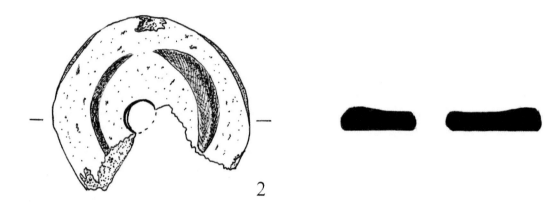

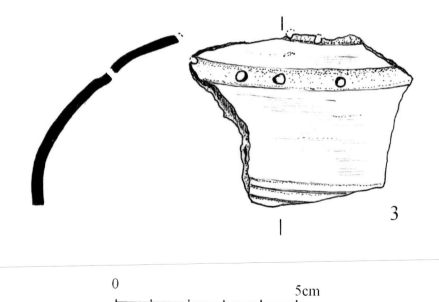

0   5cm

S.G.U.

Figure 91 Pottery objects, nos 1–2

continued simultaneously with his other productions. We do not know if the same is true for Similis 2, but it is certainly possible. This would imply, as appears to have happened with Sarrius, that a potter was sent from Similis's midland workshop armed with a die. The Lower Nene valley workshop was probably using either the die A used in the midlands or a sister die which was virtually identical. A different, but not dissimilar die, die B, was used in the Carlisle area. Dies C and perhaps D were actually made in the lower Nene valley.

The mortaria of unusual types produced in the lower Nene valley cannot be earlier than AD 150 and best fit the period AD 150–70/180. The site of production is unknown, but it was presumably at Water Newton or Castor.

Similis 2 was a multi-workshop potter and, as such, is of particular interest. His work could amply repay a programme of scientific analysis, perhaps using more than one method. Some of his products cannot be attributed with confidence without such recourse (LF2 72 LC2 +. SF 83).

3. Diameter 280mm 13% (weight 155g) Fabric: hard cream fabric; self-coloured. Inclusions: fairly frequent, tiny to smallish, mostly rose quartz with opaque red-brown particles. Trituration grit: none surviving, but the few largish grits on the flange are red-brown sandstone and are likely to be accidental strays from the gritting process.

The left-facing stamp is almost complete, but was not impressed with uniform pressure. It reads, from left to right, IVNIVS, initial I barely impressed and the S only partially impressed. When complete, an F for *fecit* follows the S. This is from one of at least twenty-three dies attributed to him.

Iunius worked in the Mancetter-Hartshill potteries. Many of his stamps were found along with those of Bruscius in a kiln at Hartshill (H63 kiln 34) and with Sarrius in a kiln in the workshop in the parish of Mancetter, outside Manduessedum (M64 Kiln 1) (both unpublished). The evidence suggests that he was probably using these two kilns in common with the above potters. Most of his stamps from the Hartshill kiln were from the same die as the Lynch Farm stamp.

Up to 130 mortaria of his have been recorded, excluding those found at the potteries. His mortaria also appear in those Pennine forts such as Bainbridge and Brough-on-Noe that are believed to have been unoccupied AD 120–60. He belongs to the latest generation of potters at these potteries to stamp their mortaria and he is the only one of these to have any stamps recorded from the Antonine occupation of Scotland (Castlecary and Duntocher). His work, however, also overlapped with that of Sarrius and Bruscius, who are both commonly recorded in Scotland.

Since he was one of the most prolific of the potters stamping mortaria in the Mancetter-Hartshill potteries, these facts suggest that his activity began too late for him to be more than marginally involved with the supply of Mancetter-Hartshill mortaria to Scotland.

He was also one of the small number of potters who were introducing the new, near-hammerhead rim profiles that were to become popular after the practice of stamping ceased. The rim profiles he sometimes used also make it possible that he continued producing mortaria after the practice of stamping had ceased. The evidence as a whole points to activity *c.* AD 145–75, with optimum importance *c.* AD 150–70+. The Lynch Farm mortarium is not likely to be among his latest products if he was working in conjunction with Bruscius at Hartshill, since Bruscius is a typical potter of the period AD 140–65 (LFC 72 C 3 from the fill of Ditch C7, see Fig. 50 Period 7 SF 245).

IV. Amphorae
by Roy Friendship-Taylor

Seven fragments of amphorae were found during the excavations. All were of form Dr 20 and seem to be from the valley of the river Guadalquivir between Seville and Cordoba in the southern province of Baetica. Two fragments each came from the bottoms of two military pits from Period 2 (LF2 72, 22 Pit 1; Fig. 11 S45 and LF2 72,

IV, 49; see Fig. 11 S123), the remaining three fragments were found in contexts that dated to Period 5.

V. Other pottery finds

Figure 91 nos 1–3

1. Part of a face mask in LNVCC with a cream fabric throughout and a light chocolate brown colour coat. The mask comes from a vase or flagon and appears to have been formed by being pressed into a mould. There are several 'faces' which are known from Nene valley kilns; that shown by Howe *et al.* (1982, no. 96) has hair touching the eyebrow over the left eye, and this example and that shown by Perrin *et al.* (1996, fig. 94, no. 339) do not have the eyelashes picked out with raised dots as on the Lynch Farm 2 example. Another face from Orton Longueville (Dakin 1961, fig. 8, no. 72) seems to have the hair shown as one smooth mass rather than individual strands of hair, as with the Lynch Farm 2 example. Two examples were found in the nineteenth century by Edmund Artis (1828, pl. XLIX, nos 2–3); both appear to have hair parted centrally, only one has stylised strands of hair and neither show the raised dots to indicate the eyebrows/lashes. Other examples in Peterborough Museum from the Wyman Abbott collection all seem to have hairstyle variations on these themes but none has the stylised eyelashes formed by dots of the Lynch Farm 2 example. All of the above mentioned examples are in cream fabrics with painted features on the faces and this, again, contrasts with the Lynch Farm 2 example, which is simply colour coated with no sign of over-painting. Clearly potters were using a variety of moulds to produce the faces and Perrin (2009, Illus. 25, no. 141) raises the idea that perhaps the production of the faces, including the whole head, was done in two stages. A kiln site at Stibbington which was producing face flagons and vases produced several 'back hair parts' but few faces, giving the impression that the faces could have been applied to already part-fired vessels. The 'face' illustrated from Stibbington has centrally parted hair in strands but no eye dots. Most examples are dated to the 4th century and the ones from Stibbington continue until the later part of this century. What these face masks are meant to represent is at present uncertain. The Lynch Farm face could represent a deity with the radiating lines above the parted hair indicating some form of diadem; alternatively, the diadem-like feature may simply have represented part of the hairstyle. Centrally parted hair seems to have been fashionable from the 2nd century onwards (Houston 1931) and the radiating lines above the eyes on the Lynch Farm face may be a similar attempt to show a 4th-century fashion and match the style shown on a late bone pin from Ashton (Upex 2008a, fig. 35) (LF2 72, F2, +. SF 48).

2. Part of a LNVCC ware base from a late 3rd- to early 4th-century beaker which has been used as a spindle whorl. Both the upper and lower surfaces have been abraded to a smooth finish, leaving only residual traces of the original colour coating of the vessel. The hole has been drilled slightly off centre (LF2 72, B, F4, +. SF 115).

3. Sherd of possible 'military ware' from Longthorpe (?) although similar vessels are not illustrated in either Dannell (1987) or Frere and St Joseph (1974). The sherd is from the shoulder of the vessel and has evidence for four holes pierced around a slight decorative depression in the wall of the vessel and a further band of holes (of which two are evident) 16mm above. The holes were formed by a thin tool being pushed from the outside of the vessel when the clay was plastic. Possibly part of an incense burner (LF2 72, unstrat. SF 34).

Unillustrated

4. Rim of mortarium in Oxford ware with one side of the spout surviving. The surface finish of the vessel has been totally worn away. The grit consists of rounded grit (max. diameter 3mm) in oranges/white/pink (LF2 72, unstrat. SF 82).

5. Base or pedestal of a pottery vessel in a poorly fired terracotta fabric throughout with no surface coating. This may belong to the Claudio-Neronian series described by Dannell (1987, 133–68) which comes from Longthorpe, although there is no precise parallel either for the fabric or the form of the vessel (LF2 72, unstrat. SF 74).

Chapter 8. Tree-ring analysis of timbers from Well I at Lynch Farm

by Ruth Morgan

Four sections of timber from the foundation raft of Well I at Lynch Farm 2 were made available for dendrochronological analysis at the University of Sheffield with the aim of assessing the relationship of timbers to each other, as two appeared to have been reused, and to establish a mean tree-ring curve that would form part of a framework of floating chronologies for the Roman period.

The four timbers from Well 1 were all of oak (*Quercus*), an excellent wood for tree-ring analysis since each annual ring is formed of two distinct zones — large vessels in the early wood and small dense elements in the late wood — and is thus clearly visible. The relationship of

the timbers to the original trees were clear on each sample: samples 1 and 2 included less than one quarter of what must have been a large trunk 0.5m or 0.6m in diameter (Fig. 92). One sample showed a very slight curvature to the rings, showing that the pith area, in addition to the soft outer sapwood which is susceptible to insect and fungal attack, has been totally removed. Such beams could easily have been prepared by cleaving with an axe and wedges along the line of rays (at right angles to the rings), in which direction oak splits naturally.

Samples 3 and 4 had been cut in a different way; they both had the appearance of originally consisting of the

Sample Number	Number of Rings	Number of Sapwood Rings	Dimentions	Sketch	Comments
No 1	83	-	12-20x15.5cm	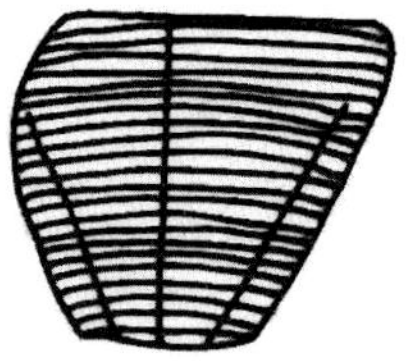	Rings 1-3mm wide, very sensitive
No 2	82	-	15-22x14.5cm		Rings 1-3mm wide, very sensitive, same tree as No 1
No 3	56	17	13x17cm, radius 8cm		Rings 1-2mm wide
No 4	54	7	16x17, radius 12.5cm	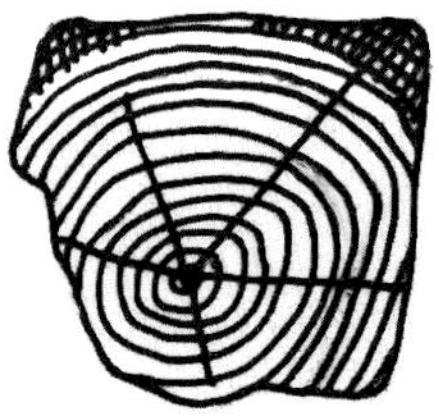	Rings 1-2mm wide

Figure 92 Details of the four samples submitted for dendrochronological analysis from Well I

144

entire trunk hewn down to a square or rectangular cross section, from which parts have since been worn away. Sapwood remains at two corners of each of these samples and was easily recognisable by its paler colour and slight structural variations. The presence of sapwood on oak is important as it retains a uniform width of about twenty-five years, and so even if only one sapwood ring remains it is possible to estimate the felling date of the tree. If all the sapwood has disappeared, as in timbers 1 and 2, it is impossible to ascertain how many heartwood rings have been lost (Fig. 93).

Sections cut from each timber were deep-frozen for about twenty-four hours in order to provide a firm cutting surface on the soft waterlogged wood; one or two radii were cut with a sharp knife so that each annual ring boundary could be clearly seen. The ring widths were then measured to the nearest 0.1mm and the value plotted on semi-logarithmic paper; the resulting curves showing the growth pattern were compared visually on a light-table and by computer, which gave an objective value for the degree of similarity between pairs of curves.

The four timbers provided only short sequences of annual rings; for absolute certainty of dating it is preferable to have at least 100 rings. The ring patterns are very sensitive — that is, the ring widths fluctuate considerably from year to year as a result of the conditions they grew in — and this is essential for successful cross-dating. Comparison of the ring patterns immediately showed that 1 and 2 were almost identical — a computer comparison gave a similarity value of 84% (at 99.9% level of probability), which is very high — and these two timbers were almost certainly cut from the same tree. Since timber 2 retained features that implied reuse, this must also apply to timber 1.

The ring sequences of timbers 3 and 4 are rather too short for secure dating and not as sensitive, being from much less mature trees; their growth pattern is similar (70.2%), but not sufficiently so to suggest that they originated in the same tree.

At the time of the original analysis in 1975, there were no reference chronologies in the UK stretching as far back as the Roman period with which to compare and date the well timbers, and relative dating against other Roman material was the only option. However, in 1991 a review of undated material revealed a good correlation with an absolute chronology established on cross-dated London timbers by Ian Tyers in the 1980s, spanning 252 BC to AD 255. This dated the pattern of timbers 1 and 2 to AD 113–97 (the correlation by then was measured in t values — t=5.7). To allow for the missing sapwood, at least ten to fifty-five years must be added to this date, as well as an unknown amount of heartwood, giving an earliest felling date for the timbers of AD 207–52; the likelihood is that the tree was felled in the mid–late 3rd century and reused in the well at some point after that.

The Lynch Farm timber is surprisingly slow-grown (narrow-ringed) and sensitive for the Roman period, during which definite selection of wide-ringed complacent timber seems to have occurred. Fast growth creates a wide zone of dense latewood in each ring, which provides greater strength and durability.

Having matched the four curves (for each of the four samples), the annual values for each were averaged to give a ninety-four-year mean curve involving three trees, for use in absolute or relative dating with other mean curves of similar date. Several mean curves for Roman timbers from different parts of England have now been established, and two comparisons with the Lynch Farm curve have provided very tentative results which must await corroboration from further contemporary material. A very short and extremely tentative overlap occurred with a short tree ring sequence from a timber from Berkhampstead (similarity value 73%), making the latter some fifty years earlier than Lynch Farm. A better correlation was found with an eighty-five-year mean curve from Gloucester at 65.5%, the latter ending about twenty years after Lynch Farm. However, the likelihood of frequent reuse of timber will confuse any interpretations of temporal relationships between different sites.

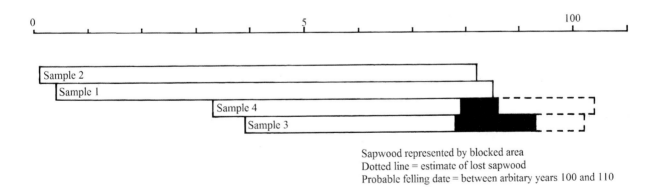

Sapwood represented by blocked area
Dotted line = estimate of lost sapwood
Probable felling date = between arbitary years 100 and 110

Figure 93 Details of the four samples submitted for dendrochronological analysis from Well I

145

Chapter 9. Faunal remains

I. Introduction

The animal bones from the site were taken and analysed by Peter W. Fifield during 1976 as part of a Masters dissertation at Sheffield University. A report was written and given to the Nene Valley Research Committee in 1977 but remained unpublished. When it was decided to publish the site during 2009 Dr Bethan Upex from the University of Durham was approached to update and revise the text and comment on the initial findings. The report below is the result of this work. The full archive of animal remains and the full text of the original report by Fifield are housed in Peterborough Museum.

II. The report

by P. W. Fifield with additions and editing by Bethan Upex

The majority of the faunal sample was recovered from a variety of ditches, pits and structural features dating from the military phase of the 1st century AD to the 4th century AD. A few bones were also recovered from pits dating to the Iron Age but these fall outside this present summary. Although all the bones were in a reasonably good state of preservation, they were mostly very fragmentary. This is to be expected if normal butchery techniques were being employed at the site. It appears likely that the bones represent the domestic refuse of the occupants of the site, although there is some evidence to suggest that a certain amount of butchery was carried out at the site prior to carcasses being sent perhaps to local markets. The faunal remains came from three main phases/contexts.

1. Military levels AD *c.* AD 44/5–60/65 This material mainly came from a series of ditches (Period 2).

2. 4th-century levels. This sample was mostly retrieved from ditches, wells, pits, 'sump'-like features and post-pits (Periods 7 and 8).

3. Ditches in continuous use. This part of the sample was recovered from a number of Romano-British ditches. However, for the purposes of this report, and owing to the sample sizes, in most cases these data sets are amalgamated (Periods 4–7).

The species represented
(Tables 11–15)
The faunal sample consisted of 2,473 stratified mammal bone fragments and 12 bird bones. Of these, 1,420 (57% of the total) were identifiable, and of the remaining bones 420 were rib or vertebra fragments (16.9%) and 645 were unidentifiable. Only the stratified, i.e. datable, fragments were included in the analysis. This is therefore a comparatively small sample and as a result many techniques developed for animal bone analysis can be applied to only a limited extent and in some cases not at all. Table 11 shows the total number of mammal and bird bone fragments identified for each species. Cattle is by far the dominant species represented in terms of both the sample as a whole as well as the individual phases identified. This is expanded upon in Table 12, which shows the percentages of the three main stock animals kept at the site: cattle, sheep and pigs. It is rarely possible to distinguish positively between sheep and goats on purely osteological grounds as the two animals are extremely similar, and therefore the term 'sheep' will be used in this report to mean sheep and/or goat. The combined total of the fragments from cattle, sheep and pigs make up nearly 80% of the assemblage.

Another and probably a more accurate way of estimating the relative importance of different animals found at the site is by calculating the Minimum Number of Individuals (MNI) present for each species. The MNI was calculated by aggregating the most abundant anatomical elements (mandible, humerus etc.) in each feature for each species. The results of this analysis are shown in Table 13, with Table 14 showing the percentages for the principal stock animals. These data clearly demonstrate the importance of cattle for the site. This fits with both a large majority of sites in the region for the Romano-British period and the long tradition of breeding cattle in the east of England (Johnstone and Albarella 2002, 14).

	Military		4th century		Ditches	
	total	*%*	*total*	*%*	*total*	*%*
Cattle	231	52.7	403	50.1	114	65.5
Sheep/goat	79	18.0	172	21.4	25	14.4
Pig	40	9.1	65	8.1	1	0.6
Bird	0	0.0	11	1.4	1	0.6
Dog	41	9.4	45	5.6	3	1.7
Cat	2	0.5	1	0.1	0	0.0
Red deer	0	0.0	42	5.2	1	0.6
Roe deer	2	0.5	2	0.2	0	0.0
Horse	42	9.6	60	7.5	29	16.7
Hare	0	0.0	4	0.5	0	0.0
Mouse	1	0.2	0	0.0	0	0.0
Totals	**438**		**805**		**174**	

Table 11 Total numbers (Number of Identified Specimens Present, or NISP) of bone fragments for all animals

	Military		4th century		Ditches	
	total	*%*	*total*	*%*	*total*	*%*
Cattle	231	66.0	403	63.0	114	81.4
Sheep/goat	79	22.6	172	26.9	25	17.9
Pig	40	11.4	65	10.2	1	0.7
Totals	**350**		**640**		**140**	

Table 12 Total numbers (NISP) for bone fragments for the three major domesticates

	Military		4th century		Ditches	
	total	*%*	*total*	*%*	*total*	*%*
Cattle	231	52.7	403	50.1	114	65.5
Sheep/goat	79	18.0	172	21.4	25	14.4
Pig	40	9.1	65	8.1	1	0.6
Bird	0	0.0	11	1.4	1	0.6
Dog	41	9.4	45	5.6	3	1.7
Cat	2	0.5	1	0.1	0	0.0
Red deer	0	0.0	42	5.2	1	0.6
Roe deer	2	0.5	2	0.2	0	0.0
Horse	42	9.6	60	7.5	29	16.7
Hare	0	0.0	4	0.5	0	0.0
Mouse	1	0.2	0	0.0	0	0.0
Totals	**438**		**805**		**174**	

Table 13 Minimum Number of Individuals (MNI) for all animals

	Military		4th century		Ditches	
	total	*%*	*total*	*%*	*total*	*%*
Cattle	21	46.7	39	49.4	5	62.5
Sheep/goat	15	33.3	25	31.6	2	25.0
Pig	9	20.0	15	19.0	1	12.5
Totals	**45**		**79**		**8**	

Table 14 Minimum Number of Individuals (MNI) for major domesticates

	Military	4th century	Ditches
Cattle	10,458	19,422	2,490
Sheep	900	1,500	120
Pig	900	1,500	100

Table 15 Edible meat weight (lbs) from animals at Lynch Farm 2

A third technique for obtaining an estimation of the three main stock animals is the conversion of the MNI into meat weight totals. This report uses the calculations of Cram (1967) (cattle 498lbs (225kg), sheep 60lbs (27kg), pig 100lbs (45kg)). It is important to bear in mind that meat is only one resource provided by the animals and that most livestock produce several others, which may have been of equal or greater importance to the occupants at Lynch Farm 2. The results of the edible meat analysis are given in Table 15. This clearly shows that cattle produced most of the edible meat. Sheep and pig each produced similar amounts of meat.

Element distribution
(Tables 16–18)
The element distributions for the three main species are shown in Tables 16, 17 and 18. It can be seen that some of the smaller bones (e.g. astragali, patelli, phalanges, carpels and tarsels) are under-represented in the sample. These smaller bones form only about 4% of the total faunal assemblage. Conversely, it is evident that mandible, teeth and skull fragments are over-represented in the sample (41%). Teeth in particular survive well under archaeological conditions and have therefore weighted this particular percentage. The larger meat-bearing bones, such as humerus, radius, femur and tibia, make up nearly 30% of the assemblage and the metapodials about 11%. These various percentages of different bones in the assemblage can be explained by differential preservation and survival; differential retrieval; and differential treatment of certain bones as a result of cooking/consumption/processing factors.

There is no clear evidence to suggest that differential preservation or survival is an important factor on this site. With a sample of this size it is difficult to draw clear-cut conclusions. However, a combination of differential recovery and some differential treatment of certain bones best explains the variations in the make-up of the sample, although the small sample size makes it difficult to interpret these patterns further.

Ageing
Ageing analysis was based on both bone epiphyseal fusion and on tooth eruption and wear. The tooth eruption data has been divided into four main groups:

Element	Military Cattle	%	4th century Cattle	%	Ditches Cattle	%	Totals Cattle	%
Mandible	35	15.2	48	10.9	11		94	12.6
Maxilla	4	1.7	3	0.7	0	9.6	7	0.9
Tooth	41	17.7	73	16.6	19	0.0	133	17.8
Skull	27	11.7	44	10.0	11	16.7	82	11.0
Scapula	13	5.6	21	4.8	16	9.6	50	6.7
Humerus	24	10.4	32	7.3	15	14.0	71	9.5
Radius	14	6.1	29	6.6	5	13.2	48	6.4
Ulna	5	2.2	9	2.1	3	4.4	17	2.3
Carpal/tarsal	0	0.0	7	1.6	0	2.6	7	0.9
Metacarpal	15	6.5	18	4.1	4	0.0	37	4.9
Atlas	2	0.9	6	1.4	0	3.5	8	1.1
Axis	1	0.4	0	0.0	2	0.0	3	0.4
Pelvis	11	4.8	17	3.9	8	1.8	36	4.8
Femur	11	4.8	24	5.5	4	7.0	39	5.2
Patella	0	0.0	0	0.0	0	3.5	0	0.0
Tibia/fibula	14	6.1	22	5.0	8	0.0	44	5.9
Astragalus	1	0.4	5	1.1	1	7.0	7	0.9
Calcaneum	1	0.4	40	9.1	0	0.9	5	0.7
Navicular cuboid	0	0.0	1	0.2	0	0.0	1	0.1
Metatarsal	11	4.8	25	5.7	6	0.0	42	5.6
Phalanx 1	0	0.0	9	2.1	1	5.3	10	1.3
Phalanx 2	1	0.4	3	0.7	0	0.9	4	0.5
Phalanx 3	0	0.0	3	0.7	0	0.0	3	0.4
Totals	231		439		114		748	

Table 16 Element distributions, cattle

1. Mandibles which have only three deciduous teeth

2. Mandibles which have only the first molar erupted but not fully in wear

3. Mandibles which have the first molar in wear and the second molar erupting

4. Mandibles with all premolars and molars in wear.

Again, it has been necessary to combine the data from the different periods to obtain a satisfactory sample. It should be remembered, therefore, that the analysis can be regarded as only a general guide to the ageing of the animals on the site.

Cattle (*Bos*)

The importance of cattle in the Romano-British economy and diet is well known and probably reflects the larger and more intensive farming practices required by an expanding population (Grant 1989, 138). Whichever method of analysis (MNI/NISP) is employed, cattle were the most abundant species at Lynch Farm 2. Cattle were extremely useful stock animals; besides producing large quantities of meat, they also provided other important products such as milk, hides and horn. Cattle were also important working animals, pulling carts and ploughs, although it cannot be said with any certainty that they were used for traction at Lynch Farm 2 given the low evidence of osteoarthritis from the site, a condition which is thought to be potentially useful in the identification of draught oxen (Bartosiewicz *et al.* 1997). Just one phalanx with evidence of osteoarthropathy was recovered from the site; however this may also reflect the ages of the animals at the site, as arthritis is also an age-related condition (Bartosiewicz *et al.* 1997). The site at Barnwell (Northants) showed that a high percentage of arthropathies were present in the cattle bones; this was

interpreted as possible evidence for the use of the animals for ploughing and may perhaps also reflect the heavy clay soil and rough terrain of the site's location (B. Upex forthcoming)

The ageing of the cattle bones through tooth eruptions and fusion revealed a fairly typical pattern of animal husbandry at Lynch Farm. Very few cattle were killed when immature (i.e. when they had only their deciduous teeth and before the glenoid cavity of the scapula fused). There seems to be a peak in killing when the third molar was in eruption and before the metapodial and tibial distal epiphyses had fused, placing the animals between 2½ and 3 years (Silver 1969). This may represent the killing of prime age animals for meat, possible young males, retaining the females for milk production and breeding. Maltby (1977) found a similar situation to this at Roman Exeter and also suggested this interpretation. Most of the cattle seem to have been kept until they had reached full maturity and were probably four years of age or more (i.e. all the teeth in wear and all elements fully fused). Contemporary Roman authors (admittedly referring to Italian stock keeping) mention that it was common for cows and bulls to be kept until they were ten to twelve years of age (White 1970).

However, the pattern of aging at Lynch Farm 2 was consistent with other Roman sites from the region. At Orton Hall Farm (Mackreth 1996b, 216) animals were slaughtered when over four years old and the same was seen at Haddon Lodge Farm (Baxter 2003, 122 and fig. 18). Both of these sites show a change from the early periods of Roman occupation (1st and 2nd centuries), when large numbers of cattle were killed off at a very young age. Possibly this was to provide veal for the military fort at Longthorpe and later the town of *Durobrivae* (Baxter 2003, 122). This change across the

Element	Military		4th century		Ditches		Totals	
	Sheep	%	Sheep	%	Sheep	%	Sheep	%
Mandible	8	10.1	24	14.0	0	0.0	32	11.6
Maxilla	3	3.8	3	1.7	0	0.0	6	2.2
Tooth	8	10.1	30	17.4	7	28.0	45	16.3
Skull	4	5.1	11	6.4	2	8.0	17	6.2
Scapula	1	1.3	6	3.5	2	8.0	9	3.3
Humerus	5	6.3	14	8.1	3	12.0	22	8.0
Radius	10	12.7	6	3.5	1	4.0	17	6.2
Ulna	0	0.0	2	1.2	0	0.0	2	0.7
Carpal/tarsal	1	1.3	1	0.6	0	0.0	2	0.7
Metacarpal	11	13.9	12	7.0	1	4.0	24	8.7
Atlas	0	0.0	1	0.6	0	0.0	1	0.4
Axis	0	0.0	2	1.2	0	0.0	2	0.7
Pelvis	2	2.5	5	2.9	3	12.0	10	3.6
Femur	7	8.9	20	11.6	1	4.0	28	10.1
Patella	0	0.0	0	0.0	0	0.0	0	0.0
Tibia/fibula	8	10.1	16	9.3	2	8.0	26	9.4
Astragalus	1	1.3	2	1.2	0	0.0	3	1.1
Calcaneum	0	0.0	0	0.0	0	0.0	0	0.0
Navicular cuboid	0	0.0	0	0.0	0	0.0	0	0.0
Metatarsal	10	12.7	12	7.0	2	8.0	24	8.7
Phalanx 1	0	0.0	4	2.3	0	0.0	4	1.4
Phalanx 2	0	0.0	1	0.6	1	4.0	2	0.7
Phalanx 3	0	0.0	0	0.0	0	0.0	0	0.0
Totals	**79**		**172**		**25**		**276**	

Table 17 Element distributions, sheep

region from the consumption of very young individuals in the 1st and 2nd centuries to much more mature cattle in the 3rd and 4th centuries suggests an increased emphasis on arable farming and as a consequence the increased use of cattle for traction (Baxter 2003, 122). The pattern of old animals being present on sites in the later periods of Roman occupation appears to be common for many sites in East Anglia; Great Holts Farm, Essex (Albarella 2003), Hacheston, Suffolk (King 2004), and Little Oakely, Essex (Bartford 2002) all display similar profiles, with over half of the cattle surviving to maturity. This is almost certainly a reflection of a region known for the breeding of cattle and for arable farming, where cattle would have been exploited for traction and not consumed as high-status veal.

There were a number of horn core fragments in the sample from Lynch Farm 2, which in some cases had been sawn or hacked off. However, they were too poor and fragmentary to allow conclusions as to breed to be drawn. In terms of metric analysis, the available data suggests that the cattle at Lynch Farm were similar in size to other animals from the region, standing at an average of 1.2m high (calculated using the measurements from von den Dreich and Boessneck 1974), with a range of 1.10–1.23m. This was similar in size to the animals from 4th-century Lincoln, which ranged from 1.05m to 1.25m tall (Dobney et al. 1996).

Sheep (*Ovis*) and goats (*Capra*)
The second most abundant stock animal at the site was sheep. The size of the sample has made it difficult to estimate the ratio between the sheep and goats kept at the site. There are a number of ways of differentiating between the two types and perhaps the simplest method is through study of the horn cores. The horn core of the goat

has a much flatter cross section and is quite distinctive. Of the eight positively identified horn cores, only two belonged to goats. Metric separation was also carried out using the method of Hole (Hole et al. 1969) on the distal condyls of the metapodials. This method indicated that all of the metapodials measured belonged to sheep. It is therefore assumed that the majority of the bones recorded belonged to sheep. As with cattle, sheep produced a wide variety of resources, including meat, wool and dairy produce. In contrast, the goat was usually kept simply for its milk. The results of the above analysis, thererfore, are not unexpected.

From the limited evidence available most sheep seem to have been slaughtered before the third molar was in wear and prior to the fusing of the distal epiphysis of the femur (i.e. before full maturity), which suggests that sheep were being reared mainly for their meat and were probably killed in their third year when they had achieved their maximum body weight. The majority of the male population would probably have been kept until they were old enough to have produced one or two fleeces and then they would have been slaughtered for meat. Females would probably have been kept as a breeding population, supplying milk and wool as well as offspring, and most likely would have been killed after three or four years. The sheep exploitation curves from other sites in the region are similar to this, with the large majority of animals being killed around three years of age (Baxter 2003; Albarella 2003).

Using the long bone measurements for the site and the calculations of Teichart (1975), a withers height of 0.56m was calculated for the sheep from Lynch Farm. This is fractionally smaller than the sheep from Lincoln, which had a withers height in the 4th century of approximately 0.60m, and the sheep from York, which averaged 0.59m (Dobney et al. 1996, 32).

Element	Military		4th century		Ditches		Total	
	Pig	%	Pig	%	Pig	%	**Pig**	%
Mandible	5	8.3	5	7.7	0	0.0	**10**	9.4
Maxilla	3	5.0	0	0.0	0	0.0	**3**	2.8
Tooth	22	36.7	15	23.1	1	100.0	**18**	17.0
Skull	10	16.7	8	12.3	0	0.0	**18**	17.0
Scapula	1	1.7	6	9.2	0	0.0	**7**	6.6
Humerus	7	11.7	5	7.7	0	0.0	**12**	11.3
Radius	2	3.3	1	1.5	0	0.0	**3**	2.8
Ulna	0	0.0	1	1.5	0	0.0	**1**	0.9
Carpal/tarsal	0	0.0	1	1.5	0	0.0	**1**	0.9
Metacarple	0	0.0	0	0.0	0	0.0	**0**	0.0
Atlas	0	0.0	0	0.0	0	0.0	**0**	0.0
Axis	0	0.0	0	0.0	0	0.0	**0**	0.0
Pelvis	0	0.0	5	7.7	0	0.0	**5**	4.7
Femur	2	3.3	4	6.2	0	0.0	**6**	5.7
Patella	0	0.0	0	0.0	0	0.0	**0**	0.0
Tibia/fibula	6	10.0	11	16.9	0	0.0	**17**	16.0
Astragalus	0	0.0	0	0.0	0	0.0	**0**	0.0
Calcaneum	0	0.0	0	0.0	0	0.0	**0**	0.0
Navicular cuboid	0	0.0	0	0.0	0	0.0	**0**	0.0
Metatarsal	0	0.0	0	0.0	0	0.0	**0**	0.0
Phalanx 1	2	3.3	3	4.6	0	0.0	**5**	4.7
Phalanx 2	0	0.0	0	0.0	0	0.0	**0**	0.0
Phalanx 3	0	0.0	0	0.0	0	0.0	**0**	0.0
Totals	**60**		**65**		**1**		**106**	

Table 18 Element distributions, pig

Pig (*Sus*)

The MNI estimates suggest that pork played a fairly limited role in diet throughout the Roman period at Lynch Farm 2. The pig was a valuable food resource; it is an extremely fertile animal that can produce several litters a year. It will also eat a very varied diet so can be fed easily. The aging evidence from the site, however, was extremely limited. Most animals seem to have been killed when the third molar was just coming into wear or was in wear but before the fusion of the distal epiphysis of the tibiae and radii, which indicates that most pigs were slaughtered in their third year. This pattern was similar at several other sites in the Nene Valley, such as Orton Hall Farm, where only limited numbers of pig bones were recovered, of which the majority were from mature animals, suggesting that they were kept only in small numbers and killed to provide meat (Mackreth 1996b). Baxter (2003, 125) reached the same conclusions about the pig remains from Haddon. Documentary sources refer to the popularity of suckling pig, and two immature pigs came from the fill of Well I, dating to the 4th century AD. However, the fact that there were no butchery marks and that almost complete skeletons were recovered, suggests that the pigs may have fallen in by accident or been deliberately thrown in.

Horse (*Equus*)

Horse bones were recovered from all the Roman periods examined. The highest percentage of bones was recovered from the military period (9.6%) and this may relate to the use of the animals as military mounts. This is supported by the ageing evidence which shows that all the bones were from mature animals. The absence of any young individuals suggests that horse breeding was not being carried out at the site and that the animals were mainly working adult animals. Using the factors outlined by Von Den Dreich and Boessneck (1974), the average withers height was calculated for the five complete long bones available, showing that the horses from Lynch Farm 2 stood at between 1.19m and 1.49m, with an average of 1.36m (11.3–14.3 hands, with an average of 13.2 hands). This means that all of the animals bar one were of sufficient stature to have been used as military mounts, which generally ranged from 13 to 15 hands (Collins 1994, 151).

Although horses may well have been a food resource when they had ended their working life, no clear evidence of butchery marks was found on the bones recovered in the sample and the consumption of horse in Roman times is not well documented.

A survey of 190 Roman sites in central England revealed that on average horses represent 5% of the total horse and cattle bones, although the ratio between the two taxa is higher on rural sites (1:10) than on urban sites (1:25) (Johnstone and Albarella 2002, 33). Lynch Farm fits into the rural end of the scale, with a ratio of 1:6, but it must be remembered that these ratios may well have more to do with waste disposal patterns than socio-economic factors; animals such as horses may well have been kept on urban sites but disposed of elsewhere.

Dog (*Canis*)

Dogs were found in all the Roman periods examined. Most parts of the body were represented and nearly all were mature individuals having full bone fusion and teeth present. One almost complete immature dog, not more than a year old, was found in Well I (Period 8).

Although no definite conclusions about individual species could be drawn, shoulder height could be calculated using the method outlined by Harcourt (1974). This showed that the complete dog bones came from animals standing between 0.50m and 0.41m high, making them fairly large animals. The modern Alsatian dog has a shoulder height of 0.63m (Harcourt 1975, 406). None of the dog bones examined showed any traces of butchery marks or pathology and these animals were most probably used as herding and watch dogs.

Cat (*Felix*)

Three cat bones were recovered in the sample, two from 1st-century (Period 2) and one from 4th-century (Period 7) contexts. The domestic cat was probably first introduced into Britain by the Romans and they were fairly common on rural sites such as Lynch Farm, where they would have played a valuable role in pest control (Branigan 1973, 86).

Birds

As Table 11 reveals, all but one of the twelve identifiable bird bones were recovered from 4th-century deposits (Periods 7 and 8). Ten of these bones were from domestic chicken species, one from goose and one from duck. Chicken would have fulfilled a similar role to that of pigs at Lynch Farm 2, being kept in small numbers to process household waste and to supplement the diet with eggs and meat. The question of whether the geese were hunted from the wild or were domestic is very difficult to answer, as there are no distinct morphological differences between the domestic birds and their wild ancestral species, the greylag goose (*Anser anser*). Domestic geese are known to have been kept by Egyptians, Greeks and Romans, and they may have been domesticated as far back as the 3rd millennium BC, but it may well be that the Romans simply fattened birds captured from the wild. Of 190 Roman sites surveyed in central Britain, only 60 have produced bones from geese.

III. Wild animals

Deer

Bones from both red deer and roe deer were found at Lynch Farm 2. A large percentage of the red deer sample came from Well 1. These bones comprised the almost complete skeletons of two immature individuals who, like the dog and piglets, had found their way down the well either through accident or design. These two deer were very young, as the deciduous teeth were hardly in wear

and the scapulae had not yet fused. Of the other deer bones, several fragments of antler and some metapodial fragments were recovered. These fragments indicate that deer played a minor role in the economy at Lynch Farm 2 and may occasionally have been consumed on the site, but this appears to have been a rare occurrence. This fits with the patterns from other sites in the Nene valley and from Roman sites in general within Britain, where wild animal remains are very scarce, antler often being the only find.

Hare

Three hare metapodials were recovered from the sample, possibly indicating that hare was another occasional addition to the diet at Lynch Farm 2.

Fish

No fish bones were recovered from the site. However, sieving was not carried out during the excavations and therefore it is not surprising that fish bones were absent from the samples.

IV. Conclusion

It is unfortunately not possible to draw many conclusions about changing economic practices over time as the small sample size meant that the data had to be combined. However, despite the small size of the sample, it is still possible to draw some conclusions about the economy of Lynch Farm 2 in the Roman period. Like many other sites in the region, the inhabitants of Lynch Farm 2 clearly practised mixed stock rearing, with cattle as the dominant species. Similar economies were also seen at the Longthorpe Garrison and Normangate Field (Wild 1969). Animals from the main domesticate groups all appear to have been raised primarily for meat, although they almost certainly all had secondary uses, such as traction, wool and milk. In terms of size all of the animals fall within the ranges of animals from other sites in the region, and it is possible that the horses from the military period of the site may be been used as military mounts, as most of them fall within the required size range. The presence of dog and cat at the site again fits with the typical pattern found at other local sites, while the presence of a small number of deer, hare, goose and duck bones indicates that there may have been some limited exploitation of wild resources.

Chapter 10. The Coleoptera from Well I

I. Introduction

When Lynch Farm 2 was excavated in 1972 a bulk sample weighing approximately 10kg was taken from Well 1 in Area B (context 104). The material was disaggregated and washed over a 300 micron sieve and then processed by paraffin flotation. The flot was sorted using a binocular microscope and the various beetle elements were mounted on card slides for preservation. In 1995 the identification and interpretation of the fauna was undertaken as an MSc thesis by V.C.E. Hughes. A synopsis of the findings is offered here and the thesis, details of the species found and their interpretation in the reconstruction of the environment of Lynch Farm 2 can be found at the University of Sheffield and in the site archive at Peterborough Museum. In total, 197 species and 835 individuals were identified.

II. The report: the Coleoptera assemblage
by V.C.E. Hughes

In 1972 a sample was taken from Well I at Lynch Farm 2 to be studied for insect survival. The initial processing was done at the time, but the identification and processing took place twenty years later. The assemblage was quite substantial and comprised 197 species and 835 individuals. Many of the species may have been part of the background fauna, but there was little evidence of an autochthonous well fauna and most of the species reflected the environment around the site. Once the habitat data had been established it was possible to group the species into habitat groups, which was partly based on modern work on Coleopteran communities. The data indicated an open environment with the following habitats of importance in the local area in order of their abundance: rotting organic matter; grassland; disturbed/arable; aquatic and bankside, and dung (see Table 19 and Fig. 94).

From this it is suggested that the site was involved in pastoral activity, that rubbish was accumulated on site and that the aquatic fauna was probably from permanent wet areas rather than from frequent flooding of the site.

Interpretation
The identification of beetle remains was important in that it formed a basis of the interpretation. However, the interpretation of local beetle fauna has been shown to require caution, as there are various aspects that must be taken into account and a simple list of the environment and conditions indicated by the beetles is somewhat naïve (Kenward 1976, 9). The main problems when attempting to interpret a death assemblage are concerned with the assemblage itself or the habitats that may have existed. In this section the problems connected with the assemblage are examined in relation to the Lynch Farm 2 data; the habitat problems are tackled in the environmental reconstruction section.

The problems are (Kenward 1978a):

1. Groups of Coleopteran that cannot be identified to species level.

2. The ecological requirements and range of habitats are difficult to determine for many species.

3. There is a predominance of eurytopic species rather than stenotopic ones.

4. Death assemblages contain foreign elements through mechanisms such as flying, wind transport, birds etc.

5. The death assemblage is comprised of individuals from the various communities in the area.

6. Some types of deposit, e.g. urban, have faunas that tend to be more uniform and therefore rely on more subtle differences.

7. The importance of species recovered in small numbers can be obscure.

8. There may be reworking from older deposits or contamination from modern Coleopteran.

The deposit would have formed over an indeterminate period of time, and would probably be of mixed origin, temporally or spatially (Kenward 1978a, 25; 1978b, 2). Therefore the relationship between the death assemblage and the conditions that existed was not a direct and simple one (Kenward 1976, 9) and modern studies of assemblages found on roof tops, in urban environments, and within buildings have shown this clearly (Kenward

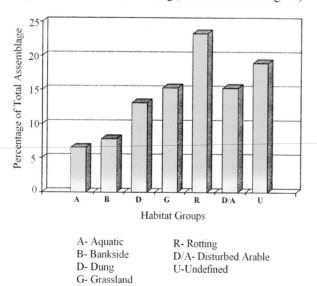

A- Aquatic
B- Bankside
D- Dung
G- Grassland
R- Rotting
D/A- Disturbed Arable
U-Undefined

Figure 94 Habitat groups

Habitat group	Number of individuals	Percentage of total
Aquatic	54	6.5
Bankside	64	7.8
Dung	109	13.1
Grassland	128	15.3
Rotting organics	194	23.2
Disturbed/arable	127	15.2
Undefined	158	18.9
Totals	**835**	**100**

Table 19 Relative abundance of habitats

1976; 1975; 1985). Kenward (1976) suggests that there may be several components to any assemblage, which he identifies as autochthonous; circumjacent; and local and regional (both contributing to the 'background' fauna). Of these the autochthonous and background elements are the most important. It is necessary, therefore, to have some means of identifying these components in an assemblage.

The evidence used to indicate that a species is autochthonous is either a 'superabundance' of numbers (over 10% is suggested (Kenward 1978a, 43)) or breeding evidence such as pale/young or deformed individuals which would not have moved far from where breeding was taking place (Kenward 1978a, 34;1978b, 8; 1976, 14). Often aquatic fauna will be considered separately from the assemblage because they are the expected autochthonous fauna in the watery conditions of most deposits such as ditches, wells and ponds and they reveal the condition of the water and thus the origin of the deposit but may not be regarded as providing relevant information about the environment of the site (Kenward 1978b, 15). In the case of Lynch Farm 2 the known presence of local watery environments and the close proximity of the river Nene, in addition to the well itself, showed that water was part of the local environment and that treating the aquatics simply as autochthonous may not have been valid.

The background fauna can be a significant part of an assemblage and can in fact be predominant, which poses difficulties in interpretation (Kenward 1976, 13). Beetles found in very low numbers can often be accounted for in an assemblage by suggesting that the habitat that they represent was less important or that they are part of the background fauna. They may arrive at a site by flying, as many beetle species have a dispersal phase in their life cycle (Evans 1975; Kenward 1975, 87). Other small species may be capable of active flight but winds will determine where they are transported (Kenward 1976, 11; 1975, 87). The wind can also carry the remains of dead insects in the same manner as inanimate particles such as sand (Kenward 1985). Birds that prey on beetles are agents of transport, as they can deposit them in regurgitated food casts and faeces. The digested remains survive and may show characteristics of having been pecked (Kenward 1985, 99; 1976, 9). Remains could be introduced from the digestive systems of other animals such as amphibians (Buckland 1976, 19) or from the corpses of dead animals put into the deposits. Water beetles and corpses may also be transported by run-off downslope and within a drainage basin. Detecting the background fauna can be done by assuming that all beetles found in low numbers may not be from the immediate vicinity, especially if their habitats support this (e.g. they are strong fliers or their usual habitat is not shared by any other species in the assemblage). In one study a species was only counted as present if it occurred in 3% of an assemblage (Kenward 1982, 76).

Both autochthonous and background components can bias an interpretation through misrepresentation. The large number of autochthones can over-represent the importance of their habitat type while background fauna will suggest habitats that may not be found in the immediate vicinity (Kenward 1975). These are also the problems facing any assemblage that may have individuals from previous deposits reworked into it or modern beetles infiltrating the deposit and contaminating it (Kenward 1978a; 1978b, 8; Buckland 1976). Dealing with these aspects in relation to the Lynch Farm 2 assemblage, it was possible to show that there were elements of both present. In all the 197 species only two reached over 3% of the assemblage; *Calathus fuscipes* and *Aphodius granarius*; while eleven comprised 2% or over of the assemblage. This would suggest that unless the area around the well was able to support a very diverse fauna, many of the species may represent background components. The published list of fauna found in a modern roof assemblage and bird droppings were compared to the Lynch Farm 2 list. This showed that of the seventy-eight species in the roof assemblage, twenty-seven were found at Lynch Farm, and of the ninety-eight species from bird droppings, thirty-seven were found at Lynch Farm. Allowing for overlaps, a total of forty-four species (22.3%) from the Lynch Farm assemblage have been found in background circumstances. Of the total number of species, 112 were represented by one or two individuals, which is a substantial amount (56.9%), but not as great as at some sites, such as Dalton Parlours = 65.5% (Sudell 1990).

There were essentially two ways in which the background fauna could be quantified and, surprisingly, results were relatively similar. The first method involved adding all the species that had been found in modern background assemblages except where ten or more had been found. This produced a figure of 635. The alternative method, in which species were regarded as background if they occurred in two or fewer individuals and the remaining species added, gave a total of 690.

Having considered these aspects it is therefore apparent that the assemblage from Lynch Farm seems to have had an autochthonous element and a substantial background fauna. These elements can be utilised to infer the environment of the site at Lynch Farm 2, not just the immediate conditions but also the surrounding area. However, Kenward states that 'where the local fauna is sparse the background fauna may be predominant and totally alter the apparent character of an area in reconstruction' (Kenward 1976, 13) and this is an important factor in trying to answer questions concerning the economy and human activities that are indicated in an area, which would be visible at a more local or even regional level (Kenward 1976).

Outdoor/indoor species
Studying an assemblage in these terms is most important when looking at material from urban sites because one of the questions that the archaeologist usually wants answered is whether the deposit was laid down in a building or not, and what type of building it was (Kenward 1985). Outdoor species are defined as those that are unable to find a habitat in which to breed in a building of any kind (Kenward 1985, 97; 1978a, 31; 1978b, 14). For a rural site such as Lynch Farm this was less important, particularly when the structure from which the deposit came was still evident. The Lynch Farm 2 sample was collected from a well and therefore the assemblage should have been dominated by an outdoor fauna, which it most certainly was, with at least 60% of the species being outdoor types and most of the remainder being likely outdoor species. Although it hardly seems necessary to examine this aspect it is worthwhile because a higher proportion of indoor species would need to be explained, perhaps, for example, by the deposition of floor sweepings in a well.

Preservation

This aspect was considered because it was a way of detecting whether there was any reworking of the sediments and temporal mix in the assemblage. If individuals showed two different preservation states then mixing would be surmised. At Lynch Farm the state of preservation was remarkably good, indicating that the sample had remained waterlogged since the deposit was formed. Nearly all individuals that have setae or scales covering their elytra, including *Appion* spp., *Phyllobius* spp., *Sitona* spp. and Ceotorhynchinae, retained some setae or scales. The iridescent colours evident in species such as *Carabus violaceus*, *Pterostichus versicolor*, *Helophorus aequalis/grandis*, *Cetonia aurata*, *Gastrophysa polygona* and *G. viridula* were easily evident and most of the elytra of the Carabidae and *Aphodius* spp. were still shiny. Overall, the condition of the beetles was very good and this suggests that the deposit formed rapidly or at least was waterlogged and therefore under anaerobic conditions quickly. Smaller beetle species had elytra that were often complete and undamaged but larger species, such as *Pterostichus* spp., had elytra and thoraxes that were broken. None showed clear evidence of having been preyed upon by birds (Kenward 1985) and the damage was probably a result of processing. Only two individuals of *Aphodius* spp. were in any way degraded. They had a peculiar grey mottled appearance which might suggest that they had passed through a digestive system, perhaps of a predating bird or of a herbivore that had inadvertently eaten them while grazing.

Environmental reconstruction

Beetles and other insects are used to reconstruct the environmental circumstances of past sites by using the modern habitat data to infer what the conditions were. The ecological requirements of all the species must first be determined and from this the species from the different habitats can be distinguished before, finally, the relative importance of the habitats present is estimated (Kenward 1976). The assumptions that beetle species have not changed their physiology, behaviour or associations are generally accepted, although it is recognised that there may have been slight changes (Kenward 1982, 71; 1976, 8; Frankie and Ehler 1978; Coope 1979; 1965, 567). As outlined above, there are three main problems connected with habitat data. The first is that some groups of species cannot easily be identified to the species level (Kenward 1982, 71; 1978a). This includes species such as *Stenus* spp., *Philonthus* spp., *Cryptophagus* spp., *Lathridius minutus* grp, *Platystethus cornutus* grp. and *Apion* spp., all of which were found at Lynch Farm. Other groups were identifiable only to families, such as Corticariinae and Ceutorhynchinae. It is difficult, therefore, to establish any precise details for preferred habitats although it is fortunate that in several cases there is an overall similarity in habitat requirements among the species forming the group.

Many species, such as *Aglenus brunneus* (Kenward 1976, 8), are able to live in a variety of habitats that are seemingly diverse but which meet the same requirements (Kenward and Allison 1995, 58; Hakbijl 1989, 83). This is particularly seen for species that can live in dung, rotting vegetation, nests, carrion and so on. Such eurytopic species usually far outnumber stenotopic ones that have requirements met only by specific habitats, such as

Cryptolestes ferrigineus (Kenward 1978b, 4). Again, this hinders the formation of a precise picture of conditions at the site.

However, the largest problem is the actual habitat data used. It is very difficult to determine the various different species' ecological requirements and the range of habitats that they prefer (Kenward 1978a, 27). The basic underlying problem is insufficient modern ecological data (Kenward 1978b, 3), which, moreover, is often included in obscure and scattered literature; and although the various 'BUGS databases' are a great help, the data is not yet extensive enough to make direct comparisons. For example, there seems to be only one modern study done of a well, at Yorkletts, near Whitstable, Kent, by Kenward (1978b, 9).

In some cases the full range of preferred habitats may not be known for a species and in others accidental records may blur the picture, as, for example, for *Trechus quadristiatus* (Kenward 1978b; 1976, 8). The data is often too coarse so that an assemblage that appears to be comprised of mainly one group of species actually reflects several ecological niches. This can be particularly seen with decomposer groups. Some work has been done to try and distinguish between decomposer groups that prefer wet (foul) or moist compost and those that prefer a more dry compost type (Kenward 1982). The problem is that the species' requirements actually fall into a continuum from foul through general decomposition to drier conditions (Kenward 1982, 76).

The solution used in many instances to compensate for insufficient habitat data and also for the problems of small numbers and background fauna is to use groups of species with similar ecological requirements (Kenward 1982, 71; 1978b, 5; 1976, 9). Basing an interpretation on such associations is a more reliable method but has its own problems in terms of the grouping of species. It is difficult to place some in any group, while other species could fit into several (Robinson 1993, 102; Kenward 1982; 1975, 86). The main drawback is that by placing an indefinite species in one group this will result in favouring one over the other and potentially misrepresenting the conditions. Some habitats also have more species adapted to them and, just as with pollen, the frequency/population levels of species varies considerably (Kenward 1978b, 3), adding to the problem. For example, the occurrence of several ground beetles may reflect the same level of environmental importance as tens of staphylinidae beetles (Kenward 1978b, 3).

The environment

The habitat data from Lynch Farm 2 was studied carefully and groupings of species were made from it, while taking into account associations suggested by modern studies and other archaeo-entomologists. The large proportion of the assemblage derived from the background fauna was not ignored, as it contained valuable information on the area around the site. The habitats of the various beetle species seem relatively diverse, but it was possible to suggest five major habitat groups that would have existed around the well when the deposit was formed. These habitats were: aquatic and bankside; dung; grassland; rotting organic matter; and disturbed/arable. Although the species are discussed in each section and are attributed to one group it is recognised that there are considerable overlaps, in addition to which there were species which implied the presence of other habitats but far less strongly.

The overlaps and alternative habitats are noted in general but it is simply not feasible to describe the entire range of every species habitat. Additionally, trying to do this from beetle habitat data is essentially a subjective exercise because there are few ways of objectively handling the data. This is where modern ecological studies and the use of numerical techniques such as Principal Component Analysis may be of value in showing more clearly the species associations and relative abundance in different habitats and 'thus sharpen the basis for our subjective decisions and provide more objective methods' (Kenward 1978b). The relative importance of habitats is suggested by proportions of the assemblage found from each, as seen in Figure 94 and Table 19. It is difficult to judge the distance from the well at which the habitats would have been found.

By combining this data with the archaeological information it is possible to pinpoint the more specific niches that would be within the usual habitat range of some beetles. And thus, in hypothesising where some beetles may have derived from, it is possible to refine and elaborate the archaeological circumstances. It is realised that the beetle assemblage is supposed to indicate the environment, rather than the archaeology suggesting possible niches to which beetles might be attributed, but the latter is not the basis of this work and has been used only to expand the picture of the environment. This is considered valid because many interpretations are often very simplistic and try to attribute many species to one habitat, whereas in most ecosystems there are complex associations and many subtly different niches which particular species take advantage of. As mentioned, it is not really feasible for most assemblages to provide detailed pictures because of the coarse nature of habitat information.

Aquatic and bankside
This ecological grouping formed quite a substantial proportion of the Lynch Farm assemblage. There were ten aquatic species comprising 6.2% of the assemblage, showing that water was present in the environs of the site and confirming what was visible from the archaeology. The species implied that water was stagnant or very slow flowing and, although most indicated fresh water (e.g. *Hydraena testacea* and *Ochthebius bicolon*), *H. testacea* inhabits water which contains duckweed and this usually grows in shallow water relatively rich in organic matter, such as a pond. Other species suggested fresh or brackish water and it would be tempting to link these to the river Nene, which would have been flowing slowly as it meandered past Lynch Farm; it was probably tidal in the Roman period and the water brackish at high tide (Pryor 1991, 37; Challands *et al.* 1972, 1). As many water beetles can be strong fliers (Girling 1989, 238; Osborne 1981a, 247) they may have flown or crawled to the site, as the distance from the river would have been relatively short. This speculation is worth mentioning as there are several individuals which may be linked to a 'coastal aspect'.

The *Helophorus* genus consists of aquatic and bankside species but also, surprisingly, some definitely terrestrial ones such as *H. nubilis*, which was found in this assemblage. The bankside species in the Lynch Farm assemblage were approximately equal in abundance to the aquatic species. The two individuals of *Lathrobium longulum* would certainly fit into this category but the one account of it in the 'BUGS database' is somewhat obscure, giving its record as 'on the surface of a pool' (Donisthorpe 1939). The bankside species found in the assemblage all inhabit the margins of often stagnant water or slow rivers where there is relatively rich, lush vegetation including moss. The genus *Stenus* has many species that would find suitable habitats in bankside situations, preferring muddy areas, often with moss.

Moss is an important aspect of habitats for *Manda mandibularis*, commonly found in bankside situations but also in woodlands. *Silpha tristis* is recorded from moss but it may also favour habitats connected with carrion. Moss in willow swamps is the usual habitat for *Anotylus inustus* and *Omalium caesum* but the four individuals present were not sufficient to suggest a significant tree component, although river banks such as those of the Nene were often places where trees remained, since agricultural activities usually stopped short of them. An interesting possibility is that moss, which was presumably available in quantity near the river, might have been required as packing material for the objects produced by the large number of pottery kilns in the Nene valley, the pottery from which has been found dispersed throughout the country.

Platystethus cornutus, P. degener/alutaceus, P. nodifrons and *P. nitens* are associated with mud and litter, which would have been present around the margins of bodies of water. These species could suggest that the area around the water bodies was trampled. *Notaris acridulus* lives on plants such as reed sweet-grass (*Glyceria aquatica/maxima*) and amphibious bistort (*Polygonum amphibium*). *Plateumaris sericea* suggests plants such as bulrush (*Typha latifolia*; *Scirpus lacustris*), sea club-rush (*Scirpus maritimus*), bur-reed (*Sparganium erectum*), sedge (*Carex* spp.) and water lilies (*Nuphur* spp.). All the plants indicated are common to slow-moving or stagnant waters which are fairly shallow (Polunin 1988; Clapham *et al.* 1987) and *Sparganium erectum* is usually found by permanent shallow water which is not subject to grazing (Robinson 1975, 168).

At approximately 14.3% of the assemblage the species related to an aquatic habitat were relatively abundant, although, even including the damp grassland species, it was not feasible to suggest that an extensive part of the environment around Lynch Farm 2 was wet. The proportion was certainly lower than Robinson showed for sites such as Mingies Ditch, Shustoke and Fisherwick (Robinson 1993, 107; 1981). The three sites studied by Robinson (1981, 93) at Appleford, Barton Court Farm and Farmoor all had species indicating damp spaces. Farmoor was shown to be the dampest of the three, which corresponds to its location on the first gravel terrace of the Thames valley and it is comparable to Lynch Farm, both in terms of the beetle fauna and also in that Lynch Farm is situated on the first gravel terrace of the Nene valley.

Perhaps this shows that the apparent drainage ditches at Lynch Farm, which covered an extensive area, worked efficiently, meaning that the only open water and bankside habitats would have been connected with the river Nene, the 'sump' (see Figs 50 and 53) and the two wells. Assemblages from other sites such as Mingies Ditch, Fisherwick and the Iron Age site at Farmoor, suggest that a higher proportion of aquatic and bankside species than species indicating marshes should have been expected if the ditches at Lynch Farm were water-filled.

It is difficult to determine whether the Lynch Farm beetles recovered were indigenous well fauna or whether perhaps they came from areas such as the 'sump' in Area C. Strong arguments against the aquatic fauna being indigenous to the well were their low numbers — even as a group the level did not reach autochthonous status (10% of the assemblage: see above). In addition, there were no recorded larvae or teneral individuals and it is entirely probable that the aquatic fauna indicated a more distant source of water.

For beetles to have entered the well at all shows that it must have been open, not covered, which the lack of aquatic fauna at Whitton seems to suggest (Osborne 1981a, 247). While the significant component of synanthropic beetles, that can be associated with household refuse at Dalton Parlours, suggests that floor sweepings were deliberately dumped, there was also the implication that the well at this site had a revetment wall or possibly a surrounding structure, which would have filtered out some of the beetles (Sudell 1990, 269).

Dung
This was a well-represented habitat both by numbers and diversity of the fauna. Although some of the species, such as *Aphodius prodromus*, *A. ater* and *A. fimetarius*, are found in background assemblages, they were not found at Lynch Farm in significant numbers (Kenward 1976, 11–12). The diversity of the species indicated that this was a real and not a spurious habitat and the additional evidence of two teneral *Aphodius granarius* individuals showed that they were breeding close by. Several of the species can inhabit either dung or rotting plant debris, but the variety of species particularly associated with dung, including *Geotrupes* sp., *Onthophagus similis*, *Aphodius sordidus*, *A. depressus*, *A. merdarius*, *A. contaminatus*, *Tachinus laticollis*, *T. marginellus* and *Hister bisexstriatus*, indicated that it was definitely present and it is reasonable to assume that the other species would also have made use of this opportune habitat, as might those found in the more foul types of rotting organics.

Grassland
Grassland species such as *Athous haemorrhoidalis*, *A. spp.*, *Agriotes lineatus*, *A. sputator*, *A. obscurus* and *Phyllopertha horticola* were found. The larvae of these species eat the roots of grasses and, where they are common, they may also be found as pests on cereals and root crops. *Hyper punctata*, *Sitona hispidulus* and *S. lepidus* are found on clover (*Trifolium* spp.), which again suggests grassland. The ground beetle fauna was a substantial part of the LF2 assemblage and this group of species have requirements that could be met by a wide range of environments, such as parks, gardens, grasslands and woodlands. Work by Eyre and Luff has shown that damp, unmanaged grasslands have an association with *Dromius linearis*, *Pterostichus strenuous*, *Trechus obtusus*, *Loricera pilicornis*, *Amara plebeja*, *Pterostichus nigrita* and *Nebria brevicollis*, which can be found together in managed upland pastures (Eyre and Luff 1990). All of these species were present within the Lynch Farm assemblage and this confirmed what is shown by other grassland species. *N. brevicollis* and *L. pilicornis* are also part of the assemblage association of managed lowland grasslands, along with *Pterostichus melanarius* and *P. madidus* (Eyre and Luff 1990). *P. madidus* is not often found in assemblages (Hall and Kenward 1980, 49) and so far it has been recovered only from Chichester, Barnsley Park, Empingham and now Lynch Farm. It is a very common species today, which is why the lack of records from the past is puzzling. It has been suggested that it has become more widespread in association with man and his environments (Hall and Kenward 1980, 49; Coope and Osborne 1968, 86). Perhaps the Roman period had the same effect on it as it did the grain beetle species (see below), and with more sites being studied and therefore a greater sample this may become apparent.

The ground fauna included very eurytopic species but it was possible to distinguish several that prefer damper grassland (with fourteen individuals found) from those which prefer drier grassland (forty-four individuals found). It is not clear which particular type of grassland may have existed around the Lynch Farm site. Species preferring damp conditions suggest plants of wet meadows, grasslands and water margins. Various substrates are indicated by the species and although the local soils are predominantly of a calcareous nature they do also have clayey, loamy and sandy attributes. The species preferring damp conditions often favour clayey soils, while the drier ones are associated with more sandy and free-draining soils. Both soil types are found around the Lynch Farm site.

Several species are decomposers that do not inhabit grassland but prefer cut and stored grass. They were represented in the assemblage in significantly high numbers and since they are eurytopic it is difficult to be precise about what they show. There may be sufficient numbers to imply more than one main habitat, and cut grass/hay could be an option. The grassland indicated may have been utilised not only to graze animals but also to produce hay for winter feed.

Rotting organic matter
This was a relatively large group of beetles but this was principally because there are many species adapted to such conditions. There are two extremes of rotting matter: one is termed 'foul', and species in this group could be found on dung, fresh corpses, and rotting vegetation under humid conditions. The other extreme is the drier conditions presented by nests, dry carcasses, compost, cut grass etc. The large range of species found at Lynch Farm and their abundance suggests that both habitats were present at the site.

Disturbed/arable
The two land uses share many similar attributes in terms of beetle requirements. There are usually areas of bare ground which suit particular predaceous species, while other species live on plants that grow in such conditions, such as common nettle. The assemblage contained a significant number of species and individuals that were associated with plants of disturbed ground, but these plants, and also therefore the beetles, can be found in other circumstances, such as grassland and cultivated areas. The diversity of species found suggests that these beetles do represent a habitat that actually existed rather than a spurious one derived from the background fauna.

Disturbed ground in this case is taken to mean areas where there was activity resulting in trampled ground and changing conditions, which could include pathways, track verges, field edges and cultivated areas. It might be possible to suggest that cultivation was taking place in the area around Lynch Farm, but the evidence suggested that it was probably not sufficiently extensive to have had a large impact on the beetle fauna. Further evidence from botanical remains would be needed before cultivation could be confirmed. Two *Zabrus tenebrioides* individuals were found in the Lynch Farm fauna and this species has only rarely been found in Roman assemblages. It is suspected to be a Roman introduction (Buckland 1981b) and is closely associated with crops. At this stage, with only the beetle data to use in an environmental reconstruction, there is insufficient evidence to confirm cultivation. All the species could have found adequate habitats on plants that would occur around buildings, wet areas, paths and other structures excavated at Lynch Farm.

Other habitats
Species associated with trees were very few in the Lynch Farm assemblage. *Phyllobius virideaeris* is found mostly on willow and poplar. Willow swamps were indicated by *Anotylus inustus* and *Omalium caseum*, but these represent only 0.6% of the assemblage, and are insufficient to imply a habitat. Species connected to dead wood could have originated from the timber buildings on the site or perhaps even the wood used in constructing the wells. In total there were twelve individuals (1.4.%) particularly associated with trees or timber, but there are many whose range of habitat includes woodland. The tree-related fauna is not a significant part of the assemblage and in agreement with most other Roman sites the assemblage indicates an open environment with very few woods or trees nearby. At Farmoor an identical level was indicated (1.4%), Appleford had a similar proportion (1.2%), while Barton Court Farm had even fewer indicators of trees (0.2%).

Throughout large areas of Britain the Roman period was one of open landscapes, as it is today (Roberts 1989, 152; Turner 1979), but in an area of many potteries and kilns, coppiced woodland might be expected as a source of fuel (Miles 1986, 23).

Two species were found that are usually associated with human activities. *Typhaea stercorea* is a mould feeder and despite there being suitable natural habitats it often frequents houses and other buildings. *Ptinus fur* seems to have general indoor tendencies and eats all manner of dried organic matter (Osborne 1983; Lindroth 1974).

Finally there were two further species which deserve mention: the first was two examples of *Sitiphilous granarius*, a grain weevil and known pest in stored products. It is usually found in stored cereals such as wheat, barley, rye, maize, millet, oats and buckwheat, and although it can overwinter in unheated buildings in Britain it is unlikely to have been indigenous and during the Roman period may have been the subject of many introductions and reintroductions (Buckland 1981b). As it does not fly these two individuals would have had to crawl to the well or have been put there accidentally or intentionally.

The other species was *Zabrus tenebrioides*. The adults of this species tend to eat cereal seeds, while the larvae eat shoots of cereals and grasses (Bullock 1993; Hyman 1992; Lindroth 1974). This species has been closely connected to cultivated plants in much of Europe and has been recognised as a pest of cereals in Britain since 1862 (Curtis 1862).

III. Discussion

The investigation of the Lynch Farm 2 beetle fauna allowed the environmental conditions on the site to be tentatively reconstructed. The fauna showed that herbivore dung was an important factor in the environment, implying the presence of animals such as cows, sheep and horses. The diversity of species, high numbers of individuals and direct evidence of breeding indicate that the dung was in close proximity to the well and this has been taken to show that the animals were actually on site at some point.

Accompanying this was a substantial grassland fauna which suggested that grazing land was available, as well as open conditions common to the Roman period (Roberts 1989, 152). The species were from damp and dry grasslands and it was suggested that this indicated a continuum from the wetter areas near the river, around the 'sump' in Area C and the ditches in all areas, to areas of drier grassland away from the river and in the better-drained land. The type of grassland was difficult to define from the beetle data alone but the calcareous nature of many of the soils and underlying substrate suggest that the grassland plant species would have been in this group.

The disturbed ground/arable category showed that there was land which was neglected waste, trackways and footpaths, or perhaps cultivated land. Cultivation was also tenuously suggested by four individuals of *Sitiphilius granarius* and *Zabrus tenebrioides*, both species that are linked to crops, the former to stored grain, the latter to growing crops. *Sitiphilius granarius* was likely to have been associated with the corn drier found in Area D. These beetles may have crawled to the well and fallen in, or may have been deliberately removed from grain about to be put into the drying oven. The individuals were not charred and so would not have been removed after parching or malting activities.

Areas of disturbed land would be expected in a rural farming settlement, and this was further shown by the rotting organics group. The substantial number of species in this group illustrated that the area was not kept particularly clean and that accumulations of rotting material were able to exist in both foul and drier compost areas. However, one other explanation of this group was that these species were often associated with flood refuse and, with the river Nene in its current position less than 600m away, some of the fauna may have reflected flooding in the area.

The aquatic and bankside species were a significant component of the assemblage and although some of the individuals may have come from the well itself, the overall habitat they implied was one of shallow, stagnant, fresh water and lush vegetation, including reeds and moss, growing at the muddy edges of bodies of water.

The relative lack of aquatic and diverse marshland type species, although negative evidence, was quite persuasive in implying that the ditches and drainage areas immediately adjacent to Well I had little standing water in them and that the area was quite successfully drained, allowing it to support grassland. In addition, faunal evidence for flooding of the site was unclear, unlike at

Sewer Lane, Hull, where a large number of aquatics on an otherwise terrestrial site was accounted for by occasional flooding (Kenward 1977, 33). There were species from Lynch Farm which are found in flood refuse habitats, but not in significantly large numbers, and other habitats could have supported them.

The whole deposit from Well I was probably accumulated over a fairly rapid period, as the state of preservation was excellent for the entire assemblage. It was formed at the bottom of the well and there were no indications that it was dumped rubbish since there was little pottery and very little animal bone from the sample context (B 104; see Fig. 90 no. 176 for a sherd of OXRW from this context (Period 8)). This suggests that the well was in use when the deposit formed and that the majority of the beetles entered the well, which acted like a pitfall trap, by accident, further implying that the well was not covered. The diversity of species was an aspect of the highly background nature of the fauna, but this seemed to enable a useful interpretation of the environment around the site. All of the species could have found suitable habitats in one of the major groups mentioned, but the various beetles could also have come from quite diverse niches throughout the site. A good example of this is *Trox scaber* which probably came from an area of dry, decaying vegetation but it could have originated, for example, from a nest in the roof of one of the buildings excavated at the site. This instance exemplifies the problems of interpretation.

There are seventy-one species on the 'BUGS database' that are of Roman origin — that is, the first record of them in Britain comes from Roman deposits. For Roman introductions there are no documentary sources, only the evidence from the beetle exoskeletons themselves (Luff and Rushton 1989). In the Lynch Farm assemblage six 'introduced' species were present, totalling twenty-two individuals (2.6%). Many were almost certainly Roman introductions, particularly those that were pests of stored products. Several other species, however, may have been earlier introductions but not yet identified or recovered from deposits from the Iron Age or Bronze Age. Determining when a species was introduced has proved difficult enough even when documentary sources are available (Lindroth 1957), and distinguishing their origins has been even harder (Sailer 1983).

The increased levels of activity in agricultural pursuits, trade and concentrations of population that accompanied the Roman period helped the spread of species (Girling 1983, 128). The influx of personnel and the need for grain to feed the military probably introduced and allowed species to establish. More areas of land may have been turned over to agriculture and larger and more widespread granaries would have encouraged pest species (Buckland 1981b). Thus not only did the Romans introduce some species but they encouraged the spread of others. On the other hand, the continuing destruction of certain environments, such as woodland, would have reduced the numbers of some species.

The site of Lynch Farm was, in the period when the well was in use (Period 7–8), not a Roman military site, although there was evidence of this in an earlier period (Period 2). The beetle data showed that the area around the site was being used for pasture, which confirmed the suggestions of the excavation evidence. The slight beetle-based evidence for cultivation may indicate that small areas were used to grow either cereals or root crops, perhaps at a subsistence level. The settlement pattern within the Nene valley indicates that each site along the Nene valley would have had a fairly even distribution of land (Wild 1974; Upex 2008a, chapter 5; Upex forthcoming b), but the overall economic organisation of the area is at present unclear.

IV. Conclusion

The sample deposit (B 104) taken from the fill of Well I appeared to show that it formed rapidly while the well was in use and that accidentally trapped beetles reflected the environment of the site. The major habitats around the site were rotting organic matter, dung, grassland, disturbed ground and an aquatic environment. The aquatic fauna appeared to show that the site was relatively damp, perhaps owing to the proximity of the river Nene. However, the Roman drainage system of local ditches was probably efficient as open, dry, grassland conditions were also present. There was plenty of evidence for the existence of animals around the site and some slight evidence for cultivation; thus mixed farming may have been practised at Lynch Farm even though the evidence suggests that the dominant activity was pastoral agriculture. The site showed no startling discrepancies from other Roman well faunas but it was evident that, accompanying the species often found at these sites, a wide range of other species was exploiting essentially the same habitats.

The insects from the well samples formed part of the basis of work carried out by Panagiotakapulus *et al.* (2015) into the dating of insect chitin, which confirmed a late 4th-century to early 5th-century date for the infilling phase of the well.

Chapter 11. Discussion

I. Introduction

The excavations at the site of Lynch Farm 2 form a significant contribution to the overall understanding of the development of the Iron Age and Roman occupation within the large meander along the lower course of the river Nene which the Royal Commission termed the 'Lynch Farm Complex' (RCHM 1969, 19). The site also adds to the broader picture of occupation within the lower Nene valley as a whole. The known extent of Iron Age occupation at the site has been increased by over a hectare and the identification of a previously unknown Roman military installation has added considerably to our understanding of the military presence in the area and poses several questions about the organisation of the army and its major base across the river at Longthorpe (see Frere and St Joseph 1974). In addition, the nature and functioning of the whole Lynch Farm complex has been opened up for further discussion, as has the relationship between other local agricultural sites such as those at Orton Hall Farm, Monument 97 and the villa site part-excavated in the grounds of Orton Longueville school in the early 1960s (Mackreth 1996b; 2001; Dakin 1961).

The Royal Commission entry for the Lynch Farm Complex as a whole says that the cropmarks extend over some 70 acres (28 hectares) and this evidence and the reporting of finds from the area show that there was certainly occupation during the late Neolithic period, if not earlier. The density of Bronze Age finds is also significant, especially the distribution of ring-ditches, of which ten are marked on the RCHM plan of the site (RCHM 1969, fig. 7). Perhaps not all of these ring-ditches are linked with former Bronze Age burial sites — the diameters of some of those marked by the Royal Commission are small (see, for example, RCHM 1969, Orton Waterville, no. 4, which is 20ft or 6.1m in diameter; see also Fig. 3, no. 4) and some of these small features may well prove to be either Iron Age or Roman structures rather than burial features. However, the general view is that during the Bronze Age the meander of the river Nene was extensively used for burial and probably settlement, and the few finds from the Lynch Farm 2 excavations would seem to support this view (see Fig. 59). Further finds from the early and middle prehistoric periods have also been made during the excavations at Lynch Farm 1 by Adrian Challands (unpublished but pers. comm.), including two Neolithic axes (Challands 1973, 22–3; 1974, 23). Bronze Age barrows have been excavated some 1.5km to the south-east of the Lynch Farm site in Orton Longueville parish, apparently demonstrating that many of the river terraces of the lower Nene were being used intensively during this period (O'Neil and Mackreth 1982; Mackreth forthcoming; French 1983).

II. The Iron Age

Iron Age occupation over the whole of the Nene's meander at Lynch Farm and within the parishes of Alwalton, Orton Waterville and Orton Longueville is extensively reported by the RCHM (1969), the unpublished record cards held by Peterborough Museum and the HER list now maintained by Peterborough City Planning Department. Chance Iron Age finds and finds from early excavations suggest that the general area continued to be very important throughout the Iron Age period. Edmund Artis appears to have excavated a 'tumulus' — possibly the remaining monument within Ailsworth parish (see RCHM 1969, fig. 10 no. 8) — during the 1820s, and he illustrated the finds in his volume of 1828 (Artis 1828, pl. XXX1, nos 1, 2, 7 and 8). More recently a series of iron objects has been recovered from the old bed of the river Nene, including nine currency bars, three swords, a spearhead, a latchlifter and a ladle. The objects may have been chance losses but it also seems that some were deliberately deposited as votive offerings (Stead 1984, 6–7). Other finds were made when 'dragging the river' during the early 1700s. These finds consisted of 'armour … and an antique sword' as well as pottery and bones and were reported by Morton, writing in 1712. These finds may be Iron Age although they could also relate to the Roman fortress at Longthorpe (Morton 1712, 515).

The cropmarks within the Lynch Farm Complex are plotted in Figure 3 and suggest a picture of earlier prehistoric occupation, or at least burial, but the larger proportion of the enclosures, trackways and field systems may well be late Bronze Age, Iron Age and Roman in origin. A full description of these cropmark features is given by the RCHM but, briefly, they consist of large, sub-rectangular enclosures (Fig. 3 nos A6, 9), smaller enclosures the complexity of which suggests that they are probably multi-period (A7, 10, 7), a complex of linked small enclosures (H), pit alignments, trackways and what are, from the excavation evidence, triple- and quadruple-ditched Iron Age (defensive?) boundaries (A9).

The complex of cropmarks (Pl. 1) is both extensive and impressive but can be paralleled by other complex settlement patterns plotted from the air in both the Welland and Nene valleys. In Northamptonshire sites have been plotted along various parts of the valley system, with some extensive settlements that are similar to the Lynch Farm arrangements (see Deegan 2007, figs 6.9, 11 and 15; see also RCHM 1975; 1979; 1981). Similarly, in the Welland valley and along the fenland edge sites have been both recorded from the air (RCHM 1960; Upex 1977, 22–3; Pryor et al. 1985, see fig. 3) and part-excavated, and show complicated chronological histories which cover both prehistoric and Roman periods (Pryor et al. 1985; Pryor 1974; 1977; 1978 and 1984).

Without further excavations of the cropmark features at Lynch Farm it would be impossible to add further valid comment regarding dates and functions to that already expressed within the Royal Commission's pages (RCHM 1969, 19), and at present this seems both unlikely and unnecessary, as the area is preserved under grassland within the Nene valley leisure park at Ferry Meadows.

Of particular interest, however, are the three pit alignments which were seen on air photographs to cross the whole complex at Lynch Farm (RCHM 1969, pl. 2b) and which are plotted in Figure 3. One can be seen to run for some 425m in an east–west orientation to the south of the large enclosure A6 and to the north of Area E, while a second alignment appears to run at right angles to this first set of pits, its northern end being obliterated by a modern trackway. A third pit alignment, running for some 500m in an east–west alignment, lies some 300m to the north and parallel with the first alignment. It is this pit alignment which was explored within the excavated area during 1972–3, when seventeen pits were located (see Fig. 5).

Pit alignments, like many linear archaeological features, have been notoriously difficult to date, but the growing consensus is that they originate during the late Bronze Age/early Iron Age. There is evidence, however, to suggest that some pit alignments were either maintained or even constructed as late as the late Iron Age at places such as Tallington (Lincs.), Langford Down (Oxford.) (Simpson 1966; Williams 1946–7) and Upton (Northants) (see Kidd 2004, figs 4.7 and 4.8). Some may have formed land boundaries, which at present are not fully understood but may represent some aspect of landscape planning or organisation, and often appear to delineate blocks of land set out in a rectilinear fashion. At Wollaston in Northamptonshire, for example, there appears to be a whole area of the side of the Nene valley which is arranged in blocks of land which are bounded, in part, by pit alignments (Deegan 2007, 82; see also the distribution of pit alignments shown as fig. 6.2). A variation on this functional theme is that the landscape divisions they formed were perhaps more symbolic than they were physical barriers to the movement of stock and populations (Carlyle 2010, 86). The general function of the pits, however, remains at present enigmatic, but they do date to a period when settlement was expanding in many parts of the east midlands and pressure on the lighter soils of the valley floors might have warranted some form of demarcation of land, territory or sub-tribal area (see Parry 2006).

The excavation and recording of the seventeen pits at Lynch Farm 2 seems to show that the pits conform to most other excavated pit alignments, in that the fills of the pits are rather homogenous, with few finds to provide dating. Most of the pits were filled with clean gravel and mixed loam, and there was little evidence for any primary silting, suggesting that the features had not been open for any length of time — either that, or they were regularly scoured and kept very clean. The pits were all shallow, flat-bottomed and roughly rectangular in plan (see Fig. 6). The pottery recovered from the Lynch Farm 2 pits seems to suggest that at least some of the alignment pits were functioning in the late Iron Age (see Fig. 80, nos 1–4 for pottery from pits F, H, L and J).

The only other point of interest within the pits came from Pit D, where a crouch burial was found lying on its left side and facing to the east (Fig. 8). The condition of the bones was poor owing to the acid soil conditions and the body was probably also subjected to some compression by earth-moving equipment on the site immediately prior to

archaeological work starting (*Northamptonshire Archaeology* 1975b, 159). No scientific reporting on this burial was made but it was assumed to be Iron Age in date because of its association with the pottery from other pits within the alignment. Similar burials were found between 1970 and 1974 at the site of a farmstead located across the river and near the site of the Roman fortress at Longthorpe (Dannell and Wild 1987, 31–2). Here two adults and an infant were found in shallow depressions. The adults were laid out in a typical crouched position, although they were orientated with their heads to the north or east of north, and both were laid on their right sides. Other similar crouched burials from a site at Cat's Water, Fengate (Pryor 1984, 116–22) also conform to this general character of late Iron Age burial as exemplified in southern and central England (see Whimster 1977; 1981; Wilson 1981). Dannell and Wild (1987, 33) suggested that the burials from the Longthorpe farmstead were the farm's inhabitants, who could have been killed by members of the military stationed at the Longthorpe fortress. This could have been the case with the Lynch Farm 2 burial, but the formality of the interment must surely counter this scenario.

Between Pits N and R there appears to be a gap in the alignment, with no pits recorded in this space. This area was fully excavated (see Fig. 5) and the absence of either three or four pits is curious. Breaks or gaps in pit alignments are, however, not uncommon and Deegan illustrates such breaks with examples from Ketton (Leics.), Pitsford and Harlestone (Northants) (Deegan 2007, figs 6.4, 6.5 and 6.7). Whether these breaks in the alignments were intended as access points or gateways through the features is, again, unclear.

The part-excavated alignment at Lynch Farm 2 probably forms the eastern end of a feature that is shown on air photographs to run for over 500m (see Fig. 3). If it continued on the same line to the east it would terminate against the present course of the river Nene. This east–west orientation is matched by the line of a triple and in some sections a quadruple line of ditches which runs some 300m to the south (see Fig. 3 and Pl. 2). These ditches (Lynch Farm 1) were part-excavated by Adrian Challands (Challands 1973; 1974a; *Northamptonshire Archaeology* 1974a, 85; see also Chapter 1 above) and found to contain material that dated them to the Iron Age, although the full analysis and publication of the site is still awaited.

Multiple-ditched systems of the sort identified at Lynch Farm 1 are now comparatively well known within the archaeological record. Jim Pickering was one of the earliest people to both identify them and contribute to the debate regarding their possible functions (Pickering 1978), and other researchers added to the geographical distribution of such features and their interpretation (Everson 1983, 16). The early view was that such features represented significant boundaries or land divisions between adjoining agricultural groups as population pressure put increased strain on land resources. Pickering went even further by suggesting that the lines of these 'multiple ditch systems' were in some way tribal or sub-tribal boundaries between significant population groups and marked the beginnings of tribal territories that became more formalised in the late pre-Roman Iron Age.

More recent work in the east midlands, however, suggests that the multiple-ditched systems may have some link with pit alignments in that they may have evolved from or replaced earlier boundaries marked out with pit alignments. As such, it has been suggested that multiple-ditched systems could either be contemporary with, or slightly later in date than, pit alignments, and thus be of a late Bronze Age/Iron Age date. At Stow-Nine-Churches (Northants: see Deegan 2007, fig. 6.6) part of a ditched system survives as a ditched and banked feature, suggesting that it formed a massive earthwork feature across the local landscape (Moore 1973; RCHM 1981, fig. 136). Other plots of triple-ditched systems from Northamptonshire and Leicestershire also suggest major boundaries at Pitsford, Moulton and Boughton, Harleston, Church Brampton and Chapel Brampton (Northants) and Ketton (Leics.) (Deegan 2007).

The function of these multiple-ditched systems is still much debated within the published literature (for example, Wilson 1978; MPP 1989; Pollard 1996; Waddington 1997; Thomas 2003). However, the basic suggestion still remains that they were set out as significant, large-scale and monumental boundaries which would have required considerable inputs of labour to construct and maintain. Such current thinking fits well with the situation at Lynch Farm, where the triple-ditched system appears to have annexed an area of land within the meander of the river, within which the most significant areas of cropmark features are known (see Figs 2 and 3). As such, the ditch lines may have acted as formal boundaries demarcating land within the meander of the Nene which was somehow different from the land to the south of the boundary and perhaps outside of the more formal arrangement to the north. In effect they could be seen as early boundary lines, albeit on a much smaller scale than those 'dyked' features which demarcated the areas of late Iron Age *oppida* at places like Silchester and Chichester (see English Heritage 2011; Cunliffe 2005). At Baldock (Herts.) part of a ploughed-out triple-ditched system was recorded from the air (English Heritage 2012, fig. 8) and appears to have formed a dyke system around a 'local *oppidum*'; this may parallel the situation at Lynch Farm remarkably well.

Other large concentrations of what appear to be Iron Age and earlier cropmarks found close to the river Nene occur at Ashton, near Oundle (Northants). Here the extensive cropmarks include multiple enclosures and a layout of trackways, some of which were later surfaced in the Roman period (Hadman and Upex 1975b; Upex 2008b, pl. 12 and fig. 22; RCHM 1975, fig. 23). Excavations over a small part of the edge of the Iron Age core of this site have produced significant finds of late Iron Age pottery, including *terra rubra*, *terra nigra* and Lyons cups and beakers, along with two coins, one minted at *Verulamium* by Tasciovanus (Hadman and Upex 1977, 9; Curteis 1996, 30). Less well-understood Iron Age settlement features were also found at Westwood to the west of Peterborough when the railway yards and railway housing were being laid out and then expanded in the late Victorian period (Walker 1899; RCHM 1969, 3–4; also unpublished record cards held at Peterborough Museum). Again, like those at the Ashton site, the finds include imported late Iron Age fine wares and significant numbers of coins, showing that the site was probably of considerable importance and status (Curteis 2001, 449–78).

However, terms such as '*oppida*' have in the past often obscured a clear understanding of the roles and functions of these dyked complexes. Moore (2012) argues from his studies of the complex at Bagendon (Glos.) that such settlement complexes have connections with other, smaller settlements within a wider landscape context. Such ideas may also be linked to the developing views of the heterarchical rather than hierarchical nature of Iron Age society. Thus the Ashton, Westwood and Lynch Farm 2 sites may represent settlements of an elevated status within the late Iron Age landscape, but their exact roles within what Branigan (1987, 6–7) suggests is a confederacy of smaller tribal groups are unclear. There is no evidence so far for imported pottery and coins from the Lynch Farm complex and the excavations reported on here did not produce anything that might suggest a high-status site. However, the multiple-ditched system, annexing the area of land within the meander of the river, and the finds of metalwork from the river itself do suggest that the site can perhaps be added to the list of important Iron Age sites within the east midlands.

The best fit for overall tribal control in the region in the late Iron Age was the *Catuvellauni*, with their centres of power based on *Verulamium* and *Camulodunum* (see Branigan 1987; Todd 1973; Whitwell 1982; Davies 1996; Upex 2008a, 22–6). The boundaries of Catuvellaunian territory are uncertain but it may be that the Nene itself or the interfluves between the Nene and Welland formed the boundary, an idea that may be supported by the line of Romano-Celtic temples at Brigstock, Collyweston and Maxey, along the Welland valley, which may parallel the situations in Gaul where temple sites follow tribal boundaries (see Rivet 1964, 134; Knocker 1965; Greenfield 1963; Pryor *et al.* 1985).

There is a growing corpus of evidence to suggest that the siting of the more significant Iron Age sites was often associated with water and river systems, which fits well with Lynch Farm's situation within a river meander (Rogers 2008; Willis 2007). The multiple-ditched arrangement would have certainly required a considerable investment of labour for its construction, but whether its function was defensive, as a status statement, as a boundary to some seasonal or cultural activity or even simply as a large agricultural enclosure, marking the limits of stock proprietorship, remains uncertain at present. All that can be said is that such features are not common in the lower Nene valley and the growing amount of recent evidence suggests that the digging of multiple-ditched systems in England is often related to sites with a high status (see Garland 2012; 2013; and Nick Garland pers. comm.).

All of this speculation regarding the status of the Lynch Farm Iron Age complex, set within its significant boundary ditches, may go some way to explain the siting of the Roman fortress just across the river to the east and away from any concentration of Iron Age power. Admittedly, the fortress site did cause the demise of local Iron Age farmsteads, which were cleared away presumably because they lay in close proximity to the fortress itself. However, if the Lynch Farm complex formed any sort of power base then it remained, as far as the archaeological evidence indicates, largely intact. The siting of the fortress may also have been influenced by more high-level political considerations if the Nene were the actual line of the tribal boundaries between the *Catuvellauni* (to the south) and the *Corieltauvi* (to the north). It may have been politic for the fortress to be sited outside of Catuvellaunian territory altogether, making a clear statement that its tribal system was not being violated in any way. However this does not explain the situation which arose with the siting of the military installation to the south of the river and on the edge of the Lynch Farm complex itself.

Much of the above discussion needs testing by further research and excavation within the area, but the whole Lynch Farm complex now needs to be seen as a major and significant site within local Iron Age studies. This makes the preliminary comments on the finds from the multiple-ditched system (Lynch Farm I) reported by Challands (Challands 1973; 1974a; *Northamptonshire Archaeology* 1974a, 85) ever more tantalising. These excavations, completed in 1974, remain after nearly forty years the most extensive investigation of any triple-ditched system in the east midlands and thus the full publication of the excavations must now be eagerly awaited so that the whole area can be more formally appraised.

III. The Roman military period
(Figs 95 and 96)

The suggestion that the Lynch Farm 2 site had links with a military phase was first made in 1972, when J.K.S. St Joseph reported seeing two parallel ditches running through the site (NVRC 1972). These features and other cropmarks photographed during 1976–7 have been plotted in Figure 3 and marked as D. The position of this feature is also shown in Figure 95 (air photographs held at Peterborough Museum with copies in the Peterborough HER). Concerns have already been expressed above (Chapter 2, II. Area A, Period 2) about the interpretation of this feature as a Roman military installation, considering that there are numbers of multiple-ditched and very regularly shaped late Iron Age and early Roman farmsteads in the region which look remarkably similar in plan. However, the excavations and the finds suggested that the most likely interpretation of the site was as a previously unknown Roman military base which, according to the air photographs, had sides of approximately 175m (north–south) by 150m (east–west), thus giving it a total area of approximately 2.8ha (7 acres). The fort, if that is what it was, was of a slightly trapezoid shape and there were no indications of any entrances or gateways into the central area.

The fort ditches consisted of a slightly wider and deeper inner ditch which had a steeper inner face and a shallower outer face (Figures 10 and 96). The outer ditch was slightly shallower and more rounded in profile and there was a gap of around 2.5m between the two ditch lines on the western side of the feature and some 2.0m on the south side. The angle or corner of the fort was not explored during the excavations but it was assumed to have been a standard (military) rounded corner as vaguely seen on the air photographs. The ditches were, in most excavated sections, less that 0.5m deep, although one section of the inner ditch was 0.95m deep (see Fig. 10 S44). These ditches are comparatively shallow when compared with the ditches at the other local auxiliary forts at Great Casterton and Water Newton, which were on average 1.5m deep, although the fort at Godmanchester had defensive ditches that were of a similar depth to the Lynch Farm 2 examples (Todd 1968, fig. 3; Upex 2013b; 2014; Green 1975, fig. 2). The ditches surrounding the fortress at

Longthorpe, which housed a detachment of the Ninth Legion, were more substantial, with the inner ditch being some 2.0m deep — although the ditch during the second phase of the fortress (Longthorpe II) was reduced down to 1.5m (Frere and St Joseph 1974, figs 5 and 6).

What is clear at Lynch Farm is that the lower fills of the ditches were comparatively clean and contained little indication of the accumulation of any primary silting, thus giving the impression that the ditches had been open for only a short period of time. There was also the impression from some of the inner ditch sections that they had been part backfilled from the inner side of the fort with a clayey loam that may represent the former rampart material (Geoffrey Dannell and John Peter Wild pers. comm.). Figure 10 shows these sections and contexts 264 in S41, 263 in S42 and 263a in S43 which may be part of this rampart material.

None of the internal features either survived or were identified during the excavations other than five pits (Figures 9 and 96) that contained finds from Period 2, the military phase of the site. What these pits were dug for is uncertain but their positions may be significant considering the conjectural layout of this part of the fort. Figure 96 shows the pits set within the corner of the fort, with conjectural lines showing the possible area covered by the rampart and, behind that, the possible line of the intervallum. The model adopted here also follows the situation found at Great Casterton (Lincs.), which shows no room for any berm between the base of the rampart and the edge of the inner ditch. The rampart width is also based on that at Great Casterton, where the reconstructed rampart was thought to have been 5m wide, with the intervallum being 6m wide (Todd 1968, fig. 4) — by contrast, the conjectural width of the rampart at Godmanchester was thought to be 3.5m (Green 1975, fig. 2). What these pits were dug for is uncertain. They do not appear to have been structural — most had rounded bottoms and did not give the appearance of being large post-holes (see Fig. 11); thus they should not be seen as some form of setting for a wooden corner tower. They might be related to the accommodation within the fort itself and may have been cesspits. The fills of several were of fine silty loam with green/brown flecking which is characteristic of former cesspits.

The question now arises as to the function and date of this fort, sitting as it does very close to the site of the fortress across the river at Longthorpe (see Fig. 95). The dating of the Longthorpe fortress, based on excavation, appears to have started by AD 48 — and possibly as early as *c.* AD 44–45 — and to have continued in a reduced form until *c.* AD 64–5 (Frere and St Joseph 1974, 36–7). At Lynch Farm 2 the evidence from the pottery alone suggests a similar date range. The early samian and the coarse wares (see Chapter 7) that come from the Longthorpe military works depot indicate that the two sites were operating at much the same time, although the evidence from the Lynch Farm military ditches suggests that this site was comparatively short-lived, perhaps in use for a matter of a few years, compared with the potential twenty years during which the fortress was operating. However, the early samian from the site and the quantity of coarse ware sherds (120 sherds; see Figs 81 and 82), along with the two fragments of quern stone (Fig. 73) and the axe head (Fig. 68), all suggest that military occupation of the site had taken place and that the installation was not

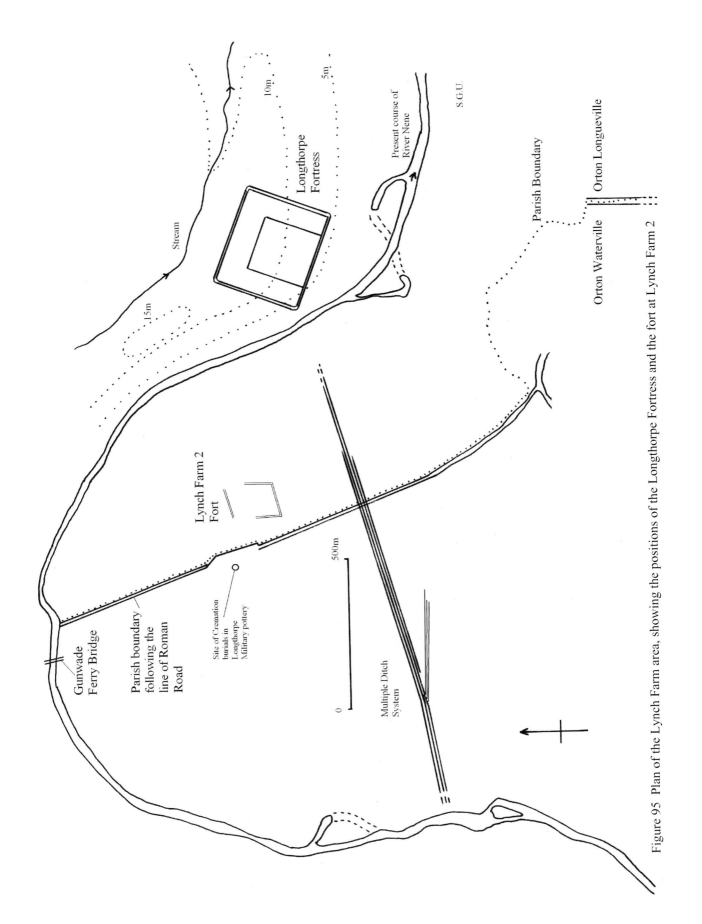

Figure 95 Plan of the Lynch Farm area, showing the positions of the Longthorpe Fortress and the fort at Lynch Farm 2

Stream

15m

10m

5m

Longthorpe
Fortress

Present course of
River Nene

S.G.U.

Parish Boundary

Orton Waterville

Orton Longueville

Gunwade
Ferry Bridge

Parish boundary
following the
line of Roman
Road

Lynch Farm 2
Fort

Site of Cremation
burials in
Longthorpe
Military pottery

500m

0

Multiple Ditch
System

163

some form of practice or very temporary structure. However, it has been impossible to determine the make-up of the troops stationed at the Lynch Farm fort and in fact the site may not have had its own garrison if troops from the fortress were billeted here.

In addition to these finds from the LF2 excavations, Adrian Challands found three cremation burials accompanied by pottery made in the Longthorpe military works depot kilns. A fragment of a mid-1st-century brooch dated to *c*. AD 50–65 was also recovered with these finds (Wild 1973b, 21; NVRC 1973; *Northamptonshire Archaeology* 1973, 9). These cremations lay some 80m from the fort ditches and to the west of Ham Lane (Fig. 95). One burial contained at least four vessels and the excavator commented that the 'burning around the edge of the burial pits echoed a mode of cremation practiced in the Roman Rhineland in the 1st century' (*Northamptonshire Archaeology* 1973, 9).

How these burials link with the site of the Lynch Farm fort is unclear but it is surely significant that the cremations were placed within pottery produced at the military works depot (G.B. Dannell and A. Challands pers. comm.) operating just outside the fortress at Longthorpe. As such the best, although unprovable, explanation is that the cremations were those of individuals connected with the Longthorpe fortress or more likely perhaps the Lynch Farm fort, the interments thus taking place along the line of the early course of the Roman road which ran past the site (see below and Fig. 95).

The functions of the military installation at Lynch Farm are far from clear and the use of the term 'fort', although employed within this report for convenience, is by no means either satisfactory or a firm assessment of the site's actual use. The proximity of the fortress at Longthorpe could indicate that the Lynch Farm military area was simply used as some form of annex. Annexes are well known and are found attached to all forms of military sites for the holding of stores, transport waggons and animals (Campbell 2009, 45–6; Bidwell 2007, 87–9; Jones 2012, 101–5). Locally, at Great Casterton, aerial photographs show an annex extending to the south of the auxiliary fort and covering an area of approximately two acres which Todd suggests the garrison used to keep and water animals (Todd 1968, 23–4, figs 1–2 and pl. I).

It would be tempting to see the Lynch Farm fort as being perhaps a construction camp, used while the main Longthorpe fortress was under construction. The Lynch Farm site is clearly south of the river and within, one might argue, Catuvellaunian territory, which in the early years of the invasion may have been considered safer than building to the north of the river. As such, the indications of the site being rather short-lived may fit with an interpretation as a construction camp that was no longer required when the main fortress had been constructed, and was then demolished. However, Rebecca Jones wisely points out that although the interpretation of a construction camp, with its close proximity to a larger/main camp makes sense, it need not mean that that camp housed troops involved in construction (Jones 2012, 24). The size of such camps does little to help either, with there being great variation in the size of so-called construction camps. The same problem with size is also inherent in interpreting the Lynch Farm site as a marching or campaign camp of some form, as here the range of known sizes, shapes and

defences is considerable (Jones 2012, 19–20; see also Bidwell 2007, chapter 2).

An outside possibility for the Lynch Farm fort's use might relate to the aftermath of the revolt of AD 60. Troops from the Ninth Legion based at Longthorpe had attempted to head off the Icenian army under Boudicca before they reached and lay waste to Colchester. This tactic failed catastrophically, as the Icenian army routed the Roman troops, whose 'entire infantry force was massacred, while the commander escaped to the camp (Longthorpe) with his cavalry and sheltered behind its defences' (Tacitus 1974, 329). This neatly explains the reduced size of the military works at Longthorpe in its later (post-Boudiccan) second phase (Frere and St Joseph 1974, 38–9). In the aftermath of the revolt and when the Roman troops had regained control and defeated the Icenian army in battle, the Ninth Legion was strengthened by additional troops from overseas. Tacitus records that after the revolt two thousand 'regular troops' (legionaries?) were brought in from Germany, 'which brought the Ninth division to full strength'; the additions also included eight auxiliary infantry battalions and a thousand cavalry which were stationed in 'new' winter quarters (Tacitus 1974, 331). Clearly the dating for these troops to come to Britain would be after AD 60, and it is just possible that the Lynch Farm fort may relate to this phase in the military development of the area, perhaps acting as a base from which these new troops could prop up the Ninth Legion, who were, after all, only based across the river. The excavations at Longthorpe clearly showed how the original size of the fortress had been considerably reduced, perhaps as a result of the large number of the original force that had been massacred. Thus one might assume that this reduced defensive circuit involved the destruction of the internal arrangements of the abandoned part of the fort. In addition, the slighting of the outer defences of the original part of the fortress may have occurred in favour of the new inner defences. Any new troops being brought into the area to prop up the Ninth, therefore, would require either a brand new fort or some refurbishment of the old fortress, which was not detected by Frere and St Joseph during their excavations at Longthorpe.

In general terms the coarse pottery recovered from Period 2 deposits at LF2 is linked with the productive life of the 'works depot' at Longthorpe where it was made and which was dated to the duration of activity within the fortress itself. There are clearly problems with using the pottery alone to provide the dating here. Given the paucity of other pottery supplied to the site before the 2nd century it is perhaps obvious that the 1st-century pottery supplied to the site will have been dominated by the local (military) kilns. Once these kilns ended production in the early AD 60s the supplies to Lynch Farm will have also ended, but this should not imply that occupation of the site ceased at the same time and the site's assemblage could have been dominated by the vessels already in circulation.

Dannell and Wild point out that the foundation of this works depot started somewhat later than the foundation of the fortress, 'but that such working is most unlikely to have continued on the spot after the fortress was abandoned'. Thus, pottery production probably ceased by *c*. AD 61–2 (Dannell and Wild 1987, 61) and any military installation to house troops new to the province would thus have to fit at the very end of not only the working life

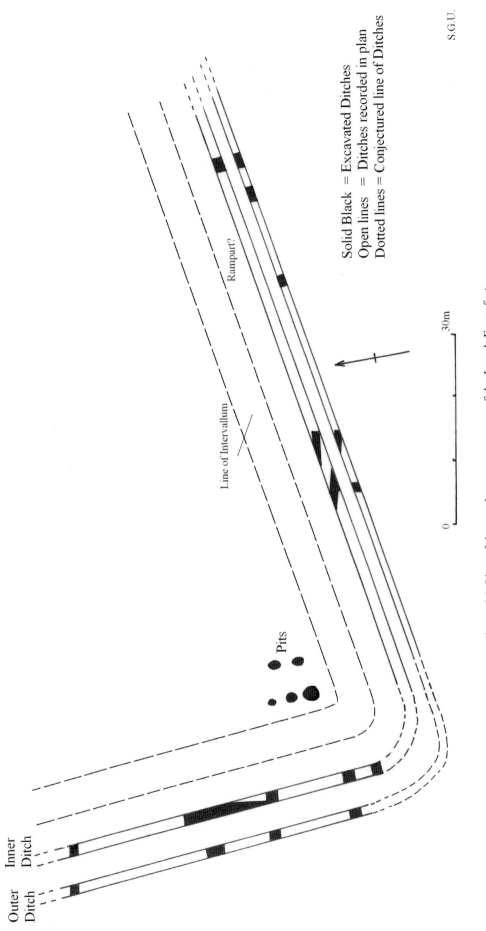

Outer Ditch

Inner Ditch

Pits

Line of Intervallum

Rampart?

Solid Black = Excavated Ditches
Open lines = Ditches recorded in plan
Dotted lines = Conjectured line of Ditches

0   30m

S.G.U.

Figure 96 Plan of the south-western corner of the Lynch Farm fort

165

of the local military pottery production but also the pottery sequences found at LF2. The problem with following this line of argument any further is the problem posed by precise dating, and all that can be said at present is that the Lynch Farm fort could be of the right date to link with new troop movements in Britain after Boudicca. This idea for the fort's use is thus merely a possibility that is worthy of consideration, but may be stretching the evidence a little too far.

However, it is worth noting that at Great Casterton the fort was remodelled in the early Flavian period and Todd has suggested that the smaller garrison introduced was 'probably an *ala quinqenaria*'. Todd goes on to outline the possible troop withdrawal from the fort of legio IX during the governorship of Cerealis and the reassembly of the entire legion at York (Todd 1968, 39–40). The suggestion is that the second fort at Great Casterton did not last long after *c.* AD 80. Perhaps the thing to note from the Great Casterton site is that although *c.* AD 80 seems perhaps too late to link with the evidence from both the Longthorpe and the Lynch Farm military sites, there was activity within the general area during the early Flavian period. Thus the links between military installations within the east of England warrant closer scrutiny to determine whether they represent some form of formal post-Boudiccan reorganisation that could, perhaps, be linked with the subjugation of the Iceni or some aspects of the central control of areas of fenland.

It is interesting to note that both the Longthorpe and the Lynch Farm forts were probably served by an early road system that ran from Godmanchester along the line of Ermine Street to Norman Cross, continued through the modern parish of Alwalton and then followed a line adopted by the later parish boundary between Orton Waterville and Orton Longueville parishes (Frere and St. Joseph 1974, 5; see Fig. 95). This line headed for a crossing of the river Nene at some point close to the medieval Gunwade Ferry and the later still Gunwade Ferry Bridge. How the river was crossed at this point is uncertain but there has to be doubt over its being left to a ford, which would have been open to seasonal flooding that would have left the fortress dangerously exposed. A wooden bridge is more likely.

It has been suggested that this line of a 'proto-Ermine Street', serving both the fortress at Longthorpe and the fort at Lynch Farm, was later abandoned and realigned from a point near Norman Cross (TL 158917) to lead to a new crossing of the Nene between Water Newton and Castor parishes, where the establishment of a bridge provided a better, all-weather crossing of the river. The Nene was almost certainly tidal during the Roman period up to, if not beyond, Alwalton, and thus the early crossing at the head of the meander to the north of the Lynch Farm site may have been either difficult at certain times due to tidal runs or simply flooded for parts of the year. The abandonment of the fortress at Longthorpe during the mid AD 60s, along with the establishment of significant military bases and settlements at Lincoln and then York, may simply have been the catalyst for the reorganisation of the road system and its bridges in the Nene valley (Upex 2008a, 34–47 and fig. 10).

Recent excavations at the site of the Water Newton fort undertaken during the summer of 2012 suggest that this fort may have been part and parcel of this general reorganisation within the area. The best evidence from these excavations suggests that the Water Newton fort was only occupied for a very short time and may have been linked with the realigning of Ermine Street and the construction of both a bridge at the river crossing and a causeway to carry the road across the low-lying flood plain (Upex 2013b; 2014).

IV. The post-military occupation

The best evidence from Lynch Farm 2 suggests that the military withdrawal occurred at some point between *c.* AD 60–65, roughly contemporary with the withdrawal of troops from the Longthorpe fortress (Frere and St Joseph 1974, 38–9). The archaeological deposits indicate that occupation took place immediately afterwards, with the construction of a pit (Pit 6), later enlarged (Pit 7), which was then part-filled and cut through by Ditch 3 (Figs 12 and 13). The line of Ditch 3 appears to have formed an enclosure which on its western side followed the line of the already levelled inner ditch of the fort. This former fort ditch was in part re-excavated (see Fig. 10 S41, context 275; S42, context 275 and S43 context 275). It is possible that the enclosure was formed in what was the abandoned south-western corner of the fort, although this was not tested during the excavation. However, if this were the case then the enclosure would have been of the order of 38×38m, forming a rough square.

At some point the ditches of this enclosure were either recut by Ditch 4 in the north-western sector or realigned totally in the north-eastern sector and along the eastern side of the feature (Fig. 12). What this enclosure was for is not clear, but the quantities of pottery that filled the ditches (Figs 81–82) and that can only be associated with this phase of the site suggest that settlement was taking place either within the area of the feature or very close by. The excavations failed to show any structures which could be associated with this enclosure other than a pottery kiln (Figs 12 and 18 and Pl. 59) which is one of the earliest non-military kilns known from the Nene valley and appears to have been operating at some point in the late 1st or possibly early 2nd century. It seems to be of Wood's Type IC (Woods 1974, fig. 2) and Swan's 'Type iii' kilns (Swan 1984, fig. II), with a stokehole and bowl of fairly equal size. It is similar to the military kilns from Longthorpe and a kiln from Haddon (Dannell and Wild 1987, 41–8; Evans 2003, 75–81) dated to the 1st century. However, the kiln found at Water Newton in a late Flavian context was of a completely different form in that it was sunk some 0.6m into the ground (Perrin 1999, 40). The Lynch Farm and Water Newton kilns both appear to have been making grey wares, while the Haddon example seems to have been associated with shell-tempered vessels. At present all that one can say about pottery production at this early stage of development within the Nene valley is that the size and style of kilns perhaps shows an influence from the military works depot at Longthorpe, where both surface and sub-ground kilns were being operated. Whether some potters stayed after the military moved on is debatable but unanswerable at present, but it would seem that this may be the likely scenario.

What is interesting at Lynch Farm 2 is that the post-military phase of the site appears to have been immediately resettled, suggesting that either military officials had released the site for use by a local native or civilian population or that perhaps the site somehow continued under a form of quasi-military jurisdiction or control once the actual troops had withdrawn. There was no evidence that any immediate and similar occupation within the Roman period had occurred at the Longthorpe fortress; in fact, the next stratigraphical sequence at Longthorpe appeared to consist of Saxon burials (Frere and St Joseph 1974, 112–3). The military works depot outside the fortress was similarly abandoned and not reused for some time, and it was not until c. AD 150 that any new features appeared on this site (Dannell and Wild 1987, 82).

V. Late 2nd- and early 3rd-century expansion

The enclosure ditches of the late Flavian and early 2nd century expanded to include a side ditch (Ditch 5) which headed to the east and whose function was unclear. However, there appears to have been a remodelling of the site in the late 2nd century. The early military pits and the large pit (Pit 6/7) and ditches of the post-military enclosure were being filled and consolidated (see, for example, Fig. 12). Across the eastern part of the post-military enclosure a ditch was dug (Ditch 6; Fig. 19) and at about the same time an aisled building was constructed with stone foundations and what would appear from the evidence to be a wooden superstructure (Building 1; Fig. 19). There was, up to this period, little activity over the rest of the excavated parts of the site but ditches and pits were dug at some point during the late 2nd century in Areas B and C (see Figures 44 and 50). Their functions are unclear, other than to say that they were probably related to the drainage of the site and may have formed some eastern line or limit beyond which settlement did not spread.

The aisled building (Fig. 20) was of a typical early Nene valley form with two rows of four posts which were set within stone-packed post-holes. The outer wall lines were all probably of pitched limestone, of which fragments in the north-eastern corner and part-way down the western side remained. On this wall foundation would have been fixed a timber sill beam into which the timber upper walls were set. There was no indication of roofing material, but thatch has to be likely and the proximity to the river and its reed beds would have provided such material.

At the north-eastern end of this building was a short stub wall some 2m long with two post-holes set along its line. This is best interpreted as some form of lean-to, which may have had a similar stub wall at its western side — but of this no trace survived. Nor was there any trace of an entrance into the main building or between the lean-to and the main building.

Inside this aisled building six small ovens or furnaces were found (see Fig. 22). None of them contained evidence for metalworking and they were possibly intended for some domestic use linked with cooking or baking. However, Furnace 5 did have three fragments of briquetage within the bowl of the feature which may have been linked with salt production. The river would have been tidal up to and beyond the Lynch Farm 2 site during the Roman period and salt may have been produced from the military period onward; certainly, finds of briquetage came from one of the military pits (Pit 1; Fig. 11 S45). If salt was being produced within Furnace 5 and some of the

other furnaces with Building A1 then this would represent the most upstream site along the Nene valley where this has been detected.

There is some debate about whether salt was considered to be a commodity that was totally under the control of the state or the military (Shotter 2005, 43; see also Millett 1990, 121). Around modern Middlewich (Cheshire) there were numerous sites linked with salt production which have been associated with a nearby military site (Garner 2005; Dodds 2005), and the proximity of the Longthorpe fortress and the Lynch Farm fort may have initially stimulated and controlled organised salt production in the Nene valley which perhaps even superseded earlier late Iron Age salterns (Every 2006; Morris 2008). However, at present there is no firm evidence to suggest that salt was in any way centrally organised within the fenlands. The distribution of saltern sites does show a concentration along Roman roads, including the Fen Causeway (Lane 2005, 54). This in turn may offer some form of explanation as to how the salt-making was organised by suggesting that the production of salt, or perhaps more especially salted products such as hides and meat, was part of an export market from the fenland, rather than for just local consumption. Tom Lane perhaps best sums up the situation within the fenland by commenting that the 'official response to indigenous salt workers is unrecorded, but [...] concessions to private lessees is no problem and is recorded elsewhere and thus formal state control would not be necessary' (Lane 2005, 54; see also Potter 1981). However, it should not be forgotten that the exploitation of salt within the empire was an imperial prerogative and control by civil servants at the *civitas* level or by the army may have occurred (De Clercq 2011, 250). It thus remains unclear whether the whole process of salt-making was driven by any form of state control and, if so, whether dues and rents were paid eventually into imperial coffers, or whether salt extraction was only partly controlled by officialdom and remained largely an essentially peasant production.

The dating of the salterns within the fenland to the 1st and 2nd centuries does match the dating evidence for salt production from Lynch Farm remarkably well, with a general fenland decline in evidence after this date (Potter 1989, 170; Lane 2005, 47). This later decline may be rather more due to climatic and geomorphological changes that to an actual reduction in production. The environmental conditions of the early Roman period changed in the later periods (Bromwich 1970, 114; Potter 1981, 132; Pryor 1984, 204; Pryor *et al.* 1985, 309) forcing populations onto higher ground, and changes in water levels would have changed tidal flows, forcing many salt workers to move closer to the coastal margins, where salinity was greater (Lane 2005, 50–53).

VI. 3rd- and 4th-century developments

How long Building 1 remained in use is difficult to deduce from the available evidence, but at some point probably around c. AD 200 it was demolished and a second building (Building II; see Fig. 25) was erected on a different alignment, this time with a long axis orientated east–west. This new aisled building partly overlay the southern part of Building I but was larger and longer, being some 16×10.5m and having four pairs of posts, set like those of the earlier arrangement in stone-packed post-holes (see Fig. 25, Pls 20–22). Like the earlier structure, this building had walls composed of pitched limestone masonry which presumably held a sill beam into which was pegged a timber superstructure. There was some evidence along the southern wall line to show that post-holes had been dug along the line of the wall, but whether these formed part of the original wall structure or were more likely some form of modification or repair remains uncertain. The roof was supported on the internal posts and was presumably either thatched or even perhaps pegged with wooden shingles. At this stage of the building's life there was no evidence to suggest any entrances.

The internal arrangements are also uncertain, as there was no indication as to what activities went on in this new building. The floor levels did not survive, but in the make-up above the building there was little to suggest any form of industrial activity and no evidence for furnace debris or salt-making.

Away from the building the north–south ditch line, Ditch 6, which was dug during the life of Building 1, seems to have been maintained (Fig. 25). There remained a gap of about a metre between the end of the building and the termination of this ditch, which could have provided access from the west to the north of the structure.

Further to the east there was little activity on the site. In Area B there was some evidence for narrow ditches which were probably dug at this period. Ditch B5 (Fig. 44) seems to date from this phase of the site's history but its function is unclear. Similarly, there is little evidence for any organised use of the landscape in Areas C and D, where the only feature located from this period was Ditch C4 (Fig. 50).

VII. Significant expansion and landscape organisation
(Fig. 97)

It is only during Period 6 that significant landscape developments occurred at the site, including a western extension to Building II. This aisled building which originally had four pairs of posts was expanded by the addition of three extra pairs of posts to form a structure with seven pairs of posts. In terms of the structure there was little difference between the new post-holes and those from the first phase, although the gaps between the new posts were slightly different to those between the earlier posts. However, the outer wall line was very different in that it consisted of a much less substantial limestone foundation and instead included substantial amounts of gravel (Fig. 26).

Internal arrangements were, again, not detected archaeologically, although a small furnace or oven was found on the north side of the central aisle between Posts 1 and 3 (Fig. 28). At this point, too, a furnace was inserted against the south wall of the building between Posts 10 and 12 (see Figs 26 and 31) and appears to have been used for metalworking.

There was some suggestion at this stage of the building's life that entrances had been formed. There was a break in the limestone walling in the long axis of the south wall opposite Post 6 (Fig. 26), which may have given pedestrian access. Along the north wall opposite Post 5 there was a similar break in the limestone walling associated with a spread of limestone which could have

been laid to consolidate an entrance, perhaps of slightly wider proportions. However, some of this material may have been make-up over the top of the earlier Ditch 6 (Fig. 19), which had been filled by this stage but might have needed consolidation as the deposits settled.

The occupants of the building seem to have been concerned about the stability of the whole structure, perhaps with ageing timbers needing replacing and the building possibly tilting or shifting. To this end buttresses were added to all four corners of the building, presumably in an attempt to support or prop up the superstructure. Perhaps the threat of collapse warranted the deposit of a horse skull as some form of offering to the deities for the safe protection of the building (Pl. 25).

Whatever was going on inside this building in its now expanded form coincided with activity in other parts of the site. To the north of Building II a fence line was erected which ran from close to the north-western corner of the building in a roughly northern direction (Fig. 36) close by a small square building with pitched limestone foundations (Building III; see Figs 28 and 32 and Pl. 27). This fence line may have partly reorganised the area to the north of Building II once Ditch 6 had been filled in and the western extension to Building II completed (Building II Phase II).

Building III was approximately 4m square and appeared to have an entrance in its eastern wall marked by a post-hole that presumably held a door jamb. Inside there was a small central limestone spread that part-filled an underlying hollow. Around the site, which was already badly damaged when excavations started, there were considerable spreads of wall plaster (Fig. 35) and mortar and the general view was that this building was painted on the inside with a scheme largely of red but also of some orange paint. Around the outside of the building were several post-holes which were interpreted as representing a veranda or walkway which may have extended around the whole structure, although again machine damage had obliterated large areas of potential archaeological evidence here.

Various functions for this building were suggested by the excavators of the site, including its being a small mausoleum similar to that found within Normangate Field at Castor (*Northamptonshire Archaeology* 1969, 7); another suggestion was that it formed a small milling chamber, with the central stone spread acting as the emplacement for the millstones (*Northamptonshire Archaeology* 1974b, 95). However, the structure is best seen as a small rural shrine with a central, solid — perhaps squat — tower forming the *cella*, which was surrounded by a veranda walkway. If this was indeed the original form of Building III then it appears to conform to the style of Romano-Celtic temples of which the literature has many examples (Lewis 1966).

Rural shrines within the east midlands are not uncommon (see Taylor 2007, 35) and vary in shape from circular or penannular layouts to rectangular forms. Two shrines from Brigstock (Greenfield 1963) and those from Collyweston (both Northants) excavated by Knocker (1965) are of the circular or irregular circle form. The closest local parallel to the Lynch Farm 2 shrine comes from Chesterton, found in part of the suburbs of *Durobrivae* excavated during 1956–7. Here a small rectangular shrine went through three separate phases of construction. The earliest phase, dated to the 2nd century, had a *cella* which was 5.5m square; this was later replaced by a structure 3.9m square, slightly smaller than the *cella* at Lynch Farm 2. The latest phase at Chesterton was so badly damaged that little could be said of its exact form other than it, like the second phase, was constructed in the 3rd century. Around the *cella* were sets of post-holes which would have held posts supporting a roofed walkway or ambulatory (Perrin 1999, fig. 35; Greenfield 1958, 2–6)

In the Welland valley Structure 12 at Maxey appears to represent the basic layout of a similar rectangular Romano-Celtic shrine (Gurney 1985, fig. 63). Here there were two concentric rectangular ditches set out with an entrance opening to the west. The innermost of these ditches (9×10m) probably held a palisade or portico of posts which surrounded an inner timber shrine set on sill beams, of which no trace was found (Gurney 1985, 104). This would make the Maxey example larger than that at Lynch Farm, and the orientation of the entrance was also different. However, the orientation of entrances at such sites varies, though east- and south-facing predominate (Gurney 1985, 103; Wilson 1975, 13–27; de la Bédoyère 1991, 177–95).

At Godmanchester Michael Green found another structure interpreted as a shrine which went through three distinct phases of which the second phase, although larger, is remarkably similar to the Lynch Farm example in layout (Green 1986, fig. 3). The Godmanchester example, approximately the same size as that from Maxey, appears to have had a timber inner wall enclosing the *cella*, while the ambulatory was set out with large timber posts 2m apart. The floors were of gravel and the structure was roofed with either tiles or Collyweston slates. Green (1986, 33 and fig. 10) suggests that the shrine was dedicated to the god Abandinus, who is recorded on an inscription found nearby.

The shrines from Chesterton, Maxey and Godmanchester are shown along with five other rectangular shrines from southern Britain in Figure 97. All seem to follow the basic form, consisting of either single or double concentric circuits of construction the innermost of which represent the *cella*, which would have risen above the roof level of the outer, ambulatory walkway. Within this group the Lynch Farm shrine is the smallest and also the only example in which the *cella* is constructed of stone with floors that may have been mortared, although the Godmanchester example did have gravel floors.

There were no votive finds from the Lynch Farm shrine to add further detail to the working of the structure or give any dedicatory information, but the lack of finds is not uncommon on sites that are considered to have been shrines. The Maxey shrine produced no evidence of any religions function and the same was true at Lancing Down, which yielded nothing in the way of any religious link (Gurney 1985, 103; Bedwin 1981, 46).

How a shrine of this form fitted into the general religious situation during the late 3rd and early 4th centuries is debatable. Shrines or temples associated with farm-type buildings are not uncommon in the Roman world, and there are continental parallels and examples from Britain (*Northamptonshire Archaeology* 1974b, 95; Percival 1976, 183–97; Smith 2000, 266–92; Walters 2009). However, the late date of the Lynch Farm shrine provides an interesting perspective on what was

happening within the countryside at this time. Pagan shrines certainly did flourish in the countryside in the 4th century despite, and probably in direct opposition to, a growing Christian influence. The shrines at Brigstock have coin issues associated with them that run well into the 4th century and that indicate that the use of the shrines was probably continuous from the middle years of the early 2nd century until *c.* AD 380, when coin use ceases (Greenfield 1963, 239). Millett (1990, 195–6 and fig. 83) points out that rural temples mirror the distribution of villas and that their numbers increase throughout the Roman period, reaching a peak in the middle of the 4th century. The Lynch Farm shrine would fit perfectly well with this known pattern of dates and contexts.

To the south-west of the shrine another building (Building IV; see Fig. 28) was discovered, although this structure was so badly damaged that little could be recovered of its plan or form other than to say that it had pitched limestone foundations and was associated with wall plaster. Because of the poor state of preservation the dating of this building was insecure, but the best interpretation of the evidence is that it was erected at the same time as the expansion of the aisled building (Building II, Phase II) and the construction of the shrine, and formed part of substantial development in this part of the site. This also fits with the considerable expansion of ditch systems and shallow pools in Area B (see Fig. 44) and the use of one small length of ditch in Area C (Ditch C3, see Fig. 50). The excavations in Area B also cut a section across what appeared to be a wooden walled structure with a clay floor (Building B1; see Fig. 45 was 46). This structure was, like Building IV, impossible to date directly but was aligned with nearby ditches dated to the 3rd century. If this is any indication that the building was of a similar or slightly later date to these ditches then this building would also fit into the general expansion that appears to be going on at the site during Period 5 or possibly Period 6.

The ditched features within Area B and the large shallow ponds (Fig. 44) are difficult to assess in terms of function. In some cases the ditches seem to have been very long-lived, with recuts taking place over a considerable length of time and with each cut following a slightly different orientation (see, for example, the situation with Ditches B12, shown in Fig. 44 and in section in Fig. 49 S120). In other areas the ditches appear to have been first laid out during Period 6 and to have followed some form of planned layout. This is especially true in the western part of Area B, where Ditches B2 and B3 follow a parallel course for some 30m across the site and form what can only be described as side ditches for a track or drove way. Elsewhere within Area B the destruction caused by the contractor's machinery after the initial topsoil was stripped away had truncated the archaeological features so that little was left of any interpretive features that may have existed within the upper levels of the site. It is interesting to note, however, that along some of the ditch lines there were attempts to revet the sides of the ditches. This was especially so along Ditches B2 and B3. An attempt to secure the sides of the ditches in the friable gravel subsoil of the site against the erosion of the banks by stock walking along the trackway between the two ditches is likely, but one might ask why, if these ditches did form a trackway, a greater space was not allowed between the ditches so that revetting would have been unnecessary.

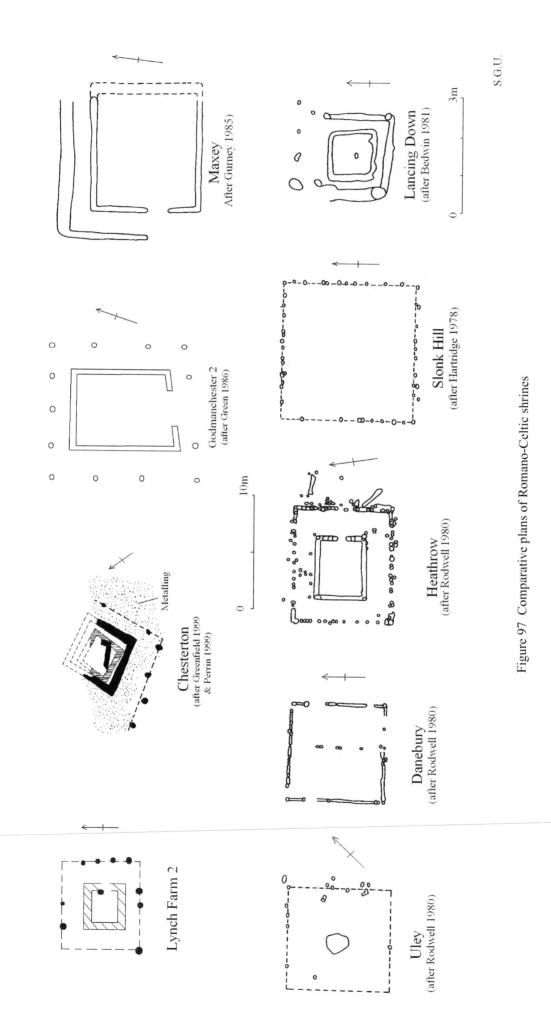

Maxey
After Gurney 1985

Lancing Down
(after Bedwin 1981)

3m

0

S.G.U.

Godmanchester 2
(after Green 1986)

Slonk Hill
(after Hartridge 1978)

10m

0

Chesterton
(after Greenfield 1999
& Perrin 1999)

Metalling

Heathrow
(after Rodwell 1980)

Danebury
(after Rodwell 1980)

Lynch Farm 2

Uley
(after Rodwell 1980)

Figure 97 Comparative plans of Romano-Celtic shrines

The intention of the revetting might also be linked with the need for a clean flow of water into or out of the site; the original excavators did propose that some parts of the site were set aside for fish farming, which would have needed or benefited from such hydrological works (Wild 1973a). However, there is now little firm evidence to support claims for fish production at the site and the area and the site as a whole are probably best seen as operating some form of agricultural economy orientated towards stock management rather than fish farming. The report by Fifield and Upex (above) shows no evidence of fish bones within the faunal assemblage (accepting that sieving was not carried out during excavation work), but suggested an agricultural economy based on stock rearing.

The shallow pools or ponds that were found in Area B appear to have been too shallow for fish farming, even allowing for the fact that their depth was reduced by the pre-excavation removal of topsoil and other upper layers. Ponds A and B appeared simply to be shallow areas of what might have been natural flooding. They had little regular shape, appeared to overlie filled-in ditches of a stratigraphically earlier period and, in the case of Pond C, appeared to have covered isolated post-holes (Fig. 44 context 32) of uncertain date and use. The possibility of these pools having any links with the salt production referred to above can probably be discounted. There were no links with any briquetage or other materials which might have suggested salt production and the pools were late within the stratigraphic sequence of the settlement, when these areas of the site appeared to have been partially abandoned and when flooding was an increasing problem. However, Fincham does point out that the switch from briquetage to wooden containers — which do not survive within the archaeological record — for salt production may mask the extent of late salt production (Fincham 2004, 132–5).

VIII. Late developments
(Fig. 98)

Building II in Area A seems to have continued in use until some point toward the end of the 4th century when it was demolished and a rubble spread, presumably from the walls, was levelled over an area within the middle of the structure (Fig. 39). Much of this deposit was very disturbed when archaeological work began but enough survived to show that some of this levelled stonework had formed a flooring surface for a structure which had been constructed over the demolished area of Building II. A wall to the west of this flooring area may have been part of this late structure, but nothing more was found to indicate that it was anything more than a very rough shed-like construction which was linked to some of the latest pottery on the site and formed the end of the occupation sequence.

It is not clear from the dating if this demolition of Building II (Phase II) was linked in some way with the construction of Ditch 7 (see Fig. 37), which was dug and filled in at some point during the late 4th century. The line of this ditch, which is roughly north–south and ran close to the eastern, short axis wall of the building, may have marked a boundary line that separated the demolition going on within the building from the developments which were happening to the east.

Most of the ditches in Area B appear to have been allowed to silt up naturally or were partly filled with rubbish, augmenting the silting. This was happening during the late periods of the site's history, when only the ditch in the south-western corner of Area B had pottery which indicated that some form of late deposits (Period 7) were being made. It is possible that this debris and rubbish was associated with the late phases within Area A, including the removal of Building II and the shed-like structure built over the demolition rubble.

There seems to have been an almost deliberate emphasis at the site on levelling the area to the west while at the same time there was growing activity to the north-east in Areas C and D. Here a series of three ditches was dug during Period 7, all draining from the west to the east and following the general slope of the ground (Ditches C5, C7 and C8, shown in Fig. 50). In addition, there was a large shallow 'sump'-like feature that may have acted as a pond or watering hole and was probably linked to Ditch C8, which may have acted as some form of overflow channel. This 'sump' was very different to the areas termed 'ponds' in Area B, which were probably entirely natural flooded areas. Here in Area C the 'sump' was dug out to over 1m deep, although it is possible that it was in part formed out of a natural depression in the ground. Whether the formation of this 'sump' was linked to increased stock rearing regimes at the site is not clear and the small sample of faunal remains fails to help here, other than to say that cattle were still dominant within the economy.

Ditches C5 and C7 do seem to form a narrow track-like feature to the south of the 'sump', with Ditch C7 terminating some 3m away from the edge of this feature. This arrangement may have formed a means of moving stock around the 'sump' and either further to the east and down toward the Roman course of the Nene, or in the opposite direction from the Nene, around the 'sump' and towards the west.

Considering developments during the previous periods at the site, including the general decline and the demolition of buildings, it is somewhat astonishing to find that there was considerable activity during Period 8 in Areas C and D. For whatever reason the 'sump' and the ditches were filled in with rubbish containing very late sequences of pottery and buildings were set out along with large areas of limestone rubble which formed working surfaces and floors. All of this activity is linked to late coin losses which are emphasised by Walton (Chapter 6, II. The Roman coins).

The wall lines of three structures (Buildings C1, C2 and D1; see Fig. 52) were plotted, although the precise lines of the walls and the nature of the buildings generally were difficult to visualise as the whole area had been churned up and badly disturbed by heavy machinery prior to the archaeological work (see, for example, the situation in Pls 4 and 5). However, what sense can be made of the area suggests that Building C1 was the first in the series. This was followed by the setting out of Building C2, which then appears to have had a room, lean-to or further structure added at its eastern end. The building sequences were very unclear, however, and any differentiations regarding date were not recovered. As such, the three buildings have been treated as being all roughly contemporary, although the orientation of Building C1 probably makes this the earliest.

The walls of all three structures were formed from limestone rubble which in some parts was pitched in a herringbone fashion, as along the north wall of Building II. This building also had evidence for two post-holes along its southern wall line, which could have been in some way linked with a timber superstructure or doorway. Along the south wall of Building D1 there was some attempt to provide facing stones to an inner core of rubble. This building also contained an oven-like feature which was interpreted by the excavators as a corn drier. The functions of such features have been well set out by Morris (1979, 6–9), who outlines ten major groups or types which all use gentle heat to part-dry grain, either for seed corn or more especially malt (Morris 1979, 88–103). The Lynch Farm 2 corn drier is small when compared with larger local examples from Orton Hall Farm and Haddon (Mackreth 1996b, 75–80; Hinman 2003), and it is difficult to know how it functioned in detail. The sooting and heat marks shown along the limestone flue must have come from a fire which was channelled from this flue and under a suspended floor to the south, marked by the rectangle of limestone rubble. The amount of grain being processed at any one time must have been small.

It is also possible that alternative uses could have been made of this feature; for example, the proximity to the Nene and its fisheries may have encouraged the smoking of fish, for which the Lynch Farm 'drier' would have been equally suited (Mattingley 2007, 322; Lawrence 2010, 36).

The biggest problem with the description of these three structures as buildings is the manner of the roofing. Buildings C1 and D1 are both small enough to have been roofed over easily, although it is uncertain how a roof over Building D1 might have been organised. This structure had a surviving south wall but there is only slight evidence for a north wall owing to the damage done to the site before excavation commenced. It may be that this structure was simply a lean-to arrangement against the south wall and remained open to the north, with the eaves supported on a series of timber posts of which nothing remains.

However, the chief problem in this regard relates to Building C2, which appears to have had no internal supports for any posts. The structure is 13.75m wide, 29m along its northern wall and 31m along its southern wall, making the whole layout slightly trapezoid. This skewing in the wall lines may, however, be the result of damage by machinery prior to excavation. Along the southern wall line the wall appeared to have been shifted into sections curved slightly to the north, possibly where the wheels of machines had skidded sideways as they passed over the area. The building's overall size of 13.75×30m makes it slightly larger than would be expected if it were an aisled building of standard Nene valley type. The largest of the aisled buildings known from the Nene valley, found at Orton Hall Farm (Mackreth 1996b, fig. 35), had six pairs of internal posts and was 13m wide and 25m long. This compares with Building II (Phase II) at Lynch Farm, which was 11×22.75m. A building at Wakerley

(Northants) was 12m wide by 20m long with eight pairs of aisle posts (Jackson and Ambrose 1978, fig. 15). Other smaller structures from the area are known and their comparative plans are shown by Upex (2008a, fig. 46). Thus, with an outline of 13.75×30m, Building C2 at Lynch Farm falls beyond the standard size for local aisled buildings and, although the width is almost matched by the width of 'Barn 1' at Orton Hall Farm, the length exceeds the longest known length of such structures by 7m. If Building C2 were an aisled structure, therefore, the spacings of posts at other known structures suggest that it would need some nine or perhaps ten pairs of internal posts to support the roof. There was no evidence for any internal supports for nave posts in the form of either post-holes or post pads, although this is not to say that any such internal posts were not set on wooden pads which have simply disappeared from the archaeological record.

An alternative view is to see this structure as one of a growing number of known walled enclosures, which may at some point have been roofed or partly roofed, but which remain difficult to explain. At Orton Hall Farm a 'rectangular building' was found which was 20×25m (see Table 20) with an entrance or doorway 2.5m wide set into its southern side. Again, there was little to explain how this structure was roofed and the best interpretation is to see the wall as encircling an open yard. The function of this building remains uncertain, as it contained no evidence for any domestic occupation and the absence of drains would have made it very unsuitable for containing stock of any kind (Mackreth 1996b, 72). A structure of similar size, measuring some 17.5×25m and termed by the excavator a 'walled enclosure', was found in 1957, set back slightly from Ermine Street on the south side of the Roman town of *Durobrivae*. This structure was bounded by side roads which came off the line of Ermine Street and led to the rear of adjoining house plots. There was an entrance set into the south-western corner of this structure but nothing to indicate that it was ever roofed over and its function remains enigmatic (Perrin 1999, figs 2 and 34). A third structure, possibly similar to that at Lynch Farm, comes from excavations undertaken in Normangate Field at Castor in 1962–3 by Graham Webster (Perrin and Webster 1990, fig. 2). It was 16×22m and again without any indication of internal roof supports, although this excavation was very limited and detailed excavations inside the structure were not undertaken. This point may also account for the fact that there is no known entrance into the area marked out by the walls at this site.

Dating of these structures is somewhat mixed, with little evidence being recorded for either the Normangate Field example or the structure outside *Durobrivae*. However, the example from Orton Hall Farm appears to have been used during the 4th century (Mackreth 1996b, 70), and this date would match the Lynch Farm example. The Orton Hall Farm structure also appears to have been in part floored with gravel, at least in its early phase, and this corresponds with the situation at Lynch Farm where part

No.	Site	Structure size	Reference
1	LF2	13×30m	This volume
2	Orton Hall Farm	20×25m	Mackreth 1996, 72
3	Durobrivae's Suburbs	17×25m	Perrin 1996, figs 2 and 34
4	Normangate Field, Castor	16×22m	Perrin 1990, fig. 2

Table 20 Large open walled enclosures within the Nene valley

of the interior of Building C2 was covered in limestone rubble. This rubble spread is shown in Figure 52 and Pls 45 and 47, and may have been an attempt to provide both a hard standing or surface for some activity taking place within the area of the walls and packing for the underlying 'sump' from Period 7, which would have settled as the soft fills of the feature compacted, causing a hollow to develop.

The rubble spread within Building C2 was very similar to that which was being made within the area of the nearby demolished aisled building (Building II), and the source of both sets of rubble may well have been the same. It is difficult to know how high the walls of Building II extended, and the general view is that Roman aisled buildings within the local area perhaps only ever had dwarf stone walls that acted as a form of damp-proofing for the timber superstructure that would have been fitted over the top of these solid and dry foundations. However, there are now enough examples to show that Roman builders were easily able to build to eaves or even full roof height (King and Potter 1990; Roy Friendship-Taylor pers. comm.), and it is possible that the debris from Building II's walls was considerable and could have formed the bulk of both the spread within Building II (Fig. 39 context 33) and Building C2.

What the function of this large walled structure was remains enigmatic. It was claimed by the original excavators that it could have served as a fish pool for the breeding of fish (Wild 1973a, 21 and fig. 10) but it is difficult to see how the whole structure would have operated in this form. Pools for fish breeding would have required leets to take water into and out of holding tanks and a head of water would have been desirable (see Higginbotham 1997, 9–49), besides which the need to line a tank with walling and to pave the bottom may seem unnecessary when ponds to hold fish could easily have been dug into the ground without any additional groundworks.

In addition to the absence of leets or channels able to feed water into the area defined by the encircling walls of Building C2, it is worth pointing out that those channels that were encountered at this period in Areas C and D, such as Ditch C9, were at a lower level than the area inside Building C2 (see Fig. 50, also Fig. 55 was 56 S92) and, as such, would seem to have been dug to try to drain the area of Building C2 or to stop water coming into the area from this northern side.

It may be that the builders were more intent on the demarcation of an area and that within the walls of Building C2 there were lean-to-type structures with light roofs which did not require heavy posts to carry their weight and which could have been either fixed onto post pads or on sill beams that have left no trace in the archaeological record. However, it remains unclear what the area was used for in this late period but activity within the whole of the excavated area was either concentrated here or over the demolished remains of Building II, where some form of shed-like structure appears to have been constructed.

Roughly contemporary with the construction of the buildings in Areas C and D and the levelling of Buildings II and III in Area A appears to be the construction of two wells (see Figs 4 and 40–43). The better evidence for dating came from Well I, which cannot have been constructed before the middle of the 4th century as a coin of Helena (AD 337–41) came from the fill of the construction trench (see Walton above). The dating of Well II was less secure but the best evidence suggests that, for whatever reason, they were very close in date, probably in both their construction and the date at which they were filled in, which was late in the 4th century or at the beginning of the 5th. This final filling of both wells, which included late assemblages of pottery, matches the material from the late sequences within the 'sump' in Area C and seems to fit a pattern of late reorganisation of sites which is growing ever more familiar within the lower Nene valley (see, for example, Upex 2008a, 240–57; 2008b, 320–29, 2). The deposition of young pigs, deer and dogs within the fill of Well I fits with recent research into forms of votive deposition (Morris 2011) and can be paralleled locally at Bretton Way, Peterborough (Pickstone and Drummond-Murray 2013, 62).

The fragmented sections of excavated ditches at Lynch Farm 2, which show no apparent indication that they formed enclosures in which buildings or other features were constructed, may give the slightly false impression that the site lacked any planning whatsoever. A summary of the 1972–3 season of work at the site does refer to Buildings II, III, B1 and C2 as being laid out around 'a courtyard'-type space (NVRC 1973, 8), but this 'disjointed' arrangement may simply reflect the poverty of the archaeological record that it was possible to extract from the site itself, especially given the circumstances in which the excavation was first undertaken. What is clear is that there was some degree of planning at the site when it came to the orientation of the buildings, which were laid out in either a north–south (Building I) or an east–west (Buildings II, B1, C1, C2 and D1) orientation. The 'formal' orientation of aisled buildings in the Nene valley has already been commented on by Upex, who points out that this class of building was generally set with the long axis aligned to the cardinal points (see Upex 2008a, fig. 47). Why such buildings were orientated in such a way is uncertain, but may in some way be linked with the functions of the buildings and the need to consider either light or perhaps draught, if industrial processes were being carried on inside (Upex 2008a, 130–39). It would be interesting to know whether such a basic 'orientation' of buildings, apparent within the excavated group at Lynch Farm, extended to the other buildings within the whole Lynch Farm complex; at present, all that can be said is that the cropmark and fieldwork evidence suggests that this could be the case (see Fig. 98).

The late history of the site appears to be characterised by periodic flooding or at least the accumulation of standing water, and this must account for the build-up of sediments over the rubble surfacing within Building C2. This was seen most clearly within the sections taken of the 'sump' (Fig. 53), where a silty layer (context 1) appeared to have been fluvially deposited. The general impression of the whole site during Periods 6–8 is of a gradually rising water table with ditches in Areas B, C and D all silting up and being abandoned.

Such a problem may be linked with the general problems of flooding that were experienced within the local fenlands, which may have been caused by a variety of factors. The changing climate, the silting of rivers flowing out and over the fens into the Wash and relative changes in sea level all appear to have played their part. Perhaps, too, the organisation of Roman drainage

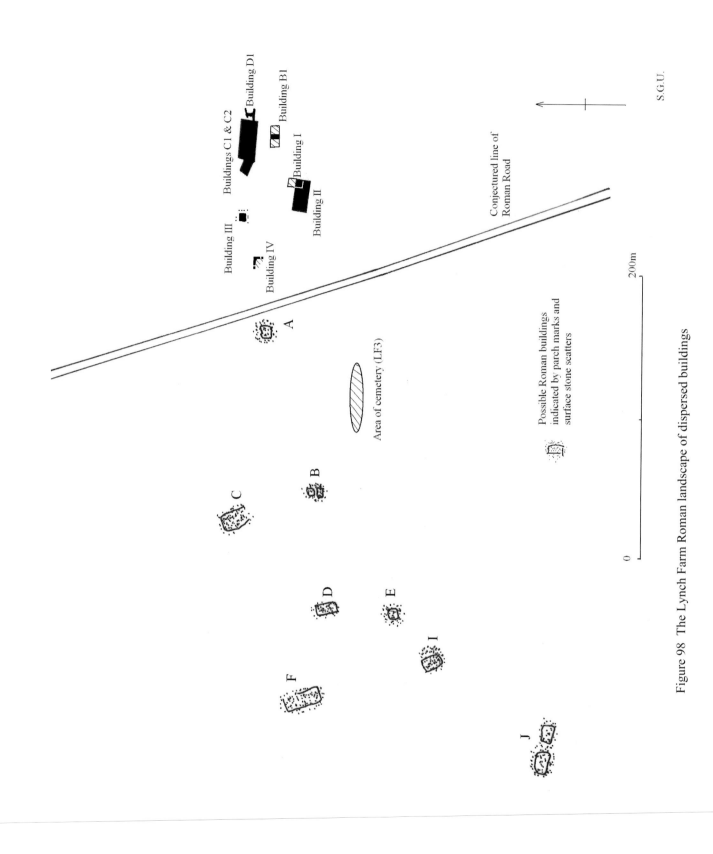

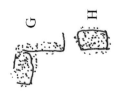

Figure 98 The Lynch Farm Roman landscape of dispersed buildings

174

schemes, which might have been administered locally but backed by political will nationally, had also changed. Salway (1981, 268) has suggested that the lack of maintenance of private estate schemes, especially in the southern fenland, could have played a part, citing the disastrous diversion of the Ouse at Willingham as an example. In addition, the problems on the continent and the general switch of Roman focus away from the province may have also played their part, with less state funding for projects including fenland drainage and its maintenance (Salway 1981, 207). Admittedly, the detailed history of the late Roman fenland is poorly understood, but what evidence there is suggests that flooding was and continued to be a major problem throughout the 4th century and many settlements were inundated (Hayes 1988; Phillips 1970; Hall and Cole 1994; Waller 1994; Upex 2008a, 176–210).

Fenland flooding, river silting and drainage problems in the 3rd and 4th centuries would have simply backed water up the river systems which flowed out across the fen and into the Wash, and it is only to be expected that sites situated by the side of rivers such as the Nene would have suffered as a consequence of this change in hydrology. The Lynch Farm 2 site sits some 500m from the present course of the river Nene and, with a more abraded set of shallow channels forming the course of the river in Roman times, it would follow that flooding across the flood plain near the site could have been frequent (Chatwin 1961; Steers and Mitchell 1962; Grove 1962; Taylor 1963; Williamson 2003).

Even allowing for a rising water table, there was still some very late activity within Area C; one of the very latest features on the whole site was a pit (Fig. 52 context 46 and Fig. 53 S73) dug into the deposits of silt caused perhaps by flooding (context 1) which had accumulated over the top rubble fill (context 2) within Building C2.

The pottery assemblages from the site's late deposits, including the wells, the 'sump' from Area C and the rubble spread (Fig. 39 context 33) over Building II in Area A, all follow a sequence similar to those recovered from other late Nene valley deposits. The well at Stibbington, excavated in 1969, produced a very late sequence of pottery along with a coin of Honorius (AD 393–423) while the latest coin from the stone-lined cistern at Bretton, dug during 2010, was of the House of Valentinian (AD 364–78), although the pottery was remarkably similar in date to that from the Stibbington well (Todd 2008, 314; Pickstone 2011, table 12; Pickstone and Drummond-Murray 2013; Upex 2011a; Upex 2013a). Similar late deposits have been recorded at Haddon (Phases 6 and 7) and at Orton Hall Farm (Period 5) (Hinman 2003; Mackreth 1996b), and all show that occupation was undergoing some general form of reorganisation, with buildings not being maintained or being demolished and rubble (presumably from the demolished buildings) being levelled over sites. Some of these rubble spreads appeared, as within the area of Building II at Lynch Farm 2, to be forming the floors of shed-like structures. The best examples of such late structures, the levelling of walls and the reuse of wall rubble for floors and surfaces was found at Ashton over the earlier metalled surfaces of roads (Hadman and Upex 1975b; 1977; Upex 2008a, fig. 80).

Exactly what this reorganisation within the Nene valley at all the sites so far described in the literature means is unclear, unless it is a reflection of the general breakdown of local administration, tax collection and organisation. The population perhaps felt released or at least eased from the enforcement of a demand economy and the need to produce surpluses, both agriculturally and industrially, and had moved to a more relaxed subsistence economy where buildings were just not maintained. Additionally, the make-up of the local population may have been changing, with immigrants either taking up any surplus land or working alongside an indigenous late Roman population who were farming in a much reduced or less intensive way. This paradigm is perhaps the situation seen at Orton Hall Farm where the chronology of Roman and Saxon structures seems to overlap slightly, and it is tempting to see the two cultural groups living side by side or at least being aware of each other, with the result that a 'working farm passed, largely intact, to a new type of occupant' (Mackreth 1996b, 237).

There is no indication of such Migration Period continuity at Lynch Farm; for example, no Migration Period pottery has been recognised from the site. Instead, from the excavations so far carried out over what appears to be an extensive series of Roman buildings (see Fig. 3), settlement shifted away from the area of Lynch Farm 2 and perhaps by the 6th century had become more focused around the site of the later medieval church and the core of the present village, which was firmly established by the time of the Domesday survey of 1086 (Morris 1975).

However, the laying-out of the landscape in the post-Roman period does appear to show some aspects of continuity, and the conjectured line of the Roman road, which may have had a military origin (see Fig. 95), became the line of the later parish boundary between Orton Waterville and Orton Longueville; as such, it may have been set out as a land boundary from the middle Saxon period onwards (Roffe 1984, 117; Taylor 1983, 104).

IX. The Roman occupation at Lynch Farm within a local and regional context

The plan of the excavated Roman buildings at Lynch Farm 2 can be added to the evidence from the cropmarks and the reported stone scatters of other buildings to give an overall view of the extent of Roman structures in the immediate area. The plots of all these features are shown in Figure 98, along with the conjectured line of the early Roman road and the position of the cemetery excavated in 1972 (Jones 1975). The sites of potential Roman buildings are given as A–J in Figure 98, and it must be recognised that such a plot is based on either directly observed stone scatters, which were plotted during the grading down of the area by machines to level the site for the creation of the country park, or reported stone scatters found within the record cards held at Peterborough Museum. These reports have been linked with the air photographic evidence to produce an overall plot of potential buildings at the site. For example, one significant stone and pottery scatter reported during fieldwalking in 1973 was probably that of 'a substantial rectangular building of coursed, dressed, stone' which was located some 250m to the west of the LF2 site (*Northamptonshire Archaeology* 1974b, 95). This report seems to match the position of one of the possible buildings seen on air photographs and marked as either B or C on Figure 98.

Thus it is possible, if all the reported stone scatters and parchmark features are buildings, that there is a total of twelve structures to the west of the excavation site of Lynch Farm 2 that are considered to be Roman. If the five excavated structures are added to this list this gives a total of seventeen structures — allowing for the fact that some buildings, such as C1, C2 and D1 appear, potentially, to be part and parcel of the same building and that Buildings I and II occupy much the same ground. In addition, these buildings are spread over an area in excess of 600m from east to west. It is impossible to say which of the cropmarks showing as ditched features on the air photographs are Roman, and thus linked with these buildings, without excavation. However, the evidence from the excavated buildings, which are clearly associated with ditched areas, suggests that it is probable that some of these cropmarks represent Roman enclosures within which buildings are situated. This could be the case with F, shown in Figure 98, which appears to sit within a sub-rectangular enclosure shown on air photographs (see Fig. 3) and marked on a plan published by the Royal Commission in 1969 (see RCHM 1969, fig. 7). The outline of the potential building marked as I also appears to be within an encircling ditched enclosure (see Figs 3 and 98).

The collection of buildings within the area shown in Figure 98 thus seems to consist of a somewhat scattered settlement that may include aisled buildings similar to those excavated during the early 1970s at Lynch Farm 2. The dimensions of structure F, taken from the air photographs, seem to match approximately the dimensions of the latest phase of Building II. Other buildings seen only as parchmarks seem to be of a smaller size and it is impossible at present, without further fieldwork in the form of geophysical surveys or excavation, to make any detailed comment about the nature and form of these potential buildings.

What is clear, assuming that all of the structures marked in Figure 98 are in fact Roman, is that the site does not conform to a standard farmstead or villa plan. It seems unlikely that the buildings form several loose-knit farmsteads as they are too close together. Roman farmsteads are known in fair detail within both the Nene and the Welland valleys, where they are often set within ditched enclosures and have structures built of either timber or stone. They appear to be regularly spaced across the landscape and, according to air photographic and fieldwalking evidence, they extend up from the terrace gravels along the valley and onto the heavier clay soils with equal density (Upex 2008a, 116–21 and fig. 42). Often such farmsteads have Iron Age origins and their chronology extends to the end of the Roman period, with a few exceptions, such as the site in Orton Longueville known as 'Monument 97', falling out of use during the Roman period (Mackreth 2001).

The plans of Roman villas within the area are becoming better understood with the research of recent years, with both the reappraisal of formerly known sites (Wild 1969; Upex 2008a, Chapter 5; and Upex forthcoming b) and the discovery of new sites such as the villas at Upton and Itter Crescent in the middle of Greater Peterborough (Paul Middleton pers. comm.; Pickstone 2012). Some of the larger villa sites first explored by Edmund Artis (Artis 1828) in the 1820s proved with the advent of air photography to be substantial structures set within courtyards, with both domestic and probably agricultural elements (see, for example, Upex 2001; Scott 1993). However, the plan of the structures at Lynch Farm does not bear any resemblance to the layout of a local 'villa-type' establishment. The rather loose-knit arrangement of structures spread across a large area is more reminiscent of types of villas found on the continent, in France, Germany and the low countries where villa buildings are ranged over considerable distances of up to 500–600m (Smith 2000, 159–65; Percival 1976, 67–91). The continental examples are, however, almost always set out with an axial and formal arrangement (Roymans and Habermehl 2011) whereas the Lynch Farm buildings appear both haphazardly arranged and set out with slightly differing orientations.

At Lynch Farm there is no evidence of any central, major or important building associated with the settlement, and it perhaps matches similar arrangements of dispersed buildings set out without any formal arrangement which occur in the category of Roman settlements now termed 'villages' or 'non-villa nucleated settlements' (Hingley 1989, 76–81) that are found at sites such as Chisenbury Warren, Wilts. and Catsgore, Somerset (Leech 1982; see also Hanley 1994, fig. 34). Loose-knit settlements are well known in the fenland region and were first systematically discussed by Sylvia Hallam in 1970 (Hallam 1970, see especially pls II–VIII and XXI–XXIII; see also Hanley 1994, 39, fig. 30). In almost all fenland cases there is a lack of any centrally placed or high-status villa arrangement associated with these settlements.

Other arrangements similar to those at Lynch Farm were found at the villa at Stanwick (Northants), where there was a rather haphazard distribution of circular buildings interpreted as the houses of estate workers. These houses were spread over a broad area and set out with no apparent formal arrangement, with the exception that at Stanwick there was a large, well-appointed and centrally placed 'house' with mosaic floors, wall plaster and heated rooms (Neal 1989, see figs 2, 3 and 4). At Stanton Low in Buckinghamshire possibly six separate substantial stone buildings were constructed over an area of 250m in the early–mid-2nd century; additions were made up to the early 3rd century, and there was a final early 4th-century phase of industrial working (Woodfield and Johnson 1989, see especially figs 4 and 5). The generally loose-knit nature of the arrangements of structures at this site is puzzling but suggests that the structures form the core to an estate area. At other sites, such as that at Kingscote in Gloucestershire, a single high-status house was surrounded by seventy-five 'outbuildings', all in a very loose-knit arrangement. Again, it is difficult to know what the actual organisation or layout of the site represents here other than, as Jane Timby has suggested, a Roman estate centre and small town (Timby 1989).

Another similar but more local arrangement is that known from Fotheringhay (Northants), where a series of small Roman enclosures is set out along a trackway. The site is known only from air photographs, but the small enclosures may have acted as house plots and contain Roman structures. However, here a large villa lies some 600m from the southern end of the trackway and it may be that the settlement acted as a 'village' for estate workers

(Hingley 1989, fig. 55; RCHM 1975, fig. 50; Upex 2008a, fig. 50). In this case the population was perhaps under the employ of the villa owner, whereas at Lynch Farm there is no known villa in the vicinity. The nearest large structure to the Lynch Farm site, with heated rooms, wall plaster and baths, was that found during the construction work for new schools in 1960 at Orton Longueville (Fig. 2), and this is 3km away (Dakin 1961), while a site with similar domestic arrangements was found at Botolph Bridge, some 5km from the Lynch Farm site (Spoerry and Atkins 2015). On the other side of the river there is a villa site at Mill Hill (Castor) and two within Water Newton parish (see Fig. 2), as well as the palatial structure underneath Castor village which, it has been argued, may be something much more substantial than a villa (Upex 2011a).

The Lynch Farm site, therefore, seems to fall within the category of 'non-villa nucleated settlements' outlined by Hingley (1989, 76–81) and Taylor, who shows the trend towards rural settlement nucleation throughout the Roman period (Taylor 2007). The cropmark evidence does not suggest that there was a series of trackways or linking routes to unify the site and yet the presence of the cemetery at Lynch Farm 3 shows that there must have been a long-term and fairly large population (Jones 1973; 1975). The evidence of the concentration of furnaces (or ovens) within the first phase of Building I suggests some form of large-scale and specialised process, whether for salt or some other form of production, and this would be entirely consistent with what we know about the development of large landholdings and private estates within the Roman world. In many respects the production capacity shown by the numbers of Lynch Farm furnaces can be paralleled locally at Orton Hall Farm, where the processing of corn and the milling of flour dominated (Mackreth 1996b, 2205–31).

Mackreth argues that one structure with a dedicated 'milling' function and a large milling capacity (called by him the 'Mill House') may have been under some form of military or state control, saying: 'it is hard not to think of another body of people who would have needed a special supply of it (grain/flour) if it were not the military, army or navy' (Mackreth 1996b, 236). He goes on: 'at Orton Hall Farm there could have been a civilian population under the control of officials who did not themselves have to be members of the army as such' (Mackreth 1996b, 236). The whole site at Orton Hall Farm demonstrates the presence of extended accommodation and a storage, brewing and milling capacity that far outweighed its probable 'in-house' needs and Mackreth interprets the site, at least from the period c. AD 300–325 onwards, as being a farmstead that had passed into the hands of either the army 'or the res private' (Mackreth 1996b, 236). However, such claims seem, on reflection, somewhat exaggerated and are very speculative. The Roman town of Durobrivae is only 4.5km away from Orton Hall Farm and it is difficult to agree with the claim that 'It seems unlikely that flour was being supplied to the townsfolk of Durobrivae from so far away' (Mackreth 1996b, 236), as it would actually be only an hour or so away by Roman cart.

It is also interesting that within the lower Nene valley area there is growing archaeological evidence to suggest that not only were farmsteads being remodelled but also the size of landholdings may have been increasing. At Monument 97 it would seem that land was taken over by the rise of developments at Orton Hall Farm, and a similar situation may have been happening at Werrington to the north of modern Peterborough, and on the fen-edge gravels, where small farmsteads seem to have given way to the expansion of larger establishments (Mackreth 1988; 1996b; 2001). If such amalgamations were in fact taking place they could have been caused by a population influx or some form of military or state influence or reorganisation but, equally, they could be attributable to some other economic or social development of which at present we are unaware.

Clearly the settlement at Lynch Farm is not a straightforward villa site but it may have been part of, or formed the core of, a villa estate and been linked to the buildings known to exist in Orton Longueville (Dakin 1961) in a manner similar to the situation at Fotheringhay (see above). The archaeological evidence from the excavations at Lynch Farm shows that in the aftermath of the military withdrawal the site was taken over immediately by what one can only guess was a civilian workforce. The question here is whether this workforce was entirely autonomous or was, as suggested for Orton Hall Farm by Mackreth, under the auspices of either state or military control. Certainly it would be easy to see the two sites, which are only some 3.5km apart, as falling under the same sphere of control if native farmers were not making the decisions. If the state did have control at Orton Hall Farm, which is the scenario favoured by Mackreth (Mackreth 1996b, 236), then with the original military influence at Longthorpe and early military occupation on the site at Lynch Farm, it would be easy to see that influence extending not from Orton Hall Farm to Lynch Farm but in the opposite direction!

However, there are considerable problems in taking this line of argument any further, as it begins to stretch the archaeological evidence. The lack of military finds, including metalwork, at Lynch Farm after Period 2 (the site's military period) is perhaps significant and the degree to which the coin evidence from Lynch Farm is representative of the whole settlement site is debatable and awaits further excavation of additional buildings in the area. Philippa Walton's comments (above) about late coin use are, however, instructive in suggesting that 'the continued use of coinage at such sites indicates an association with the late Roman administration and particularly with the collection of taxation' (see also Walton 2012).

It would perhaps be much easier to see how the civilian centre of the Roman town of Durobrivae could stretch out and influence production on local villa estates. It is possible that some senior person, magistrate, large landowner or industrial entrepreneur based within Durobrivae could have held sway over the area on the south side of the Nene and thus had control over the scattered Lynch Farm settlement and its economic regime. Durobrivae clearly became a significant and wealthy centre for a late Roman population, with the town being defended by walls with bastions. The wealth of the town seems to have been based on its geographical location and communications by road and river; its market function; its surrounding rich agricultural land which gave rise to a number of large 'status' villas; its localised mineral wealth which founded pottery and ironworking industries; and its proximity to the fenland, where it appears to have acted as a conduit for goods coming out of the fens and the control, organisation and administration being applied to that area.

The late wealth of the area is hinted at by the major hoard of Roman gold coins, dated to after AD 350, which was found in 1974 (Johns and Carson 1975), and even more spectacularly by the find of the hoard of early Christian silver plate (Painter 1976; 1977; 1999; Hartley *et al.* 2006). The wealth of the town and its area thus seems to have been considerable, and it may have been that the local magnates who signed the *Durobrivae* Christian treasure and their successors had some input into the economic area in which the Lynch Farm settlement clearly developed.

X. The site of Lynch Farm 2 today

The line of the parish boundary between Orton Waterville and Orton Longueville, and thus the line of the Roman road dating to the early Roman period, is partly maintained today in the form of Ham Lane. This lane leads down to Ferry Meadows Country Park, which was created out of the gravel workings from which gravel was taken for use within the developments of Peterborough New Town in the 1970s and early 1980s. Much of the area of cropmarks within the meander of the Nene which was first systematically recorded in 1969 (RCHM 1969; see Fig. 3) was set aside for long-term preservation. This now forms part of the recreation area within the Park and is a scheduled ancient monument. During the archaeological work at Lynch Farm 2 undertaken between 1972 and 1974 the importance of the excavated Roman remains became ever more apparent and it was agreed with the Peterborough Development Corporation and the gravel contractor (ARC) that the overall extent of gravel workings should be modified slightly so that part of the site could be preserved *in situ*, including Well I and Buildings II and III within Area A. These structures were consolidated and are now displayed within the Park where they are open to public access with an information board outlining the history of the site.

Appendix 1. List of sections

Most sections were drawn after the topsoil had already been removed by mechanical digger and where it was impossible to estimate how deep this topsoil cover was. Thus sections show a dotted line which is an estimate of this topsoil cover. Compression and compaction of the archaeological deposits was observed over the entire site and this is referred to within the section drawings as 'ruts' or 'compression marks' within individual drawings. For details of which Figures sections appear in see Appendix 2 (below).

Sections within Area A
S1. Post-hole 3 looking north
S2. Post-hole 4 looking north
S3. Post-hole 9 looking north-west
S4. Post-hole 14 looking north
S5. Post-hole 11 looking west
S6. Furnace 1 looking north
S7. Furnace 2 looking north
S8. Furnace 3 looking north
S9. Furnace 4 looking north
S10. Furnace 5 looking east
S11. Furnace 6 looking west
S12. North-eastern buttress looking north
S13. South-eastern buttress looking north, A
S14. South-eastern buttress looking north, B
S15. Post-hole 5, Phase I aisled building, looking south
S16. Post-hole 6, Phase I aisled building, looking north (see also S4)
S17. Post-hole 7, Phase I aisled building, looking north
S18. Post-hole 8, Phase I aisled building, looking north
S19. Section through 7 and wall line within temple (?) structure
S20. Post-hole 9 within Temple (?) structure
S21. Post-hole 17, portico of temple structure?
S22. Post-hole 11, portico of temple structure?
S23. Post-hole 12, portico of temple structure?
S24. Post-hole 25, fence line to south of temple
S25. Post-hole 26, fence line to south of temple
S26. Post-hole 28, fence line to south of temple
S27. Post-hole 27, fence line to south of temple
S28. Section of Trench 56 showing Iron Age Pits F and G, south channel of double ditch and 'inner' fort ditch
S29. Section of Trench 55 showing north channel of double ditch and 'inner' fort ditch
S30. Section through Pit A looking west
S31. Section through Pit B looking west
S32. Section through Pit C looking west
S33. Section through Pit D looking west
S34. Section through Pit T looking west
S35. Section through Pit L and double ditches looking west
S36. Section through Pit H and double ditches looking west
S37. Section through Pit J and double ditches looking west (drawn as a mirror image)
S38. Section through Pit I and double ditches looking west
S39. Section through Pit K and double ditches looking west
S40. Trench 45. Section through Military Ditches looking north
S41. Trench 44. Section through Military Ditches looking north
S42. Trench 49. Section through Military Ditches looking north
S43. Trench 50. Section through Military Ditches looking north
S44. Trench 71. Section through Military Ditches looking west
S45. Section through Military Pit 1 within area of later aisled building (3m from S wall and 2.5m from W wall)
S46. Section through Military Pit 2 within area of later aisled building (1.0m from W wall/2.5m from N wall) (see also S122–S124 for pits 3, 4 and 5)
S47. Trench 11/12/20. Section through northern ditch extension to the east
S48. Trench 23. Section through northern ditch extension to the east, at junction of southerly extension
S49. Trench 22. Section through northern ditch extension to the east including Iron Age Pit R
S50. Trench 7. Section through late ditch to east of aisled building
S51. Trench 24. Section through late ditch to east of aisled building

S52. Trench 5. Section through late ditch to east of aisled building
S53. Trench 36. Section of ditch running N–S terminating at north wall of aisled building
S54. Trench 32. Section of ditch running N–S terminating at north wall of aisled building
S55. Trench 28. Section of ditch running N–S terminating at north wall of aisled building
S56. Trench 25. Section of ditch running N–S terminating at north wall of aisled building
S57. Trench 15. Section of ditch running N–S terminating at north wall of aisled building
S58. Trench 10. Section of ditch running N–S terminating at north wall of aisled building
S59. Trench within aisled building. Section of ditch running N–S terminating at north wall of aisled building
S60. Trench 7. Double ditch running N–S and under aisled building
S61. Trench 31. Double ditch running N–S and under aisled building
S62. Trench 9. Double ditch running N–S and under aisled building
S63. Trench against north wall of aisled building. Double ditch running N–S and under aisled building
S64. Trench in central area of aisled building. Double ditch running N–S and under aisled building
S65. Trench against south wall of aisled building. Double ditch running N–S and under aisled building
S66. Trench 71. Double ditch running N–S and under aisled building
S67. Sections of stonework within Well I
S68. Sections of west and north faces of stonework in Well II
S69. Section of the fill of Well I
S70. Section of the fill of Well II

Sections within Areas C and D
S71. Section of 'Sump' area in Area C, north face
S72. Section of 'Sump' area in Area C, central area
S73. Section of 'Sump' area in Area C, south face (mirror image)
S74. Section of 'sump/pit' 58, Section A–B
S75. Section of 'sump/pit' 58, Section C–D
S76. Section of Pit 60
S77. Section of Ditch 63
S78. Section of Gully 49
S79. Section through shallow Gullies 52 and 44
S80. Section through Gully 44
S81. Section through Post-hole 47
S82. Section through Gully 42
S83. Section through Gully 42
S84. Section through Ditch 3
S85. Section through Ditch 3
S86. Section through Ditch 3
S87. Section through Ditch 3
S88. Section through Gully 45
S89. Section through Ditch 7
S90. Section through Ditch 35/26
S91. Section through Ditch 35/26
S92. Section of Ditch 8
S93. Section of Pit 13
S94. Section of Pit (?) 9
S95. Section of Pit 22
S96. Section of Ditch 29
S97. Section across flue of corn drier

Sections within Area B
S98. Section of Ditch 93
S99. Section of Ditch 91
S100. Section of Ditch 11 (mirror image)
S101. Section of Ditch 7 (mirror image)
S102. Section of Ditch 19 (mirror image)
S103. Section of Ditch 20 (mirror image)
S104. Section of Ditch 18 (mirror image)
S105. Section of Ditch 23/23a (mirror image)
S106. Section of Ditch 37 (mirror image)
S107. Section of Ditch 5 (mirror image)
S108. Section of Ditch 4
S109. Section of Ditch 6
S110. Section of Ditches 1, 2 and 3
S111. Section of Ditches 88 and 88b

Appendix 2. Description of section contexts/layers

Section 1. Post-hole 3 (Fig. 27)
25. Limestone packing and brown earth
26. Dark brown earth and small fragments of limestone
27. Limestone packing in sandy/gravel mix
28. Dark brown clayey earth and small limestone fragments

Section 2. Post-hole 4 (Fig. 27)
29. Small limestone packing and brown earth
30. Brown earth and large limestone packing
31. Brown sandy earth and limestone packing
32. Brown sandy/gravelly earth
33. Limestone in brown earth and patches of blue clay
34. Black/brown earth with limestone

Section 3. Post-hole 9 (Fig. 27)
32. Brown earth and gravel
32a. Limestone packing
34. Dark brown earth with limestone fragments
34a. Dark brown loamy earth

Section 4. Post-hole 11 (Fig. 27)
38. Brown loamy earth with limestone
41. Yellow gravel and limestone
42. Dark brown loam with limestone packing
48. Brown gravelly earth with limestone packing
49. Fine brown earth and gravel (upper filling of earlier ditch)
50. Sandy gravelly earth (lower fill of earlier ditch)
54. Grey clayey earth

Section 5. Post-hole 14 and Post F103 (Fig. 27)
11. Heavy limestone packing set in brown earth
98. Brown silty/sandy earth and limestone packing
99. Fine orange gravelly sand
100. Limestone packing in brown sandy earth
101. Brown earth and limestone packing and charcoal flecks
102. Grey/brown sandy earth
103. Brown sandy earth and small limestone fragments
104. Blue clay
105. Light brown sandy earth

Section 6. Furnace 1 (Fig. 23)
3. Black ashy earth in bowl of hearth and limestone packing
8. Red burned sand lining bowl of hearth
12. Black ash and charcoal

Section 7. Furnace 2 (Fig. 23)
1. Dirty brown sand and limestone and charcoal
2. Brown earth
3. Sandy brown earth

Section 8. Furnace 3 (Fig. 23)
17. Black earth and charcoal and limestone packing
23. Yellow sand
24. Brown/grey earth

Section 9. Furnace 4 (Fig. 23)
20. Burnt limestone and black ash

Section 10. Furnace 5. (Fig. 23)
2. Yellow clay and burned reddened clay and limestone fragments and briquetage fragment
14. Burnt limestone and black ashy material
29. Ashy grey/black layer and pockets of grey clay
31. Brown loam

Section 11. Furnace 6 (Fig. 31)
30. Heavily burned limestone
30a. Large flat and smoothed limestone flags, burned on one edge
31. Red burned clay and sand
36. Fragments of crushed tile and limestone
44. Limestone burnt to a blue/black colour
45. Black ashy earth with flecks of charcoal and burnt clay and sand with some hammerscale

Section 12. North-eastern buttress of Phase II aisled building (Fig. 30)
6. Limestone packing set in dark gravelly loam, also including a horse skull (see Pl. 25)

Section 13. South-eastern buttress of Phase II aisled building (Fig. 30)
97. Limestone packing set in dark gravelly loam

Section 14. South-eastern buttress of Phase II aisled building (Fig. 30)
97. Limestone packing set in dark gravelly loam

Section 15. Post-hole 5 of Phase 1 aisled building (Fig. 21)
7. Limestone packing in brown gravelly loam
31. Brown gravelly loam
57. Brown/grey silty loam, brown flecks and limestone
59. Grey/brown silty loam, with limestone

Section 16. Post-hole 6 of Phase I aisled building (Fig. 21, see also section 5)
103. Brown sandy earth and small limestone fragments
104. Blue clay
105. Light brown sandy earth

Section 17. Post-hole 7 of Phase I aisled building (Fig. 21)
39. Dark loam and gravel with limestone
52. Grey/brown loam with green/brown flecks and limestone packing
43, 66, 74 = all from earlier feature

Section 18. Post-hole 8 of Phase I aisled building (Fig. 21)
55. Sandy brown loam with limestone packing
60. Brown silty earth with limestone packing
64. Light brown loam and gravel
76. Brown gravelly earth and limestone fragments
77. Red/brown gravelly earth (redeposited natural?)

Section 19. Section through 7 and wall line within temple (?) structure (Fig. 33)
2. Brown sand and gravel and flecks of burnt daub and white wall plaster
5. Dirty brown sand/gravel and mortar, clay fragments and wall plaster
6. Limestone walling
7. Limestone set in dark earth
20. Brown sand and pebbles and flecks of daub
21. Dirty brown sand/gravel
22. Dirty brown sand and flecks of daub

Section 20. Post-hole 9 within temple (?) structure (Fig. 33)
18. Limestone set in brown loam

Sections 21–23. Post-holes 17, 11 and 12 around temple (?) structure (Fig. 34)
S21. 17. Limestone packing set in dark brown loam
17a. Dark brown loam (rotted-out post?)
S22. 11. Limestone packing set in dark brown loam
11a. Dark brown loam (rotted-out post?)
S23. 12. Limestone packing set in dark brown loam
12a. Dark brown loam (rotted-out post?)

Sections 24–27. Post-holes 25, 26, 28, 27 in fence line S of the Temple structure (Fig. 34)
S24. 25. Limestone fragments set in dark brown loam
S25. 26. Limestone fragments set in dark brown loam
S26. 28. Limestone fragments set in dark brown loam
S27. 27. Limestone fragments set in dark brown loam

Sections 28–29. Pits F and G, inner fort ditch and double ditch (Fig. 14)
S28. 269. Clayey sand and gravel mix
274. Silty sand with clay flecks and gravel
275. Silty sand with gravel
278. Brown loam sand and gravel mix
282. Light brown sandy silt
291. Light brown sandy silt
S29. 269. Clayey sand and gravel mix
270. Dark grey/brown sand and gravel mix
275. Silty sand with gravel

276. Silty sand with clay flecks and gravel

302. Dark brown silt

Sections 30–34. Pit alignment sections of Pits A, B, C, D and T (Fig. 7)
S30. 1. Dark loam infill and machine compression?

2. Soft brown silty sand and burnt daub and charcoal

3. Gravel and sand with some loam

S31. 1. Gravel consolidation layer/machine compression?

2. Soft brown silty sand with burnt daub and charcoal

3. Silty loam and gravel

S32. 1. Soft silty brown/grey loam and burnt daub and charcoal

2. Silty brown loam/gravel

S33. 1. Burial

2. Soft grey/brown silty loam and burnt daub and charcoal

S34. 94. Soft brown silty loam

334. Sand silty loam

Sections 35–39. Pit alignment sections and sections of double ditch (Fig. 15)
S35. 122. Black/brown silty loam

171. Brown silty loam and gravel

193. Sand and gravel with some loam

284. Brown loam

287. Brown sandy silt and clay mix and gravel

289. Silty sand with a little gravel

290. Very silty brown sand

296. Silty sand and gravel

297. Light brown silty sand and gravel

300. Loamy silt/sand/gravel mix

315. Silty gravel

316. Dark grey loamy sand

S36. 1. Loamy sand and gravel

2. As above, but more gravel

279. Silty gravel and sand

281. Silty sand with small gravel inclusion

330. Gravel (slumping ?)

331. Silty sand and gravel

331a. Grey silt

332. Sand gravel and larger gravel pieces

354. Consolidation by machines?

356. Consolidation by machines?

S37. 301. Greyish brown sandy clay and gravel

303. Greyish brown silty sandy and gravel

307. Silty sand and small gravel

309. Silty sand and gravel

310. Brown silty sand and gravel

311. Brown loam with some sand inclusion

319. Gravel lens (slumping?)

320. Light brown sandy loam

S38. 243. Silty grey loam

267. Grey/brown sandy loam and gravel

268. Orange clayey sand and large gravel

271. Orange sandy clay and small gravel

272. Grey/yellow sandy loam and small limestone fragments

S39. 215. Clayey loam

218. Grey/brown silt and sand

245. Dark brown loam

227. Dark grey loam and gravel and silt

342. Gravel, sand and silt

Sections 40–44. Sections through the military ditches (Fig. 10)
S40. 250. Loamy sand and gravel

249. Loamy sand and gravel

S41. 3. Sandy loam

248. Loamy sand and gravel

247. Loamy sand and gravel

264. Reddish brown clayey loam with gravel

275. Silty sand with gravel

S42. 3. Sandy loam

248a. Loamy sand and gravel

263. Reddish brown clayey loam with gravel

275. Silty sand with gravel

S43. 247a. Loamy sand and gravel

263a. Reddish brown clayey loam with gravel

275. Silty sand with gravel

S44. 1. Dark brown loamy earth

10. Brown loam and limestone fragments

11. Brown grey silty loam

12. Silty grey/brown loam

13. Silty grey loam

Sections 45–46. Sections through Military Pits 1 and 2 (Fig. 11)
S45. 4. Limestone packing set in brown loam and mortar

10. Fine silty brown loam

15. Orange/brown silty loam and green flecks and limestone fragments

15a. Brown silty earth and green flecks

15b. Brown/grey silty earth and green flecks

19. Brown/grey silty loam and limestone fragments

21. Grey clayey loam with brown/green flecks

22. Grey/brown silty loam with brown/green flecks

24. Orange/brown silty loam and green fleck and small limestone fragments

S46. 8. Limestone set in brown loam

9. Dark brown loam and limestone fragments

11. Dark brown/grey loamy earth and brown/green flecks

12. Grey silty loam

Sections 47–49. Sections through eastern extension of north ditch/its southerly return and Iron Age Pit R (Fig. 17)
S47. 72. Dark brown/black sandy clay

82. Dark brown loam

83. Silty grey/brown loam

83a. Silty grey loam

84. Yellow sandy loam

S48. 146. Yellow/brown silty loam

147. Brown silty loam

S49. 1. Sandy loam and gravel

96. Limestone packing set in brown loam

126. Brown silty loam

127. Sandy brown loam

186. Light brown silty loam

Sections 50–52. Sections through late ditch to east of aisled building (Fig. 38)
S50. 1. Brown loam with limestone packing

2. Brown silty loam with limestone fragments

S51. 133. Brown loam

141. Dark brown loam and charcoal and hammerscale and gravel

S52. 7/31. Limestone surfacing and packing set in silty/gravel mix

29. Grey/black silt and gravel

30. Black silt and charcoal = hammerscale and gravel

Sections 53–59. Sections of Ditch 6 (Fig. 24)
S53. 200. Fragments of limestone set in gravel

201. Grey/brown silty loam

202. Brown silty loam

S54. 185. Brown silty loam

187. Brown clayey loam

195. Yellow sandy silt

S55. 122. Black silty loam

S56. 138. Brown silty loam

144. Dark brown silty loam

S57. 98. Grey/brown loam

99. Light brown fine silty loam

100. Clayey orange loam and limestone fragments

105. Clayey brown loam

S58. 53. Grey/brown loam

54. Limestone packing set in gravel

55. Light brown fine silty loam

69. Orange/brown clayey loam with limestone

S59. 40. Brown clayey loam with limestone

41. Brown loam with some limestone

43. Brown sandy loam

Sections 60–66. Sections of double ditch running N–S and under aisled building (Fig. 16)
S60. 46. Dark brown silty loam

67. Brown loam and gravel mix

68. Brown loam and gravel mix

S61. 203. Silty loam

203a. Silty loam and gravel

204. Brown silty loam and gravel

218. Grey silty loam

219. Light brown loam and gravel

222. Light brown clayey loam

222a. Light brown clayey loam

223. Reddish brown clayey loam

223a. Brown/grey silty loam

S62. 52. Light brown loam

77. Light brown loam with sand inclusion

78. Light brown loam with sand inclusion set in lenses

S63. 9. Brown sandy loam

10. Limestone walling of aisled building set on dark brown loam and gravel
13. Brown loam and gravel
18. Brown loam and gravel with charcoal flecks
19. Brown loam with green flecks
22. Grey silty loam with green flecks
27. Charcoal and black ash
35. Brown loam and gravel
35a. Brown loam and gravel
65. Yellow sand clay mix
69. Clayey brown loam with limestone
70. Brown sandy loam and gravel
72. Dark brown/black clayey loam
73. Dark brown/black clayey loam
S64. 40. Skid mark from modern machine
43. Reddish brown loam
43a. Reddish brown sandy loam
63. Red/brown clayey loam and gravel
66. Reddish brown clayey loam
67. Brown sandy loam
74. Brown silty loam
75. Yellow clayey loam
S65. 61. Dark brown/black silty loam
80. Brown loam with limestone
81. Red/brown silty loam
82. Dark brown silty loam
83. Silty grey loam
84. Yellow sandy loam
85. Dark brown silty loam
86. Red/brown clayey loam
88. Red/brown/black clayey loam
S66. 1. Light brown sandy loam
2. Light brown silty loam
3. Light brown sandy loam
4. Dark brown loam and small limestone fragments
5. Light brown sandy loam
6. Brown clayey loam

Section 67 of the stonework in Well I (Fig. 40)
S67. 90. Limestone lining within the well
90a. Timber cradle within the well

Section 68 of the west and north faces of stonework in Well II (Fig. 41)
S68. 2. Limestone lining within the well
7. Timber cradle within the well

Sections 69–70. Sections of the fills of Wells I and II (Fig. 42)
S69. 90. Limestone lining of well
90a. Timber cradle within the well
99. Large limestone blocks, gravel, set in brown loam
101. Limestone set in sandy loam and pottery and bone
103. Small limestone fragments within silty loam and pottery and bone
104. Dark brown silty loam
S70. 2. Limestone lining within the well
3. Brown earth and gravel and heavy limestone packing
4. Gravelly/sandy earth with heavy limestone packing
5. Brown silty sand with limestone fragments
6. Grey/black silty and pottery/bone/leatherwork
7. Timber cradle within the well

Sections 71–73. Sections across the main 'sump' area of Area C (Fig. 53)
S71. 1. Black silt with some clay inclusions
2. Limestone packing
27. Black silt with organic content
S72. 1. Black silt with some clay inclusions
2. Limestone packing
27. Black silt with organic content
28. Orange/brown clay
29. Grey sandy silt
S73. 1. Black silt with some clay inclusions
2. Limestone packing
27. Black silt with organic content
28. Orange/brown clay
29. Grey sandy silt
46. Limestone capping for 46a
46a. Grey clay/silt mix
48. Brown sandy silt
49. Brown sandy silt

Sections S74–S78. Areas C and D 2nd-century features (Fig. 54)
S74. 58. Grey silt and oxidised flecks
64. Black silt
S75. 58. Grey silt and oxidised flecks
58a slip?
64. Black silt
S76. 60. Grey silty sand
66. Black silt
S77. 63. Grey/brown silty sand
S78. 49. Brown sandy silt

Sections 79–81. Areas C and D 3rd-century features (Fig. 55)
S79. 44. Light brown sandy silt
52. Grey silty sand
S80. 44. Light brown sandy silt
S81. 3. Black sandy silt
47. Grey silt with limestone packing
54. Black silt with limestone packing

Sections 82–83. Areas C and D late 3rd-century features (Fig. 55)
S82. 42. Brown sandy silt with some limestone fragments at base
S83. 42. Brown sandy silt with some limestone fragments at base

Sections 84–91. Areas C and D mid-4th-century features (Fig. 55)
S84. 3. Black silt
S85. 3. Black silt
S86. 3. Black silt
S87. 3. Black silt
3a. Black silty clay
S88. 45. Light brown sandy silt
S89. 7. Brown clay and yellow flecks
14. Iron stained sand
17. Grey clayey loam with gravel
S90. 35. Grey silt with charcoal flecks
S91. 26. Grey silt with charcoal flecks

Sections S92–S95. Sections through Pits and Ditches in Area C and D (Fig. 56)
S92. 8/1. Brown sandy silt and iron staining
8/2. Grey sandy clay
8/3. Black silt
8/4. Sandy grey silt

Sections S93–S96. Areas C and D late 4th-century features (Fig. 56)
S93. 13. Grey clayey loam
15. Dark grey clay mixed with silt patches
S94. 9. Light brown/grey clay/silt mix
S95. 22. Grey silty loam
S96. 29. Dark loam
30. Dark clayey loam

Section 97. Area D, corn drier (Fig. 58)
S97. 1. Mixed sandy loam
5. Limestone flagging, heavily burned, forming floor to corn drier
12. Limestone 'packing' (burned) and gravel — may be part of the demolished sides of the feature
16. Black ashy deposit
17. Sandy gravel make-up layer/redeposited natural?

Sections 98–107. Area B – ditches running N–S in south-eastern section of area (Fig. 47)
S98. 93. Dark blue/grey clay
93a. Dark blue silt
S99. 91. Dark blue/grey silt/clay
91a. Dark blue silt
S100. 11. Dark blue/black silt
11a. Black silt
11b Black silt
S101. 7. Black/blue silt
22. Grey clayey silt
S102. 19. Grey/orange clayey silt
19a. Black silt
S103. 20. Black silt
21. Grey clayey silt
S104. 18. Blue/grey silt
18a. Black silt
S105. 23. Grey silt turning blacker in lower fill
23a. Clayey silt turning into black silt in lower fill
S106. 37. Light blue silt
37a. Black silt
S107. 5. Grey/blue silt

14. Dark clayey silt turning to black silt in lower fill

Sections 108–115. Area B (Fig. 48)
S108. 4. Blue/grey clayey silt
4a. Blue/black silt
4b. Black silt
4c. Gravel and sandy mix over black silt (possible side slip over deposit)
S109. 6. Grey/black clayey silt
6a. Grey clayey silt
6b. Blue/black silt
S110. 1. Blue/black silt
1a. Blue/black silt
2. Grey silty clay
3. Dark grey silt becoming black in lower fills, many lenses
S111. 51. Dark blue silt
88. Grey clayey silt merging into black silt in lowest fill
88a. Dark blue clayey silt merging into black silt in lowest fill
S112. 24. Dark blue/black silt
25. Dark grey clayey silt
26. Black silt
S113. 81. Yellow dirty clay
81a. Grey/blue silt becoming back in lower fill
100. Blue/grey clayey silt becoming black in lower fill
S114. 10. Dark blue/black silt
44. Light grey gravelly loam and sand
45. Black silt
78. Grey silt becoming darker in lower fills and black in bottom fill
S115. 42. Grey silt becoming darker in lower fill
42a. Grey silty clay

Sections 116–120. Area B (Fig. 49)
S116. 94. Dark grey silt
95. Grey silt with iron staining
95a Black/blue silt
S117. 47. Grey clayey silt in lenses with blue/black bottom fill
S118. 41. Grey silt
41a. Blue/black silt
S119. 40. Mixed sandy clay becoming black silt in lowest fill
52. Dark sandy silt with lenses of clayey silt and darker silts
S120. 38. Dark blue silts in lenses
38a. Grey clayey silt
38b. Dark blue silts in lenses
38c. Light grey clay

Section 121. 1st-century kiln in Area II (Fig. 18)
S121. 54. Limestone packing within stokehole (former flue cheek?)
79. Charcoal and ash
97. Sandy loam with gravel (surface?)
104. Ash, charcoal and fire bars and dome plates
111. Burnt clay lining to kiln

Sections 122–124. Military Pits 3, 4 and 5 (Fig. 11)
S122. 47. Dark brown silt and small stones
S123. 48. Dark brown silty loam
49. Green/grey silt
S124. 16. Brown loam and gravel with limestone fragments
50. Pale brown silt

Sections 125–127. The northern extension of Area B (Fig. 46)
S125. 53. Blue/black clay
53a. Light grey clay
54. Dark grey/blue silt and gravel
54a. Light grey silt and gravel
73. Dark grey clay
73a. Dark loamy silt
98. Light blue clayey silt
S126. 1. Limestone and rammed gravel walling set within mason's trench
2. Blue/grey clay (flooring)
S127. 89. Sandy silt with some gravel
105. Dark blue/black clay and sand and gravel

S128. Pits 6 and 7 in Area A (Fig. 13)
71. Yellow/brown sandy clay
72. Dark brown/black sandy clay
76. Brown sandy loam
76a. Dark brown sandy loam
163. Brown/black clayey loam
164. Grey silt
165. Yellow/grey silt
176. Yellow silt flecked with charcoal
177. Yellow/brown silty clay
180. Brown clay
188. Yellow/brown/green clay
192. Blue/black silt
206. Grey/brown sandy silt
232. Lenses of brown clay/red clay/sand and silts

Bibliography

Albarella, U., 2003 — 'Zooarchaeological evidence: animal bone', in Germany, M., *Excavations at Great Holts Farm, Boreham, Essex, 1992–1994*, E. Anglian Archaeol. 105, 193–200

Alexander, J.S., 1995 — 'Building stone from the east midlands quarries: sources, transportation and usage', *Medieval Archaeol.* 39, 107–35

Allason-Jones, L., 1996 — *Roman Jet in the Yorkshire Museum* (York, Yorkshire Museum)

Allason-Jones, L., 2002 — 'The jet industry and allied trades in Roman Yorkshire', in Wilson, P. and Price, J. (eds), *Aspects of Industry in Roman Yorkshire and the North* (Oxford)

Allen, J.R.L., Fulford, M.G. and Todd, J.A., 2007 — 'Burnt Kimmeridge shale at early Roman Silchester, south-east England, and the Roman Poole–Purbeck complex agglomerated geomaterials industry', *Oxford J. Archeol.* 26/2, 167–91

Anderson, S., 1973 — 'The differential pollen productivity of trees and its significance for the interpretation of a pollen diagram from a forested region', in Birks, H.J.B. and West, R.G. (eds), *Quaternary Plant Ecology*, (Oxford, Blackwell), 109–15

Artis, E.T., 1828 — *The Durobrivae of Antoninus* (London)

Ashurst, J.A. and Dimes, F.G., 1990 — *Conservation of Building Stone, Vol. I* (London, Butterworth-Heinemann)

Atkinson, D., 1914 — 'A hoard of samian ware from Pompeii', *J. Roman Stud.* 4, 27–64

Barford, P.M., 2002 — *Excavations at Little Oakley, Essex, 1951–78: Roman Villa and Saxon Settlement*, E. Anglian Archaeol. 98

Bartosiewicz, L., Van Neer, W. and Lentacker, A., 1997 — *Draught Cattle: Their Osteological Identification and History*, Musee Royal de l'Afrique Central. Tervuren, Annales Sciences Zoologique 281

Baxter, I., 2003 — 'Fauna and flora: the mammal and bird bones', in Hinman, M., *A Late Iron Age Farmstead and Romano-British Site at Haddon, Peterborough*, Cambridge County Council Archaeological Field Unit Monograph 2. Brit. Archaeol. Rep. British Ser. 358 (Oxford), 119–32

Bédoyère, de la, G., 1991 — *The Buildings of Roman Britain* (London, Batsford)

Bedwin, O., 1981 — 'Excavations at Lancing Down, West Sussex', *Sussex Archaeol. Collect.* 119, 37–56

Bidwell, P., 2007 — *Roman Forts in Britain* (Stroud, Tempus)

Blackford, J.J. and Chambers, F.M., 1991 — 'Proxy records of climate from blanket mires: evidence for a Dark Age climatic deterioration in the British Isles', *The Holocene* 1, 63–7

Boon, G.C., 1974 — *Silchester: the Roman town of Calleva* (Newton Abbot, David and Charles)

Boutwood, Y., 1998 — 'Prehistoric linear boundaries in Lincolnshire and its fringes', in R. Bewley (ed.), *Lincolnshire's Archaeology from the Air* (Lincoln, Soc. Lincolnshire Hist. Archaeol.), 29–46

Branigan, K., 1973 — *Town and Country. The Archaeology of Verulamium and the Roman Chilterns* (Bourne End, Spur Books)

Branigan, K., 1987 — *The Catuvellauni* (Gloucester, Alan Sutton)

Briggs, S., 1979 — 'The stone of Group VI rock from Lynch Farm: a reconsideration', *Durobrivae: A Review of Nene Valley Archaeology* 7, 14–15

Breeze, D., 2016 — *Bearsden; A Roman Fort on the Antonine Wall*, Soc of Antiq of Scotland

Brodribb, A.C.C., Hands, A.R. and Walker, D.R. 1971 — *Excavations at Shakenoak Farm, near Wilcot, Oxfordshire, Part II: Sites A and D* (printed privately)

Brodribb, G., 1987 — *Roman Brick and Tile* (Gloucester, Alan Sutton)

Bromwich, J., 1970 — 'Freshwater flooding along the fen margins south of the Isle of Ely during the Roman period', in Phillips, C.W. (ed.), *The Fenland in Roman Times: Studies of a Major Area of Peasant Colonization with a Gazetteer Covering All Known Sites and Finds*, Royal Geographical Society Res. Ser. 5 (London), 114–26

Buckland, P.C., 1976 — *The Archaeology of York Vol. 14: Past Environment of York Fasc. 1: the Environmental Evidence from the Church Street Roman Sewer System*, (London, Council for British Archaeology for York Archaeological Trust)

Buckland, P.C., 1981a — 'An insect fauna from a Roman well at Empingham, Rutland', *Trans. Leicestershire Archaeol. Hist. Soc.* 60, 1–6

Buckland, P.C., 1981b — 'The early dispersal of insect pests of stored products as indicated by archaeological records', *Journal of Stored Product Research* 17, 1–6

Buckland, P.C., Hartley, K.F. and Rigby, V., 2001 — *The Roman Pottery Kilns at Rossington Bridge 1956–1961: A Report on Excavations carried out by J.R.Lidster on behalf of Doncaster Museum. Journal of Pottery Studies*, 9 (Oxford: Oxbow Books for the Study Group for Roman Pottery)

Bullock, J.A., 1993 — 'Host plants of British beetles: a list of recorded associations', *Amateur Entomologist* 11a, 1–24

Bushe-Fox, J.P., 1913 — *Excavations on the Site of the Roman Town at Wroxeter, Shropshire, in 1912*, Rep. Res. Comm. Soc. Antiq. London 1 (Oxford)

Campbell, D.B., 2009 — *Roman Auxiliary Forts 27 BC–AD 378* (Oxford, Osprey)

Carlyle, S., 2010 — 'An Iron Age pit alignment near Upton, Northampton', *Northamptonshire Archaeol.* 36, 75–87

Carson, R.A.G., 1994 — 'Coins', in Greenfield, E., Poulsen, J. and Irving, P., 'The excavation of a fourth-century AD villa and bath-house at Great Staughton, Cambridgeshire, 1958–1959', *Proc. Camb. Antiq. Soc.* 83, 97–8

Chadwick-Hawkes, S., 1976 — 'A late-Roman nail cleaner with peacock', *Durobrivae: A Review of Nene Valley Archaeology* 4, 17–18

Challands, A., 1973 — 'The Lynch Farm complex: the prehistoric site', *Durobrivae: A Review of Nene Valley Archaeology* 1, 22–3

Challands, A., 1974a — 'The Lynch Farm complex: recent work', *Durobrivae: A Review of Nene Valley Archaeology* 2, 23

Challands, A., 1974b — 'A Roman industrial site and villa at Sacrewell, Thornhaugh', *Durobrivae: A Review of Nene Valley Archaeology* 2, 13–16

Challands, A., Dannell, G. and Wild, J.P., 1972 — 'Lynch Farm, Site 2: Roman buildings and fishpond', unpublished report, Nene Valley Research Committee Bulletin 3.

Chatwin, C.P., 1961 — *British Regional Geology: East Anglia and Adjoining Areas* (4th edn, London, Her Majesty's Stationary Office)

Clapham, A.R., Tutin, T.G. and Moore, D.W., 1987 — *Flora of the British Isles* (3rd edn, Cambridge, Cambridge University Press)

Clarke, G., 1979 — *Pre-Roman and Roman Winchester: Pt II The Roman cemetery at Lankhills*, Winchester Studies 3 (Oxford, Clarendon Press)

Collins, P., 1994 — 'The animal bone', in French, C.A.I., *The Archaeology along the A605 Elton–Haddon Bypass, Cambridgeshire*, Cambridgeshire County Council and Fenland Archaeological Trust Monograph 2 (Cambridge), 142–54

Condron, F., 1997 — 'Iron production in Leicestershire, Rutland and Northamptonshire in antiquity'. *Trans. Leicestershire Archaeol. Hist. Soc.* 71, 1–20

Connor, A. and Buckley, R., 1999 — *Roman and Mediaeval Occupation in Causeway Lane, Leicester*. Leicester Archaeol. Monographs 5 (Leicester)

Coope, G.R., 1965 — 'Fossil insect faunas from Late Quaternary deposits in Britain', *Advancement of Science* 21, 564–75

Coope, G.R., 1979 — 'Late Cenozoic fossil coleoptera: evolution, biogeography and ecology', *Annual Review of Ecology and Systematics* 10, 247–67

Coope, G.R. and Osborne, P.J., 1968 — 'Report on the coleopteran fauna of a Roman well at Barnsley Park, Gloucestershire', *Trans. Bristol Gloucestershire Archaeol. Soc.* 86, 84–7

Corder, P., 1951 — *The Roman Town and Villa at Great Casterton: First Interim Report* (Nottingham)

Corder, P., 1954 — *The Roman Town and Villa at Great Casterton: Second Interim Report* (Nottingham)

Corder, P., 1961 — *The Roman Town and Villa at Great Casterton: Third Interim Report* (Nottingham)

Cram, C.L., 1967 — 'The animal bones', in Salway, P., 'Excavation at Hockwold-cum-Wilton, Norfolk 1961–2', *Proc. Cambridge Antiq. Soc.* 60, 75–80

Crosby, A., 2001 — 'Briquetage', in Lane, T. and Morris, E.L. (eds), *A Millennium of Salt Making: Prehistoric and Romano-British Salt Production in the Fenland*, Lincolnshire Archaeology and Heritage Reports Series 4 (Heckington), 290–301

Crummy, N., 1979 — 'A chronology of Romano-British bone pins', *Britannia* 10, 157–63

Crummy, N., 1983 — *The Roman Small Finds from Excavations in Colchester 1971–9*, Colchester Archaeol. Rep. 2 (Colchester)

Cunliffe, B., 1971 — 'Other objects of bronze and silver', in Cunliffe, B., Excavations at Fishbourne, 1961–1969. Vol.2 The Finds, Rep. Res. Comm. Soc. Antiq. London 27 (London), 107–53

Cunliffe, B., 2005 — *Iron Age Communities in Britain* (London, Routledge)

Curteis, M., 1996 — 'An analysis of the circulation patterns of Iron Age coins from Northamptonshire', *Britannia* 27, 17–42

Curteis, M.E., 2001 — *The Iron Age Coinage of the South Midlands with Particular Reference to Distribution and Deposition* (unpubl. PhD thesis Univ. Durham) Available http://etheses.dur.ac.uk/1231/ Accessed: 15 July 2015

Curtis, J., 1862 — *British Entomology: Being Illustrations and Descriptions of the Genera of Insects Found in Great Britain and Ireland, Coleoptera Part 1* (London, Lovell Reeve and Co.)

Dakin, G.F., 1961 — 'A Romano-British site at Orton Longueville, Huntingdonshire', *Proc. Cambridge Antiq. Soc.* 54, 50–67

Dannell, G.B., 1973 — 'The potter Indixivixus', in Detsicas, A. (ed.), *Current Research in Romano-British Coarse Pottery*, Counc. Brit. Archaeol. Res. Rep. 10

Dannell, G.B., 1974 — 'Roman industry in Normangate Field, Castor', *Durobrivae: A Review of Nene Valley Archaeology* 2, 79

Dannell, G.B., 1987 — 'Coarse pottery', in Dannell, G.B. and Wild, J.P., *Longthorpe II. The Military Works-Depot: An Episode in Landscape History*, Britannia Monogr. Ser. 8, 133–68

Dannell, G.B. and Wild, J.P., 1987 — *Longthorpe II. The Military Works-Depot: An Episode in Landscape History*, Britannia Monogr. Ser. 8

Dannell, G.B., Hartley, B.R., Wild, J.P. and Perrin, J.R., 1993 — 'Excavations on a Romano-British pottery production site at Park Farm, Stanground 1967–8', *J. Roman Pottery Stud.* 6, 51–93

Dannell, G., Dickinson, B. and Vernhet, A., 1998 — 'Ovolos on Dragendorff form 30 from the collections of Frédéric Hermet et Dieudonné Rey', in Bird, J. (ed.), *Form and Fabric: Studies in Rome's Material Past in Honour of B.R. Hartley*, Oxbow Monogr. 80 (Oxford: Oxbow Books), 69–109

Dark, K.R., 1996 — 'Pottery and local production at the end of Roman', in Dark, K.R (ed.), *External Contacts and the Economy of Late Roman Britain and Post Roman Britain* (Woodbridge, Boydell Press), 53–65

Darling, M., 2004 — *Guidelines for the Archiving of Roman Pottery*, London. Study Group for Roman Pottery

Davies, J., 1996 — 'Where eagles dare: the Iron Age of Norfolk', *Proc. Prehist. Soc.* 62, 63–92

Davis, H.F., 1936 — 'The shale industry at Kimmeridge', *Archaeol. J.* 93, 200–213

De Clercq, W., 2011 — 'Roman rural settlements in Flanders. Perspectives on a "non-villa" landscape in *exrema Galliarum*', in Roymans, N. and Derks, T. (eds), *Villa Landscapes in the Roman North* (Amsterdam, Amsterdam University Press), 235–57

Deegan, A., 2007 — 'Late Bronze Age, Iron Age and Roman settlements and landscapes', in Deegan, A. and Foard G., *Mapping Ancient Landscapes in Northamptonshire* (London, English Heritage), 81–124

Deegan, A. and Foard, G., 2007 — *Mapping Ancient Landscapes in Northamptonshire* (London, English Heritage)

Dickinson, B.M. and Hartley, B.R., 2000 'The samian', in Rush, P., Dickinson, B., Hartley, B. and Hartley, K.F., *Roman Castleford, Excavations 1974–85, Vol. III, The Pottery*, Yorkshire Archaeology 6 (Wakefield, West Yorkshire Archaeology Service), 5–88

Dobney, K., Jaques, S.D. and Irving, B.G., 1996 *Of Butchers and Breeds: Report on Vertebrate Remains from Various Sites in the City of Lincoln*, Lincoln Archaeol. Stud. 5 (Lincoln: City of Lincoln Archaeology Unit)

Dodds, L.J., 2005 'Saltmaking in Roman Cheshire pt 2: discoveries and re-discovery: excavations along King Street, 2001–2', in Nevell, M. and Fielding, A.P. (eds), *Brine in Britannia: Recent Archaeological Work on the Roman Salt Industry in Cheshire*, Archaeology North West 7, Univ. Manchester Archaeol. Unit (Manchester), 25–30

Donisthorpe, H. St. J.K., 1939 *The Coleoptera of Windsor Forest* (London)

Downes, J., 1993 'The distribution and significance of Bronze Age metalwork in the North Level', in French, C. and Pryor, F., *The South-west Fen Dyke Survey Project 1982–86*, E. Anglian Archaeol. 59, 21–30

English Heritage, 2011 *Introductions to Heritage Assets, Oppida*. Available https://content.historicengland.org.uk/ images-books/publications/iha-oppida/oppida.pdf. Accessed 7 September 2016

Evans, G., 1975 *The Life of Beetles* (London, Allen and Unwin)

Evans, J., 2003 'The later Iron Age and Roman pottery', in Hinman, M., *A Late Iron Age Farmstead and Romano-British Site at Haddon, Peterborough*, Cambridge County Council Archaeological Field Unit Monograph 2. Brit. Archaeol. Rep. British Ser. 358 (Oxford), 68–107

Everson, P.L., 1983 *The Impact of Aerial Reconnaissance on Archaeology*, Counc. Brit. Archaeol. Res. Rep. 49

Every, R., 2006 'Briquetage and fired clay', in Andrews, P., 'Romano-British and medieval saltmaking and settlement in Parson Drove, Cambridgeshire', *Proc. Cambridge Antiq. Soc.* 95, 35–7

Eyre, M.D. and Luff, M.L., 1990 'The ground beetle (Coleoptera Carabidae) assemblages of British grasslands', *Entomologist's Gazette* 41, 197–208

Fairless, K.J., 2009 'Objects of jet, shale and similar materials'. Available http://www.barbicanra.co.uk/ shopimages/Documents/DigCh11contents.pdf Accessed: 15 July 2015

Fincham, G., 2002 *Landscapes of Imperialism: Roman and Native Interaction in the East Anglian Fenland*, Brit. Archaeol. Rep. British Ser. 338 (Oxford)

Fincham, G., 2004 *Durobrivae: A Roman Town between Fen and Upland* (Stroud, Tempus)

Forrer, R., 1911 *Die römischen Terrasigillata-Töpfereien von Heiligenberg-Dinsheim und Ittenweiler im Elsass* (Stuttgart)

Frankie, G.W. and Ehler, L.E., 1978 'Ecology of insects in urban environments', *Annual Review of Entomology* 23, 267–87

Fraser, S., 1994 'Other small finds', in French, C.A.I., *The Archaeology along the A605 Elton–Haddon Bypass, Cambridgeshire*, Cambridgeshire County Council and Fenland Archaeological Trust Monograph 2 (Cambridge), 135–41

French, C.A.I., 1983 *An Environmental Study of the Soils, Sediments and Molluscan Evidence Associated with Prehistoric Monuments on River Gravels in North-west Cambridgeshire* (Unpubl. PhD thesis Univ. London)

French, C.A.I. (ed.), 1994 *The Archaeology along the A605 Elton–Haddon Bypass, Cambridgeshire*, Cambridgeshire County Council and Fenland Archaeological Trust Monograph 2 (Cambridge)

French, C.A.I., and Wait, G.A., 1988 *An Archaeological Survey of the Cambridgeshire River Gravels* (Cambridge, Cambridgeshire County Council/Fenland Archaeological Trust)

Frend, W.H.C., 1968 'A Roman farm-settlement at Godmanchester', *Proc. Cambridge Antiq. Soc.* 61, 19–43

Frere, S.S. and St Joseph, J.K., 1974 'The Roman fortress at Longthorpe', *Britannia* 5, 1–129

Garland, N., 2012 'Boundaries and change: the examination of the late Iron Age–Roman transition', in Duggan, M., McIntosh, F. and Rohl, D., *TRAC 2011: Proceedings of the Twenty First Theoretical Roman Archaeology Conference, Newcastle 2011* (Oxford, Oxbow Books), 91–104

Garland, N., 2013 'Territorial oppida: late Iron Age settlements and landscapes', *Society for Landscape Studies Newsletter* (Winter 2012/13), 2–3

Garner, D., 2005 'Salt making in Roman Middlewich: Pt I. Discoveries before 2000', in Nevell, M. and Fielding, A.P. (eds), *Brine in Britannia: Recent Archaeological Work on the Roman Salt Industry in Cheshire*, Archaeology North West 7, Univ. Manchester Archaeol. Unit (Manchester), 15–24.

Geological Survey, 1972 'Peterborough Sheet', being part of sheets TF00/10/20/and TL09/19 29 (Geological Survey of Great Britain)

Girling, M.A., 1983 'The environmental implications of the excavations of 1974–1976', in Brown, A.E., Woodfield, C. and Maynard, D.C. (eds), 'Excavations at Towcester, Northamptonshire: The Alchester Road Suburb', *Northamptonshire Archaeol.* 18, 128–30

Girling, M.A., 1989 'The insect fauna of the Roman well at the Cattlemarket', *Chichester Excavations* 6, 234–41

Goodburn, R., 1974 'Objects of bronze', in Frere, S. and St Joseph, J., 'The Roman fortress at Longthorpe', *Britannia* 5, 42–68

Goodburn, R., 1984 'The non-ferrous metal objects', in Frere, S.S., *Verulamium Excavations, Vol. III*, Oxford Univ. Comm. Archaeol. Monogr. 1 (Oxford)

Grant, A., 1975 'The animal bones in excavation at Porchester Castle', in Cunliffe, B., *Excavations at Portchester Castle. Vol.1 Roman*, Rep. Res. Comm. Soc. Antiq. London 32 (London), 378–408

Grant, A., 1989 'Animals in Roman Britain', in Todd, M. (ed.), *Research on Roman Britain 1960–1989*, Britannia Monogr. Ser., 11, Society for the Promotion of Roman Studies (London), 135–47

Green, H.J.M., 1975 'Roman Godmanchester', in Rodwell, W. and Rowley, T. (eds), *The Small Towns of Roman Britain: Papers Presented to a Conference, Oxford, 1975*, Brit. Archaeol. Rep. British Ser. 15 (Oxford), 183–210

Green, H.M.J., 1986 'Religious cults at Roman Godmanchester', in Henig, M. and King, A. (eds), *Pagan Gods and Shrines of the Roman Empire*, Oxford Univ. Comm. Archaeol. Monogr. 8 (Oxford), 29–55

Green, H.M.J., 2005 'Stonea: a temple sanctuary', in Malim, T., *Stonea and the Roman Fens* (Stroud, Tempus), 130–32

Greenfield, E., 1958 'Interim report of Water Newton excavations, Huntingdonshire', unpublished typescript held in Peterborough Museum

Greenfield, E., 1963 'The Romano-British shrines at Brigstock, Northants', *Antiquaries J.* 42, 228–63

Greenfield, E., Poulsen, J. and Irving, P., 1994 'The excavation of a fourth-century AD villa and bath-house at Great Staughton, Cambridgeshire, 1958–1959', *Proc. Camb. Antiq. Soc.* 83, 75–127

Greep, S.J., 1995 'Objects of worked bone, antler and ivory from C.A.T. sites', in Blockley, K.M. and P., Frere, S. and Stow, S. (eds), *The Archaeology of Canterbury Vol.5, Excavations in the Marlowe car park and surrounding areas*, Canterbury Archaeological Trust (Canterbury), 1112–69

Greep, S.J., 1996 'Objects of worked bone and antler', in Jackson, R.P.J. and Potter, T.W., *Excavations at Stonea, Cambridgeshire 1980–85* (London, British Museum), 525–38

Grove, A.T., 1962 'Fenland', in Mitchell, J.B. (ed.), *Great Britain: Geographical Essays* (Cambridge: Cambridge University Press), 104–22

Grove, J.M., 1988 *The Little Ice Age*, London

Groves, S., 1973 *The History of Needlework Tools and Accessories* (Newton Abbot, David and Charles)

Gurney, D., 1985 'Romano-British features', in Pryor, F., French, C., Crowther, D., Gurney, D., Simpson, G. and Taylor, M., *The Fenland Project, No. 1: Archaeology and Environment in the Lower Welland Valley* (2 volumes), E. Anglian Archaeol. 27, 88–113

Guy, C.J., 1977 'The lead tank from Ashton', *Durobrivae: A Review of Nene Valley Archaeology* 5, 10–11

Hadman, J., 1978 'Aisled buildings in Roman Britain', in M. Todd (ed.), *Studies in the Romano-British Villa* (Leicester, Leicester University Press), 187–95

Hadman, J. and Upex, S.G., 1975a 'A Roman pottery kiln at Sulehay near Yarwell', *Durobrivae: A Review of Nene Valley Archaeology* 3, 16–18

Hadman, J. and Upex S.G., 1975b 'The Roman settlement at Ashton near Oundle', *Durobrivae: A Review of Nene Valley Archaeology* 3, 12–15

Hadman, J. and Upex, S.G., 1977 'Ashton 1976', *Durobrivae: A Review of Nene Valley Archaeology* 5, 6–9

Hadman, J. and Upex, S.G., 1979 'Ashton 1977–8', *Durobrivae: A Review of Nene Valley Archaeology* 7, 28–30

Hains, B.A. and Horton, A., 1969 *British Regional Geology: Central England* (London, HMSO)

Hakbijl, T., 1989 'Insect remains from Site Q, an early Iron Age farmstead of the Assendelver Polders project', *Hellenium* 29, 77–102

Hall, A.R. and Kenward, H.K., 1980 'An interpretation of biological remains from Highgate, Beverley', *J. Archaeol. Sci.* 7, 33–51

Hall, A.R., Kenward, H.K. and Williams, D., 1980 *The Archaeology of York Vol. 14: Past Environment of York Fasc. 3 Environmental Evidence from Roman Deposits in Skeldergate* (London, Council for British Archaeology for York Archaeological Trust)

Hall, D. and Martin, P., 1980 'Fieldwork survey of the Soke of Peterborough', *Durobrivae: A Review of Nene Valley Archaeology* 8, 13–14

Hall, D.N., 1985 'Survey work in eastern England', in Macready, S. and Thompson, F.H. (eds), *Archaeological Field Survey in Britain and Abroad*, Soc. Antiq. London Occas. Pap. 6 (London), 25–34

Hall, D.N., 1987 *The Fenland Project, No. 2: Fenland Landscapes and Settlements between Peterborough and March*, E. Anglian Archaeol. 35

Hall, D.N., 1992 *The Fenland Project, No. 6: The South Western Cambridgeshire Fenlands*, E. Anglian Archaeol. 56

Hall, D.N., 1996 *The Fenland Project No. 10: Cambridgeshire Survey: The Isle of Ely and Wisbech*, E. Anglian Archaeol. 79

Hall, D.N. and Cole, J., 1994 *Fenland Survey: An Essay in Landscape and Persistence* (London, English Heritage)

Hallam, S., 1970 'Settlement around the Wash', in Phillips, C. (ed.), *The Fenland in Roman Times: Studies of a Major Area of Peasant Colonization with a Gazetteer Covering All Known Sites and Finds*, Royal Geographical Society Res. Ser. 5 (London), 22–113

Hanley, R., 1994 *Villages in Roman Britain* (Princes Risborough, Shire)

Harcourt, R.A., 1974 'The dog in prehistoric and early historic Britain', *J. Archaeol. Sci.* 1, 151–76

Harcourt, R.A., 1975 'The dog bones', in Cunliffe, B., *Excavation at Porchester Castle Vol.1 Roman*, Rep. Res. Comm. Soc. Antiq. London 32, 406–8

Hartley, B.R. 1960 *Notes on the Roman Pottery Industry in the Nene Valley*, Peterborough Museum Occas. Pap. 2 (Peterborough, Peterborough Museum Society)

Hartley, B.R., 1974 'The samian', in Frere, S.S. and St Joseph, J.K., 'The Roman fortress at Longthorpe', *Britannia* 5, 91–6

Hartley, B.R. and Dickinson, B., 1990 'Samian ware', in Perrin, J.R., *The Archaeology of York Vol. 16: The Pottery Fasc. 4 Roman Pottery from the Colonia 2: General Accident and Rougier Street* (London, Council for British Archaeology for York Archaeological Trust), 275–303

Hartley, B.R. and Dickinson, B.M., 2008–12 *Names on Terra Sigillata: An Index of Makers' Stamps and Signatures on Gallo-Roman Terra Sigillata (Samian Ware)* (London, Institute of Classical Studies)

Hartley, E., Hawkes, J., Henig, M. and Mee, F., 2006 *Constantine the Great* (York: York Museums and Gallery Trust)

Hartley, K.F., 1990 'The mortaria', in McCarthy, M., *A Roman, Anglian and Medieval Site at Blackfriars Street, Carlisle: Excavations 1977–9*, Cumberland and Westmorland Antiq. Archaeol. Soc. Res. Ser. 4. (Kendal, Cumberland and Westmorland Antiquarian and Archaeological Society), 237–63

Hartley, K.F., 1996 'A type series for mortaria in the Lower Nene valley', in Mackreth, D., *Orton Hall Farm: A Roman and Early Anglo-Saxon Farmstead*, E. Anglian Archaeol. 76, 199–204

188

Hartley, K.F., 1997 'Mortaria', in J. Monaghan, *The Archaeology of York Vol. 16: The Pottery Fasc. 8 Roman Pottery from York* (London, Council for British Archaeology for York Archaeological Trust), 930–43

Hartley, K.F., 2016 'Mortaria', in Breeze, D.J., *Bearsden: A Roman Fort on the Antonine Wall*, (Soc. Antiq. Scotland), 280–84

Hartley, K.F. and Hartley, B.R., 1970 'Pottery in the Romano-British fenland', in Phillips, C.W. (ed.), *The Fenland in Roman Times: Studies of a Major Area of Peasant Colonization with a Gazetteer Covering All Known Sites and Finds*, Royal Geographical Society Res. Ser. 5 (London), 165–9

Hartley, K.F. and Healey, H., 1987 'Stamped mortarium from South Kyme, Lincs', *Lincolnshire Hist Archaeol.* 22, 44–5

Hartley, K.F. and Perrin J.R., 1999 'Mortaria from Excavations by E. Greenfield at Water Newton, Billing Brook and Chesterton 1956–58' in J. Perrin, *Roman Pottery from Excavations at and Near to the Roman Small Town of Durobrivae, Water Newton, Cambridgeshire, 1956–58*, J. Roman Pottery Stud. 8 (Oxford, Oxbow Books)

Hartridge, R., 1978 'Excavations at the prehistoric and Romano-British site on Slonk Hill, Shoreham, Sussex', *Sussex Archaeol. Collect.* 116, 69–141

Hattatt, R., 1982 *Ancient and Romano-British Brooches* (Sherbourne, Dorset Publishing Co.)

Hawkes, C., 1939 'The Roman camp near Castor on the Nene', *Antiquity* 13, 178–90

Hayes, P.P., 1988 'Roman to Saxon in the south Lincolnshire fens', *Antiquity* 62, 321–6

Higginbotham, J.A., 1997 *Piscinae: Artificial Fishponds in Roman Italy* (Chapel Hill, NC, University of North Carolina Press)

Hingley, R., 1989 *Rural Settlement in Roman Britain* (London, Seaby)

Hinman, M., 2003 *A Late Iron Age farmstead and Romano-British Site at Haddon, Peterborough*, Cambridge County Council Archaeological Field Unit Monograph 2. Brit. Archaeol. Rep. British Ser. 358 (Oxford)

Hole, F., Flannery, J.V. and Neely, J.A., 1969 *Prehistory and Human Ecology of the Deh Luran Plain*, Memoirs of the Museum of Anthropology, University of Michigan 1 (Ann Arbor, MI, University of Michigan)

Horton, W., Lucas, G. and Wait, G., 1994 'Excavation of a Roman site near Wimpole, Cambridgeshire, 1989', *Proc. Cambridge Antiq. Soc.* 83, 31–74

Houston, M., 1931 *Ancient Greek, Roman and Byzantine Costume* (London, A. and C. Black)

Howe, M., Perrin, J. and Mackreth, D., 1982 *Roman Pottery from the Nene Valley: A Guide* (Peterborough, City Museum and Art Gallery)

Hyman, P.S., 1992 *A Review of Scarce and Threatened Coleoptera of Great Britain Part 1*, revised and updated by M.S. Pearsons (Peterborough, UK Joint Nature Conservation Committee)

Jackson, D.A. and Ambrose, T.M., 1978 'Excavations at Wakerley, Northants 1972–75', *Britannia* 9, 115–288

Jackson, D.A. and Tylecote, R.F., 1988 'Two new Romano-British Iron working sites in Northamptonshire: a new type of furnace?' *Britannia* 19, 275–98

Jackson, R.P.J., 1996a 'Other copper-alloy objects', in Jackson, R.P.J. and Potter, T.W., *Excavations at Stonea, Cambridgeshire 1980–85* (London, British Museum), 339–59

Jackson, R.P.J., 1996b 'Iron objects', in Jackson, R.P.J. and Potter, T.W., *Excavations at Stonea, Cambridgeshire 1980–85* (London, British Museum), 359–70

Jackson, R.P.J. and Potter, T.W., 1996 *Excavations at Stonea, Cambridgeshire: 1980–85* (London, British Museum)

Johns, C., 1996 *The Jewellery of Roman Britain* (London, Routledge)

Johns, C. and Carson, R., 1975 'The Water Newton hoard', *Durobrivae: A Review of Nene Valley Archaeology* 3, 10–12

Johnson, A.G., 1987 'Fineshade Abbey', unpubl. report for Northants Archaeology Unit

Johnstone, C. and Albarella, U., 2002 *The Late Iron Age and Romano-British Mammal and Bird Bone Assemblage from Elms Farm, Heybridge, Essex* (Portsmouth, English Heritage)

Jones, M., 1996 *The End of Roman Britain* (New York, Cornell University Press)

Jones, R., 1973 'A Romano-British cemetery and farmstead at Lynch Farm', *Durobrivae: A Review of Nene Valley Archaeology* 1, 11–13

Jones, R., 1974 'A Roman and Saxon farm at Walton, North Bretton', *Durobrivae: A Review of Nene Valley Archaeology* 2, 29–31

Jones, R., 1975 'The Romano-British farmstead and its cemetery at Lynch Farm, near Peterborough', *Northamptonshire Archaeol.* 10, 94–136

Jones, R., 2012 *Roman Camps in Britain* (Stroud, Amberley)

Kenward, H.K., 1975 'Pitfalls in the environmental interpretation of insect death assemblages', *J. Archaeol. Sci.* 2, 85–94

Kenward, H.K., 1976 'Reconstructing ancient ecological conditions from insect remains: some problems and an experimental approach', *Ecological Entomology* 1, 7–17

Kenward, H.K., 1977 'The insect remains', in Armstrong, P., *Excavations in Sewer Lane, Hull, 1974*, Hull Old Town Report Series 1, East Riding Archaeologist 3, 33–5

Kenward, H.K., 1978a 'The value of insect remains as evidence of ecological conditions on archaeological sites', in Brothwell, D.R., Thomas, K.D. and Clutton-Brock, J. (eds), *Research Problems in Zooarchaeology*, Institute of Archaeology, University of London Occas. Publ. 3 (London), 25–38

Kenward, H.K., 1978b *The Archaeology of York Vol. 19: Principles and Methods Fasc. 1 The Analysis of Archaeological Insect Assemblages: A New Approach* (London, Council for British Archaeology for York Archaeological Trust)

Kenward, H.K., 1982 'Insect communities and death assemblages past and present', in Hall, A.R. and Kenward, H.K., *Environmental Archaeology in the Urban Context*, Counc. Brit. Archaeol. Res. Rep. 43, 71–8

Kenward, H.K., 1985 'Outdoors–indoors? The outdoor component of archaeological insect assemblages', in Fieller, N.R.J., Gilbertson, D.D. and Ralph, N.G.A. (eds), *Palaeobiological Investigations: Research Design, Methods and Data Analysis*, Brit. Archaeol. Rep. Int. Ser. 266 (Oxford), 97–104

Kenward, H.K. and Allison, E.P., 1995 'Rural origins of the urban insect fauna', in Hall, A.R. and Kenward, H.K. (eds), *Urban–Rural Connexions: Perspectives from Environmental Archaeology*, Oxbow Monogr. 47 (Oxford), 55–77

Kenyon, K.M., 1948 *Excavations at the Jewry Wall Site, Leicester*, Rep. Res. Comm. Soc. Antiq. London 15 (London)

Kidd, A., 2004 'Northamptonshire in the first millennium BC', in Tingle, M., *The Archaeology of Northamptonshire* (Northampton, Northamptonshire Archaeology Society), 44–62

King, A., 2004 'Mammal bone', in Blagg, T., Plouviez, J. and Tester, A. (eds), *Excavations at a Large Romano-British Settlement at Hacheston, Suffolk, in 1973–4*, E. Anglian Archaeol. 106, 188–95

King, A.C. and Potter, T.W., 1990 'A new domestic building-facade from Roman Britain at Meonstoke', *J. Roman Archaeol.* 3, 195–204

Knocker, G.M., 1965 'Excavations in Collyweston Great Wood, Northamptonshire', *Archaeol. J.* 122, 52–72

Knorr, R., 1952 *Terra-Sigillata-Gefässe des ersten Jahrhunderts mit Töpfernamen* (Stuttgart)

Lane, T., 2005 'The wider context of the Cheshire salt industry: Iron Age and Roman salt production around the Wash', in Nevell, M. and Fielding, A.P. (eds), *Brine in Britannia: Recent Archaeological Work on the Roman Salt Industry in Cheshire*, Archaeology North West 7, Univ. Manchester Archaeol. Unit (Manchester), 47–54

Lane, T. and Morris, E.L. (eds), 2001 *A Millennium of Salt Making: Prehistoric and Romano-British Salt Production in the Fenland*, Lincolnshire Archaeology and Heritage Reports Series 4 (Heckington)

Lane, T., Morris, E.L. and Peachey, M., 2008 'Excavations on a Roman salt-making site at Cedar Close', *Proc. Cambridge Antiq. Soc.* 97, 89–109

Lawrence, R.R., 2010 *Roman Britain* (Oxford, Shire)

Lawson, A.J., 1976 'Shale and jet objects from Silchester', *Archaeologia* 105, 241–75

Leech, R., 1982 *Excavations at Catsgore 1970–1973: A Romano-British Village*. Western Archaeological Trust Excavation Monograph 2 (Bristol)

Lewis, M., 1966 *Temples in Roman Britain* (Cambridge, Cambridge University Press)

Lindroth, C.H., 1957 *The Faunal Connections Between Europe and North America* (New York, J. Wiley and Sons)

Lindroth, C.H., 1974 *Coleoptera Carabidae*, Handbooks for the Identification of British Insects 4/2 (London, Royal Entomological Society)

Liversidge, J., 1968 *Britain in the Roman Empire* (London, Routledge)

Lott, G. and Smith, D., 2001 'Shining stones: Britain's native "marbles"', *The Building Conservation Directory*. Available http://www.buildingconservation.com/articles/shining/shining.htm Accessed: 15 July 2015

Luff, M.L. and Rushton, S.P., 1989 'The ground beetle and spider fauna of managed and unimproved upland pasture', *Agriculture, Ecosystems and Environments* 25, 195–205

MacGregor, A., Mainman, A.J. and Rogers, N.S.H., 1999 *The Archaeology of York Vol. 17: Small Finds Fasc. 12 Craft, Industry and Everyday Life: Bone Antler, Ivory and Horn from Anglo-Scandinavian and Medieval York* (London, Council for British Archaeology for York Archaeological Trust)

Mackie, D., 1993 'Prehistoric ditch systems in Ketton and Tixover, Rutland', *Trans. Leicestershire Archaeol. Hist. Soc.* 67, 1–14

Mackreth, D.F., 1981 'The brooches', in Partridge, C., *Skeleton Green. A Late Iron Age and Romano-British Site*, Britannia Monogr. 2, 130–51

Mackreth, D.F., 1988 'Excavation of an Iron Age and Roman enclosure at Werrington, Cambridgeshire', *Britannia* 19, 59–151

Mackreth, D.F., 1996a 'Brooches', in Jackson, R.P.J. and Potter, T.W., *Excavations at Stonea, Cambridgeshire 1980–85* (London, British Museum), 296–327

Mackreth, D.F., 1996b *Orton Hall Farm: A Roman and Early Anglo-Saxon Farmstead*, E. Anglian Archaeol. 76

Mackreth, D.F., 2001 *Monument 97, Orton Longueville, Cambridgeshire: A Late Pre-Roman Iron Age and Early Roman Farmstead*, E. Anglian Archaeol. 97

Mackreth, D.F., 2011 *Brooches in Late Iron Age and Roman Britain*, 2 vols (Oxford, Oxbow Books)

Mackreth, D.F., forthcoming *Prehistoric Burials at Orton Meadows, Peterborough*, E. Anglian Archaeol.

McCarthy, M.R., 1990 *A Roman, Anglian and medieval Site at Blackfriars Street*, Cumberland, Westmoreland Antiq Archaeol Soc, Res Ser, 4, Kendal

Malim, T., 2005 *Stonea and the Roman Fens* (Stroud, Tempus)

Maltby, J.M. 1977 *The Animal Bones from Roman Exeter*, unpubl. MA thesis Univ. Sheffield.

Manning, W.H., 1973 'Three iron tools from Lynch Farm', *Durobrivae: A Review of Nene Valley Archaeology* 1, 29–30

Manning, W.H., 1985 *Catalogue of the Romano-British Iron Tools, Fittings and Weapons in the British Museum* (London)

Mattingley, D., 2007 *An Imperial Possession: Britain in the Roman Empire* (London, Penguin)

May, J., 1985 'The finds', in Pryor, F. and French, C., *The Fenland Project No 1: Archaeology and Environment in the Lower Welland Valley*, vol. 2, E. Anglian Archaeol. 27, 261–4

Mees, A.W., 1995 *Modelsignierte Dekorationen auf südgallischer Terra Sigillata*, Forschungen und Berichte zur Vor- und Frühgeschichte in Baden-Württemberg Band 54 (Stuttgart)

Miles, D., 1986 *Archaeology at Barton Court Farm, Abingdon, Oxfordshire*. Counc. Brit. Archaeol. Res. Rep. 50

Millett, M., 1990 *The Romanization of Britain: An Essay in Archaeological Interpretation* (Cambridge, Cambridge University Press)

Monaghan, J., 1997 *The Archaeology of York Vol. 16: The Pottery Fasc. 8 Roman Pottery from York*, (London,

Council for British Archaeology for York Archaeological Trust)

Moore, T., 2012 — 'Beyond the oppida: polyfocal complexes and late Iron Age society in southern Britain', *Oxford J. Archaeol.* 31/4, 391–417

Moore, W.R.G. 1973 — 'Note', *Northamptonshire Archaeol.* 8, 27

Moritz, L.A., 1958 — *Grain Mills and Flour in Classical Antiquity* (Oxford, Clarendon Press)

Morris, E.L., 2001 — 'Briquetage', in Lane, T. and Morris, E.L. (eds), *A Millennium of Salt Making: Prehistoric and Romano-British Salt Production in the Fenland*, Lincolnshire Archaeology and Heritage Reports Series 4 (Heckington), 33–63

Morris, E.L., 2008 — 'Briquetage', in Lane, T., Morris, E.L. and Peachey, M., 'Excavations on a Roman salt-making site at Cedar Close', *Proc. Cambridge Antiq. Soc.* 97, 93–102

Morris, J., 1975 — *Domesday Book. 19. Huntingdonshire* (Chichester, Phillimore)

Morris, J., 2011 — *Investigating Animal Bones: Ritual, Mundane and Beyond*, Brit. Archaeol. Rep. British Ser. 535 (Oxford)

Morris, P., 1979 — *Agricultural Buildings in Roman Britain*, Brit. Archaeol. Rep. British Ser. 70 (Oxford)

Morton, J., 1712 — *The Natural History of Northamptonshire* (London)

MPP (Monuments Protection Programme), 1989 — *Wooton Hill Style Enclosures. Monument Class Description*: http://www.engh.gov.uk/mpp/mcd/whl.htm. Accessed 2012, no longer available online

Neal, D.S., 1989 — 'The Stanwick Villa, Northants: an interim report on the excavations of 1984–88', *Britannia* 20, 149–68

Neal, D.S. and Butcher, S.A., 1974 — 'Miscellaneous objects of bronze', in Neal, D.S., *The Excavation of the Roman Villa in Gadebridge Park, Hemel Hempstead 1963–8*. Rep. Res. Comm. Soc. Antiq. London 31 (London), 128–50

Northamptonshire Archaeology, 1969 — 'Bulletin of the Northamptonshire Federation of Archaeological Societies', *Northamptonshire Archaeology* 3, 7–9

Northamptonshire Archaeology, 1973 — 'Archaeology in Northamptonshire 1972', *Northamptonshire Archaeology* 8, 9–12

Northamptonshire Archaeology, 1974a — 'Archaeology in Northamptonshire 1973', *Northamptonshire Archaeology* 9, 85

Northamptonshire Archaeology, 1974b — 'Archaeology in Northamptonshire 1973', *Northamptonshire Archaeology* 9, 92–5

Northamptonshire Archaeology, 1975a — 'Archaeology in Northamptonshire 1974' *Northamptonshire Archaeology* 10, 149

Northamptonshire Archaeology, 1975b — 'Archaeology in Northamptonshire 1974' *Northamptonshire Archaeology* 10, 158–61

Northamptonshire Archaeology, 1976 — 'Archaeology in Northamptonshire 1975' Northamptonshire Archaeology, 11, 186–191

NVRC, 1972 — 'Nene valley excavations 1972 Bulletin III', unpubl. typescript held in Peterborough Museum

NVRC, 1973 — 'Nene valley excavations 1973 Bulletin I', unpubl. typescript held in Peterborough Museum

O'Neil, F. and Mackreth, D., 1982 — 'Orton Meadow, Orton Longueville', Nene Valley Res. Comm. Annual Report 1981/2, chapter 5.1.2

Osborne, P.J., 1981a — 'The insect fauna', in Jarett, M.G. and Wrathwell, S. (eds), *Whitton: an Iron Age and Roman Farmstead in South Glamorgan* (Cardiff, University of Wales Press), 245–8

Osborne, P.J., 1981b — 'The insect fauna', in Stanford, S.C. (ed.), *Midsummer Hill: an Iron Age Hillfort on the Malverns* (Leominster), 156–7

Osborne, P.J., 1983 — 'An insect fauna from a modern cesspit and its comparison with probable cesspit assemblages from archaeological sites', *J. Archaeol. Sci.* 10, 453–63

Oswald, F., 1936–37 — *Index of Figure Types on Terra Sigillata*, University of Liverpool Annals of Archaeology and Anthropology, Supplement (Liverpool, Liverpool University Press)

Painter, K.S., 1976 — 'The Waternewton silver treasure', *Durobrivae: A Review of Nene Valley Archaeology* 4, 7–9

Painter, K.S., 1977 — *The Water Newton Early Christian Silver* (London, British Museum)

Painter, K.S., 1999 — 'The Water Newton silver: votive or liturgical?' *J. Brit. Archaeol. Assoc.* 152, 1–23

Panagiotakapulus, E., Higham, T.F.G., Buckland, P.C., Tripp, J.A. and Hedges, R.E.M., 2015 — 'AMS dating of insect chitin — a discussion of new dates, problems and potentials', *Quaternary Geochronology* 27, 22–32

Parry, S., 2006 — *Raunds Area Survey: An Archaeological Study of the Landscape of Raunds, Northamptonshire 1985–94* (Oxford, Oxbow Books)

Payne, S., 1972 — 'Partial recovery and sample bias: the results of some sieving experiments', in Higgs, E.S., *Papers in Economic History* (Cambridge, Cambridge University Press), 49–64

Peacock, D.P.S. and Williams, D.F., 1986 — *Amphorae and the Roman Economy: An Introductory Guide* (London, Longman)

Percival, J., 1976 — *The Roman Villa: An Historical Introduction* (London, Batsford)

Perrin, J.R., 1980 — 'Pottery of "London Ware" type from the Nene valley', *Durobrivae: A Review of Nene Valley Archaeology* 8, 8–10

Perrin, J.R., 1981 — 'The late Roman pottery of Great Casterton – thirty years on', in Anderson, A.C. and Anderson, A.S. (eds), *Roman Pottery Research in Britain and North-West Europe*, Brit. Archaeol. Rep. Int. Ser. 123 (Oxford), 447–63

Perrin, J.R., 1988 — 'The pottery', in Mackreth, D., 'Excavation of an Iron Age and Roman enclosure at Werrington, Cambridgeshire', *Britannia* 19, 104–41

Perrin, J.R., 1999 — *Roman Pottery from Excavations at and Near to the Roman Small Town of Durobrivae, Water Newton, Cambridgeshire, 1956–58*, J. Roman Pottery Stud. 8 (Oxford, Oxbow Books)

Perrin, J.R., 2008 — 'The Roman pottery', in Upex, S.G., 'The excavation of a fourth-century Roman pottery production unit at Stibbington, Cambridgeshire', *Archaeol. J.* 165, 282–313

Perrin, J.R. and Webster, G., 1990 'Roman pottery from excavations in Normangate Field, Castor, Peterborough 1962–3', *J. Roman Pottery Stud.* 3, 35–62

Perrin, J.R., Wild, F. and Hartley, K.F., 1996 'The Roman pottery', in Mackreth, D., *Orton Hall Farm: A Roman and Early Anglo-Saxon Farmstead*, E. Anglian Archaeol. 76, 114–204

Phillips, C.W. (ed.), 1970 *The Fenland in Roman Times: Studies of a Major Area of Peasant Colonization with a Gazetteer Covering All Known Sites and Finds*, Royal Geographical Society Res. Ser. 5 (London)

Pickering, A., 1978 'The Jurassic spine', *Current Archaeol.* 64, 140–43

Pickstone, A., 2011 *Iron Age and Roman Remains at Bretton Way, Peterborough: Post Excavation Assessment*, Oxford Archaeology East Rep. 1230, 41–56

Pickstone, A., 2012 'Peterborough's lost Roman villa', *Current Archaeol.* 23/5, 28–33

Pickstone, A. and Drummond-Murray, J., 2013 'A late well or cistern and ritual deposition at Bretton Way, Peterborough', *Proc. Cambridge Antiq. Soc.* 102, 37–66

Pollard, J., 1996 'Iron Age riverside pit alignments at St Ives, Cambridgeshire', *Proc. Prehist. Soc.* 62, 93–115

Polunin, O., 1988 *Collins Photo-guide to Wild Flowers of Britain and Northern Europe* (London, Collins)

Potter, T.W., 1981 'The Roman occupation of the central fenland', *Britannia* 12, 79–133

Potter, T.W., 1989 'The Roman fenland', in Todd, M. (ed.), *Research on Roman Britain*, Britannia Monogr. Ser. 11 (London), 147–73

Potter, T.W., 1996 'Discussion and conclusions', in Jackson, R.P.J. and Potter, T.W., *Excavations at Stonea, Cambridgeshire 1980–85* (London, British Museum), 671–94

Potter, T.W. and Potter, C.F., 1982 *A Romano-British Village at Grandford, March, Cambs*, British Museum Occas. Pap. 35 (London)

Potter, T.W. and Robinson, B., 2000 'New Roman and prehistoric aerial discoveries at Grandford, Cambridgeshire', *Antiquity* 74/283, 31–2

Pryor, F.M.M., 1974 *Excavations at Fengate, Peterborough, England: The First Report*, Royal Ontario Museum Archaeol. Monogr. 3 (Toronto)

Pryor, F.M.M., 1977 'Fengate 1976', *Durobrivae: A Review of Nene Valley Archaeology* 5, 14–17

Pryor, F.M.M., 1978 *Excavations at Fengate, Peterborough, England: The Second Report*, Royal Ontario Museum Archaeol. Monogr. 5 (Toronto)

Pryor, F.M.M., 1980 *Excavations at Fengate, Peterborough, England: The Third Report*, Northamptonshire Archaeol. Soc. Monogr./Royal Ontario Museum Archaeol. Monogr. 6 (Toronto)

Pryor, F.M.M., 1984 *Excavations at Fengate, Peterborough, England: The Fourth Report*, Northamptonshire Archaeol. Soc. Monogr. 2/Royal Ontario Museum Archaeol. Monogr. 7 (Toronto)

Pryor, F.M.M., 1991 'Archaeology in the Peterborough area', in Pryor, F.M.M., *Flag Fen: Prehistoric Fenland Centre* (London, Batsford), 25–40

Pryor, F.M.M., French, C., Crowther, D., Gurney, D., Simpson, G. and Taylor, M., 1985 *Fenland Project, No. 1, Archaeology and Environment in the Lower Welland Valley*, 2 vols, E. Anglian Archaeol. 27

RCHM (Royal Commission on Historic Monuments), 1960 *A Matter of Time: An Archaeological Survey of the River Gravels of England* (London, HMSO)

RCHM (Royal Commission on Historic Monuments), 1962 *Eburacum, Roman York* (London, HMSO)

RCHM (Royal Commission on Historic Monuments), 1969 *Peterborough New Town – A Survey of the Antiquities in the Area of Development* (London, HMSO)

RCHM (Royal Commission on Historic Monuments), 1975 *An Inventory of the Archaeological Sites in North East Northamptonshire* (London, HMSO)

RCHM (Royal Commission on Historic Monuments), 1979 *An Inventory of Archaeological Sites in Central Northamptonshire* (London, HMSO)

RCHM (Royal Commission on Historic Monuments), 1981 *An Inventory of Archaeological Sites in North West Northamptonshire* (London, HMSO)

Reece, R., 1972 'A short survey of the Roman coins found on fourteen sites in Britain', *Britannia* 3, 269–76

Reece, R., 1991 *Coins from 140 Sites in Britain*, Cotswold Studies 4 (Cirencester)

Reece, R., 1995 'Site finds in Roman Britain', *Britannia* 26, 179–206

Ricken, H., 1948 *Die Bilderschüsseln der römischen Töpfer von Rheinzabern*, Tafelband (Speyer)

Rivet, A.L.F., 1964 *Town and Country in Roman Britain* (2nd edn, London, Hutchinson)

Roberts, N., 1989 *The Holocene: An Environmental History* (Oxford, Blackwell)

Robertson, A., 2000 *An Inventory of Romano-British Coin Hoards*, Royal Numismatic Soc. Special Publ. 20 (London, Royal Numismatic Society)

Robinson, M.A., 1975 'The environment of the Roman defences at Alchester and its implications', *Oxoniensia* 40, 161–70

Robinson, M.A., 1981 'Roman waterlogged plant and invertebrate evidence', in Hinchliffe, J. and Thomas, R. (eds), *Archaeological Investigations at Appleford*, *Oxoniensia* 45, 90–106

Robinson, M.A., 1983 'Arable/pastoral ratios from insects?' in Jones, M. (ed.), *Integrating the Subsistence Economy*, Brit. Archaeol. Rep. Int. Ser. 181 (Oxford), 19–55

Robinson, M.A., 1993 'The scientific evidence', in Allen, T.G. and Robinson, M.A. (eds), *The Prehistoric Landscape and Iron Age Enclosed Settlement at Mingies Ditch, Hardwick-with-Yelford, Oxfordshire* (Oxford, Oxford University Committee for Archaeology for Oxford Archaeological Unit)

Rodwell, W.J., 1980 'Temple archaeology: problems of the present and portents for the future', in Rodwell, W. (ed.), *Temples, Churches and Religion: Recent Research in Roman Britain*, Brit. Archaeol. Rep. British Ser. 77 (Oxford), 211–42

Roffe, D., 1984 'Pre-conquest estates and parish boundaries: a discussion with examples from Lincolnshire', in Faull, M. (ed.), *Studies in Late Anglo-Saxon Settlement* (Oxford, Oxford University Dept. for External Studies)

Rogers, A., 2008 'Religious places and its interaction with urbanisation in the Roman era', *J. Social Archaeol.* 8/1, 37–62

Rogers, G.B., 1974 *Poteries sigillées de la Gaule Centrale I: les motifs non figurés*, Gallia Supplement 28

Rogers, G.B., 1999 *Poteries sigillées de la Gaule Centrale II: les potiers*, premier Cahier du Centre Archéologique de Lezoux

Rollo, C.J.S., 1981 'Excavations at Elmlea House, Castor 1980', unpubl. ms report, Peterborough Museum

Rollo, L., 1994 'The pottery', in French, C., *The Archaeology along the A605 Elton–Haddon Bypass, Cambridgeshire*, Cambridgeshire County Council and Fenland Archaeological Trust Monograph 2 (Cambridge), 89–131

Rollo, L. and Wild, F., 2001 'The Iron Age and Roman pottery', in Mackreth, D., *Monument 97, Orton Longueville, Cambridgeshire: A Late Pre-Roman Iron Age and Early Roman Farmstead*, E. Anglian Archaeol. 97, 46–77

Roymans, N. and Habermehl, D., 2011 'On the origins and development of axial villas with double courtyards in the Latin west', in Roymans, N. and Derks, T. (eds), *Villa Landscapes in the Roman North* (Amsterdam, Amsterdam University Press), 83–105

Rudd, G., 1968 'Notes', Counc. British Archaeol. Group 7, *Bulletin of Archaeological Discoveries* 15, 2–3

Rudd, G., 1969 'Notes', Counc. British Archaeol. Group 7, *Bulletin of Archaeological Discoveries* 16, 3

Sailer, R.I., 1983 'History of insect introductions', in Wilson, C.L. and Graham, C.L. (eds), *Exotic Plant Pest and North American Agriculture* (New York, Academic Press), 15–83

Salway, P., 1970 'The Roman fenland', in Phillips, C.W. (ed.), *The Fenland in Roman Times: Studies of a Major Area of Peasant Colonization with a Gazetteer Covering All Known Sites and Finds*, Royal Geographical Society Res. Ser. 5 (London), 1–21

Salway, P., 1981 *Roman Britain* (Oxford, Clarendon)

Schrufer-Kolb, I., 1999 'Roman iron production in the East Midlands', in Young, S.M.M., Polland, A., Budd, A.M. and Ixer, P. (eds), *Metals in Antiquity*, Brit. Archaeol. Rep. Int. Ser. 792 (Oxford), 227–33

Schrufer-Kolb, I., 2004 *Roman Iron Production in Britain: Technological and Socio-economic Landscape Development along the Jurassic Ridge*, Brit. Archaeol. Rep. British Ser. 380 (Oxford)

Scott, E., 1993 *A Gazetteer of Roman Villas in Britain*, Leicester Archaeological Monogr. 1 (Leicester)

Shaffery, R., 2009a 'Rotary querns', in Lawrence, S. and Smith, A., *Between Villa and Town: Excavations of a Roman Roadside Settlement and Shrine at Higham Ferrers, Northamptonshire*, Oxford Archaeology Monogr. 7 (Oxford)

Shaffery, R., 2009b 'The other worked stone', in Howard-Davis, C., *The Carlisle Millennium Project: Excavations in Carlisle, 1996–2001, Vol II, The Finds* (Lancaster, Oxford Archaeology North), 873–87

Shotter, D., 2005 'Salt production in Roman Cheshire: realities and possibilities', in Nevell, M. and Fielding, A.P. (eds), *Brine in Britannia: Recent Archaeological Work on the Roman Salt Industry in Cheshire*, Archaeology North West 7, Univ. Manchester Archaeol. Unit (Manchester), 41–6

Silver, J.A., 1969 'The ageing of domestic animals', in Brothwell, D. and Higgs, E.S., *Science and Archaeology* (London, Thames Hudson), 283–302

Sim, D., 2012 *The Roman Iron Industry in Britain* (Stroud, The History Press)

Simpson, W.G., 1966 'Romano-British settlement in the Welland valley', in Thomas, A.C. (ed.), *Rural Settlement in Roman Britain*, Counc. Brit. Archaeol. Res. Rep. 7, 15–26

Skidmore, P., 1991 *Insects of the British Cow Dung Community*, Field Studies Council Occas. Pap. 21 (Shrewsbury)

Smith, J.T., 2000 *Roman Villas: A Study in Social Structure* (London, Routledge)

Spain, R.J., 1996 'The millstones', in Mackreth, D., *Orton Hall Farm: A Roman and Early Anglo-Saxon Farmstead*, E. Anglian Archaeol. 76, 105–13

Spoerry, P. and Atkins, R., 2015 *A Late Saxon Village and Medieval Manor: Excavations at Botolph Bridge, Orton Longueville, Peterborough*, E. Anglian Archaeol. 153

Stead, I., 1984 'Iron Age metalwork from Orton meadows', *Durobrivae: A Review of Nene Valley Archaeology* 9, 6–7

Stead, I.M., 1986 'The brooches', in Stead, I. and Rigby, V., *Baldock: The Excavations of a Roman and Pre-Roman Settlement*, Britannia Monogr. 7, 109–25

Stead, I. and Rigby, V., 1986 *Baldock: The Excavations of a Roman and Pre-Roman Settlement*, Britannia Monogr. 7

Steers, J.A. and Mitchell, J.B., 1962 'East Anglia', in Mitchell, J.B. (ed.), *Great Britain: Geographical Essays* (Cambridge, Cambridge University Press), 86–103

Sudell, T.L., 1990 'Insects from the well', in Wrathmell, S. and Nicholson, A. (eds), *Dalton Parlours: Iron Age Settlement and Roman Villa Site*, Yorkshire Archaeology 3 (Wakefield, Yorkshire Archaeological Service), 267–71

Swan, J. and Metcalfe, A., 1975 'Roman leather shoes from Lynch Farm', *Durobrivae: A Review of Nene Valley Archaeology* 3, 24–5

Swan, V.G., 1984 *The Pottery Kilns of Roman Britain*, RCHM Supplementary Ser. 5 (London)

Swift, E., 2000 *The End of the Western Roman Empire: An Archaeological Investigation* (Stroud, Tempus)

Tacitus, 1974 *The Annals of Imperial Rome*, translated with an Introduction by Michael Grant (London, Penguin)

Taylor, C.C., 1983 *Village and Farmstead: A History of Rural Settlement in England* (London, George Philip)

193

Taylor, J., 2007   *An Atlas of Roman Rural Settlement in England*, Counc. Brit. Archaeol. Res. Rep. 151

Taylor, J.H., 1963   *Geology of the Country around Kettering, Corby and Oundle*, Geological Survey of Great Britain (London, HMSO)

Teichart, M., 1975   'Osteometrische Untersuchungen zur berechnung der Widerristhohe bei Schafen', in Clason, A.T. (ed.), *Archaeological Studies* (Amsterdam, Elsevier), 51–69

Thomas, C., 1993   *Christianity in Roman Britain to AD 500* (London, Batsford)

Thomas, J., 2003   'Prehistoric pit alignments and their significance in the archaeological landscape', in Humphrey, J. (ed.), *Re-searching the Iron Age* (Leicester, University of Leicester School of Archaeology and Ancient History)

Timby, J.R., 1989   *Excavations at Kingscote and Wycomb, Gloucestershire: A Roman Estate Centre and Small Town in the Cotswolds with a Note on Related Settlements* (Cirencester, Cotswold Archaeological Trust)

Todd, M., 1968   *The Roman Fort at Great Casterton, Rutland* (Nottingham, University of Nottingham)

Todd, M., 1973   *The Coritani* (London, Duckworth)

Todd, M., 2008   'The coins', in Upex, S.G., 'The excavation of a fourth-century Roman pottery production unit at Stibbington, Cambridgeshire', *Archaeol. J.* 165, 313–14

Tomlin, R.G.O. and Hassall, M.W.C., 2001   'Roman Britain in 2000', *Britannia* 32, 288

Turner, J., 1979   'The environment of northeast England during Roman times as shown by pollen analysis', *J. Archaeol. Sci.* 6, 285–90

Upex, B., forthcoming   'The animal bones', in Upex, S., 'A Roman farmstead at North Lodge, Barnwell, Northamptonshire 1973–1988', *Northamptonshire Archaeol.*

Upex, S.G., 1977   'Recent aerial photography', *Durobrivae: A Review of Nene Valley Archaeology* 5, 22–3

Upex, S.G., 1993   *Excavations at a Roman and Saxon Site at Haddon, Cambridgeshire, 1991–1993* (privately printed)

Upex, S.G., 2001   'The Roman villa at Cotterstock, Northamptonshire', *Britannia* 32, 57–91

Upex, S.G., 2008a   *The Romans in the East of England: Settlement and Landscape in the Lower Nene Valley* (Stroud, Tempus)

Upex, S.G., 2008b   'The excavation of a fourth-century Roman pottery production unit at Stibbington, Cambridgeshire', *Archaeol. J.* 165, 265–333

Upex, S.G., 2011a   'The *Praetorium* of Edmund Artis: a summary of excavations and surveys of the palatial Roman structure at Castor, Cambridgeshire 1828–2010', *Britannia* 42, 23–112

Upex, S.G., 2011b   'The pottery', in Pickstone, A., *Iron Age and Roman Remains at Bretton Way, Peterborough: Post Excavation Assessment*, Oxford Archaeology East Rep. 1230, 41–56

Upex, S.G., 2013a   'The pottery', in Pickstone, A. and Drummond-Murray, J., 'A late Roman cistern and ritual deposition at Bretton Way, Peterborough', *Proc Cambridge Antiquarian Soc.* 102, 48–53

Upex, S.G., 2013b   *Excavations at Roman Fort at Water Newton, Cambridgeshire, Post Excavation Assessment* (Peterborough, Nene Valley Archaeological Trust)

Upex, S.G., 2014   'Archaeological excavations on the site of the Roman Fort at Water Newton', *The Five Parishes Journal: More History of the Villages of Castor, Ailsworth, Marholm, Upton, Sutton, Stibbington and Water Newton* 2, 5–10

Upex, S.G., forthcoming a   'A Roman farmstead at North Lodge, Barnwell, Northamptonshire 1973–1988', *Northamptonshire Archaeol.*

Upex, S.G., forthcoming b   'The Roman villas of the lower Nene valley and the *Praetorium* at Castor', in Soffe, G. and Henig, M. (eds), *Roman Villas: The Proceedings of a Conference held at the British Museum in 2009* (Oxford, Oxbow Books)

Von den Driesch, A. and Boessneck, J., 1974   'Kritische anmerkungen zur widerristhohenberechung aus langenmassen vorund fruhgeschichtlicher Tierknochen', *Sausetierkundliche Mitteilungen* 22, 325–48

Wacher, J.S., 1978   *Roman Britain* (London, Dent)

Waddington, C., 1997   'A review of "pit alignments" and a tentative interpretation of the Milfield Complex', *Durham Archaeol. J.* 13, 21–34

Walker, T.J., 1899   'The traces of the Roman occupation left in Peterborough and the surrounding district', *J. Brit. Archaeol. Assoc.* ns 5, 51–62

Waller, M., 1994   *The Fenland Project, No. 9: Flandrian Environmental Change in Fenland*, E. Anglian Archaeol. 70

Wallis, H., 2002   *Roman Routeways across the Fens: Excavations at Morton, Tilney St Lawrence, Nordelph and Downham Market*, E. Anglian Archaeol. Occas. Pap. 10

Walters, B., 2009   'Roman villas in Britain: farms, temples or tax depots?' *Current Archaeol.* 230, 30–35

Walton, P., 2012   *Rethinking Roman Britain: Coinage and Archaeology*, Collection Moneta 137 (Wetteren)

Walton Rogers, P., 1997   *The Archaeology of York Vol. 17: Small Finds Fasc. 11 Textile Production at 16–22 Coppergate* (London, Council for British Archaeology for York Archaeological Trust)

Waugh, H. and Goodburn, R., 1972   'The non-ferrous objects', in Frere, S., *Verulamium Excavations, Vol. I* Rep. Res. Comm. Soc. Antiq. London 28 (London), 114–62

Webster, G., 1975   *Romano-British Coarse Pottery: A Students Guide*, Counc. Brit. Archaeol. Res. Rep. 6

Wessex Archaeology, 2012   *Bedford Purlieus Wood, Thornhaugh near Peterborough, Cambridgeshire: Archaeological Assessment and Evaluation*, Wessex Archaeology Rep. 71512.01

Whimster, R., 1977   'Iron Age burial in southern England', *Proc. Prehist. Soc.* 43, 317–27

Whimster, R., 1981   *Burial Practices in Iron Age Britain: A Discussion and Gazetteer of the Evidence c.700BC–43AD*, Brit. Archaeol. Rep. British Ser. 90 (Oxford)

White, K.D., 1970   *Roman Farming*, Thames and Hudson

Whitwell, J.B., 1982 — *The Coritani: Some Aspects of the Iron Age Tribe and the Roman civitas*, Brit. Archaeol. Rep. British Ser. 99 (Oxford)

Wild, F., 1985 — 'Samian ware', in Hurst, H.R., *Kingsholm, Gloucester Archaeological Reports* 1 (Gloucester), 56–67, 105–6, 121–6

Wild, J.P., 1970 — *Textile Manufacture in the Northern Roman Provinces* (Cambridge, Cambridge University Press)

Wild, J.P., 1974 — 'Roman settlement in the lower Nene valley', *Archaeol. J.* 131, 140–70

Wild, J.P., 1973a — 'The Roman fishpond at Lynch Farm', *Durobrivae: A Review of Nene Valley Archaeology* 1, 20–21

Wild, J.P., 1973b — 'Longthorpe, an essay in continuity', *Durobrivae: A Review of Nene Valley Archaeology* 1, 7–11

Wild, J.P., 1987a — 'Objects of clay', in Dannell, G.B. and Wild, J.P., *Longthorpe II. The Military Works-Depot: An Episode in Landscape History*, Britannia Monogr. Ser. 8, 113–14

Wild, J.P., 1987b — 'Objects of stone', in Dannell, G.B. and Wild, J.P., *Longthorpe II. The Military Works-Depot: An Episode in Landscape History*, Britannia Monogr. Ser. 8, 97–9

Williams, A., 1946–7 — 'Excavations at Langford Down near Lechlade, Oxfordshire in 1943', *Oxoniensia* 11 and 12, 44–64

Williamson, T., 2003 — *Shaping Medieval Landscapes: Settlement, Society, Environment* (Macclesfield, Windgather Press)

Willis, S., 2004 — 'Research Framework document for the Study of Roman Pottery in Britain', *Journal of Roman Pottery Studies* 11, 1–20

Willis, S., 2007 — 'Sea, coast, estuary, land and culture in Iron Age Britain', in Haselgrove, C. and Moore, T. (eds), *The Later Iron Age in Britain and Beyond* (Oxford, Oxbow Books), 105–29

Willis, S., 2011 — 'Samian ware and society in Roman Britain and beyond', *Britannia* 42, 167–24

Wilson, C.E., 1981 — 'Burials within settlements in southern Britain during the pre-Roman Iron Age', *Bull. Instit. Archaeol.* 18, 127–70

Wilson, D.R., 1975 — 'Romano-Celtic temple architecture', *J. Brit. Archaeol. Assoc.* 38, 3–27

Wilson, D.R., 1978 — 'Pit alignments: distribution and function', in Bowen, H.C. and Fowler, P.J. (eds), *Early Land Allotment*, Counc. Brit. Archaeol. Res. Rep. 48, 3–5

Wilson, M.G., 1974 — 'The other pottery', in Frere, S.S. and St Joseph, J.K., 'The Roman fortress at Longthorpe', *Britannia* 5, 96–111

Woodfield, C. and Johnson, C., 1989 — 'A Roman site at Stanton Low, on the Great Ouse, Buckinghamshire – Excavated by Margaret Jones 1957–58', *Archaeol. J.* 146, 135–278

Woodland, A.W., 1942 — *Water Supply from Underground Sources of the Oxford–Northampton District, Pt II*. Geological Survey wartime pamphlet 4 (London)

Woods, P.J., 1974 — 'Types of late Belgic and early Roman-British pottery kilns in the Nene valley', *Britannia* 5, 262–81

Woodward, H.B. and Thompson, B., 1909 — *The Water Supply of Bedfordshire and Northamptonshire*, Memoirs of the Geological Survey (London)

Wyman Abbott, G., 1910 — 'The discovery of prehistoric pits at Peterborough', *Archaeologia* 62, 333–9

Young, C.J., 1977 — *The Roman Pottery Industry of the Oxford Region*, Brit. Archaeol. Rep. British Ser. 43 (Oxford)

Young. C.J., 1980 — *Guidelines for the Processing and Publication of Roman Pottery from Excavations*, Directorate of Ancient Monuments and Historic Buildings, Occasional Paper 4

Young, C.J., 1981 — 'The late Roman water-mill at Ickham, Kent and the Saxon shore', in Detsicas, A. (ed.), *Collectanea Historica: Essays in Memory of Stuart Rigold* (Maidstone, Kent Archaeological Society), 32–41

195

Index

East Anglian Archaeology

is a serial publication sponsored by ALGAO EE and English Heritage. It is the main vehicle for publishing final reports on archaeological excavations and surveys in the region. For information about titles in the series, visit **http://eaareports.org.uk**. Reports can be obtained from:
    Oxbow Books, 10 Hythe Bridge Street, Oxford OX1 2EW
or directly from the organisation publishing a particular volume.

Reports available so far:

No.1, 1975 Suffolk: various papers
No.2, 1976 Norfolk: various papers
No.3, 1977 Suffolk: various papers
No.4, 1976 Norfolk: Late Saxon town of Thetford
No.5, 1977 Norfolk: various papers on Roman sites
No.6, 1977 Norfolk: Spong Hill Anglo-Saxon cemetery, Part I
No.7, 1978 Norfolk: Bergh Apton Anglo-Saxon cemetery
No.8, 1978 Norfolk: various papers
No.9, 1980 Norfolk: North Elmham Park
No.10, 1980 Norfolk: village sites in Launditch Hundred
No.11, 1981 Norfolk: Spong Hill, Part II: Catalogue of Cremations
No.12, 1981 The barrows of East Anglia
No.13, 1981 Norwich: Eighteen centuries of pottery from Norwich
No.14, 1982 Norfolk: various papers
No.15, 1982 Norwich: Excavations in Norwich 1971–1978; Part I
No.16, 1982 Norfolk: Beaker domestic sites in the Fen-edge and East Anglia
No.17, 1983 Norfolk: Waterfront excavations and Thetford-type Ware production, Norwich
No.18, 1983 Norfolk: The archaeology of Witton
No.19, 1983 Norfolk: Two post-medieval earthenware pottery groups from Fulmodeston
No.20, 1983 Norfolk: Burgh Castle: excavation by Charles Green, 1958–61
No.21, 1984 Norfolk: Spong Hill, Part III: Catalogue of Inhumations
No.22, 1984 Norfolk: Excavations in Thetford, 1948–59 and 1973–80
No.23, 1985 Norfolk: Excavations at Brancaster 1974 and 1977
No.24, 1985 Suffolk: West Stow, the Anglo-Saxon village
No.25, 1985 Essex: Excavations by Mr H.P.Cooper on the Roman site at Hill Farm, Gestingthorpe, Essex
No.26, 1985 Norwich: Excavations in Norwich 1971–78; Part II
No.27, 1985 Cambridgeshire: The Fenland Project No.1: Archaeology and Environment in the Lower Welland Valley
No.28, 1985 Norfolk: Excavations within the north-east bailey of Norwich Castle, 1978
No.29, 1986 Norfolk: Barrow excavations in Norfolk, 1950–82
No.30, 1986 Norfolk: Excavations at Thornham, Warham, Wighton and Caistor St Edmund, Norfolk
No.31, 1986 Norfolk: Settlement, religion and industry on the Fen-edge; three Romano-British sites in Norfolk
No.32, 1987 Norfolk: Three Norman Churches in Norfolk
No.33, 1987 Essex: Excavation of a Cropmark Enclosure Complex at Woodham Walter, Essex, 1976 and An Assessment of Excavated Enclosures in Essex
No.34, 1987 Norfolk: Spong Hill, Part IV: Catalogue of Cremations
No.35, 1987 Cambridgeshire: The Fenland Project No.2: Fenland Landscapes and Settlement, Peterborough–March
No.36, 1987 Norfolk: The Anglo-Saxon Cemetery at Morningthorpe
No.37, 1987 Norfolk: Excavations at St Martin-at-Palace Plain, Norwich, 1981
No.38, 1987 Suffolk: The Anglo-Saxon Cemetery at Westgarth Gardens, Bury St Edmunds
No.39, 1988 Norfolk: Spong Hill, Part VI: Occupation during the 7th–2nd millennia BC
No.40, 1988 Suffolk: Burgh: The Iron Age and Roman Enclosure
No.41, 1988 Essex: Excavations at Great Dunmow, Essex: a Romano-British small town in the Trinovantian Civitas
No.42, 1988 Essex: Archaeology and Environment in South Essex, Rescue Archaeology along the Gray's By-pass 1979–80
No.43, 1988 Essex: Excavation at the North Ring, Mucking, Essex: A Late Bronze Age Enclosure
No.44, 1988 Norfolk: Six Deserted Villages in Norfolk
No.45, 1988 Norfolk: The Fenland Project No. 3: Marshland and the Nar Valley, Norfolk
No.46, 1989 Norfolk: The Deserted Medieval Village of Thuxton
No.47, 1989 Suffolk: West Stow: Early Anglo-Saxon Animal Husbandry
No.48, 1989 Suffolk: West Stow, Suffolk: The Prehistoric and Romano-British Occupations

No.49, 1990 Norfolk: The Evolution of Settlement in Three Parishes in South-East Norfolk
No.50, 1993 Proceedings of the Flatlands and Wetlands Conference
No.51, 1991 Norfolk: The Ruined and Disused Churches of Norfolk
No.52, 1991 Norfolk: The Fenland Project No. 4, The Wissey Embayment and Fen Causeway
No.53, 1992 Norfolk: Excavations in Thetford, 1980–82, Fison Way
No.54, 1992 Norfolk: The Iron Age Forts of Norfolk
No.55, 1992 Lincolnshire: The Fenland Project No.5: Lincolnshire Survey, The South-West Fens
No.56, 1992 Cambridgeshire: The Fenland Project No.6: The South-Western Cambridgeshire Fens
No.57, 1993 Norfolk and Lincolnshire: Excavations at Redgate Hill Hunstanton; and Tattershall Thorpe
No.58, 1993 Norwich: Households: The Medieval and Post-Medieval Finds from Norwich Survey Excavations 1971–1978
No.59, 1993 Fenland: The South-West Fen Dyke Survey Project 1982–86
No.60, 1993 Norfolk: Caister-on-Sea: Excavations by Charles Green, 1951–55
No.61, 1993 Fenland: The Fenland Project No.7: Excavations in Peterborough and the Lower Welland Valley 1960–1969
No.62, 1993 Norfolk: Excavations in Thetford by B.K. Davison, between 1964 and 1970
No.63, 1993 Norfolk: Illington: A Study of a Breckland Parish and its Anglo-Saxon Cemetery
No.64, 1994 Norfolk: The Late Saxon and Medieval Pottery Industry of Grimston: Excavations 1962–92
No.65, 1993 Suffolk: Settlements on Hill-tops: Seven Prehistoric Sites in Suffolk
No.66, 1993 Lincolnshire: The Fenland Project No.8: Lincolnshire Survey, the Northern Fen-Edge
No.67, 1994 Norfolk: Spong Hill, Part V: Catalogue of Cremations
No.68, 1994 Norfolk: Excavations at Fishergate, Norwich 1985
No.69, 1994 Norfolk: Spong Hill, Part VIII: The Cremations
No.70, 1994 Fenland: The Fenland Project No.9: Flandrian Environmental Change in Fenland
No.71, 1995 Essex: The Archaeology of the Essex Coast Vol.I: The Hullbridge Survey Project
No.72, 1995 Norfolk: Excavations at Redcastle Furze, Thetford, 1988–9
No.73, 1995 Norfolk: Spong Hill, Part VII: Iron Age, Roman and Early Saxon Settlement
No.74, 1995 Norfolk: A Late Neolithic, Saxon and Medieval Site at Middle Harling
No.75, 1995 Essex: North Shoebury: Settlement and Economy in South-east Essex 1500–AD1500
No.76, 1996 Nene Valley: Orton Hall Farm: A Roman and Early Anglo-Saxon Farmstead
No.77, 1996 Norfolk: Barrow Excavations in Norfolk, 1984–88
No.78, 1996 Norfolk:The Fenland Project No.11: The Wissey Embayment: Evidence for pre-Iron Age Occupation
No.79, 1996 Cambridgeshire: The Fenland Project No.10: Cambridgeshire Survey, the Isle of Ely and Wisbech
No.80, 1997 Norfolk: Barton Bendish and Caldecote: fieldwork in south-west Norfolk
No.81, 1997 Norfolk: Castle Rising Castle
No.82, 1998 Essex: Archaeology and the Landscape in the Lower Blackwater Valley
No.83, 1998 Essex: Excavations south of Chignall Roman Villa 1977–81
No.84, 1998 Suffolk: A Corpus of Anglo-Saxon Material
No.85, 1998 Suffolk: Towards a Landscape History of Walsham le Willows
No.86, 1998 Essex: Excavations at the Orsett 'Cock' Enclosure
No.87, 1999 Norfolk: Excavations in Thetford, North of the River, 1989–90
No.88, 1999 Essex: Excavations at Ivy Chimneys, Witham 1978–83
No.89, 1999 Lincolnshire: Salterns: Excavations at Helpringham, Holbeach St Johns and Bicker Haven
No.90, 1999 Essex:The Archaeology of Ardleigh, Excavations 1955–80
No.91, 2000 Norfolk: Excavations on the Norwich Southern Bypass, 1989–91 Part I Bixley, Caistor St Edmund, Trowse
No.92, 2000 Norfolk: Excavations on the Norwich Southern Bypass, 1989–91 Part II Harford Farm Anglo-Saxon Cemetery
No.93, 2001 Norfolk: Excavations on the Snettisham Bypass, 1989
No.94, 2001 Lincolnshire: Excavations at Billingborough, 1975–8
No.95, 2001 Suffolk: Snape Anglo-Saxon Cemetery: Excavations and Surveys
No.96, 2001 Norfolk: Two Medieval Churches in Norfolk
No.97, 2001 Cambridgeshire: Monument 97, Orton Longueville